The Water of Life

Illustration for cover
De Antro Nympherum, tempera, 1821

Based on the 3rd century Neo-platonist philosopher Porphyry's mystical treatise on the homecoming of Odysseus (Ulysses), De Antro Nympherum or The Cave of the Nymphs, combines two events—one from Book V and the other from Book XIII of the Odyssey.

Odysseus, kneels with averted head as he throws back the "girdle" of protection lent to him by the sea-goddess Leucothea, also known as the White Goddess. Leucothea can be seen out at sea guiding four dark stallions through the waves.

After wandering for ten years after the Trojan War, Odysseus has finally arrived home. Next to him stands the goddess Athena in her aspect as Sophia or Divine Wisdom. As protector of culture and mistress of mentoring Athena's raised hand points to the heavens above where the Cycle of the Life of Mankind is depicted as a reflection of the course that the sun follows each day.

In the upper right-hand corner of the image is the Cave of the Nymphs. Standing inside the cave are the Naiades, the spirits who inhabit all springs, rivers, streams, fountains, lakes, and marshes. Some of the water spirits carry urns filled with the Water of Life, others hold bowls containing the honey of regeneration.

In the waters below Odysseus and Athena the Three Fates weave and measure the threads of each human life giving each a "twist of fate" that makes each soul unique and irreplaceable. They are assisted by Phorcis who appears as the "old man of the sea."

The painting by William Blake was found at Arlington Court in Devonshire, England where it had been unnoticed for many years. It appears here with the permission of the National Trust at Arlington Court.

THE WATER OF LIFE

INITIATION AND THE TEMPERING OF THE SOUL

Michael Meade

*To Brent,
Much peace, many
blessings, Michael Meade*

GREENFIRE PRESS
An Imprint of Mosaic Multicultural Foundation

GREENFIRE PRESS
An Imprint of Mosaic Multicultural Foundation

Cover illustration: THE ARLINGTON COURT PICTURE by William Blake
(1821), Arlington Court, The National Trust. ©NTPL/Derrick E. Witty.

Contents

The Forest of Stories

Whether in the monumental epics of Homer... or in the charming wonder stories of the folk tradition... the powers have to be consulted again directly, again and again. Our primary task is to learn, not so much what they are said to have said, but to evoke fresh speech from them, and understand that speech.

HEINRICH ZIMMER, *THE KING AND THE CORPSE*,
EDITED BY JOSEPH CAMPBELL

PREFACE

WHEN I WAS A CHILD in school we practiced hiding under our little wooden desks in order to save ourselves from atomic bombs. The idea was that distant and evil enemies were about to attack us and we had to be prepared to duck under our desks. Those exercises affected our world view as we all grew up imagining that the world could end at any moment. It seems strange to say, but those were simpler times. Today, the use of school desks for defense seems quaint, but the threat to the existence of the world has grown more immediate and palpable.

The desk exercise came to mind when my four-year-old granddaughter told me that she needed a "dreamcatcher" because she was having nightmares. She heard that a dreamcatcher could block out the bad dreams while allowing good dreams to pass through. I remembered a Native American story from the Anishnabe tribe that told the origin of dreamcatchers. It seems that the early people were having a hard time. They were not sleeping well because most were having intense nightmares. The leaders of that time were troubled and tired from lack of sleep and they made bad decisions, causing things to go from bad to worse.

The elders and the medicine people tried to solve the problem, but they couldn't stop the incursion of bad dreams. Eventually, a council of all the people was convened. During that council an elder had a vision in which he saw a hoop with a spider's web stretched across it and a feather and bead attached to it—a dreamcatcher. Once people learned to make and use these dreamcatchers, which would trap the bad dreams but let good dreams through, their nightmares became quite infrequent. People began to rest easier, there was less anxiety, and life went in a better way.

I found myself thinking about a dreamcatcher that might intercept the nightmares that currently plague the entire human tribe. These days many people believe that the dream of the world will end soon either because of weapons of mass destruction or through global warming. The modern world seems to be in the same state as my granddaughter and the early people who were just learning how to be in this world.

Some of the oldest myths of the origins of life describe this earthly world as a dream floating on the eternal waters of time. Many traditional cultures consider each person to be the incarnation of a unique dream, each soul a living microcosm of the cosmic dream of life. The nightmare version of the world takes over whenever the number of people having bad dreams increases and those genuinely living out the dream of their life decreases. In this sense, humans are the makeweights on the scales where the dream of life is weighed. The dream of life is in the hands of those people who happen to be alive at a given time. The Anishnabe people knew this, all the ancient people knew it, and most of the old stories remind us of it.

I thought of the dreamcatcher again when I read that the president of Iran believes that the legendary Islamic savior, the Imam Mahdi, will return at the end of time to convert all humans to Islam. The legend says this savior will return when there is enough chaos in the world. The president of Iran believes that it is his divine mission to help generate the required level of chaos. At the same time, the president of the United States revealed that "god has spoken to him," directly giving him the mission to invade Iraq and Afghanistan in order to save the world from dangerous tyrannies and "extremist religions."

The president of Iran is living in a dream that requires extreme chaos in the world in order for salvation to become possible; the president of the United States is living in a dream where god tells him where to invade and whom to destroy. The deepening nightmare has the two of them facing off over the issue of nuclear arms. Each is dreaming of massive destruction in order to save their dream of the world. And they are not the only ones having such dreams.

The issue isn't simply a global war on terror, but also the global terror of modern war. Whether it be a savior story or a crusade story, a vengeance story or a final justice story, humans repeatedly fall into the shadows of ideas and beliefs that attempt to justify everything or solve everything. People will invest in and proselytize for stories that predict the end of the world as long as there is a caveat that implies that they will be among those saved from total perdition.

I find myself searching for a dreamcatcher that can deflect the nightmare visions of the end-times long enough for people to recall how to dream life forward and live out the dream each person came to life to live. In today's struggles the true enemy—the enemy behind the enemy—is the collapse of imagination that causes people to take stories as literal. The real enemy is the collapse into literalism and fundamentalism and the nightmare of fixed doctrines. The real problem is a loss of faith in the dream of life and the immediacy of the spirit that animates the world.

It's the job of myth to have a story for everything that happens and might happen in the world. In the great body of human stories, legends, and tales there are many myths of the end of the world. The fact that there are many and that they are different from each other holds the clue to the idea that they are stories to learn from, not historical predictions to literalize. The world depends upon this multiplicity and upon diversity and variety; it's true for the ecologies of the earth and it's true for the earthlings, as well. There cannot be a single religion or a single idea or a sole style of governing that works for everyone—not on this earth where each soul carries a living dream across the threshold of life and where each person and each culture needs to fashion their own dreamcatcher.

We are in a struggle for the presence of genuine imagination in the face of the hardening of ideas and the narrowing of hearts that ensues when people make god one-sided and consider their own beliefs to be literally true and universal. Mythic imagination is a primordial resource of the human heart that combines heart-felt intelligence with a reverence for life in its myriad forms. When times become tragic and dark with uncertainty, what is missing is the touch of eternity and a mythic sense of being woven within the ongoing story of the world.

An old idea says that each soul chooses when to be born. If that is so, we have each chosen to be born to a dark time when the sleep of the human tribe is troubled by the dual nightmare that includes both global terror and global warming. Human tragedies and natural disasters knock us out of the story we thought we were living, throwing us into a confusion of endings and beginnings. War does that, so does terrorism. Hurricanes and earthquakes do that, so does global warming.

Another old idea states that it is the same to live in a tragic time as to live in a tragic place. Tragedy transcends time and place, especially in an age of mass communication. The tragic sense of life is increasingly everywhere, flooding our physical and temporal world. Yet tragedy is never simply an ending, it's more of a dark birth, a somber road where pretensions of innocence must be replaced by a darker knowledge or else another tragedy ensues. And tragedy begets more tragedy, especially when blood crimes are involved. The first offspring of tragedy is often blind retribution, but during dark times something different—something beyond simple fear and blind outrage—is ultimately trying to be born. In the long run, the tragic sense would deepen both un-reflected innocence and bloody vengeance into a darker knowledge and bring forth a wisdom that holds and understands both sorrow and survival.

Amidst the modern rush and confusion something ancient and primordial is trying to catch up with us, an inner wisdom that alone can decipher a path through the mind-boggling dilemmas presented by both culture and nature. Myths involve primordial thinking, through which original ideas present at the very beginning return in order to begin it all again, even as it seems about to end.

The fabric of a culture tends to unravel in two places at once, where its young people are rejected and where its old people are forgotten. Conversely, a culture becomes creative where the dreams of its youth are revealed and the visions of its elders are revered. Youth and elder are each visionary states, each mythic conditions more attuned to the threads of eternity than to the strictures of time.

Youth and elders meet where the dream of life-ongoing tries to awaken in the hard-edged world of reality. When a culture rejects the dreams of its youth and forgets the visions of its elders it becomes destructive to life regardless of its heralded ideals. A culture that rejects the spirit of its youth will come to lack spirit and imagination when faced with life's almost impossible challenges. A culture that forgets the necessity of converting "olders" into genuine elders will have leaders who can't learn from the past and, therefore, can't imagine a meaningful future.

Youth are ever the *first responders*: They answer the call; they instinctively seek a greater sense of life and often do it through brushes with death. They speed in cars as if trying to drive into another world; they risk giving birth in order to become reborn themselves. They experiment with drugs in order to reach a higher world. They respond to calls from the extreme borders where life and death commune, be it extreme sports or questionable wars. They even respond to extremist religions that offer suicide and terrorism as ways to find salvation.

The elders, on the other hand, are those who have survived little deaths and have learned something of the beauty and meaning of being fully alive. Many people live longer now—but that simply makes people older, not necessarily elder. An old proverb states that white hair doesn't make an elder. Those who grow old without learning the story that is trying to live through them don't become "old enough" or ancient enough to serve the dream of life.

A culture deteriorates—regardless of its professed standards of living—when those old enough to know better seek to solve complex problems with force and political manipulation. Those who grow old without finding a genuine sense of meaning in their lives tend to become repositories for fear and anxiety, while those who find an inner sense of meaning and purpose tend to become keepers of medicine and healing ideals.

Perhaps the United States, with such a large population of potential elders, is trying to awaken to a darker knowledge and a deeper sense of wisdom. America—no longer outside the tragedy of being human or innocent of the dangers and delusions of handling power—cannot afford to wrap itself in a pretentious cloak of innocence while the complications of tragedy and disaster force a darker knowledge upon the world. Either the United States will learn from the lived knowledge of its elders and the nascent dreams of its youth or it will stay the course and blindly follow the predictable path of hubris and tragedy into the desert of time.

One way to consider the struggles of youth, the troubles of the aged, and the changes and dangers sweeping through both culture and nature is through the lens of initiation. The sense of an initiatory process intensifies whenever and wherever radical changes disrupt the flow of life. The Water of Life approaches the issues of war, cultural conflict, and the struggle to be fully human through the images and ideas of initiation.

One purpose of initiation was to awaken the elder within a person. Through a symbolic second birth a person would become psychologically aware—double-minded—and thus able to see the play of opposites in themselves and in the world. Elders are those who can see many sides of an issue. They also know their own shadows well enough to see the hidden and mistaken motives in others.

Seeking ways to sustain the dream of life and cool the flames of conflict requires an ability to suffer the pressure of opposing forces. Be it in an individual or a culture, genuine maturity involves an increasing capacity to tolerate inner as well as outer oppositions. Whereas many might argue that success in political affairs involves proving an unyielding will in the face of enemies, the elders know that wisdom lies in a deeper place than will and that courage lies in a more profound place than force.

Weapons may become more and more sophisticated, but the battle in the human heart remains the same. It is an ancient battle that cannot be won by better weapons. Neither can it be decided by any dogma or doctrine, be it religious or political. The trigger for all weapons resides in the human heart. The heart is the most tormented country, where each person must battle with their own darkness, with their own incapacity to believe in life, and with their own inability to forgive themselves and others. The deepest meaning of *jihad* is not a war against unbelievers but the ethical struggle in the human heart. Crusade comes from the root for *cross* and *crux*, the underlying idea being to bear the oppositions of life long enough to find a third way, a path with heart. The real war takes place in the human heart, as does the real peace.

Seen this way, those who plan for war and those who hope that war will solve the dilemmas and tragedies of life are young regardless of their years.

There have been societies where those over a certain age become "practice elders" who cannot plan for or contribute to the making of war. After a certain age people are required to serve the greater sense of life-ongoing rather than participating in the ongoing war.

When leaders declare an endless war, be it a *jihad* or a crusade, they have become blinded by the red fog that war engenders. At that point, cooler heads must be found. Elders are those who know the heat of battle, yet also know how and when to carry water that cools and heals. During dark times those who have survived their own battles become the guides to finding a renewed sense of life amidst the gathering shadows.

A culture dies when its dream becomes lost, when the march of history crushes its dream in the dust of time. When a culture hardens into an economy of facts and figures, or fashions its imaginative power into mass weapons and harsh policies, its dream is dying, its story is already becoming lost. All that happens has happened before, as in the period before people discovered dreamcatchers. The surface may be new, but the eternal drama of the human soul remains the same. That is what the old stories show. In the deeper levels of the soul it is always the last-minute in which life and death conflict, in which destruction and creation battle. In the forest of imagination it is always the crucial time, it is always the creative moment on earth.

This book began as an attempt to revive the ideas and ideals of creative initiation in order to re-imagine the importance of youth and the necessity of elders for a healthy society. Through ancient and recent stories it seeks a double-minded sense of humans as creators of culture and companions of nature. At this time, both young and old advocates are needed in order to find ways forward that return a sense of the sacred to the halls of culture and to the cycles of nature.

I wrote the first draft of The Water of Life partly as a reaction to the first Gulf War and partly as a reflection on years of work with severely at-risk youth in the ghettos and barrios of America. I felt compelled to try to help and understand the increasing number of young people becoming lost in the firestorms of violence, in the confusion of drugs, and in the dull throes of depression.

While writing I was visited by many ghosts from my own nightmarish experience of coming of age during the Vietnam War. Soon enough that story had worked itself into the text. At the time, I was also working with groups of men, trying to do "soul work" in order to offset the affect of mass cultures on modern men who tend to become increasingly isolated and hard-hearted as they age. On one hand I was working with the overheated psyches of youth and on the other I was encountering a hollowness in the midst of manic modern culture. What was common to both works was the need for soul and for stories, for the greater depth of feeling and meaning that the soul gives to the moment and for stories that help return wisdom and healing to the course of life.

The stories that shape this book are "soul stories," dilemma tales that challenge a person's character and understanding and tales of quests that require the entire reach of human spirit and depth of human soul. Behind each tale is the sense that a person must give themselves fully to the adventure of life or fail to find the story they came to life to live. According to the old stories, failing to discover and live the dream of one's life is a fate worse than death.

Despite appearances and arguments to the contrary, we are all in this together. Each person now stands at the edge of darkness like the elder in the Native story who envisioned a dreamcatcher and helped shift the dreams of the people just enough to change the imagination of the times. Since we know it's a mythic not a literal story, we can intuit that it isn't a solitary person or a single savior needed to save everyone, but a mythical elder trying to awaken inside people. If enough people awaken from the nightmare and find their dream and the medicine in their hearts, then our grandchildren may yet have a chance to make their own dreamcatchers.

Stories, like dreams, are the way that people understand the world and their own place in it. In the midst of the worst trouble imaginable, stories can restore the sense of continuity in life that is necessary for discovering creative solutions. Mythic stories are like big dreams caught in a collective dreamcatcher. I sincerely hope that the stories in this book can help to catch some of the imagination needed to restore the living dream of life.

Michael J. Meade
July, 2006, Seattle, Washington

INTRODUCTION

MYTHIC STORIES relate the origins of all that exists in the world. What comes to be "real" begins outside reality as each beginning has mythic undertones, more often felt than seen. Children play with "unseen" aspects of life quite naturally; whereas modern adults often suppress the subtle play of imagination and dreams, which remain as the daily presence of myth. Youth live somewhere between adult reality and childhood fantasy, in a territory of betwixt and between that once was considered deeply initiatory, and an essential condition for sustaining the imagination of human cultures. Seen this way, the intensity and recklessness of youth can serve as a source of vitality for renewing and cultivating culture. When ignored, the same vital energy tends toward either apathy or violence.

Since young people are bound to take up the adventure of life and stumble into its enduring mysteries, the struggles they encounter become the necessary troubles around which genuine community can form. Youth tend to embody both the persistent symptoms and the ongoing dreams of a culture. Ignoring the inevitable crises through which young people try to learn who and what they are in this world intensifies cultural symptoms while diminishing the amount of genuine imagination available for healing and making community.

To this day, I can feel the edges of living mystery that I encountered in youth and the shock of learning that modern culture has a blind eye for myth and its essential connection to meaning.

Before entering high school I felt a deep division between the world of parents and the realm that my friends and I inhabited. A widening gap existed between classrooms and the street corner we claimed as our own. We moved dutifully through the daily world governed by teachers and family, but our real lives took place on a different plane, where our instincts, feelings, and imagination took precedence. The dull restrictions of daily life fed rebellious feelings as many youth felt left out of the post-war celebration of materialism. The modern idea that held adolescence to be simply a 'phase' on the way to being grown up left the raw energies, passionate desires and spiritual longings of youth out in the cold.

During the 1950s in New York City, local neighborhoods became redefined as "turfs" by the street gangs and local crews that roamed restlessly through them. Instinctively, the streets were re-visioned as native territories partially hidden from adults and authorities and needing to be defended against outsiders. Gangs took the names of royalty—the Dukes, Crowns, Kings, Knights—or of animal totems—the Blackhawks, Sharks, Cobras. The names represented an opposition to the banality of daily life, but also revealed that besides overheated hormones and animal intensity, youth had instincts for nobility as well.

Left to our own vices and devices, we created a realm that existed in the same physical space as the worlds of family and society but was somehow on a different plane. Our world coincided with the neighborhood, but its boundaries were not simply physical. A stranger could enter it completely unawares and violate its rules unknowingly. In an untutored way, the city was a mythical place for us, "concrete" to be sure, yet full of imagination and drama at the same time.

It was a baffling, shifting world of light and dark with sharp edges and sudden triggers. One moment we were suffused with the warmth of friendship and thankfully contained in our little band. The next instant we were a reckless crew animated by our symbolic name, prowling our mythical turf, just looking for trouble and defying anyone to enter our territory or deny our supremacy. Our bodies followed our imaginations as we leapt at the feeling of belonging to something, especially something primal and immediate enough to separate us from parents, from school, from *the* authorities—from history itself!

We felt new, even original as we entered an unguided experiment that involved mysterious elements and hints of ancient initiations, although we didn't realize that. We did know that Friday night involved rites of attraction to and fear of gang fights; that Saturday meant dances and costume-drama romances and that Sunday morning fell quiet with the mystery of churches. For a while, that was enough of a rhythm, enough range of danger and potential to feel engaged in life and on the edge of something undiscovered.

Friday night rumbled with preplanned or impromptu battles with rival crews. Whether there was an actual battle, the air was thick with expectation and untested testosterone, with the rhythms of handshakes and the sounds of challenges and boasts. Better be fast with your hands or fast on your feet. On Saturday, we gathered to review the night before, to make a story of it—what happened, what could have happened, what would happen the next time.

Soon, it was time to get ready for the heart of Saturday night. There would be a dance, a party, or just hanging out—but somehow music, and, if possible in any way, girls, and, if lucky, pretty girls, and, if this was really "it," sex. But if not actually sex, then talking about it, preparing for it, using the language of it. Not just sex, but the romance of it, telling stories of finding it, and making them up as well, entering the compelling imagination of it with music and dance as doorways into the darkly lit rituals of desire. We shaped costumes from everyday clothes, polished shoes as if to shine the flashing feet within them. We wore socks to match our shirts, as if to say we were subtle and contrasting pants to say we were not. Hair was slicked up and back as if to show the speed at which our minds were moving. Our shirts were open to the winds whether summer or winter, for these were instinctive rituals of exposure and display as something inside had to find ways to be lived out.

Tentative dances led us into the mysterious world of girls, where 'slow songs' could soften all the edges of the mind. Girls whose shapes had barely been visible hours before were voluptuous now as the world became measured by the inches between bodies. Caught in another mystery, we entered a different temple where another dance was required. New fears and surprising rituals of self-revelation accompanied dreamy songs which chanted compelling promises of *always* and *forever*.

Sunday morning broke the spell of Saturday as we gathered to exchange stories of what had or hadn't happened. Retelling the events of Friday and Saturday was a way to mythologize our experiences. We embellished the facts, enlarging them to mythic proportions, and we slipped unknowingly into the mythic aspects of ourselves. Sometimes, we hung around the local church, making our myth outside as the faithful inside revisited theirs. At that time, Sunday was still God's day. Religiously speaking, it was the beginning of a new week, the rising of a new Sun. Functionally, it was the end of the week, the last day of creation. God rested; the rest of us paused uncertainly.

In those days, Sunday held the presence of God. The newspaper appeared as a great, heavy tome, a summary of the creations and destructions of the week. Stores closed in honor or in fear of God. Another world appeared, a godly realm with its own songs and hushed silences. In our church, the father God was distant and hard to see, but the infant Son of God was gently held by the regal Mother Mary. The central altar held the sacramental presence of the Christ, while all who entered became surrounded by a pious confusion of saints and the deliberate, bloody Stations of the Cross. The effect was dramatic and magnificent in many ways. Even when we mocked it, we knew that this world was sacred, a realm that had power by rite, by movements repeated by ancestors, by secrets confessed, by births blessed, by deaths mourned, and by marriages celebrated.

We learned the ways of the church as children, innocently compelled by the grandeur and precision of the ceremonies. Yet we increasingly felt exiled from the sanctuary as the dogmas and teachings failed to meaningfully address the immediate and growing dilemmas of our lives. Our aggressions and transgressions, as well as the intensity of our imaginations seemed to place us outside the church proper and beyond the reach of its rites. So we would hang outside inhabiting a space between the sacred and the profane.

Monday would arrive with its insistence upon elaborate profanity. School seemed constructed to deny the vital intensities and turbulent complexities of other realms that we glimpsed and inhabited both passionately and uncertainly. Occasionally, something said or read in class would cause the room to vibrate for a moment and a window to open to an inner realm or something beyond the ruling banality. But most of the time one world didn't even recognize the existence of the other as the instinctive rhythms and essential longings of our lives remained at odds with the demands and considerations of family, church and school.

Another view of the world suddenly opened up for me on my thirteenth birthday. My aunt, mistakenly thinking it a book on classical history, gave me a copy of Edith Hamilton's *Mythology*. Reading it that night, I was stunned by the array of Greek myths and legends. Time stopped as one story led to another and the tales of gods and goddesses, of humans and animals caught in extreme and mysterious situations leapt off the pages. The tales did not "explain" things in the sense of making life plain and clear; rather, they mirrored the dramas and dilemmas I was experiencing. The stories gave form to my internal life, opening a vast dwelling place within.

That book reshaped my mind. I felt more meaningfully in the daily world, yet less bound by it. Imagination and emotions denied and rejected by family, school, and church found a territory of acceptance with endless nuances and frequent hints of divine energies attending to the drama of being human. Inside those stories I found the stuff we are made of, not simply the heroic, but also the Homeric, a poetic resonance echoing through time and space.

I had a habit of reading while soaking in a hot bath, which was often the only refuge in a crowded house. I became drenched in the poetics of story and awakened to the presence of deities standing at the edges of awareness. In many ways, that was my first immersion in the Waters of Life, a literal, mythical baptism in myth and story.

Later that year, I had another encounter with stories that changed my understanding of people altogether. At the time, the other arena for storytelling was the local movie theater, which my friends and I would visit on most Saturdays. We were trying to be a "crew," a small, neighborhood gang. We were trying to be *cool*. We had a street corner where we hung out and some older guys to watch and emulate. We had our own rules, ways to look and act. One of our rules stated that we couldn't pay to enter the movie theater. I think the rule started because money was scarce, but it also became an adventure and eventually an issue of honor. Since we went to see almost every new film, the management of the movie house had figured out our ritual approach to theater and watched and waited each Saturday to stop and catch us.

We created ruses and distractions that allowed us to slip in with the paying customers, like Odysseus and his crew slipping past the Cyclops while under the sheep. As the entry game escalated, the theater managers placed hired guards at the entrance, forcing us to find other approaches. Right behind the theater there were elevated railroad tracks and, not far along, a station. One day we jumped the turnstiles and walked along the train tracks to a place above and behind the theater. We hopped over a fence, slid down a hill, and jumped from the top of a wall to an alley. We tapped on the rear fire door until some kid opened it. We slipped in and once again took our seats in the dark.

During the movie I headed up the aisle to the bathroom and found myself surrounded by six older guys. They escorted me upstairs behind the projection room to the restroom. They threw everyone else out and shoved me onto the floor by the white urinal. While one guarded the door, the others stood over me holding knives and short pipes. I recognized the leader who held a sharpened monkey wrench in my face; he had a reputation for hurting people and for carrying a zip gun. The wrench in his hand shook as he angrily accused my crew of calling his gang punks. Now he was going to show us what happened to anyone who messed with them.

At first I was too startled to understand what he meant; then I realized they had mistaken me for a friend who had recently tangled with them and got away. This was payback; they were going to mess me up for what he had done. As my eyes went back and forth between the sharp, curved edge of the monkey wrench and the mad eyes of the guy holding it, my tongue began to speak, as if of its own accord.

I quickly explained that I wasn't the one who had called them names. Why would I be fool enough to challenge them? They were older and armed, and everyone knew they were tough. Our crew was just forming; we wouldn't challenge them. But listen, I went on; my friend curses everyone. He's crazy, I said, he does this shit all the time. His older brother beats on him, and it makes him crazy. Actually, their father beats both of them all the time. Now the older brother takes it out on him, too. So, he's crazy, what he says doesn't make sense. He's just going around yelling. It doesn't mean anything.

I was talking fast, and elaborating anything that seemed to catch their attention. I could see the leader's eyes waver and the wrench drift a little away from my head. The more I talked, the more they calmed down and the more the cold stare left their eyes, replaced by flickers of recognition. They got caught up in the story of this guy's family, because it was their families as well. It was a story each of us felt in one way or another; the story of how anyone could wind up on edge and enraged and looking for trouble. They listened despite themselves, and listening made them lose the bloody edge of their anger. They let me go unharmed. I was to tell my friend to apologize; they would be waiting for us outside the theater after the show.

Still in great fear, I walked back to my seat and told my friends. We crawled out on the sticky floor of the theater, pushing everyone's legs out of the way until we reached a side door. We burst through the door, and tore down the street. Before the screen said The End, we were standing on our corner discussing what had happened, figuring out what to do next.

Years later, when someone once asked me how I became a storyteller, the encounter with that gang came right to mind. I saw it all again—the tool converted to a weapon, the mistaken identity, the strange way in which I became just as caught up in the story I told as my attackers did. And the way in which telling of one tragedy seemed to avert another. Faced with the cutting edge of the monkey wrench, in the proximity of a thorough beating, I instinctively placed a wound that already existed in the space between us. Naming one of the wounds we already carried made it possible to stop the wounding for a minute. For a moment, the wounds that were being passed around in each of our lives became a story we each could reflect upon. These elements were compelling to me, but other parts were more important to my friends. They wanted details on the weapons and descriptions of the gang members. They wanted to retaliate, to do some damage, and the sooner the better.

My friend became especially angry because I had talked about him and his family. He wanted to go right back and have it out with them. I argued that they could kill him, or at least cut him up, and that would accomplish nothing. What happened next was strange. He went home and wildly attacked his older brother. He put the blame back on him. If his brother hadn't beaten him, he wouldn't have cursed that crew. The protective side of the older brother awakened. He gathered his crew and they confronted the monkey-wrench gang. Those guys didn't want to mess with the bigger, older guys, so they agreed to drop the whole thing. It was over. No one got hurt, and we could even go back to the theater… as soon as we devised another way in without paying.

Meanwhile, I tried to understand what had happened to me in the bathroom of the theater. To me, there were stories within stories and strands which reminded me of the myths in my book. A real-life drama was being enacted inside a theater where a larger than life story marched across the screen. As the movie flickered on the screen, I struggled to make up a story in the bathroom. Each tale tried to recast life to make a point, to suspend harsh reality, to alter the blind course of things.

Something was trying to awaken in me. I could feel it and tried hard to reflect on what I saw and felt. In telling about my friend and his family, I told the truth; yet I also lied. I dramatized and elaborated things to make the tale more immediate and real. I lied to tell the truth. Facts, psychology, and myth were all mixed together. I couldn't sort it out and didn't know anyone who could. I began to see how the world offered an endless tangle of stories with complicated layers of meaning. At the same time, I felt more alone, separate from my friends—a little like old Odysseus wandering about after the Trojan War.

That same year I began to ride the subway train from my neighborhood to a high school in the middle of Manhattan. I caught the train where it ran on elevated tracks, rattling along above the city streets. At a certain station, the train plunged from daylight into darkness as it rushed into the underground. For me, this became the underworld of Hades, described in the mythology book as a place inhabited by departed souls who remained interested in those living above. One of them was Tiresias, who had given up normal sight in order to see more deeply. As a blind seer, he foretold how Odysseus would wander through many strange places and foreign lands in his search to find a way home. I took that as encouragement to wander beyond my neighborhood and learn the ins and outs of the whole city.

Most days I climbed up from the underground along with the hordes of workers who surfaced in the middle of Manhattan at Grand Central Station, then walked to school. Sometimes something unseen seemed to pull me toward the unknown and I would stay on the train, ride under the streets and surface in another part of the city. At that time in New York most of the old ethnic neighborhoods still existed. I could descend into the underworld and ascend into Little Italy, Germantown, Spanish Harlem, Chinatown, and on and on. Each neighborhood offered an experience of an entire culture, each another world connected by an underworld of blind commuters and the ghosts of departed souls.

Each area had unique foods the smells of which filled the air. Old immigrants from distant lands spoke their native languages; some wore clothes that defied modern styles. Snatches of traditional music leaked out of storefronts where unusual costumes hung in the windows. Newspapers offered stories of distant worlds, some written in scripts that appeared only as designs to my untutored eye. It was like finding remnants of old civilizations and lost tribes encamped throughout the city.

The city became a school beyond school, a maze of cultural shapes in which some people struggled to preserve traditions while others invented themselves anew each day. Here was the true commerce of the city, the living layers of multi-ethnic heritage and cultural invention that seemed parallel to the many-layered stories of myth. Each place and each group had rites of entry that secretly wove its members together and each held bits of myth that could still speak to those who had ears to listen. Although I continued to live in the neighborhood, I also came to feel that I was a citizen of a world where each place and each occasion held hidden meanings and mysteries that wanted to be revealed.

Through a series of after-school and summer jobs, I came to know many areas of the city, each with its own mysteries and histories. For a time I worked amidst the sweat shops and dark elevator shafts of the old buildings in the garment district. Amidst the machinery and traffic, dark-skinned men labored to shepherd racks of bright, newly designed clothes between trucks and buildings. They spoke a language which was unintelligible to the people who designed the clothes and they were invisible to those who purchased the latest fashions in Uptown stores.

At first, I thought these intense black men represented another foreign group. I recognized the touch of Harlem in the *do-rag* on their heads, but couldn't follow their rapid, rhythmic speech. Only after weeks of delivering freight and listening closely in the dark elevators could I penetrate the complex weaving of common English with African tones and words. After they noticed my willingness to sweat into the work and intuited my interest in the rapid speech, they clued me in and taught me how it worked.

They mixed common speech with phrases from the deep South that brought along African intonations and added slang words that changed every week. They laced it all together with syncopated rhythms and fired the whole thing back and forth in high speed exchanges as the carts and racks pushed quickly past each other in the noisy streets. It took as much attention to learn their language as it did to learn Cicero's Latin in class. One was a dead language still trying to speak its measured thoughts in school; the other, a street Latin being invented with Shakespearean wit in the vital streets and shadows of the city. The idea that you had to keep up because words were being invented daily and added to the language helped me to understand the compelling nature of mythic stories in which very old tales come to life again when they are mixed with the language and issues, and with the signs and symbols of the present.

Although I eventually left my old neighborhood and left friends behind, I never completely left the questions that arose during youth. In college I majored in literature and philosophy, but continued to read and study myths. Stories could settle my mind, as if the track laid out in a traditional tale allowed me to rearrange the otherwise chaotic experiences of modern life. The confusions and defeats of marriage, becoming a father and seeking a career made more sense when reflected against the contours of the eternal drama reflected in primordial stories.

Being full of stories, I eventually experimented with ways of telling them to audiences. One day, while working on a European fairy tale, a remarkable thing happened. I had found a story that was compelling, yet something about it didn't work. It had been altered in some way that made it hard to tell. I couldn't easily figure how to correct the problem and wasn't even sure if I had the right to do so.

During the same period I was learning to play certain rhythms from Africa and Brazil on hand drums. As I puzzled over the broken part of the story, I began to play, somewhat absently, a rhythm that I favored. All of a sudden the story appeared before my eye as if it had become a movie. I could *see* the story I was thinking about. That was dramatic enough, but I also could see where the story went off course. And, I could see a way to fix the broken part. For me, that was an epiphany, a revelation in which a secret connection between stories and rhythms became palpable and visible.

In one open moment I had an insight into the soft structure of stories and a discovery of how to tell them while drumming. I could see the story before me, see into it more deeply and see—all at once—many different ways to tell the same tale. After that, I felt I was a storyteller as much as I was a person fascinated by stories.

Stories need to be told in order to remain alive, and this one had a new life to try out. With my Cuban-styled drum, an African rhythm, and the patched-up European story, I went looking for an audience. I offered it at a gathering of the local folklore society. I gave a version of the story that showed its newly repaired bones. Under the influence of the drum and the surprising visual presence of the story, I added whatever words spontaneously appeared in my mouth. For me, this was exciting and risky and fully alive. It wasn't a recital or a rehearsed performance. I didn't know exactly what I would say, but just described the story as I saw it before my eye while I held it present through the rhythm.

After telling the tale I tried to offer a sense of what intrigued me about the story, how I felt it had needed rehabilitation and what it could mean in the contemporary world. I invited a discussion of the themes in the story and any reactions to it. The first speaker asked if the drum came from the same place as the story. "No," I answered. Was the rhythm traditionally associated with that drum or that story? "No." Then, it was inappropriate to tell the story in that manner. A discussion followed in which most folks agreed that stories should be reproduced as close as possible to their original context. They also suggested that I had no right to tamper with the shape of the story.

I found myself reflecting back on my experience with the gang in the bathroom of the movie theater. It was twenty years later, yet there was something similar. I felt myself on the edge of revelations about storytelling and the living powers of spontaneous speech, while those I tried to share it with remained focused upon other issues, which seemed less immediate and less meaningful.

For me, the story could come back to life if told in a creative and spontaneous way. Something ancient, yet still alive, tried to slip into the room through the meeting between the old shape of the story and the breathing presence of the audience. Somewhere between the ancient images and the immediate conditions people silently carried into the room, a *living myth* could arise. Although myth has come to mean something false, its true meaning is closer to emergent truth.

Telling a story in an enlivened way was like releasing water to run down an old and dry riverbed, so that people could drink at the endless stream of knowledge and imagination again. That's what I found at the living edge of stories where the "real world" meets the more than real world. I became determined to find others who sensed the way myths and old stories carried living water to those thirsty for meaning.

In the course of studying stories and poems, I went to hear the poet Robert Bly. After delivering a barrage of poems he told a fairy tale and launched into an interpretation of it. He asked people to consider how the tale reflected issues in their own lives. He used theories of Freud and Jung to connect the old story with contemporary issues. Afterward, he talked with me about stories and myth and about William Butler Yeats and the role of rhythms in poetry. He invited me to teach rhythm at a workshop for writers and I gladly accepted.

Somehow all the pieces began to make sense. If people were willing to enter the moment with full attention and open emotion, then their exact troubles become the context wherein stories and poetry, psychology, and philosophy could all become personally important and vitally alive. Not a matter of academic interest, or the preservation of folklore; not simply psychological theory, or indulgence in one's feelings, but a spontaneous arrangement and coincidence of artistic and mythic elements, which can melt the opposition of ancient and modern, make myths come back to life, and allow emotions to flow and language to sing.

Evoking the echo of fairy and folk tales caused people to experience the story of their own life in mythic terms. Where mythic symbols and important events in a person's life meet, strong emotions arise and release memories long held in the body. The story comes to life through the listeners who relive their own lives in ways that can be compelling and profound. Besides being *homo erectus*, humans are also *homo symbolicus*, as the human soul longs to participate in the symbolic life, and needs to encounter the great passions in relation to mythic themes. In doing so, time collapses and people can find again the continuing story of the age-old chain of being.

Modernity's obsession with progress and blind rush to create a future based in technology seems to require a thorough departure from the past. Yet the past secretly travels along with us. The past, especially the ancient imagination that caused humans to stand and walk with heads in the heavens and feet on the goat's earth, holds keys that can unlock the literalism of the present and open the future to greater meaning. That which is ancient has no expiration date and its value resides exactly in its enduring oldness. Hidden in the soul of all peoples—something ancient and mythic—continues to be the source of both survival and originality.

Mythic imagination and the story-mind dwell in the ancient core of human beings, generating the instinct to seek meaning both individually and culturally. People used to know that the future is in the past. A person can only go as far forward as their soul can reach back. The role of myth is to give meaning to what people experience. Without a sense of myth and story, life increasingly becomes a pointless series of experiences that cannot add up to either meaning or wisdom.

When Robert Bly called again to say he wanted to hold some retreats to consider the increasing sense of isolation amongst modern men and address the problems of fathers raising children in a culture increasingly devoid of art and meaning, I was right there. I had been collecting stories from many traditions and looking for ways to consider both myth and cultural rituals in relation to the unfinished initiations of youth and the loss of elders in the chaos of contemporary culture.

Thus began a long series of experimental events that, while though mostly involving men, aimed at the heart of culture, seeking ways to attend to the "making of soul" in the modern world. It was both fearful and heartening to encounter groups of men who were desperate enough to be emotionally open and savvy enough to seek more meaning than modern life dares to consider. For me, it allowed a return to my first intuitions of the connections between youthful exploits and the mythic, questing bands that roam through the old stories of cultures the world over.

It was startling to find that, given the chance, many men would throw caution to the wind and boldly enter mythic territories in order to explore neglected levels of emotional and spiritual life. It was a great and welcome surprise to learn that behind the boardroom, the waiting room, the locker room, and the barroom, there was a ground of spiritual longing and emotional immediacy that modern men were willing and able to enter. That, upon entering that forest of imagination, the armor that choked off emotional and spiritual needs could loosen and crack and fall clattering to the ground.

Just as in the adventures of youth, there was a reckless, heartfelt willingness to experiment in the study and practice of myth, music, emotional expression, and ritual forms. It was as if a territory lost amidst the clutter of modern life had been found again, as if a path had opened in the tortured present that led to the age-old grounds of the psyche. Old wounds were opened in attempts to heal and change, while unique aptitudes and inner gifts awakened, as well. To my continuing surprise, executives and ex-cons, priests and war veterans, doctors and healers of all kinds, students, craftsmen, professors, and artists of every description struggled to sing and even drum, but mostly to wander and work in the ancient forest of stories.

"A man's work is nothing more than to rediscover, through the detours of art, those one or two images in the presence of which his heart first opened."
ALBERT CAMUS

If we open up the word "art" to include its roots in myth and ritual, if we use "man" in its old sense of mankind so that it includes women as well as men, then the real work of life involves meaningful attempts to rediscover the doorways to the human heart and the territories of the soul. The heart first opens when a person encounters in the world elements of an imagination already existing in the soul. Tribal cultures throughout time used art, rituals, and mythic stories to sustain connections to those unique moments in which the heart and mind fully open to life. Rites of passage and initiations of all kinds were invented to make detours to the ground of the soul and hold open the heart within.

Seen with an eye for that which opens the heart and reveals life's inherent purpose, the period of youth becomes less an awkward phase and more an essential detour in life. Whereas childhood is mostly about growth, youth is more about radical change. In addition to obvious growth spurts and physical maturation, the psyche seeks to know itself and can only do so in contrast to both the simple play of childhood and the impending duties of adulthood. The period of youth represents a radical diversion from the typical limits of social life. Before youth can become old enough to be responsible, they must become ancient enough to awaken to who they are at heart.

Initiations and rites of passage were ways in which traditional societies consciously assisted and enhanced life's essential patterns of change. When a culture forgets to assist its members through necessary changes, the passage happens with less awareness, usually with less consciousness and eventually with a loss of continuity throughout the society. When young people are not invited into a conscious rite of transition and self-discovery, they attempt to invent their own ceremonies to fill the void. Since both life and death are involved at every major transition, things can go darkly awry.

Our neighborhood crew back on the corner could be reckless and destructive. Yet we didn't simply intend to destroy things or self-destruct. Rather, we felt driven and pulled into all the gaps and alleys and detours of life. Unconsciously, we sought to encounter ourselves in a deeper way. We sought to crack open our hearts and our minds. Instinctively, we broke rules to break the spells of childhood and to avoid being captured in the dull trance of normality.

Unwittingly, we sought initiatory breaks in order to find out who we were in the face of life, even in the face of death. We didn't so much wish to die as to be born into a greater life where we could feel significant and meaningful. Our clumsy rituals and reckless adventures were attempts to encounter the mysteries of the world and measure ourselves against the energies of life and through brushes with death.

"Little death" was an old term for a brush with death that generates greater life. "Creative death" is another term which distinguishes initiation from actual death while indicating that something must die in order for life to grow and continue on. The sense that each life-stage grows out of the death of what existed before was common to ancient peoples living closer to the natural cycles of life and death. At certain crucial levels, the human psyche remains ancient and continues to attend to the pattern of life-death-renewal, even if modern thought fails to recognize the indelible pattern.

Despite the loss of initiatory ways and the modern tendency to deny the presence of death, the psyche reacts to radical alterations in life as if an initiation were underway. Thus, any break or loss or severe separation can evoke the sense of initiation in a person's psyche or soul. Whatever severely alters the overt patterns of life, also opens a person to psychological and mythical levels of unusual depth. Accident, divorce, abortion, the death of a loved one, the loss of a career, even eruptions of nature which destroy and reshape the landscape, all can precipitate the psyche's expectation of a thorough rite of passage. They are the detours that keep the heart and the mind open to growing and learning who we are and what we are meant to do in the world.

Initiation is the dramatic style in which the psyche shifts the ground and inner orientation of an individual or group in response to the expected and the unexpected breaks in the skin of life. Initiation is the psyche's response to both the severe struggles and the great opportunities found in the course of life. Success as well as failure can shift the psychic ground in a person and awaken the old pattern of separation, ordeal, and return to life as a new person.

Whether it be the trauma and shock of a loss in life, or the drama and exhilaration of success, whatever interrupts, breaks us open, or breaks us down also initiates us into a greater knowledge of ourselves, particularly of the nature and style of our given soul. Initiation opens pathways to the center of the self, where a person encounters the mysteries of life and death and learns of their unique participation in them. Once such an opening occurs, the psyche becomes animated with an expectation that the change will culminate in a different status in life.

Each individual carries an expectation of and a desire for self-revelation. What seeks to be revealed is extreme by nature and can only reach awareness through radical circumstances. Whether formal or informal, certain events touch the inner realities of a person. Initiatory events are those that mark a person's life forever, that pull them more deeply into the waters of life than they would normally choose to go. What initiates us also strips us down to the inner essentials and releases qualities and powers that were hidden within.

In the soul, the style of life-death-renewal remains primordial, axiomatic, and archetypal. Initiatory ceremonies and rites of passage tend to elaborate the pattern of life-death-renewal through three basic steps: first, a departure and separation from daily life; secondly a period of suffering ordeals and dramatic episodes which breakthrough to the heart and soul of the initiate; finally, a return marked as a different person and recognized by a knowing community. Initiation includes a felt sense that a person changes completely; they become as if another, a new and renewed person.

Initiatory experiences inhabit the same deep psychic ground as birth and death. Instead of normal circumstances, radical conditions prevail and are essential for real change. As with circumstances of life and death, a person steps outside the normal rules and beyond their own beliefs. For the one experiencing separation, the abnormal becomes the norm; the ordeal becomes the only way through, and a proper welcome upon return confirms the reality of the changes experienced.

Just as growth involves growing pains and healing requires abnormal and unusual treatments, initiations tend to involve pain and suffering. Tribal initiations often include intentional wounds, visible markings or scars. The bodies of initiates are visibly altered to literally impress a new condition upon them and leave outer evidence of the inner changes. What happens inside also appears on the surface and becomes visible to others, for it was understood that initiation changes a person's relationship to everyone else. Indelible physical markings such as tattoos indicate a thorough change which alters the entire person. Lines are drawn, marks are made, and there can be no going back to an unblemished or innocent place.

Initiation involves an increase of knowledge, especially self-knowledge, as well as a loss of innocence. Knowledge cuts through and opens the skin of innocence that keeps a person unknowing. After childhood, innocence about oneself and the world becomes an obstacle to growing and learning, as well as a danger to others. Initiation involves a knowledge of the presence of death that fosters a greater knowledge of life. Seen through the eye of initiation, death is not the opposite of life, death is the opposite of birth;

both are aspects of life and part of the patterns of renewal.

When life's inevitable stages and dramatic events go unmarked and unreflected, the world seems more chaotic and less meaningful. Intense feelings of emptiness or chaos at certain points in life can be seen as calls from areas of unfinished initiations. Knowledge of how life opened and initiated a person gives meaning to life experience; without it old age can be filled with irrational fears, strange nostalgia, and chaos. The little deaths that make renewal on the road of life possible also prepare a person for death's final embrace. Traditionally, initiation was considered to make both life and death more intelligible and dignified.

Whereas rites of passage used to provide occasions for generations to connect, modern cultures generate gaps instead. Generation gaps, gender gaps, even leadership gaps become more pronounced because events intended to open the hearts and minds of people go unexamined and unmarked. Nevertheless, people carry scars and markings that indicate where life has taken them. Psychological scars and emotional traumas exist where life tried to break a person open to the heights and depths of the human soul. The places where we each suffer in life can become the metaphorical ground on which we reflect upon our "informal initiations."

The heart opens where life breaks it open, be it through love or loss or both. Those events that touch us deeply make us take heart or else lose heart. Either way, what reaches to the soul and gives us a change of heart, marks us and makes us who we are in the world. The eye of initiation sees darkly and sees in the darkness of suffering the glint of survival and the glimmer of a spirit that would come to know itself. To be human means to be wounded. The story of one's life grows around wounds that open to what is truly, deeply human. By "wounds," I mean those blows from life that stun a person, that stop the daily round of life, that lacerate the tissues of the soul, that make a person feel other than who they were or thought they should be.

Using a "psychology of initiation," we can see that experiences that change a person's life and mark them as an individual can be opened up and re-examined to learn what tries to live into the world through them. When seen through the "eye of initiation," the exact wounds a person carries turn out to be openings to a greater imagination and deeper understanding of that life. Where native people might say, "that ceremony made me," a modern person might consider, "that life-changing experience made me who I am." Returning to the places which first opened one's heart, or even first broke it, can continue to reveal hidden aspects of the story trying to live through him or her. Initiation means to begin, to take a step, to step further into life; what initiates us can continue to educate us.

Rites and symbols of initiation are intended to open the life of each young person to the sense of meaning and purpose already dwelling in them as their god-given, spirit-blessed, passion-fed soul tries to awaken. The need for initiation and soulful education of young people doesn't disappear because mass societies ignore the age-old expectation to find purpose and meaning in life. But a culture that denies the innate inclinations of its young will itself become aimless and pointless. The great injustices of this world begin where the innate nobility of those who are young becomes sacrificed to the monumental greed and cowardice of those who inherit worldly power simply by becoming old enough to do so.

The most lost and dangerous people in this world are those not emotionally bonded to family, community, and humanity as a whole and those who acquire power without being initiated to a genuine sense of the source of that power and the value of individual human life. The spread of mass industrial societies produces increasing numbers of unbonded children and adults uninitiated to the purpose and meaning of their own lives. The loss of shared myths and rites that invite the individual into a "knowing community" leaves increasing numbers of youth at a loss and feeling lost in the sea of life.

In many cases, boys will act out the collective wounds of a culture, often in seemingly pointless violence. News reports of murderous child-soldiers, drive-by shootings, increased racism and religious intolerance, the spread of child abuse, and the steady increase in the rape and mistreatment of women in the very centers of culture are bulletins from uninitiated child-men whose bodies grow apace while their psyches remain outside the touch and blessings of human community.

Life is not tame and each generation bears a fire of individual and collective heat that only learns its purpose by burning into the world. In many tribal cultures it was said that if the boys are not initiated into manhood, shaped and guided by the skills and love of knowing elders, they would destroy their own culture. When the passions and imagination innately burning inside youth are not intentionally and lovingly added to the hearth of community, they become a negligent rage that can hollow out or burn down the structures of culture. But the most certain signals for lighting the fires of destruction are sent when those old enough to know better fail to find meaning and purpose in their own lives.

In trying to leave the past behind, people walk blindly into it again. In seeking to dominate Nature and control life, modern mass cultures also tend to divorce people from their own "inner nature." In over-committing to that which is literal and seemingly logical, people lose touch with the great imagination for life, which ever lives in the soul. Each person is "mythic by nature," each a story trying to participate in the ongoing creation of both culture and nature. What waits to awaken in each person is ancient and surprising, mythic and meaningful. This book considers ways to view the conflicts and dilemmas of modern societies against a background of myth and imagination in the way of the Old Mind, the ancient, poetic mind through which each soul seeks to know itself more fully, and to find at least moments of genuine human community.

I

The Road of the Two Fathers

...two old roads, curving and white.
Down them my heart is walking on foot.
CESAR VALLEJO

THE HUNTER AND HIS SON

Pay heed to this tale of a father and son!

A hunter and his son went to the bush one day to pursue their occupation. They hunted all morning and found nothing to sustain them but one small bush+. The father gave the rat to the son to carry. It seemed of no consequence to the son, so he threw the rat into the bush. The rest of the day they saw no other game.

At dusk the father built a fire and said, "Bring the rat to roast, son; at least we will have something to eat." When he learned that the son had thrown the rat away, he became very angry. In an outburst of rage, he struck the son with his ax and turned away. He returned home, leaving his son lying still on the ground.

Late in the evening, the son rose up and returned to his father's village. He stood at the edge of the village until everyone was asleep. Then he went quietly to his parents' hut, gathered up his few belongings, and left. He walked into the night, following a long path that led to another village.

The son arrived at this large village in the dark of the night. Everyone was asleep. He went to the center of the place and came to the chief's hut. The chief was awake. The son of the hunter entered the hut of the chief naked, without trousers.

The chief said, "From where do you come?"

"From that other village," the son told him.

The chief asked, "How goes it with you?"

The son spoke, "My father and I went to the bush to hunt. We found only one small rat. He gave it to me to carry and I threw it into the bush. In the evening, we built a fire. He told me to roast the rat. I said I had thrown it away. He became angry and struck me with his ax. I fell down. In the night, I rose up, left that village and came here. That's how it is with me."

The chief said, "Will you keep a secret with me?"

The son said, "What secret?"

The chief explained that there had been a war in which his only son had been killed. He said, "Now I have no son. How can that be, a king with no son? I wish to say that you are my son who was captured in the war, that you have escaped, and that you returned home. Will you keep that secret?"

The son said, "This will not be difficult."

Then the chief began to play his drum—boom, boom, in the middle of the night. The mother of the house was awakened; she came out and said, "Oh King Lion, he who causes fear, what is the drum you are playing in the middle of the night?"

The king announced, "My son has returned."

Then the mother raised the sound of joy, the whole village was awakened. Everyone was saying, "What has happened at the king's hut that they are playing drums and singing in the middle of the night?" A messenger was sent around, telling everyone that the king's son had come, he who had been captured in the war had returned. Some of the people were joyful; others doubted it, saying, "Indeed, indeed."

At dawn, the son was bathed, anointed with oil, and dressed in fine new clothes. The chief gave him gifts and brought him before the whole village to be welcomed. Some of the chief's counselors said, "It is not his son." Others said surely it was. The doubts of some grew; they said, "Indeed, indeed."

Soon the counselors summoned the sons of the village, dressed them in fine garments, and called for their great war-horses. The counselors said, "Go to the house of the chief. Call the chief's son. Tell him to bring his horse and a sword. Say you are taking the horses for exercise. Ride out to the great clearing. Dismount there, take your swords and slay your horses. Observe what the son of the chief does, and report to us here." Each counselor gave a sword to his son, and the young men set off for the chief's hut.

Now, there was a talebearer present who heard the counselors' plan and quickly informed the king. The king made preparations, saying, "If the naked man can dance, how much better can the man with a cloak?" He called the son to him and said, "Take this horse and sword. When the sons of the village call for you, go with them. Whatever they do, you do it as well." The sons of the counselors came and called for the king's son. They all set off. They rode to the clearing and dismounted. When the son of the king saw the other sons slay their horses—well, he did it, too.

The sons of the counselors returned to their fathers and reported that the king's son had slain a valuable mount, saying, "Only the son of a king would display such magnificent disregard for property and wealth."

The counselors still had doubts and said, "Indeed, indeed." They decided on further tests. The next day they gave each of their sons a slave girl. They instructed them to invite the son of the chief to bring a slave girl and go with them to the clearing. Once there, they should slay the slave girls and observe what the son of the chief did. Once again, the talebearer was present. He informed the king, who told the son to take his slave girl when they called for him, and "Whatever you see they have done, you do it as well." In the clearing, the sons of the counselors took their swords, and each slew a slave girl. The son of the king? Well, he did it, too. And the sons returned to the counselors and reported what had happened, saying, "Only the son of a king would act as he has done." This time the counselors were satisfied. They offered no more tests.

Time went on. The son lived with the king. Then one day the hunter came looking for his son. He questioned people, saying, "Have you seen one who looks like this, who acts like such and such?" The people said, "No, we don't know him, we haven't seen your son. But there is a son in the king's hut who looks like that." He was sent to the hut of the king. He entered and greeted the king, who was seated with the son at his side.

The hunter said to his son, "Will you get up and return with me and live as before?" The son remained silent. The king said, "Hunter, if you will keep the secret with me, I will give you whatever gold you wish." The hunter refused. The king offered one hundred times whatever gold the hunter would request. The hunter refused despite all the entreaties of the king. The son? Well, he remained silent.

Then the king called for three horses to be saddled and one sword to be brought. The three of them—the hunter, the king, and the son—then rode off to the clearing. When they reached that place, the king gave the sword to the son. He said, "We are here unarmed, but you hold a sword. There is nothing else left to do. Either you must slay me and take my goods and return with your father to his village and his world, or you must slay your father and return with me and live as we have been in my village."

The son did not know what to do. If it were you, what would you do? Kill the father, or kill the king? What would you do?

Off with the rat's head!!

CHAPTER 1

THE HUNTER AND HIS SON

THERE'S A STRANGE relationship between a storyteller and a story. Looking for a story to tell easily becomes like hunting. I often set out seeking a story for a certain occasion, only to wind up being hunted down myself by a different kind of story. I found The Hunter and His Son in a paperback collection of African stories hidden in a dark corner of a used bookstore. The book had been out of print for more than twenty years; the pages of this copy were torn and yellow from age and neglect. The book cost me fifty cents. I read all the stories and put it away.

At the time, I wanted a story that could engage a class of high school students who were prone to distractions and mostly disinterested in what school offered to them. To hold their attention, a story would need to be immediate and compelling. I thought that African "dilemma tales" might surprise them and intrigue them to consider some age-old questions.

One story told the tale of a young woman who was undervalued by her father, disrespected by her husband, and mistreated by a would-be lover. The students jumped into that story and a passionate discussion ensued. Everyone had their own story of being rejected, undervalued, and overlooked. Boys and girls spoke willingly and knowingly from the position of the under-valued woman as the sense of each person's inner worth became more evident.

Meanwhile, the hunter and son story kept appearing in my mind as I waited for a street light, or prepared to leave the house, or when I thought of the open-heartedness of my own children. I noticed that the tale would catch me in one direction as a son, in another as a father. I kept trying to toss this story aside. But just as the rat in the story comes back at the end, I knew that in the end I would have to tell this tale and learn why it followed me around.

After I told the "rat's tale" to the students, they sat still in a quizzical silence. Then the toughest guy in the class announced that he would kill the father: "Definitely would do that. You know, you have to fight back. That's the way it is…" Once he opened the door, most of the kids wanted to say how they perceived the wound that the son received. It was as if the story created the opportunity for everyone to acknowledge their own wounding. I felt a tremendous sympathy for the pain and courage of those kids. It was as if they were just waiting for an excuse to open up and reveal deep things that they carried inside the way they posed at school. I also found myself tasting again my own intense feelings from experiences of being hurt and abandoned as a youth. The more I stayed in touch with old wounds I still carried, the younger I felt and the more sympathy I had for younger folks.

The more I told the story, the more present and clear the shape of the inner wound became. The image of father and son setting out together struck me repeatedly. I could see my father's back as he disappeared after dropping me off at the induction center during the Vietnam War. I could feel the uncertainty in my own back as I walked away from my sons after an angry exchange. And I could see that what held those images together was a hidden wound that secretly passed from generation to generation.

The road that leads from boyhood to manhood begins where a father's footsteps can be seen. It's an old road in the psyche and modern men wander on it just as the ancients did. Sons can't help but hunt the spirit of the father who walks the road before them. Returning to pay attention to initiatory steps for men seems to require tracking back the footprints left where each father and son encounter the intense puzzle placed between them.

When the opportunity came to tell stories to a group of grown men, the tale of the father and son, of the wound and the king, was the clear choice. At the end of the story there was an uproar. Everyone wanted to speak once. The room filled with emotion and confusion. The most common entry point was the scene where the father delivers a blow to the son. Men of all ages identified with the son knocked to the ground or rising from the unconscious state caused by the blow. It became clear that there were volumes of stories which could readily arise from the place where a father and son become forever joined and yet separated by this inevitable wound.

A person can only meet the symbolic narrative of a genuine story with their own genuine life experience. When confronted with the symbolic wound between fathers and sons the whole group became wounded, each listener eventually finding an exact injury. Because the appearance of the wound comes so early in the story, the sense of a shared wound enters the group. Instead of the competitive ground of heroics, men began to connect through a sense of vulnerability and loss. Father and son may begin the journey on the hunt, but something also hunts them and requires that they turn to a shared knowledge of wounds if they would come to know each other in ways that soften the heart and produce tears of forgiveness.

The son receives a blow which staggers him on the road of life. He isn't simply hurt or offended; rather he is forced to enter the path of his own life through the wound received from his father. All the son's actions—indeed, the whole rest of the story—are generated by that wound. If the wound from the father seems an unfortunate accident, it's an accident that happens to every man. Although it may surprise some, a genuine community of men forms around an awareness of wounds experienced, of blows that knock a person backward or push them further than they expected to go. To be human is to be wounded; this turned out to be a deeply human and humanizing story.

The body secretly carries and carefully remembers the blows we receive throughout life. Whether it be the back of a hand or the more subtle injury made by absence, the wound between father and son shapes a dwelling place in each man. After telling the story, I would pose the question, "Where did the father strike the son?" A man answers, "Right in the head." "With which part of the ax?" "The blunt end on the left temple." "Is that what everyone saw?" "No!" Then, an onslaught of blows pour out: right side of head, from behind, top of the head, sharp end of the ax in the heart, in the genitals, flat of the ax in the face, on the right shoulder blade, and so on. Each man touches the area he names with the kind of impulsive gesture resembling someone just injured. The wounds are present, just under the skin of awareness from where they continue to ache and bleed into projects and relationships.

More than once someone insisted that I had stated in the story where the ax hit the boy. I argued that each listener carries wounds, and blessings as well, in specific places as the body helps remember important occurrences. Since some events were recorded, we could play the tape back and listen. It was quite a shock for many to learn that they supplied the details that they thought they heard from me. There was no mention of the head or how the boy fell, etc. Simply, the father struck the boy and left him. Similar to witnesses at an accident or a crime, each observer mixes outward events with inner contents. Images within the tale stir emotions and awaken memories of the story that each person carries within, as each meets the symbolic images with their actual life. There is no other way to hear a story except by meeting it with the story carried inside.

The wound in the story opens the "territory of the fathers" and brings remembered fathers into the room. It also brings the eternal anguish between fathers and sons into the atmosphere. A composed audience becomes an angry, sorrowful, resentful, fearful group connected by a shared and living wound. In such open moments, typical divisions and hierarchies disappear. Differences now consist of distinctions between the shapes and feelings of a shared human wound. Most recall the age when a particular blow was received and each feels an increasing pressure to reveal, even amongst strangers, stunning memories and painful feelings.

At one end of the spectrum there are stories of sons brutally and repeatedly beaten by a father or a series of stepfathers. Whenever a crisis develops, they feel the presence of the ax nearby. They feel ready to strike back or run off regardless of whether the situation warrants it. At the other extreme stand those whose fathers were either physically absent or emotionally distant. Here, the "blow" is more subtle, consisting of the absence of touch, the omission of a passionate mistake. Often as a result of wounds of omission, men can feel indecisive and only vaguely connected to the world around them. Even if their career moves forward, something remains missing. They may envy those with vivid stories of sharp blows from a raging father, preferring the clarity of a physical wound to the invisible blows of omission. Some are wounded by too much presence, others by too much absence.

Some listeners are surprised that the son in the story recovers at all and rises up again. They felt sure he had received a death blow and didn't even hear the rest of the story. Something in them was crushed in childhood and driven under the ground. Inside, they remain stunned and disoriented, not sure of what might be happening around them. In fear that he might be left behind again, a man yells, "Wait!" He wants to stay at the scene where the boy lays all alone on the ground. He describes being beaten daily by a father who was way out of control. For years he has run from the pain inside, now he doesn't want to rush ahead. His insistent pain evokes an isolation and dark earth in everyone. The rage and sorrow invited by the story and buried in busy daily lives becomes palpable. It's as if each one present sits across the fire from their father, who in turn sits amongst the long line of fathers and their sons stretching back through time. Clearly Oedipus is there, old Saturn who devoured his sons, Abraham still uncertain about Isaac, even Christ who called to the empty forsaken heavens.

From the beginning of the story, from the beginning of time, fathers and sons have been hunting each other. Both are aimed at an inevitable fire of expectation, although the expectations of the father and son are often radically different. They see each other through flames of love and flickers of hate, through high hopes and bitter disappointments. Each son follows his father's footsteps to some degree. The father, be he clumsy or adept, offers the skills and techniques he has learned. But the sense of the hunt eventually throws them into a tension of opposing states. The fire and the rat are a father's gifts—warmth, protection, food. Yet they can never be enough to meet the son's burning desire for the full feast of life. At some level the father knows that, and he strikes out or walks out because of a wound already burning within him.

This story is very old, and the situation primal. If the hunt is successful, something will die to sustain the lives of father and son. Thus, the father's footsteps inevitably lead the son into the issues of life and death. Meanwhile, the son seeks to learn the purpose of his life by tracking signs of meaning and purpose in his father. He believes he can find himself by following his father. The father usually comes to believe this as well—until, one day, he hands the son a rat. The son expects more than is offered, he already sees beyond the father, though he may not realize that. Some form of failure is inevitable; there's a rat in each version of the story. Somehow the temperament and human weakness of the father will be revealed to his son.

The father has been to the bush many times. Some days he has returned tired, empty-handed, carrying only his disappointment home. The father's expectations have been changed by his exchanges with the bush and with life. For him, the rat represents survival. He knows from experience that the bush may withhold anything more for days. He has been learning the art of survival and how to negotiate with the uncertainties that life presents.

The father may be willing to accept the rat, but the son is certain that bigger and better game waits ahead. The son has received the benefits of the father's efforts without experiencing the father's struggles. His eyes are big with the future, filled with the potentials of life. The rat seems inconsequential. What is a rat when an elephant or an elegant antelope lies ahead? The whole day is ahead, an eternity in which anything can happen, even at the last minute game might appear. The son seeks the wonders of life, and the possibilities only increase with closeness to the father. If something great were to occur they would share in it together. That might explain their relationship, change it, heal it resolve it, give it meaning. It's easy for the son to throw the rat away; it's even an act of faith in his father and faith in his father's world.

Meantime, the father has been forced to learn limitations, how dreams can become secondary to survival, how responsibilities can diminish desires. Perhaps the son will learn something of the uncertainty of this life where a person must sometimes simply accept what is given. In the life of a hunter, there isn't an antelope behind every bush. Hunting involves the art of survival; they will survive this day, and survive it better because of the gift of the bush rat. So thinks the father as he goes all the way through the act of preparing the fire. Of course, the son waits all the way to the last minute to admit tossing away the rat. When the story comes out, each thinks the other has failed in some way, and each has indeed failed the other's expectations. The son imagined that there would be some great treat for dinner, that his own sense of life's great potential would be experienced in the presence of his father. The father imagined that there would be something to share between them, that his effort would at least satisfy the basic needs. After all, something is better than nothing, especially better than a father and son with nothing between them but increasing disappointment.

Neither expected that there would be only an awkward fire, a burning sense of failure, an emptiness and exasperation between them. The father becomes speechless. There's nothing to say, maybe it's all been said before. Maybe the father would have been able to face an evening of nothingness alone, but not this way, not in front of his son. Maybe he had invested more in the rat than he realized. Maybe he had lived with his own unfulfilled promises for too long. Somehow, the rat becomes the last straw. He strikes out at the closeness, at the distance, at all that is incomprehensible, at the past, at the future. He strikes the son down and walks away.

If we allow a story to enter into us, we also enter the psychic ground held in that tale. A story reads us as much as we read it. As the aboriginal hunters of Australia say, "You can't hunt in the tribal lands until the country knows you!" By surrendering to a story we find a way to its interior where gifts of knowledge become ours for the taking. By entering the symbolic scene that compels us the most, the story becomes embodied and the depths of the human soul can open. Through the emotions and memories of those tending to a story, it comes to life and can become a source of genuine community, a communing place where people can share and heal and learn. A story is a storehouse which continues to give gifts as long as it is told boldly and people respond to it honestly.

Once we had laid out the story of the hunter and son in a wide old hall. Roughly one hundred men arranged themselves throughout the room, each taking a place according to the scene which moved them the most. A large group gathered at the scene of the ax blow, an even larger group crowded up where the son stands with sword in hand facing the dilemma of whether to strike his father or the king. But on the road between the village of the father and that of the king there stood only one lonely man. For some reason, no one else felt drawn to that place. While the two large groups stood like villages full of people, the lone figure between them looked lost and in exile.

When we turned to him, he described how a couple of years before he had separated from his wife and children. As he began to live more and more by himself, he felt an increasing isolation. Eventually he came to be overcome with shame, so much so that he couldn't explain his disappearance to his own children. Only now, finding himself a solitary man in a room full of men, did he realize how insular and lonely he had become. Everyone felt drawn to the deep sadness in his voice. Another man spoke, he too, was at that place in the story, but wouldn't admit it, even to himself, until he felt the other man's sorrow and drew courage from that admission.

The second man moved next to the solitary man. He told of growing up without a father. Initially, he felt he wasn't even in the story, or was stuck at the very beginning still looking for some footsteps to follow. Hearing the sorrow in the other man's voice evoked an old melancholy that had been his road as a child. Was it sorrow that had fathered him? Was that both the blow that struck him down as well as the style which connected him to the world? We all followed the sad men back along the dark road to the place where the son looks carefully at the hut of his parents. After a while, it became more clear that each of us left the hut of our parents with a collection of feelings and moods, with the longings and belongings we still carry out in the world.

At first the parents' hut and the home village are the whole world for a child. The parents, big and powerful appear as royalty, even as gods. Inevitably, harshly in some cases and mysteriously in others, the father gives a blow that shakes the world of the son. The wound that results may be literal; it certainly is psychological, and it has mythic dimensions as well. The crown that the son sometimes saw on his father's head falls as the ax swings through time. The head of the son turns away from the realm of childhood and toward the wide world beyond. Sadly or sternly, the son walks into the darkness at the edge of childhood looking for another head to crown. Although he feels empty and betrayed and completely alone, he walks the same road all other sons have walked. It's a necessary road made of uncertainty, of few belongings, and of many shadows.

CHAPTER 2

THE KING'S HUT

THE YOUNG SON left the village in which everyone was asleep and unaware of how he became wounded. The next village sleeps as well with one significant difference: at the center a chief waits in the middle of the night. The story puts it strangely—"everyone was asleep... the chief was awake." Old stories often have illogical aspects as if to alert irrational parts of the psyche. Stories are like dreams in that respect; the rules differ from those of the waking world and the value and status of things can change all of a sudden.

Before the son approaches the hut of the king, the story could be read as a report of something factual: a hunter struck his son over a misunderstanding and the boy ran away from home. There's little of the psychological and nothing of the mythical in the narration. As the son enters the village where everyone sleeps but the chief, he crosses a line and another level of the psyche opens. The chief is also "King Lion, he who causes fear," and the queen-mother accepts a youth she has never seen before as if he were her own offspring.

In the language of the story, the presence of the wound, the separation from all he knows, and the night journey awaken something in the son that resonates with a king who waits at the center of the psyche. Like the inevitable wounding between father and son, another primordial pattern of the psyche appears in the unvarnished folk tale. In leaving the father's realm, the son has awakened a king. Or, when the father turns away from the son, the psyche of the son turns towards someone who can bless him where he has been wounded. Loss of the father he wanted keeps the son awake, while loss of the son he needs keeps the king from sleeping.

Each son of man leaves home in search of something that can parent what is noble and royal within him. Sons act as kingmakers in order to find more fully a nobility hidden within them. Meanwhile, the kingly part of a grown man would have his achievements reflected back in the eyes of a prince. From the village of father and son, the story has necessarily shifted to the realm of the king and the prince. The world has been set this way; were it not so, children might remain at home in the shadow of their parents, unaware of the wide world with its strange presentiments of surprise and danger.

The dynamics of the story reflect the instinctive depths of the human psyche, where accepting the blows of fate and entering the road of the unknown allow hidden possibilities to arise. As the wounded child walks the uncertain road that extends away from the family, he walks toward that which the family cannot see in him. It's difficult for parents to see through the veil of their own expectations to the inner nature of the child born to them. And each child carries something that waits to be born in the world beyond the parent's door.

Opposite the door of the family hut with its literal history and limitations, another door waits to be opened. In the new place, as yet unknown qualities of the son can be announced and confirmed. He can be anointed to a new position in life. Here, it makes odd sense to enter naked, for even the painful conditions of being alone, unknown, and dispossessed can be useful in this world.

In this hut different aspects of the son's psyche will be questioned and considered. Here, it is not enough to be the good son. The first two questions are as simple as a doorway: "From where do you come? How goes it with you?" Yet such questions require some reflection on the part of the youth. Huts like this exist in the psychic forest. They appear when genuine change is possible. If the hut belongs to the Baba Yaga, the old and powerful hag of Russian tales, the first question will pose a dilemma, "Are you running toward something or away from something?"

A simple enough question, yet much depends on the skill with which it is answered. These huts have their rules and their dangers. A person who picks one horn of the dilemma becomes stuck on that horn and stuck in life. Answer that you are running away and you might go straight back from where you came. State that you are running toward something and you might enter a wild goose chase that leads nowhere at all. Sometimes, choosing either answer results in your head being removed from its perch on the body and placed as a decoration on a fence post in the old Baba Yaga's yard.

A person is never simply running away, nor are they simply going straight ahead. Only unsophisticated, un-psychological folks see life in such fundamentalist terms. The Old Woman of the psyche doesn't like that kind of simplicity, neither does King Lion Who Causes Fear. His simple questions lead somewhere while most folks sleep away. The son being naked suggests that he is supposed to bare his soul to this king who waits in the middle of the night to ask questions of strangers. He is supposed to speak to both the past and the future, tell the story of what drove him from home and imply that he also seeks something different in the world.

Like the Baba Yaga's hut, this is a place of radical change. If the son can't tell a meaningful story, he can't go forward. If he denies his wound he becomes stuck in the past. If he can't bare his ambitions in the world, the future won't open for him. Becoming aware of this two-sided wound makes him a candidate for the opening as son of the king. Surprising as it may be to some, there is a deep and abiding connection between that which is wounded in a person and that which is noble in them. The boy can only be the son of a king if he knows how he is wounded in this world. Denying his wound will deny him access to the king and the nobility in his own psyche.

In modern terms the chief's hut can be seen as a place of therapy, a kind of "therapy hut." As in therapy, the questions of the chief induce a recapitulation of the son's life so far: what were his origins; what has happened that marked him in some way; how is he coping with his wounds? Therapy is called the "talking cure" and it is usually the wounds and blows of life that need to be talked over. Inner wounds form part of one's inner life; bringing them out in the open is one of the few ways of curing them and keeping them from festering. Wounds to the soul have a blessing hidden within. Opening the wound in the right way helps to reveal the secret of why it hurt so much that it had to be hidden and held.

In the midst of a sleeping world, a person hears a question: "Can you keep a secret?" Something stirs, for the soul grows around a secret. The soul grows around wounds and secrets, and from roots difficult to unravel and explain. The story of the father and son is old and rough, yet it offers a view of a living secret of this world: where the wound resides, blessings can appear. It could be said that there are two kinds of secrets: those that should be revealed because they damage the inner life of a person and those that are difficult to share because they shape the deepest aspects of a soul.

The son reveals how he was wounded by his father and stands exposed before the king. The king has a secret as well: "I wish to say that you are my son... returned home. Will you keep that secret with me?" The exposure of the king is that he has lost a son. In many cultures, a king could not continue to rule without a son to inherit the kingdom. A king without offspring could also lack the ability to create and generate life. What the king lacks the land will soon suffer. A king without a son would not be keeping a careful enough eye on the future of the realm, and a king who was not preparing for the future of the realm would be dangerous to his subjects.

Once the hunter's son agrees act as a prince, the queen awakens. The realm needs an heir and the queen-mother can overlook differences between this boy and her actual son. She raises the sound of joy and the whole village gets involved, the whole psyche awakens. The son is washed and anointed, given new clothes and brought out before all the people. A great celebration ensues. Everyone rejoices at the return of the prodigal son... except some of the counselors, who say "Indeed, indeed."

Well, some of those in the chorus of listeners seem upset as well. "King's son indeed." What's going on? Is this a secret or simply a lie? Is the chief a legitimate king or a betraying old man misusing his power? If the king's son is dead, why does the king want a pretend son? Is the son entering an abusive situation where the secret is not to reveal the abuse? Why should the son pretend he's better than he actually is? How can anyone trust a chief who makes secret deals? Why doesn't everyone just tell the truth and get on with their lives? Isn't this just more fatherly falsehood? Isn't the village just another patriarchal set-up secretly intended to harm everyone?

The chorus stirs into action—arguments go back and forth as a meeting of the counselors has begun. The group divides sharply over the secret proposed by the king. The angle from which each man perceives the dialogue between son and king reveals much about where he stands with questions of authority and self-worth.

A man says, "It's simply a lie. I'm not the son of a king or a chief, I never was. I'm simply the son of a rat hunter, and he couldn't even accept me." There's a factual directness to this man's position. Yet it rings harsh and literal. The phrase 'never was the son of a king' has both a sound of despair and an air of longing to it. As this man works the story through his imagination, it becomes clear that his hopes were crushed early on. His capacity for trust in himself and in others has atrophied severely. He rejects any possibility of a touch of royalty within him. He carries too much of his father's attitude, his psyche still flattened by the blow from his father's ax. As a result, he continues to cut off his own imagination and with it any sense of a noble purpose inherent in his soul.

A man nearby adds that even if there was any truth to him being the son of a king, no one else would believe it. If people did believe it, that could only lead to more troublesome burdens. Others speak up—a man beaten often by his father, another sexually abused by a stepfather—the deal with the king is one more seduction leading to one more betrayal and further mistreatment. How can they trust anyone who offers pleasure, wealth, or power?

From the opposite side of the king's hut, a man says, "Why shouldn't I lie and just take whatever I can? I've been hit so many times from so many directions that I don't know who I am anyway. The whole deal is phony. All the rules are made by fools to be followed by fools. Truth is in the eye of the beholder. What you grab is what you get. If this fool is willing to make me a prince, I'll take it. In a world as unjust as this, that I don't know where I come from, don't know who my father really was, don't know what he did, what kept him alive or if he's dead, what's the difference? All deals are crooked. I may as well benefit from this crooked system as any other."

Others chime in: "Whenever I became excited or high-spirited, my father would point to something he thought was more important than me." "As soon as I started to feel good, my father would cut me down to size." "My father dismissed everything I did with a platitude." "Mine said I'd never amount to anything." "At least the king will give him something. So what if it's not completely true."

How many stories begin with a child born amongst animals or abandoned to a river or on a mountain? Those destined to become models of nobility often begin in obscurity, either they must be hidden from dangers or else exposed to the extremes of Nature. The old stories try to remind that each child arrives uniquely gifted and potentially able to realize their inner value. Even the child of a 'rat hunter' has a claim to a royal heritage and an inherent inclination to a mythic life.

In old Celtic imaginings, the birth of each person involved three dynamic forces: the bodily union of mother and father, the wish of an ancestral spirit to be reborn, and the presence of a god or goddess. This was taken to mean that at a core level each person carries ancestral desire for life and a touch of something divine. Whether high-born or of lowly birth, each person enters the world imbued with inner nobility born both of ancestry and of eternity.

Yet it is also the nature of this world that the innermost qualities of a person remain mostly hidden from family and self until extraordinary circumstances call them forth. The path that leads the soul away from home and the family fate, also leads each child out to the world and deeper into the inner realms where their inherent nobility waits to be discovered. There comes a time when secrets must be sorted out. Every family has skeletons in the closet and deals under the kitchen table. Carrying shameful family secrets requires a psychic effort that blocks genuine imagination and, like a spell, limits growth. Underneath inherited guilt and shame waits a guarded belief that somewhere in the core of the soul there exists a seed of royalty. Around that core the soul grows. The life of the soul is a slow revelation, with occasional outbursts, from that mostly hidden core.

Deep feelings of rejection and abandonment can cause a person find the deeper secret at the core of life. What else does it mean that the son 'enters naked' and secrets are discussed? Many things must become lost and abandoned in order that the inner life be revealed. That which truly belongs to a person cannot be completely lost, only we can become lost to ourselves. At this level, king and queen are emblematic royal parents; it is not their own son being considered.

As the poet William Stafford wrote in "A Story That Could Be True"
"Who are you really, wanderer?"-
and the answer you have to give
no matter how dark and cold
the world around you is:
"Maybe I'm a king."

Each person becomes a wanderer again and again in the course of life, as we find our true self by becoming lost. Each person carries within a "story that could be true." Each crossroads in life secretly asks the question: Who are you really?

In the space between childhood and the adult world, young people encounter both their gifts and their wounds. Facing the wound from the father helps to reveal the unfulfilled longings that try to awaken during youth. Accepting the nature of the inevitable wound makes one's inner life more real. It's as if each man has to talk to a king or a chief about longings which his father couldn't or wouldn't bless. For a father only rarely can see with accuracy that which is potential and grand in his son. The king becomes a "second father" by acknowledging the grand imagination that seized the son and caused him to toss away the rat. The wound resides where the grandness of the son tried to awaken and must be opened for the desire behind it to become known. Until a man can talk clearly of the rat that passed between him and his father, potential kings will keep turning out to be wounding fathers.

The inner nobility of a person and their deepest wounds dwell together. Opening the wounds in the right circumstances helps to heal and renew life's potential for fulfillment. Yet even occasions of renewal can be complicated. While part of us exults, it is only human to have doubts and questions. Doubt is a companion of one's dreams, just as folly accompanies one's certitude. There are always doubts in the psyche as the genuinely lived life remains a story that could be true. Our inner counselors and critics become activated and remind us of who we were before the anointing began. There are parts of the psyche that ever remain uneasy with change.

The hunter's son may take on royal clothes but still must face the doubting counselors who attend any court. The counselors represent the psychic status quo, they are enamored of tests, and distrustful of everything.

The counselors operate in the outer, as well as the inner, worlds—in schools, corporations, family businesses, and sports, for example. Political parties and entire nations can become obsessed with the question, "Is this the king's son or not?" Even in the United States, where there is no monarchy, candidates for major office are examined for signs of royal qualities as well as common weaknesses. The media supports both the queen-mother who anoints and the doubting ministers. They are quick to raise the sound of joy and anoint the new candidate. They are also quick to say, "Indeed, indeed." Those whom the village lionizes often come to be vilified later.

A gathering of men also involves a crowd of inherited inner critics who try to stifle attempts to open the doors of the soul, particularly when the possibility of descending into genuine sorrow arises. The inner critics can drown out the subtle voices trying to express wounds that must be hidden in the daily world. The inner critics can act as an extension of the wrathful side of the father. They can keep a man from even entering any king's hut. They can block the route that leads to help, be it therapy, a mentor, a genuine friend of one's self, or path which helps awaken one's inner life. The overly rational, fiercely practical orientation of the modern world tends to deny the presence of the soul and the necessity of a genuine inner life.

At a certain point in the interview in the king's hut, the son, the rat, the wound, the king, and the secret are all present. The scene refers to the inner life without which the son of the rat hunter cannot come to be of noble birth. The change from one to the other requires genuine insight, a suspension of literal-mindedness, and the willingness to imagine a secret self hidden in the heart.

To be modern often means to be caught in a narrow, literal view of the world. The mystery of birth becomes reduced to biology, the dilemma of illness reduced to genetics, the struggle with one's fate replaced with a dull acceptance of hard facts. "Things happen, get over it. Put it behind you." Yet the psyche moves a different way, the soul inclines toward circling back and coming around to unfinished aspects of growing up and becoming oneself.

From the view of the soul, going forward turns out to depend on being able to reach back. Returning to the past traumatic events in order to grow further into the world is one of the great movements of the psyche. It's as if bottles wash up on the shores of consciousness with little messages curled inside calling for help. Through dreams and reveries bottles float toward the shore of awareness. One day, while the critics are asleep, we notice one and open the message. Besides the linear march of days and nights, time, is also an ocean, a tide that can wash ashore things cast away long ago. Like the rat that appears again at the end of the story, the wound keeps resurfacing, especially when the possibility of learning or healing come near.

When the secret of the inner life does come out, some people will be ready to celebrate it, while others will gather to criticize it no matter what. Messengers spread the news; the horses of the psyche begin to stir; the whole village awakens. Soon the rumor mill begins running, the counselors listen to conspiracy theories, and somewhere swords are being gathered. Releasing the secret of the soul's noble heritage awakens the whole psyche and generates a new tension as the talebearer keeps even the doubting critics connected to the grand sense of self.

Meanwhile, the king instructs his new son, "If the naked man can dance, how much better can the man with a cloak?" In other words, if a man has a sense of what the tests in life are about, there's the possibility of taking the right steps and passing through. Some situations require being naked to the world and baring one's soul completely; on other occasions the test involves being prepared to be resourceful. The king and the queen in the psyche represent the inner resourcefulness of the soul and the innate generosity of a person's spirit.

CHAPTER 3

TWO TESTS, TWO SLAYINGS

W̲E̲ ̲R̲E̲A̲C̲H̲ ̲T̲H̲E̲ ̲P̲O̲I̲N̲T̲ in the story where the counselors insist that the new son of the king be tested. Dealing with the tests of the counselors becomes a great test for those working with the story. Until this point, personal and family issues have been the ground for discussion. The test has been accepting the presence of father-son wounds. Entering the field where horses and slave girls are slain shatters any sense of unity that the chorus of men have achieved through recognition of a shared sense of being wounded.

The new dilemma involves the field of gender issues and cultural wounds. Outrage, anger, and confusion fill the room. How can the test for royalty consist of the mindless cruelty of slaying innocent horses and executing slave girls? Isn't this exactly the destruction of animals and women that modern life condones and encourages? Isn't this exactly the way men act in the world? Aren't the ministers, the sons, and the king all guilty of outrageous destructive behavior? How can any king allow this cruelty? And who wants to be the inheritor of this aberrant bloody mess?

A man says, "I dropped out of the story at that point. I wouldn't kill a horse or strike a woman—I'd rather die." Another is an animal rights activist, "This is exactly what we're against—the arrogant, bloody attitude that endangers all species. The need of men to feel superior by destroying innocent animals and acting as lords of nature!" Others point out that this is typical of the destructive behavior into which young men feel pressured by their peers; loss of personal choice and mob mentality are being sanctioned. Others rail against a story which seems to justify violence against women and the persistent violence of slavery.

A man describes how swords of abusive power are being passed from fathers and kings and ministers to sons everyday. This is the cause of war and all the violence in this world. It's time for a new village that has no swords and no violence toward women, children, or animals! The arguments are heating up and sharp words fly everywhere.

Strangely, even those outraged at the idea of killing the horses are often able to imagine killing the counselors or slaying whoever makes the weapons. Literal and symbolic, social and personal issues have become all tangled and at odds. The feeling that something needs to be slain prevails. Some say, "Kill the ministers"; others, "Kill their sons," or "Kill the talebearer who keeps it going," or even "Kill the storyteller." Everyone seems to have a sword in hand and an issue to press. Clearly, another sore point in the psyche has been touched.

Some feel tricked and upset to find themselves caught in a place where wanton slaying goes on. Others disagree, "You all already accepted the deal with the king, it's part of the deal." "No one was upset when it was a rat being killed and tossed away. Suddenly, all of life has become sacred!" "You arrived in this place on a war horse just like everyone else." "How do you know that they won't simply kill you if you don't kill the horses?" "A man's gotta do what a man's gotta do." Life is full of sacrifices. Just the image of the "great war-horses" produces a litany of violence and destruction. The chorus of men must struggle with questions of blood and history, of war and sacrifices.

Over the years, I've told the tale in all kinds of environments—in prisons amidst those who have murdered, stolen, raped, and amongst gang kids trying to grow up on brutal streets. Battle-scarred war veterans and anti-war activists have entered the field of dilemmas, retired cops and ex-gang leaders; one guy a butcher, another a veterinarian. There was an army officer responsible for giving the false daily body counts throughout the Vietnam War and the man who invented an infrared rifle-scope that changed the face of that war. Work with men in a genuine way and blood stains and soul wounds become present one way or another.

Modern people may have difficulty imagining a king, but no one has trouble imagining the mass slaying of animals, the persistent demeaning of women, and the brutalization of girls. There is no denying the ravages of racism and colonial dominance or the prevalence of and increase in the abuse of women and children. The first thing to be slain in the clearing beyond the village is the idea that the ugly facts of this life can be avoided or ignored. There is no denying the persistence of wars and the increasing slaughter and devastation exacted by the modern machinery of war.

Mass culture also means mass communication of massive brutalities. Through the spread of news reports, everyone now carries the catalogue of endless wars and mindless brutality which is the heritage of modern societies. Many can recite statistics on how many women are raped each minute, and they know that the rapes are an enslavement of women by fear and a killing of both the body and the feminine spirit. The human chorus can chant an onslaught of harsh statistics and tallies of ongoing tragedies that stun the imagination and weigh on the mind. Hard facts about human suffering and oppression's many faces—war, rape, poverty, unnecessary sickness and cold indifference—enter the room wherever people gather.

Hearing this part of the story, some women have said, "That's right—men start out as boys hurting animals and each other, then move on to women and children and whole societies." For, whatever causes this flood of violence, it is most violently enacted by men. Swords become guns and horses are replaced by high-horsepower cars. Suburban white youth die in car crashes while urban black youth dodge gunshots on abandoned streets. Meanwhile, game-boys offer violence as a game, using electronic violence as an escape from an increasingly brutal world.

When I first found this story, the wounding of the son and his dilemma between father and king spoke to me. I knew I had to tell the story in order to learn from it. Yet, I felt quite uneasy about the tests of slaying horses and slave girls; they seemed archaic, shameful, repulsive. Then I realized that these responses were also reasons to tell the story. The wound that drives the son into the world also drives him to the wounds of the world. "This world is hard," says an old African song, "mother hold me, for this world is hard."

There are wounds a boy comes to feel and wounds a man comes to know. Initiation means a loss of innocence. This story tries to teach about initiation, about wounds and dilemmas, about secrets and blood, about death and knowledge of oneself and the world. If only a literal interpretation applies to the scenes in the story, then the wound to the son would be reduced only to cuts and bruises of the body and not relate to conditions of the soul.

If a man doesn't know how he is wounded, he can deny the pain of others and the tragedies of this life. If a man doesn't know how he is wounded he can't see that others are wounded as well. More than that, he'll put his wound into others because of a vague sense that there's a wound somewhere. He'll only be able to see the wound that secretly troubles him when he puts it into someone else. Then, he'll feel strangely better for a moment. The old ideas of initiation tried to shape a wound through which each boy could come to know his own wounds and know the ways in which this world wounds everyone.

There is a strong tendency to literalize the horses and the slave girls, as if the cultural imagination gets stuck at that level. In the clearing, everyone can make a sword of the ugly facts of mass society and the oppressions of the modern world that strike them the most. The accumulation of tragedies and abuses becomes undeniable and increasingly unavoidable in modern life. But to get the whole story, the hard ground of literal facts must break open. The slayings must also be seen through the wound. Deep emotions are intended to break through the fixed and literal views of this world. If that doesn't happen real change can't occur—not in the individual and not in the world.

Stories are like dreams wherein we can die but come back in another dream. Even children's stories are full of swords and of heads rolling, for this is how the psyche changes—by being slain, then growing again. The high levels of literal violence depend upon denying the depths of inner wounds already present. The presence of violence is a dilemma for each person, for each group, for each culture.

Dilemma means two assumptions, from the Greek roots that also give us *diplomats* and *diplomas*. The point of a dilemma is to pin people in the tension of opposing views in order that a deeper level of perception might open. Part of the test of the story lies in finding the symbolic layers where the psychic wounds can be examined and healed. Part of the test of a culture lies in whether it can find an imagination stronger than war and random brutality.

Someone in the chorus shouts, "If the boy is not the literal son of a king and queen, then the horses and slave girls are not literal either." "If the point isn't literal slayings, the swords may be used to cut another way." Staying in a story, like staying in a dilemma begins to create options and alternatives to the obvious. The swords can be used to cut away at the literal ideas of horses and slave girls.

Hundreds of years after horses were common to work and war they remain present through high horse-power vehicles that men own or desire to own— the Mavericks, Broncos, and Mustangs. Modern crowds gather to watch them race right on the verge of being out of control. Horses are a metaphor for instinctive power, but also for freedom, for speed, and dominant masculine force. Indeed, the horse changed the nature of warfare, and, at one time, whoever achieved the greatest skill with horses was able to rule the widest area. To this day, the funeral of a head of state is often led by a lone horse.

In this story the son of a king must have horse-power yet also be able to slay it, as if certain instinctive drives to power and tendencies to override people must be cut down. A true royal son doesn't get on his high horse or become caught up in the trappings of power. A modern man might need to slay his attachment to his Bronco or his dreams of a Porsche. Upon reflection, each man can eventually find the "horse he rode in on."

Once out in a field clear of the pressures of career and high expectations, things can be examined and cut down to size. A man may have to cut through the habit of gambling everything on long shots in order to have a moment in the winner's circle. Another might need to outgrow obsessions with risk in order to find more genuine feelings of being special or valuable. Some need to slay a deeply ingrained inner sense of being just a workhorse, a draft animal always pressed into service of others. Another must cut through a father's repeated assessment that he is just a horse's ass. Another might need to reconsider his habit of riding off into the sunset as a means of escaping from relationships or responsibilities.

As a psychological move, slaying the horse means leaving behind a habitual attitude which keeps a man acting and reacting as a boy. No matter if a man experiences great success or common failures, there come times when habitual attitudes must be sacrificed for growth to occur. Certain attitudes that worked early in life will later block his connection to a greater life. If he is to move closer to the center of grandness and creativity in the village—and in himself—he must slay whatever image he was saddled with as a boy. Slaying the hobby horse of ego habit becomes a sacrifice that moves him closer to having a place in the center of the village.

After the first test the sons of the ministers report that the son of the chief has acted in a kingly way. The ministers say, "Indeed." They require a second test, for there remains another symbolic part of the son to be seen. The chorus of men struggles mightily over the metaphor of female slaves. At this point someone usually begins a protest that the story shouldn't be told in this way, that it demeans women and raises the deadly specter of colonial slavery. With no women present to speak for themselves, many have thought that groups of men discussing women will only indulge in fantasies and fears and make matters worse.

Yet when genuine imagination is involved and the sense of each person being present with their own wounds remains present, men feel genuine anguish and confusion over the persistent cultural patterns that mistreat women and the feminine. Most often the field of the second test generates an awkward sadness and bewilderment over the pain and suffering between women and men in modern cultures.

In the tension of the metaphorical dilemmas many questions arise. What's the connection between the slave girls in the story and the profusion of female suffering—the incest, rape, battering, and discrimination rampant in modern cultures? What could it mean psychologically if each man could having a "slave girl" issue? The literal vision is horrifying, yet people line up night after night, year after year, to watch "slasher movies" and horror films where women are terrorized, reduced to helplessness, and then killed. A movie depicting men enslaving and cannibalizing women wins best picture awards even as newspapers report actual cases of girls trapped and enslaved in hidden chambers in suburban houses.

It's as if men caught in the territory between boy and man carry an undeveloped yet threatening sense of the feminine. Something slavish and unexamined resides in men, which distorts at the same time that it desires the feminine. It's the slave girl in men which needs to become conscious or else it becomes more literalized and dangerous to actual women. In

India feminine deities are visible and worshipped in public, yet there are still "dowry slaves." Young women enter arranged marriages under family pressures with their dowries paid over time. If the dowry payments stop, the bride will be beaten and humiliated. She may even be killed for lack of the dowry. Despite the presence of feminine deities, actual women lack protection. The endangered bride also appears in fairy tales of the Bluebeard type, where hidden rooms are filled with the bones of former brides kept under lock and key. The image of slave girl lives inside people and becomes a figure projected onto actual women in the outside world.

At first men resist the idea that the slave girl could be within them. It's as if the heroic ego in the psyche must keep defining *girl* as something outside itself and subject to control—as if the ego cannot accept the idea that part of the psyche could be as a slave girl. Yet the idea that the oppression of women relates to an oppression of the feminine inside men eventually becomes compelling. The question is posed, What is a slave? Answers come readily: a property, a servant, a sexual slave, someone always ready to serve, does whatever I want, does the dirty work, always submits to me, takes care of me, works for nothing, and so on.

As each defines his own sense of slave, there are indications of what he becomes a slave to. In the psyche of the individual, the slave represents a habitual way of being and seeing. Viewed psychologically, master and slave share the chains that bind them; neither has freedom and eventually each becomes dependent on the other. In the clearing where things can be opened up and examined, each person can find aspects of life where they are at times the master, at times the slave. The man who calls the slave a sexual object turns out to be easily enslaved to objectified sex. Pornography may begin with the sense of feeling masterful, yet it increasingly involves obsessions and enslavement to certain materials and addictive patterns.

The story seems to say that the hunter's son must cut through two areas in the psyche that he habitually takes for granted: the area of instinct, force, and power, and the area of his inner feminine. The story suggests that there's a logic to the order in which the discriminating sword should be used in the psyche. If a man has never ridden his own instinctive horses or was knocked off before he felt in charge, he will carry an exaggerated view of the feminine and of women. On the other hand, if the war-horses in a man have never been cut down to size, he'll be unable to cut through his habitual views of the feminine. In the logic of the story, slaying the horses is necessary to uncover the habit of enslaving the inner feminine of the man. After consciously engaging the inner feminine, a man becomes less likely to demean others and releases himself from a too heroic attitude toward life.

What needs to be slain or sacrificed in psychic terms are literalized attitudes toward both the masculine and the feminine if a full emotional and imaginal life would be found. If a man can avoid having his horse cut out from under him, he will be overbearing to everyone, especially women. Being around him, people may have the wish to cut him down to size. The forty-year-old man who claims never to have suffered a real failure in life willfully and blindly rides the horse of youth and those in his environment suffer for it. One who denies failure in himself can't abide it in others. Only after suffering loss of the great war horses of masculinity can a man begin to see and feel certain dependencies, inner and outer, that were there all along.

The son's internal feminine aspects involve a sense of *eros*, a particular way of connecting more fully to other people and to the world. If something doesn't cut through to this greater sense of the feminine, the youth will be enslaved to a narrow sense of what it means to be alive. The "slave self" fixates a person's response to the world, replacing genuine feeling with predictable reactions. Whether it is always charming and seductive or usually haggard and overworked doesn't matter as much as the fact that it is automatic, on call, and dutiful. The slave self can't break the fetters that bind it to routines and chores that obscure both the freedoms and responsibilities of a larger life. The slave sense of self stands opposite the sense of genuine nobility and grandness of the deeper self. Slaying the sense of slavishness benefits the community as well as the individual.

By the time the chorus has argued and discussed the challenging sacrifices in the clearing, it becomes clear that each man has received a complex inheritance from the world of the fathers. Each has a wound, a war-horse, a sword, and a slave girl. Upon leaving the family hut, each son faces a world of tests and dilemmas. Wishing to be, trying to be, secretly agreeing to be the son of a king forces the troubles in each area of inheritance out into the open and makes changes in the psychic village possible.

Slaying the slave sense of self ends the second test and precipitates the return of the father into the story. The father's world and the threads of feeling between father and son seem to be affected by the son being fully recognized by the king and the critical counselors. Changes in the son seem to reawaken his father's interest in him. By consciously engaging his attitudes toward power and the feminine, the son's relationships to both father and king undergo changes. The third test will find him standing between the two of them.

The father walks back into the story as if drawn to the village where his son has awakened to a life of his own. Father and son are separated, yet still connected, particularly by the wounds they share. In common life, fathers and sons frequently drift apart. A dark road often separates them. Attempts to reach the other's village go only part way; one or the other gets lost in the darkness of unexamined wounds between them. Yet questions echo back and forth through the long roads of night: Why did something have to come between us? Why did I have to do that... say that? Where was my father when I needed him? Whose son am I?

CHAPTER 4

A FONDNESS FOR SWORDS

AFTER TWO TESTS the ministers seem satisfied, the village calms down, and the son of the hunter lives with the king. For a time, life goes on and daily patterns obscure the unfinished business between father and son. Life, however, rubs at the wound, and father issues have a way of quietly returning. One day the father arrives looking for his son. The villagers say they haven't seen such a son, yet send him directly to the chief's hut. Everyone in the village seems to recognize this double fatherhood. Inside the chief's hut, the hunter calls for the son to return with him. It's as if the father cannot see the king, cannot see his son in relation to a king or settled in another realm.

The hunter offers the son life as it was before. The chief offers the father gold and great wealth to keep secret the new life of the son. The father refuses wealth and refuses to keep the secret shared between his son and the king. He continues to call to his son. The youth sits silent, like a statue between two fathers.

Stories are related to rituals and in the logic of stories, elements repeat ritualistically, often three times. For the third time the king calls for a sword for the son and he calls for three horses. On the same ground where horses and slaves were slain, father, son, and king face each other over the edge of a sword. This time the instructions are not to do "whatever they do" but to choose what to do himself. This time the son is on his own and is the only one with a discerning sword. Something must be done; he can't be in two places at once and can't serve two masters. Either slay the king, return with the father, and live as before, or slay the father and continue to live with the king. The son has become as a sword between two fathers. His dilemma is everyone's dilemma, a human dilemma that requires some action. If it were you, what would you do?

In the magic of a story a person automatically matches the words with images and feelings from their own life. It happens unconsciously, in a split second. For each life is a story trying to find its own shape. Each time we hear a story our response could be different, for the inner landscape of emotion and images constantly shifts. Yet the psychic response will be swift and clear-cut when unhampered by outer expectations, conventional thinking, or fixed moralities. If the inner critics and ego counselors don't intervene, the answer to the question will be right on the tip of the tongue.

As the question cuts through the chorus of men, three groups emerge: a large crowd of "father slayers," a mob of "king killers," and a third, mixed group of those who refuse to do either, those who want to do both, those who seek a quick way out and those who turn the sword on themselves.

In the camp of the father slayers, each takes a turn telling his story of being wounded by the father. For some there was simply no choice when faced with the dilemma. As soon as they felt the sword in hand the decision was made, and it was off with the father's head. Their choice was clear-cut and fueled with anger: "He struck me with an ax and left me for dead. It's my turn to strike back." "He left when I was three years old, no explanation, no return; if he did come back, I'd take his head off." "He beat me every day for twelve years, and I've slain him a hundred times in my mind. For what he did to my mother, I'd kill him if he ever came back." "My father never struck me, but he didn't ever protect me from anything either. Now, he needs to feel that." "He preferred my brother and rejected everything I brought him; let's see him reject this blade." "He drank himself into a stupor, and I hate that head and that cursed mouth." "He called me a sissy and had to outdo me at everything." "His work meant more to him than anything I ever did; with the blessing of the king, I can finally feel my own rage."

In the psyche, nothing is forgotten. Long-buried memories rise up like the son in the story returning to painful awareness after being struck down. Eventually anger and rage produce tears and some voices trail off into sadness. A pool of sorrow grows along with the angry fire. Men who are less enraged but no less determined join the chorus: "Killing the father means continuing to go forward; not killing him would be a regression." "Going back means agreeing to the old deal again. It's time to move on." "If I don't strike him down, he'll come into everything I'll do." "He disowned me because I'm gay, and I almost killed myself; I could kill him for that." "If I killed the king, I'd lose all that I've struggled for." "Killing the king would mean killing my spiritual life."

On the other side, the "king killers" can't wait to speak. "Blood is thicker than water. If my father didn't truly love me, he would have taken the gold and left me with the king." "Despite everything, I just want to hear my father say he loves me." "I forgive him for the ax. No matter what, I couldn't kill my father." "If I killed him, I'd die as well." "That my father stopped what he was doing to come find me is all I need in order to go to him." "Now that I have a sword, I don't need to fear my father." "The king only offers material wealth; my father's love is greater than that." "If he weren't sorry, he would never have come after me." "My father is real; the king is a tyrant who rules by force and lies." "The king is simply a false father; he'll use me for his own purposes." "I had a mentor who led me on and then stole my ideas for himself; this king will misuse the son in the same way." "There are plenty of bad leaders in the world, but I only have one father." "The king has caused all the killing; now it's his turn to die."

In the camp of the king killers there's no lack of heads that can roll and there's a strong need to talk of painful betrayals and name false kings. "Now I can understand how I could wind up standing in an adoring crowd waiting for a guru to drive by in a Rolls Royce! Imagine how desperately I needed to be seen by a noble eye! And any more than a glance would have been too much." Another was betrayed in the inner sanctum of academia by a mentor he revered. Several with business careers tell of corporate lies and chief executives who betray everyone. An ex-army officer who volunteered for Vietnam cuts through the conversation with a piercing scream. He needs to unburden himself of betrayals that stick in his heart like a sword. He bewails having led and directed troops of men to their deaths only to find later that there was no point to it.

Any hundred men can tell a hundred stories of betrayal. Eventually the discussion moves to the lack of leadership throughout society. There is a collective realization of a broad betrayal by the false kings of politics and industry who deny the inner nobility common to men in order to appear like rulers and heads of state. The fervor for killing kings sinks into a sadness over the sense of so many lives wasted, so many talents unfulfilled. The question becomes this: when the false leaders are cut down and the naïve inner illusions put to the sword, will there be anything left of the son's capacity to trust another king, or even another man?

Meanwhile, the third camp keeps dividing into smaller more distinct groups. One subgroup contains those who simply refuse: "I just won't do it. The story tricked me into this position; I refuse to handle the sword." "I'd break the sword in pieces and walk away." "I'd bury the sword in the ground and go to another village." "I'd leave the sword with them and take all the horses so they can't follow me." "I won't be forced to decide. I'm going to a new village; they can come if they want." This group wants to settle the dilemma without using the sword. They see the sword as the cause of the trouble. They refuse to use the sword and seem to deny that something must die. Unfortunately, in the psyche, refusing to let something die leads to being unable to fully live.

A small group expresses a reluctance to relinquish the sword at all. They wield it quickly to slay both father and king. They stand willing to do this again and again. The members of this group seem as if they are in the flames of a forge. There are battle veterans in this group. They were pulled out of Asian jungles, aflame with the fires of napalm, and dropped back into the streets and back roads of America. There was no cleansing, no anointing with oils. They continue to burn, some scorched by betrayal from both sides—from fathers who led them to believe in war and chiefs who led them into the flames of hell. In this group are black men who feel the fires of injustice and oppression every day in the city streets, who ache with the knowledge of what their children will have to endure. Not many questions here; it's too hot, the swords are held too tightly, no scabbards in sight. Anyone could lose his head in this group. There's a silent call for water to cool things down.

Another group feels fragile and brittle. The tests are too much, life can't be this way. Some in this group were thrown from the horse before they even reached the clearing; the test was over before it started. They can only find pieces of their story and they want out of the field of conflicts altogether. Some say they'll just go on to the next village, or else start a village of their own. Both father and king are flawed characters, a plague on both their houses. There's always another village, a new idea, the next relationship, the next invention of their personality. They deny their ancestors and the presence of any fate which could claim them. At this point, they don't realize that the rat, the father, and the king will all appear in the next village as well.

Near them sits the quietest group. A sadness surrounds them. There's a sense that they should be approached gently. There's a solemnity and no sense of imagination. When given the sword by the king, they each felt clear that they would use it on themselves. It's difficult for them to explain it, but it's true. "I've been paralyzed since I heard the choices." "I'd wound myself and see who would offer to die so that I wouldn't kill myself." "If someone has to die, it will be me." "I'd kill myself rather than continue to suffer and see them suffer." "At least if I was gone, there'd be nothing to fight over."

Some feel they are stuck inside the horse or the slave girl, just waiting to die. There is something too sharp here, too cutting; no matter what happens they focus on their own complicity in events. They are too willing to remain stuck or else die themselves. The presence of the sword puts them in a "suicidal position." They identify with the feeling of being no one's child—neither the father's nor the king's. With no hope of being loved by the father or blessed by the king, they turn to cutting themselves down. Although most people feel suicidal at one point or another, these wounded sons dwell in a recurring suicide wherein they continually cut off their own grand desires and their connections to the world. Once it becomes clear that this wound can also be touched, many stories of contemplated suicide come out. This group takes a long time to consider the options.

In dilemmas of this sort, there can be no right answer, just learning more about the wounds and emotions, the sorrows and hopes found on the road of the two fathers. Each of the camps can teach something about fathers and kings and the slayings that go on in the psyche. Each camp can sharpen an edge of the sword of understanding. Each offers an angle on the recurring dilemma, for without a place in the heart for one's father, a person feels cut off from a source of strength and protection in life. Without a sense of royal connection, old wounds cannot heal and fears of repeating an old failure can cut off new opportunities to grow and learn.

Initiation speaks to the need for a second birth, one which reveals the indwelling spirit and temperament of a young person. The old idea was that the man does not simply grow from the boy; a man is something that must be 'made' and in the course of time made over again. There are many metaphors for the making of men, many styles of initiation. The ordeals and isolation of a vision quest serve to create an encounter with animal and dream spirits. A shamanic rite of passage involves falling apart and being dismembered in order to be put back together as a new person. A *walkabout* involves wandering ancestral lands until nature begins to speak and the wanderer learns the song and speech of his inner nature as well.

In this story an ax-blow throws a youth into a dark night-journey, followed by a series of fiery tests through which he becomes as a sword. A fire released in the son as a result of the rough ax blow from his father converts to a sword smelted in a king's forge. The father by mistake and the king by intention help shape the raw metal and inner fire of the son into a metaphorical sword, a blade that can destroy or else cut through to meaning. The original rough blow leads to more discriminating cuts as the wound reveals a temperament that must be tested again and again. The son becomes the sword being honed between the stones of father and king. They are the fathers of his temperament, progenitors of his wounds and of his blessings.

In the early imagination of sword-making, the metal of the sword and the mettle of the man were identical. The blade passed repeatedly between fire and water, it heated up and cooled down in order to temper it between strength and flexibility. Too much fire and the sword will be brittle; too much cool water and the inner metals won't marry, the sword won't be able to hold an edge. Scabbards were also part of the sword-craft; for a sword without a scabbard was unfinished. Just so, a man is unfinished if he has no ready sheath for his temper, no protection for his temperament.

In ancient Africa people imagined the forge of the smith to be inside the body of a mystical lion or leopard. The mention of "king lion who causes fear" in the story could connect to old imaginations of the mythic and mystic underworld craft through which people were smelted and reshaped in the fires of their souls. The legend of King Arthur and the magical sword Excalibur still lives in the embers of Western imagination. The wondrous sword had to be drawn from the rough stone by the one whose temperament could handle its great power in a just way. Arthur became king by virtue of the sword, and the sword became the symbol of exact virtues honed in him.

As a symbol, a sword can represent the potential for sharp awareness and capacity for discernment in an individual. Among ancient Africans and Celts, a quality sword was often cooled at least once in the blood of the man who would carry it, since his fortune and character were also being forged with the shaping of the sword. Other immersions would involve water taken from a sacred well or river, or the blade would be anointed with holy oil. In old Europe, Smith was the name for the forger of swords and of men. All the Smiths in the phone book have the echo of a forge at the back of their mind and, more than that, the hint of an alchemy through which the raw metal of a person can be transformed and shaped to serve the common needs of the realm.

Life is not tame, and a thorough education may be both the building of a fire and the carrying of water. The wounds of youth involve awakening the inner temperament of the individual and the inevitable emotional struggles between fathers and sons. The results of the psychic conflicts will be felt by the communities around them. Neglected anger and pain in the wounds of sons either turns inward and eats away at them, or erupts and becomes a danger to others. The onset of youth instigates a vision quest, regardless of whether a society consciously recognizes that or not. If the fathers and elders of a culture don't meet the sons on the grounds of their wounds and tempers, a sword hangs over everyone as the uninitiated eventually grow into positions of power and authority.

The ability of a man to discriminate between one thing and another is affected by his temperament. A well-tempered sword combines the capacity to judge with an ability to feel. The capacity to cut is tempered with the feeling to protect. Between adult and child an invisible umbilical cord waits to be cut so that the full spirit of that life can be released. The son must be remade upon leaving the village of family and entering the broader village of culture.

It isn't simple responsibility which must be learned; rather, each youth must learn to respond to an innate spirit already burning inside. Each child grows around an indelible inner expectation that one day they will learn who they are to be in this world. The wound that comes to each person turns out to be the place from which a sense of individual meaning and purpose can grow. One of the responsibilities of those who would rule, lead, or mentor involves learning to see into the wounded areas of youth and spot the blessed streak that can be shaped into genuine discernment and healthy self-awareness.

This story of father and son begins with a rat and ends with it: "Off with the rat's head!!" This story is ruled by and guided by the rat, which first runs between father and son and then hops about as the son must consider whose head should roll. The father's head must be taken off over and over until his ability to wound the son has been taken away. The king's head might have to roll a few times before it becomes clear that the son has innate nobility of soul. As he becomes more familiar with the sword of consciousness and more knowledgeable about the wound that is also the place of blessing, each sacrifice helps to reveal more of the awakened son.

The implication of the story is that the rat will continue to appear in the area of the father issues and where a man would be noble or kingly. By the time someone smells a rat, it is usually too late; the damage has already been done. All symbols present a complexity of meanings, and a rat offers extremes of disease and survival. Rats can carry diseases, yet rats endure any catastrophe. They can enter and leave through any opening. They can digest hard shells and slip through the tiniest opening. Rats leave ships before they sink and people used to believe that after a rat leaves a house, it would soon fall. In Egypt, the rat was a god that could destroy from below but that also had the wisdom to know which way to go in times of trouble.

The rat represents surviving in both the literal daily world and surviving in the grand world of spirit and emotion. It used to be considered wise to evoke the spirit of the rat at the beginning of any venture for both survival and great success. In India, no meaningful endeavor would be attempted without seeking the blessing of the elephant-headed god Ganesh, lord of wisdom and prosperity, remover of obstacles and god of language. Ganesh, however, rides upon or is accompanied by a rat. In the eye of imagination great accomplishments remain connected to the lowly intuitions of survival. Secretly, the rat of survival and the elephant god of successful endeavors work together.

In the story, the arrival of the rat forces the differences between father and son to become evident, differences that may feel as great as those between an elephant and a rat. Where the son saw big game, the father saw the rat of survival. The rat even replaced the son in the eyes of the father. At the fire, he couldn't see his son because of the rat. Later, the son can see a rat in any older man or any authority figure. The rat is the wound that won't go away and the indication of how to survive, as well. For the psychological blow that stuns the son's world also awakens something in him and marks the spot where his own sense of the grandness of life appeared.

That a father can wound or curse a child seems clear in that each father does things which the child can never forget. What remains less clear is the wild accuracy of the parental wounding. Something in the child provokes wild emotions in the father so that the one seeking a blessing receives instead a curse, a wound, a deniable but unforgettable blow. The child seeks an exact blessing, a confirmation of something already present in the soul. It seems natural that a father could recognize the gifts of his own child and confirm them. Yet where the blessing is sought a wounding will occur.

Blessing is an old word, strong word. Blessing comes from *blessure*, a French word that means wound. We each seek a blessing exactly where a wound waits; we each become wounded exactly where we seek to be blessed. That's the trouble between parent and child, the rat in the situation from the beginning.

There's a rat in it from the start. What the father passes to the son becomes changed as soon as the son handles it. This is the quantum physics of relations between fathers and sons. If children were simply satisfied with what the parents offered to them, they would remain children forever. It's not simply that parents don't give enough to the child, rather it's that whatever the parents give can never be enough for the child. Each child enters the world with a destiny beyond the attention and interests of the family. The origin of the child is a mystery that includes and exceeds the understanding of its parents.

It's stunning to the son to realize that his own father doesn't see the shape of his expectations, doesn't see the grandness in him and doesn't feel the delicate uncertainty with which he walks into life. Father and son are both shocked by the great longing they feel for each other and the way they can clash when coming close to each other. Despite and because of inner mysteries and longings, lonely distances can grow between those closest by blood. Something mysterious connects them and something awkward and painful drives them apart. Blood unites and it can separate quickly. On the road of the fathers, the task of the son is first of all to survive. Following that, to learn to use the sword that he inherits to make distinctions between the mysteries and the wounds in the world.

In the human psyche, father and king must be slain over and over in order for life to fully change. In certain ways, they're used to it, at least the ones in old stories. They recover readily and keep agreeing to further excursions to the sacrificial clearing. As part of the eternal human drama, father and king have no choice, they wound and give gifts, they suffer and keep secrets. Choice involves an edge which cuts both ways, something is chosen and something else disappears. Sons are always in quest of something and fathers are usually in question. Eventually, most sons become fathers who carry on the mixed heritage of clumsy humanity and noble potentials. On a given day, blood is thicker than water; on another occasion blood must be denied in order for the Water of Life to flow and clear the way for the next adventure.

CHAPTER 5

SPIRIT FATHERS

A s a boy, there were times when I could slip right next to my father
and sense something of the spirit and imagination that sustained
him. When he was dressing for a wedding or a party where there would be
songs and dancing, I could sense something different in the air about him. I
wanted to be near whatever transformed him from a stoic truck driver into
a quick-footed dancer. When he would strum a guitar and sing, I could get
close to something in him which I needed to know better. He knew only
four chords and he sang quietly, but his spirit would rise with each song and
I could feel it.

The other and opposite occasion in which his spirit would rise came
whenever he watched a good boxing match. He would become animated as
if he were the one feinting and trading blows. As he got inside the fight and
the fighters, I got inside him. I learned that he, too, was fighting, though
he never said what it was that he fought or if he won any rounds. Inside
that closeness, I loved him easily; what's more, I knew him. Within that
fragile, permeable space next to him, I was able to acquire some knowledge
of his spirit. Quietly, I followed his tracks, hunting with his spirit inside the
fighting and the music.

If I asked him about it, or said too much, the special atmosphere would
evaporate quickly, as if the edges in words broke some silent sound, some
secret presence almost being shared. Throughout childhood I imagined that

we would come to share more, yet my growth seemed to drive him away. As I grew older, the silence grew as well and a distance developed between us.

Children carry an expectation that fathers will give the direct stuff of love and admiration, knowledge, and guidance. Fathers expect to be able to give a child what they need. Yet neither expectation can be fully met. No matter the intentions, at critical moments something comes between fathers and sons. As the father prepares to communicate some poignant point, the son can't hear it, or thinks he already knows it. A son, wanting to be close to the father's energy, tries to learn from him—but asks the wrong question or the right question in the wrong way. Some little thing goes wrong and it all blows up. Why? How can father and son be so close yet be ever poised to knock each other far apart?

The strange resonance between fathers and sons resists being held in simple words or mere sentimentality. Although father and son can suddenly be encased within a knowing closeness, it remains hard to speak of such feelings and harder still to act upon them. How many sons have waited years to hear a father's love put into words? How many fathers have anguished over how to express their love, only to find the silence deepening? How often has the son started out to give sweet words to the father and found bitterness coming from his mouth instead? How deep the need to know something of a father's spirit as if each son is like an adopted child trying to learn who the real father might be. There is a father inside the father, a father spirit or a spirit father that can remain a mystery even to him.

Most old cultures imagined a spiritual connection between a child and the parents before the moment of conception. Some say that the spirit of the child picks the parents to whom it will be born; others that the unseen spiritual exchange between mother and father draws the particular spirit of the child to this world. Some say that the spirit child picks its mother when she is near water, as if the reflection of the mother reveals something to the spirit trying to come into the world. Others say that the spirit of the child enters the father as he hunts, then joins together the father and the mother. Some cultures believe each child to be the spirit of a grandparent or ancestor trying to enter the world again through their own descendants.

This kind of speculative imagination permeates all ancient cultures and serves to keep the ancestors present and the spirits of Nature near. This sense of secret connections with nature and the past tends to be lost in modern cultures. Positivism and the "hard sciences" depict the beginning of individual life in biological not mythical terms. Despite the obvious evidence that people are imaginative and spiritual by nature, the literalist sense of life reduces the great mystery of being to notions of genetics and microbiology. Life becomes literalized history denying mystery and factual reality denying the complications of both spirit and soul.

Older cultures conceived each child as part of an ongoing story—not simply a family history or a specific line of DNA, but a tale which began long ago. Each birth invokes certain fateful issues that constellate at the moment of birth. The tree of each family used to be imagined as being deeply rooted in the earth-bound struggle of humanity to come to know itself more fully. Each child was another attempt to solve a mystery that both unites and divides a family. The relationship between father and son would be a branch of that mystery arising from some distant place and piercing the present with more questions than answers.

There's an old African story from the Ronga people that seems to address the age-old issues of fathers and sons as a spiritual conflict. I call it "The Sweetness of Life," as it tells of a great hunter who knew all the secrets of the forest, including how to listen to the song of the honey bird. When his wife told him she was pregnant, he immediately knew it would be his firstborn son. With the aid of magic formulas he lured the unborn child from the womb and took him hunting. He showed his unborn son the bush and shared all his knowledge with him. It was the spirit of the child that went on the pre-birth expedition, while its body went on growing in the womb. Upon their return, he conjured the boy's spirit back into the womb.

After birth that child grew very quickly and soon wanted to go hunting with his father, this time in the flesh. As they went along they heard the honey bird sing and the father knew it would lead them to a tree where the bees stored honey. Once they found it, the father climbed up and told the son to receive the honeycombs as he passed them down. "But don't lick your fingers, for it is very bitter," he said. The father wanted to control the honey, but he forgot that the son knew as much about the forest as he did. By the time the father climbed down, the son had eaten all the honey.

In a rage over the offense of the son, the father sent huge animals charging at him. When the son survived that attack, the father sent him to a village of dangerous cannibals. That plan backfired when the son climbed a tree and the father became the one who miscalculated the situation and was devoured himself. After that, the son went on to start a new village and raise his own family.

Here is another strange story in the long history of estrangement between fathers and sons. When I first found this tale I was struck by the directness of the image of father and son exploring together before the literal birth of the child occurs. While mother and unborn child rest in their mutual ocean, the spirit of the son follows the spirit of the father to their mutual forest. Somehow father and son come to know each other in the spirit. Even as the child grows in the womb, son and father know each other in ways that the mother remains unaware of, in ways that secretly unite them. Yet when the son becomes old enough to approach the world of men, his spirit seems to threaten the father.

The story telescopes childhood down to a few symbolic days, for childhood is not the point here. The point is that the first father-son outing happens before birth and sets up an expectation of similar adventures to be experienced later. Yet when the son comes of age to follow the honey bird, what should be sweet easily turns sour. It's as if the nature of the father and that of the son can travel together in the spirit, but not in the flesh.

The honey bird, as the spirit in this story, guides father and son to something that is inherently sweet, but can easily turn to bitterness and opposition. Isn't that how it happens even now? Father and son in good spirits, out on an adventure; certainly there's something good ahead, something sweet or valuable to find together. How many hunting and fishing expeditions start out that way! Yet what seems easy in the abstract can become problematic, dangerous, and even tragic in embodied reality.

In the first story of the hunter and son, the boy violates his father's sensibility by completely discarding what was given to him. Here, the son takes and eats everything the father gathers. All or nothing—that's how it often stands between father and son. All or nothing. The magic through which the father first met the spirit of his son disappears when both encounter the Tree of Knowledge. Like the Old Testament God, the father becomes punishing when the son violates a rule. Be it apples, or honey or even a rat, what happens between fathers and sons readily leads to exile, for there are spirits involved and there are gods in it.

Many new fathers make a commitment not treat their child as their own fathers treated them. Yet one day, to his surprise, the new father will hear the words of his own father suddenly pour out of his mouth. What began as all giving, showing, and guiding suddenly can become forbidding, restricting, and punishing. Becoming a father means joining the line of fathers that include the old Titans as well as the old testaments, some old giants as well as some tyrannical kings. Becoming a father awakens the ancient energies of the Great Father, which can be damning and exiling as well as generous and benevolent.

Human fathers unwittingly become caught in the deep, sweeping patterns of ancient, titanic deities. As tensions and confusions rise up between parent and child, the father will feel the pull of extremes that seem out of proportion to the given situation. It's as if something other than the human connection becomes activated, especially when the son seeks to test the limits of boyhood. Even if the father possesses great sweetness, he will fail the son or deny him at a critical time or in a crucial place in his life.

Some fathers take on the devouring attitudes like the cannibal people in the story who devour even their own young. Others in the spell of patriarchs will remove themselves to heights and distances where their own child cannot reach them. While one father will move through the lives of his children like a mysterious cloud pattern they can't hold onto; another will storm about and shout, snap, and stomp through their lives so that they can't get away from him. The Greeks names for the gods of these extremes of fatherhood were Ouranos and Kronos. The Romans called them Uranus and Saturn. In more psychological terms, they can be called the "absent father" and the "devouring father."

Ouranos was a sky god who separated from the earth at the very beginning of time. In the myths, Ouranos united with Rhea, the original earth mother, and together they conceived the first children. But something about the specific natures of the offspring bothered the god, so he tried to stuff them back into their mother as he retreated to the sky above it all. Thus, the Ouranos-father tends to escape the grasp of his own child by giving vague, cloudy answers, by disappearing within abstract principles, or by hiding behind the black-and-white veil of a newspaper. Like Ouranos, the absent father leaves a gap between himself and his children, a distance that keeps them feeling abandoned and uncertain, unprotected, and overexposed to the world.

The airiness of an Ouranos father denies the earthly or earthy presence and immediate needs of the son. It also denies embodiment of the father-son emotional world. As he grows, the son feels incapable of reaching a father who can disappear into endless outside projects, or acts like a minister who only occasionally descends from the pulpit. The Ouranos-father repeatedly sends his son to the mother for answers or guidance or firmness, as if pushing him back where he came from. "Go ask your mother," is a classic move that pushes the child back and allows the father to drift or slip away.

The absent father keeps climbing out of the basic situation; where the son expects him to be, he isn't. He abdicates key aspects of his role as parent, leaving the son bound up in himself, often unable to make a start in life, tending to drift himself or try to slide by. Unable to receive proper recognition and attention from the realm of the father, a son often seeks undue attention from mother and the mother's world.

If the father claims to be holier than thou, or higher or better than thou, the son can sink into the cavities of the earth, into depressions, lonely caves, and grave visions. If the father remains distant, the potentials and possibilities of the son seem to recede at the threshold of entering the real world. Sons of Ouranos can become stuck in the material world, unable to grasp what really matters in their own lives. Or they may become overly maternal, careful, and caring for the feelings of others, yet strangely unable to live into their own emotions, their own sexuality, or their purpose in life.

The spirit of Kronos/Saturn pulls the human father the opposite way, toward dominance, active oppression, even devouring rages. Kronos, who gives us our sense of being ruled by time, was the son of Ouranos and Mother Earth. Rhea encouraged him to cut off the sky-father's genitals in order to escape being pushed back down into her matter. She also warned her Kronos that his own sons would seek to emasculate him when it came their turn and their time.

Thus, Kronos sees a threat in his own children. For the father touched by old Kronos, the presence of children feels wounding and threatens his own downfall. In this pattern, the child is not avoided, but attacked in some way. When the son reaches out to his father or toward any sweetness or reward in life, the Kronos-father sees it somehow as a threat to himself. Before the son can really get going, the father snaps at him, condemns him, and devours the effort to enter life more fully.

The Saturnian father is too present, too immediate, insensitive, and overwhelming. In the extreme, he rages, beats, and strikes at whatever tries to come out of the child. Efforts on the part of the son to be close or to be seen, can trigger a devouring rage exactly where admiring attention would be expected. If the father refrains from raging and attacking the children, he can still hold the Saturn position through outbursts of acidic waves of bitterness, cynicism, and sarcasm. Whatever the child brings to show the father becomes quickly washed in an acid bath that burns away ambition and eats away at self-worth.

A Kronos-father can tick away like a time-bomb in the house, or simply reduce each exciting possibility down to impossible, discouraging details. Where the Ouranos-father can't quite be reached, the Kronos-father bites with teeth of rage, cuts with rules that restrict and bind, and chews up the enthusiasm of the child with sarcasm and bitterness. He can act as Saturn with rings and rules around everyone, or become the old Saturnian lecher with his hands on everyone and in everything. Whether he rages fiercely or dissolves everything in alcohol, he takes the sweetness of life and turns it to bitter dregs.

The Kronos-father tends to dominate, demand, and possess. He must be accounted to and must be accounted for, or he will surprise with a sudden attack or devastating dismissal. The son of a Kronos-father can become like overly alert, and always on the edge, his teeth clenched for an attack that could come at any moment. Or else he can become sadly frozen before the overly watchful eyes of a paranoid god who sees anything new as a threat to the status quo. The father that demands decisiveness can clench the son in indecision—leaving him damned if he does, damned if he doesn't.

The sons of Ouranos can't quite get going and the sons of Kronos are punished for trying to get things going on their own. A father of either type can block the movement of the son toward the sweet things in life. Either way, the denying spirit of the father obstructs the tree which is trying to grow in the life of the son. Even where father and son relate well, one bitter occasion may turn things bitter between them. How often it is heard that a man hasn't spoken to his father in so many years and a father hasn't found a way to communicate to the son since a certain occasion when everything turned threatening and too bitter to swallow.

In the story of the honey bird, the inability of father and son to communicate leads to the devouring extremes of Kronos/Saturn. The temperament of the father becomes cannibalistic as he loses all human perspective. He becomes possessed by Saturn eating his children because he fears that they will take everything from him. Sadly, there's evidence of a sort. The son ate all the honey didn't he? The son may argue that he was lied to regarding the sweetness of honey and told that life was only bitter. Yet at some level a father does lose something as his children grow and seek to follow the bird of their own spirit. Parents sacrifice some of the sweetness of their own lives in order that children taste the honey. Meanwhile, a son can find himself caught in his own bitterness when he becomes a father himself. He may come to repeat threatening patterns similar to those of his father. Or he may set his will to be different, only to learn later that his children felt he was never there for them.

Back and forth the curse of the fathers seems to go; never there when needed or too much there for the needs of anyone else to be met. The enduring stories of fathers and sons seem to convert the Tree of Life to a cross where life feels forsaken altogether. Father and son seem destined to cross each other and to pass along the anguished pattern. An old African saying illustrates this: The grandfather and the grandson get along famously because they have a common enemy—the father. The father stands below his own father just as he looks down the family tree at his son. He has unfinished business with his father and newly discovered difficulties with his own son. Besides being a personal problem and a pattern within families, this depicts a cultural issue as well, a spiritual problem that troubles the waters between one generations and the next.

"Family is fate," people used to say when people used to consider more carefully the unseen aspects of the family trees. Each family struggles with ghosts and spirits that hang about the family tree. Each family tries to work through fated, sometimes fateful, and even fatal issues. Many cultures ease the dilemmas between parents and child by developing another branch on the family tree and placing the child in the laps of the grandparents. Grandchild and grandparent can share a certain grandness. The grandfather can be a father with a touch of grandeur. A child can more easily see grand qualities in the parents of its parents. Meanwhile, grandparents can dote on the special qualities of grandchildren without feeling their own spirit threatened.

Mothers and fathers suffer the family fate from two sides, through unresolved issues with their parents and from growing issues with their children. Many cultures offer sympathy to fathers and mothers, for they are always stuck in the middle, shaking their heads. Meanwhile, grandparent and grandchild share special feelings; one stands near the exit door, the other near the entrance to the road of life. They are distant by age, yet close because one nears completion while the other just begins.

Some cultures refer to grandfather and grandson as brothers, "spirit brothers," who can share a certain spirit for life. A grandfather, standing near the door of death, feels intimations of the end. He learns to let life take its course and can play easily with a grandchild who has only just entered the door of life. Beginning and end have a hidden closeness and share certain secrets about life. Neither the grandfather nor the grandson will ever completely understand the father; they share that also.

Grandfather, father, and son work on the similar issues, but from differing angles. The angles of grandson setting out in life can often be seen more clearly by the grandfather looking back over life's follies and secrets. The grandfather can see which way the grandson's spirit is trying to go; he can lay the ground for the grandson's initiation.

Typically, fathers do not initiate their sons directly. The father's ambivalence, be it in the absent style of Ouranos or the heavy-handedness of Kronos, obscures the mystery trying to be revealed through the son. Besides, parent and child often follow different deities. They tend to worship at different inner altars, each being "god-struck" in a particular way and seeing the spiritual paths from different perspectives. Although there can be a great sweetness between father and son, psychological and spiritual issues between them makes it easy for the father to block the direction of the son's spirit.

In traditional cultures it tends to be the uncles or unrelated older males who initiate the sons. In theory, they have fewer entanglements with the child and less need to withhold the honey of life. Through the rites of passage, the young one will leave the family and find a place amidst the community. Uncles and aunts represent a bridge for that crossing from the family circle to the community fire.

Initiation is the creative, artful container that helps each young person hear the call of spirit. In order to hear the call, a small death must come between parents and their child. From the cocoon of childhood a new stage of life begins to grow as a "second birth" involves the awakening of the unique inner life of each child. Through a conscious struggle, the young ones find the spirit sequestered in their own lives.

Among the Massai in Africa, each youth must find a honey tree and gather combs to make honey beer so everyone may celebrate and taste the sweetness of life. The son steps away from the family tree and follows the bird that calls him further into life. The one who becomes born again to the spirit has gifts to give to the whole tribe. At initiation each child becomes the honey and sweetness of life for the tribe. The initiation concludes with the youth nourishing the spirit of the whole community.

The presence of initiation rites can't solve all the issues between youth and adults. Its creative ceremonies however place the inevitable problems of family and culture in a context that allows the young ones to learn who they are at the core of their lives. The inner core contains the innate talents and gifts of the youth—gifts intended for the community as a whole. Without meaningful rites of passage, young people experience the typical troubles of youth without finding the sense of a "calling" within their struggles. This loss of self-knowledge affects both the youth and the community that depends upon their growth.

The loss of meaningful rites of passage often leaves an ambivalence between parents and children, as childhood has no clear ending. Meanwhile, youth increasingly receive either standardized education or random experience from the hands of those not fully initiated in their own lives.

Although attempting meaningful rites of transformation involves genuine difficulties and dilemmas for both youth and adults, avoiding the inevitable psychological, emotional and spiritual issues of youth generates tragic conditions for all involved.

Without the sense of initiations that reveal the core gifts of people and begin the healing of the inevitable wounds of life, it remains difficult for parents and children to find solid ground on which to meet. Something of the entanglement between parent and child must die in order for the tree of life to continue to grow.

When father and son do find a way to share the sweetness of life, there is something magical about it. The spiritual connection that existed between the spirit of the father and the unborn child can appear again and each may see the natural nobility carried by the other. Before that can happen each must find the sweet spirit hidden in their own life. Otherwise old expectations tend to be stirred up and bitter disappointments can follow again.

It's probable that a father and son must return to the bittersweet Tree of Life many times to sort things out. If the mistakes of the son are not taken too seriously and the bitterness of the father not considered too poisonous, moments occur when the honey of the heart can be shared. If the "all or nothing" extremes of Ouranos and Kronos can be avoided, the sweetness of life might be found more often. An old saying says, "Initiation makes the parents more human." The more each person becomes initiated into the shape and meaning of their own life, the less god-like and more human the "human parents" appear.

The Tree of Life stands as an age-old symbol that combines both masculine and feminine characteristics. Both the masculine and the feminine aspects of a person's soul seek to be awakened and known. The forest of initiation stretches wide and holds many secrets and surprises. The next time the son finds the tree where life can be learned, he will be in the "territory of the mothers." The end of one story is also the beginning of another.

2

Moving the Mother

*I am She who accomplishes without cease and
without end the transformation of all… I am both
She who thou namest Death, and She who thou namest Life!*

THEODORE DE BANVILLE

THE BOY AND THE HALF-GIANTESS

There was once a certain boy, a king's son, who announced that he would set out to see what existed in the world. So he started off and wandered on and on through a broad forest. Eventually he came to a clearing and saw a large lake. He walked all the way around the shore of the lake and saw no footprints except his own. He bent down and reached into the lake, took a handful of water, and drank it down. He took another handful and gave it to his dog. His dog! What dog? His dog. He decided to see who else drank at that lake. So he climbed a tree and sat in the wide branches, while his dog lay down at the base of the trunk. The youth stayed in the tree and gazed across the surface of the lake.

After a time the boy saw something coming over the horizon. He squinted his eyes and peered down as the shape came closer. Soon he could see it was a giantess coming his way—actually it was half a giantess, a Half-giantess. She came right to the shore of the lake. She lay down and began to drink the water and didn't stop until she had drained all the water of the lake and every bit of moisture from the sand in the lake bed. Then the Half-giantess began to weep, crying that her thirst was not quenched. She lamented that there was not enough to drink, that she would never satisfy her thirst because someone had stolen her water. She wept on and on; only after a long time did she calm herself down. Then she rose and strode away.

Soon the Half-giantess reached her hut. She made a fire and set a huge cauldron over it. She brought out bags of corn and poured them into the water as it simmered in the cauldron. She poured in wheat, rice, and bags of barley. She poured in beans and peas and other seeds. As this mess began to cook into a porridge, the Half-giantess caught two bulls and threw them into the cauldron. Next she caught some chickens and other small animals that happened to pass by. Finally she added a rat to season the soup.

Meanwhile, the boy climbed down from the tree by the lake and wandered over to the house of the Half-giantess. By this time, she had just finished cooking. She went into her house to dress up for dinner. The boy saw a tree near the cauldron of soup. He climbed the tree and reached down to pick some meat from the soup with his spear. His spear! What spear? His spear. He picked up a chunk of meat and, tearing it in half, he ate one piece and threw the other down to his dog, who lay at the foot of the tree.

Soon the Half-giantess came out of her house all dressed up for dinner. She sat down at the cauldron and began to eat and didn't stop until she had cleaned the pot of all the grain and had devoured every piece of meat and sucked each and every bone. She didn't stop until she had licked the entire cauldron clean. Then she began to howl and scream and curse and yell. She cried out that someone had stolen her porridge, someone had taken her meat. She fumed and cursed, shouted and screamed that there would be no end to her hunger, for her very own food had been taken from her lips. She carried on in full fury until the middle of the night; then she calmed herself and went into the house.

The boy climbed quickly down. He called his dog and began to run. He didn't stop, or pause, or look back until he had run all the way back to his parents' village. When he arrived he went to his father and said, "Father, now I have seen what is in the world."

CHAPTER 6

THE BOY AND
THE HALF-GIANTNESS

FROM THE TENSE TERRITORY between sons and fathers, the path of stories shifts to where the son of the village stumbles into the surprising realm of the Great Mother, she who gives life and can also take it away. One half of the wound of life comes from the direction of the father and the masculine energies. The other half of life's necessary wound comes from the mother world and the place of feminine energies. Where the blow of the father may feel like a curse to be overcome, the wounds from mother have the feeling of a spell that binds the soul.

Seeking to discover what there is in the world, the young son enters a primal area where some things appear as half of what they ought to be, and where a little taste or desire suddenly creates big trouble. He finds both more and less of what he expected in this world. There seems to be no balance, and there are no explanations. Everything feels out of proportion, either empty and forlorn or overflowing and overwhelming. The boy witnesses dramatic displays of sorrow and rage, which both intrigue him and terrify him. He is enthralled and shocked. Things appear and disappear; he can't understand or can only half comprehend the situation. He becomes confused, watchful, wary, fearful, awed. He says nothing, hides in trees, and finally runs out of the area. Only after retreats to a distance does he escape the spell of the great emotions and become able to speak about it.

The village son has found the territory of the mothers, the surprising land where his sense of personal mother meets the "mother behind the mother," the Great Mother of all things. Having given birth to the myriad of things at the beginning of the world, the Great Mother continues to appear in a multitude of forms. Sometimes she has many arms, sometimes a plethora of breasts, sometimes she appears as only half of what you expect to see. She answers to many names, sometimes being called Mother Nature, sometimes Mother Earth. She may be the Mistress of the Forest, the Lady of the Lake, the Mother of God, or the Lady of the Beasts. She appears as the old sisters of Fate at the cauldron of life, as the Old Hag at the well, and even as the tooth fairy claiming her bones back again.

Here she appears as first one half, then the other; first as the sorrow of the world, then as the fury of it. She paints dream-like scenes, using broad strokes of inconsolable loss and uncontrollable fury, as if to insist on the emotional content of the world. At the lake, stark loneliness prevails. There's no sign of life, even at the water's edge. There's the question of why no animals come; there's the shadow of rocks and pebbles spread across the lakebed; there's the sadness of fish floundering on the bottom. The place is lonely before she appears and completely forlorn when she leaves.

Over at the cauldron there's fire and things heat up. Many forms of life appear, only to be torn apart, all fodder for the big stew, for the rant and rage and feverish pitch that boils through the cells of life. At first there may be a sense of abundance and plenty, but soon things become over-heated, over-charged, then overwhelming. A person could become caught in the storm just by being around, become torn apart by the ferocity of feelings, swallowed up in the spinning emotions of the whole thing.

Tell a story like this to a group of men and everyone seems to fall under a spell. The atmosphere becomes heavy, thoughts become murky and unclear, as if everyone were being pulled back toward a watery womb, and the room begins to spin. Before the story people felt alert and full grown. After a while each feels more separate, alone, becoming younger, smaller… there are no footsteps to follow, even by the lake where there should be!

Those who listen to the story tend to divide into two camps: one formed at the lake of loss and sorrow, the other where the cauldron simmers and steams and boils over. Emotionally, a person can only be in one of these landscapes at any given time. I usually ask: If you had to choose, which feels closer right now? Which half of the Half-giantess draws on you—the side whose sense of loss wails with sorrow or the side which rages at something broken or missing in the world?

Given a chance to look back at this area of early life, the chorus of men has much to say. For some, the first tree in the story stands in the yard of a family which could not allow the son access to the waters of emotion. For some reason the boy had to learn that taking even a little of the Water of Life is more than the family can stand. A man says: "If I were to ask for anything extra or special, I would have broken my mother's heart. She already had so much trouble and grief, even little desires on my part seemed unbearable for her." Another says, "I was right there, too. I couldn't cry without my mother beginning to tell the story of her own troubles. How could I do this or that to her after all she had done for me? Any attempt to feel my own feelings provoked such an outpouring that I'd have to climb a tree to avoid being swamped by my mother's life overflowing." "All I recall is the bone-dry earth at the bottom of the lake. It was as if my mother had dried up. She had no capacity to give or be part of things. Everything was held back or dried up." "My house was an emotional desert, no footprints. The message I got was, "keep quiet and don't mention anything about the loneliness all around." I couldn't invite anyone over, and wasn't even allowed to have a dog."

Someone says that the lake holds the tears of the mother, that she does all the weeping and drains everyone else dry. A man says his earliest memories have him sitting in the kitchen with his mother as she tells stories of how life dealt her this disappointment or that blow. She'd weep and he would be overwhelmed by her sadness. His father was one of her disappointments, both for what he had done and what he hadn't accomplished. He realizes now that he has been drinking his mother's tears and absorbing her view, seeing both himself and his father through the salt tears of his mother's eyes. Meanwhile, he can't cry at all. His sadness seems distant and small compared with his mother's, as if he were watching himself from the top of the tree. It strikes him hard that he has only been an observer, even of his own life.

Another tells of his mother's illnesses throughout his childhood. He had to tiptoe around the house and could only go near her at certain times. It made the whole house solemn and quiet. There was nothing either of them could do to change things. Life became a careful walk around an untouchable lake, don't touch, don't desire, don't plan, because death could come at any time. Taking even a sip could precipitate her death, that's how it seemed. For him, the Half-giantess was lying on her side at the water's edge. The missing half was death, which was ever-present but unseen. When his mother did die, he couldn't grieve because he had always been awaiting her death. Now he begins to feel the grief of the boy always stuck at the edge of life's blessed waters.

"The dog was the thing that got to me," someone says. "If I hadn't had a dog, I would have had nothing. My only friend in the whole place was my dog. I shared more with that dog than anyone in my family. He'd always showed up right at my feet." "I wish I'd had a dog," says another. "My whole childhood was solitary. I still feel like I'm walking around a lake with no footprints, not even my own. It's as if the lake dried up when mother died, and I've carried this emptiness inside me ever since."

"I just decided to get in the tree and stay there. I've never come down. One look at my mother's inability to handle the little things in life sent me into the treetops. Now I have a great capacity to rise above my own pain, but I'm all alone." "I watched my mother drink herself to death, watched helplessly. It made me afraid of life and of the world. As soon as anyone starts to complain or demand or insist, I head for the trees."

Over at the cauldron, the conversation heats up. Anger and fear rule in this camp. Potential nourishment waits right nearby, but reaching for what you want means immediate danger. You could be eaten—or beaten—instead of fed. A man says being near Mom was an all-or-nothing condition; he would either be given treats, or he would be the next thing devoured. He got to where he could smell a storm brewing and would look for a place to hide.

Another says, "I saw my brother go into the stew, I didn't want to follow that. I tiptoed everywhere, and when it got hot, I'd head straight for my room." Another offers, "The whole scene at the cauldron reminded me of waiting for dinner at our house, with everyone sitting on their hands. No one could touch anything until my father got there. If you dared, you'd get whacked with the spoon." "Dinner was when my mother and father would fight, and we'd be quiet as mice because we didn't want to get blamed for whatever it was." "My mother would always find something wrong. Sometimes I didn't know what I'd done—or I hadn't even done it; I had just been nearby. Then I'd get a beating. As soon as I could, I got out of there, I ran away. Never looked back. Don't want to look at it now." "What got me was the matter-of-fact way the Half-giantess caught and cooked the animals. My mother can still devastate me with the most matter-of-fact statements, a simple phrase just tossed at me or my wife. I go numb. I'm still too stunned to do anything."

Another man says, "I thought you said the boy was in the cauldron when he got the meat! I saw the boy and dog in the stew. I became part of my mother's wrath. I've cooked in her wrath. I'm afraid that one day I'll disappear in the rage I carry. I have no sympathy for myself. All my compassion goes to animals, like the dog." "The only way I could be nourished was to steal, to wait for moments of calm and steal what I could." "I had to trick my mother to get attention and nourishment; I got it in spite of her." "I had a tremendous fear of taking anything. I still can't take the last piece of toast, the last cookie on the table. I couldn't be that selfish. I learned not to want anything, to only take what I was given, to wait. I'm a grown man, but still can't ask for what I want. I wait and get enraged, then make impossible demands."

Other voices clamor: "I was afraid the dog would bark. I felt like a boy again and could barely control my fears. What if the dog barks? We'll both be eaten. To me, the two bulls were my father and me; we were eaten up. We couldn't argue with my mother, no way. Once the rage started, I didn't listen to the rest of the story." "I spaced out as soon as the boy went near the cauldron. I've always felt half present. I started to space out, to go out of my body—I've done it ever since I was a kid." "It was exactly the opposite for me. I'm looking at the stew boiling, and then I feel it boiling inside me. I'm starting to get angry just looking at the stew. I'm getting angry now, talking about it. I get angry hearing other's stories. I get angry if someone near me is angry." "I was simply frozen in the tree. I wanted to run, but I couldn't. I just stayed right there because I felt so guilty for taking the meat. I just stayed there because it was my fault. I shouldn't ever have taken anything."

Another says, "I'm right at the cauldron, I can feel the heat of it. For a moment, I feel alive and then it's difficult to remain conscious of who I am. Any little thing can set me off. I get obliterated by my mother's rage rising up in me, and I'm gone. I don't even recall what happened, and for days I feel empty and don't know who I am. It's not the 'her' back there; it's the 'her' in me and it can blow up to the size of a Cyclops at any time." "When I hear that she's dressing for dinner, I can't stand it. How many times did it happen when I was a kid? The exact feeling: I'm waiting; I know what's coming. What's the sense of running? I can't get away." "I'm stuck in the anticipation of the trouble coming. I hate it. The anticipation still eats me up! All right, I did it! Whatever it is, I did it, just get it over with. I can't stand hearing about it over and over. Get it over with! Her questions tear me apart. I can't answer those questions. How do I know why I did it? I can't answer."

"In my house, everything was supposed to be perfect; we were supposed to have the 'perfect meal,' but it never was. Looking back, I don't even know if my father really wanted to be there. He sat there so stiff. I think he was scared, too—too scared to do anything. So it was just easiest for everyone if I got torn apart for some little thing; then he could sit still, and she could rave about how it could have been the perfect Christmas, or birthday, or whatever."

Still another man says, "The spear, I focused on the spear. I was trying to put it in carefully and take just the right amount. No matter, my mother always thought I took too much. She'd ask: Aren't you ever satisfied? What do you think I had as a kid? Does everybody owe you everything? Who do you think you are? Even now, when I want something, I have to go through an endless list of questions inside. Am I being selfish? Shouldn't I be able to do without this? Isn't there a cheaper way? It's as if any desire on my part might cause everything to unravel, one wrong move and it all falls apart." "I have the same issue. If a woman asks me what I want, I can't say. What do I want from the relationship—do I want children? Do I want anything?—I can't stand it. Either I shut down, or I blow up. Either I explode and attack everything, or I just walk out. I don't care. I won't care. It doesn't matter to me. If this is all there is, if this is what the world is, I'm gone."

By the time the entire chorus has spoken the atmosphere feels thick with spells. For the lake and the cauldron represent big spellbound areas where the Giantess keeps everything in a half-state. While alone and under the spell it becomes very difficult to understand what is happening. After the spell disappears there is a strong instinct to just avoid whatever causes it to appear. Unfortunately, the troubled area holds emotional energy, nourishment a person needs. Going there means getting in trouble, staying away means becoming dry and starved of vital energies. The Half-giantess represents basic appetites for life, the instinctive energies and desires without which life becomes a dry wasteland. The Giantess appears where a person needs to go and needs to grow. She visits whenever an important phase of life begins, and whenever we need to learn more of the world.

The first time I told the story, I felt pulled to the cauldron where the Half-giantess howled and raged. I felt increasingly angry there amidst the fuming fires. After a time it became clear to me that as a child I had been given a kind of permission to be angry, even enraged. Feeling sad… well that was another story.

As a kid I could argue with my mother by entering an intense state of anger. When I became angry it seemed to calm her and protect something in me. The story of this anger goes way back. When my mother tells stories about my childhood she inevitably comes to the place where she has to leave me at the top of some dark stairwell and I throw a fit, a long angry fit. It's a good story. She tells it to visitors as if I'm not even present. In a way, we both disappear into that story, as if the circumstances continue, as if we are both caught in a spell that the story pokes around at.

Like most mothers, my mother mythologizes episodes, especially birth and the early years. The stories aren't exactly the truth, nor are they simply made up; rather, they are pieces of personal myth and fact mingled together. They are markers on paths that lead back to the womb and the spells which envelop mother and child.

For us, the "top of the stairs" was a landing several floors up in the apartment building where we lived. The storm of World War II raged over continents and my father was away in the army. I had two sisters, one a year older and one newborn. My mother couldn't carry all three of us down the stairs by herself. When it came time to leave the apartment, she would sit me at the top of the stairs and carry my sisters down to the street. My baby sister would go into a carriage and my older sister would be assigned to watch the infant. As the story goes, by the time my mother climbed the stairs to retrieve me, the halls were filled with wailing, screaming, and howling. I was throwing a tantrum.

This happened repeatedly and apparently disturbed the neighbors. No matter—I screamed and howled every time. My little sister would often be crying in the carriage as well, while my other sister attempted to watch over an infant she wasn't tall enough to see. My mother rushed up and down the flights of stairs. Neighbors were watching, complaining, and slamming doors. She's doing all she can do, but it's never enough to stop the howling and crying.

The family tableaux shows where each family member stands in relation to the core dilemma of too many children and not enough help in the storm of life. That's the way the world was at the time. That was the dilemma surrounding and impacting both mother and children. It reminds me of the type of dilemma story in which someone must transport three unlike animals across a river. Say there are a fox, a chicken, and a dog. There's only room for one person and one animal in the little boat. How do you cross back and forth without allowing one animal to be eaten by another? You can't leave the fox with the chicken or the dog with the fox, and so on. How do you distribute the capacities, tendencies, and emotions of each child and manage to carry them to the other side of childhood?

In our family the distribution was clear: baby sister cries sorrowfully in the carriage, big sister holds onto the carriage and her emotions, brother howls the frustration and rage of the family, while mother runs between the two scenes repeatedly and father suffers another dilemma off at war.

There are, of course, practical reasons for my mother's solution to the dilemma. The baby had to be carried down and protected in the carriage. The oldest child would be the best guardian—at least she would be able to stand the longest and speak if necessary. Someone had to be left behind for a while. Eventually everyone settles down, but what has happened regarding the waters of emotion during the passage?

It's a puzzle that may be turned this way or that. A lot is expected of a mother; certain things are required of a child. Someone had to absorb the sorrow of the family; someone had to howl at the pain; someone had to witness. My mother allows some sense that she feels sorry over the scene. Yet she also implies that the distribution of children and emotions makes sense somehow, that something in each child related to their position from the beginning. What then does it say of me, I have wondered. Does anger come as a natural disposition? Am I inclined to lonely places? Was I a reminder of my father and his comings and goings, how he had left her with three babies and too many flights of stairs? Are men and, therefore, boys better able to cope on their own?

My mother claims to have known beforehand that I would be a hurricane of a child. She tells the story of my birth like a current prophecy. The night she went into labor was a dark, stormy night in the middle of winter. Thunder echoed and lightning struck revealing the snow falling against an offended sky. She felt scared and alone, worried about my father and in doubt over how she would handle another child. It was a difficult pregnancy, a hard labor, a long night pierced by thunder and a persistent storm, which seemed to reflect the nature of the pregnancy, the alchemy of the birth and the trouble of the times.

The story helped to make some sense of the temper I carried as a kid, suffered as a man, and struggled with as a parent. Whose storm is it though? Is it the fury of a young mother pregnant again and alone, the rage of a generation born to war, the pain of a child learning that there won't be enough to go around? Answers may have come more readily and made more sense back in Ireland or some ancestral place where fate remains a consideration and people seem to intuit that each soul suffers emotions in spells and torrents and storms.

Every family has plenty to be angry about and plenty to be grief-stricken over. Faced with the immensity and complexity of life, a family is like the little boat in the river of great emotions. Feelings and psychic conditions must be distributed or no one will make it across. Although each child inherits the full range of emotions, parents can't usually afford to allow them to be lived out—not if they all live in the same house, and not if the parents can't live them fully themselves. Not when certain displays of emotion were forbidden in their childhood; not when raw feelings are a painful reminder of their own continuing vulnerability. Inevitably, taboos and prohibitions become established in the psychic hut of the family. Eventually, the family dwelling has emotional zones, like the lake and the cauldron in the story. Each child finds silent permissions for certain attitudes and emotional territories and taboos for others.

While I related to the cauldron of the Half-giantess and to her rage against a world that withholds certain things, it occurred to me that I had been prohibited access to the lake of sorrow. I could come and go around the boiling cauldron, examining and entering the rituals of rage, but I left no footprints at the lake. The stillness and lack of traffic said, "Don't go there. Keep away, walk on tiptoes, off limits to you." For me, grief was a place without footprints, a land where a stinging wind blew. Later, when I learned how to face grief, it seemed like a huge lake in which I would certainly drown.

In another family, the "Do Not Enter" sign prohibits access to the cauldron of frustration and howling anger. When something goes wrong, well, it's just too bad; we're all sorry, but there's nothing to do or say. Getting angry will only make it worse; no sense crying over spilled milk, they say.

The trouble is that both lake and cauldron can be sources of the Water of Life. Each emotion acts as an entryway to the cleansing, healing waters of the psyche. The depths in which life renews can be entered through the lake of sorrow or through the boiling waters of anger. These are two of the great seas of emotion, two of the places where life energies may become lost and then again found. They are two pools for learning to temper the human heart and each family enacts its rituals of prohibition, inhibition, and exhibition in relation to them. Approaching these areas activates the "emotional body" of a person and stimulates any spells connected to it.

Like the Half-giantess, the psyche notices each occurrence in life, and the slightest thing can have great emotional importance. Seeing what's in the world includes learning to see into the inner world of subtle feelings and grand emotions. The innocent foray of the son in the story has led him to a world where huge, often blind forces are at work, where little desires awaken huge issues, where it becomes important to have a place for reflection. He sees the other side of Mother Nature and aspects of his own inner nature, which, if not made conscious, can stop all progress and devour life.

Psychologically, the story stirs the "mother complex," the great complexity in which the archetypal Great Mother overlaps and becomes confused with the human mother as she was experienced while a child. The Great Mother gives life and nourishes from her own body, yet she can overwhelm and smother; she can devour instead of feed; she can consume her child's feelings and still feel unfulfilled. The Half-giantess aspect of a mother knows right away what *her boy* is doing, whether he is dipping into the cookie jar, touching the waters of sorrow, or beginning to stew in his room. The primal energies of the Great Mother can overwhelm both mother and child and leave both in a confused and fused state.

Initiation practices often had the purpose of taking the child from the lap of the personal mother and placing them in the lap of the Mother Nature, who can be seen to manifest both as womb and as tomb. How men view mothers and sisters and the feminine deep within them affects an entire culture as well as their individual emotional lives. Will the boys learn to suffer their own confusions and overwhelming emotions, or will they tend to conflate the complexities and demonize women as representatives of the feminine and the irrational aspects of emotion? Are the spells from the mother-world going to be undone a little, or will there be an increase of hatred and fear towards literal mothers and other women?

Typically, the feminine aspects in men are denied and/or projected completely onto actual women. Denying the presence and importance of the feminine leads to undervaluing actual women and being dismissive towards them. Blindly projecting everything feminine upon actual women generates fears of them and violence toward them. The presence of poetic metaphor and mythic stories helps to break the spell of literalism that otherwise blames the evils of the world on Eve's handling of the apple in the garden. The same people who denigrate Eve because she was derived from Adam's rib, suddenly exaggerate her power when it comes to biting the apple and beginning to consider good and evil.

On one side the feminine suffers reduction and dismissal, on the other side it can be blamed for everything seemingly evil in the world. The appearance of the Half-giantess disrupts both attitudes. She can't be literalized because she's only half visible; she has to be imagined through reflection on one's own life. She can't be dismissed because she's aware of each nibble at the apple and each sip at the Waters of Life, be they the sea of emotions or the pristine lakes of great Nature.

Eventually the issues of the great feminine must be considered in mythic proportions. The Half-giantess has relatives throughout the world of myths, from Grendel's mother in the Beowulf epic to the Hindu Black Kali, who in the end devours everything during the time of the Kali Yuga. She is half and half because she is both womb and tomb, "she whom thou namest life and she whom thou namest death." In the guise of Maya, she is the spell of the world and the spinner of the world's spells.

CHAPTER 7

THE SPELL

A CHILD FEELS a distinct emotional atmosphere when near its mother. After all, mother and child shared everything during pregnancy. A boy feels it when he runs to the mother's body as a toddler and still feels it later, when approaching mother and home as a grown man. For a young child the mother is partly the center of the world and partly an atmosphere that affects everything that matters. The origins of the word "spell" include story, charm, or magical incantation. Between mother and child there exists a magical tale, a shared mythic condition that enchants or en-spells both of them. Such a spell intensifies near the mother's body, for that's wherein it began. But it also travels. Like the son in the story, wherever a person stops long enough the emotional spells from childhood will eventually catch up and quietly settle around him.

At birth, an invisible caul encases each newborn; it contains an emotional aura that doesn't wash off with the afterbirth. This atmosphere or emotional covering carries over from feelings in the womb and includes tendencies to become caught in certain moods or emotional styles. When a person becomes hard to reach, chances are that they have retreated within the emotional caul that entered the world with them. Such moods overcome both women and men, but men can remain stuck in a mood for a long time, like the boy in the tree staring uncomprehendingly at the Half-giantess.

Everyone has "troubles with mother," because mother is a complexity that can never be simply personal. The spell of mothering begins deep inside the mother-to-be and one of the great difficulties in trying to work on mother issues derives from the preconscious, preverbal nature of the mothering spell. Similarly, mothers often have great difficulty hearing about emotional issues from a grown child. Mother and child once had a long, unspoken relationship. Once upon a time they participated in everything together, as only the thinnest membrane separated them, and it was permeable. A mother literally knows her child from the inside out. Converting that magical story to common language becomes a genuine challenge for both mother and child.

Until the mother's water broke, the child grew on an inland sea within the life of its mother. Each child absorbs life from the mother's bloodstream, from the conditions of her internal lake bed, from the cauldron of her dreams and her nightmares. The dreams of a mother surround her sleeping child from the beginning and seep into its growing form. The fetus, with its transparent skin, absorbs everything from the mother in an extended feast of subjectivity. The child grows from a single cell to great complexity inside the biological, psychological, and mythological systems of the mother. Thus, the famous and infamous complexities of the mother complex.

During pregnancy, the mother becomes unusually absorbent as well, and the psychic atmospheres of the family and the surrounding culture make distinct impressions upon her womb world. The fetus floats on oceanic waters that receive the moods of the mother like calms and storms at sea. Mothers know this at some level; they have intimations of patterns that affect the child growing within. For both mother and child, complex involvements begin long before birth, as the embryo moves from the simple cells to the unique distinctions of an infant. A story silently shapes itself around the inner lake of the womb where the growing fetus is fed by the streams of mother's diet, her relationships, and her mythic imagination.

Everything that happens to mother passes unconditionally through the cell walls to the child in the womb. The child becomes acquainted with the inner rhythms of life while sharing the rhythms of the mother's life. This intimate sharing provides the child with its first sense of the world and its first experiences of love. All subsequent relationships will be affected by the first relationship with mother. Each person becomes an offspring of the biological womb, the psychic weather patterns, and the ic tides of Mother.

Mother and fetus merge so thoroughly that all embryos appear female for the first six weeks in the womb. In that sense, mother and child share the same body as well as the inner atmosphere. A shock occurs in the womb when a rapid release of hormones causes the development of a male embryo. Further shocks wait down the road when the son enters the world on his own. For the rest of his life shocks will tend to precede and accompany meaningful changes.

From this point of view, life involves a series of encounters that can shock a person into remembering who they are in essence and why they came to life. Initiatory practices try to emulate such shocks and images such as the Half-giantess represent the complexities of mother and the feminine forces in the individual soul and in the world beyond oneself.

Primitive, raw, and enormous, the Half-giantess seems a symbol of things half-formed, only half-human and hardly understood. Her extreme appearances reflect back to the boy his own half-conscious psychological condition. Ecologically, she demonstrates that every little thing in the realm of Nature remains connected to every other thing; even little sips at life alter the balance at the end of the day. Mythically, the Half-giantess shows how leaving the area of the personal mother means stepping into the great womb of the world where the fervid, libidinous forces of the life must be encountered in order that the psychic fullness sleeping inside be discovered.

Someone asks, "Does the Half-giantess put you under a spell or help break the spell by shocking you awake?" The Half-giantess loves either/or questions. Is Nature beneficent or devouring? Are intense emotions positive or negative? She loves that line of questioning and the innocence behind it. She always answers the same way: Yes! Most things are half and half, most things can be seen this way or that. Too much of a *good thing* and everything *goes to hell*. Most medicines turn poisonous if overdone. It's often the feeling-tone in a situation that distinguishes good from bad.

The Half-giantess appears where a person hasn't learned to distinguish their own feelings about the world and their unique place in it. She appears where the personal mother, the inner feminine of the son, and the Great Mother of the world all meet. The Half-giantess is made of radical "halves"—half personal mother, half "inner feminine" and half Great Mother.

Three halves make her whole. That's her style of math and her humor and her shocking, irrational form of logic.

Where the personal mother fails to satisfy the needs of the child or where she erupted with her own needs and unfulfilled desires, there the Half-giantess sets up camp and settles in as a spell of broken emotions, unconscious cravings, and exaggerated fantasies. The less a person looks in her direction, the bigger she grows. When everything seems quiet and still, virginal and untouched… she is right nearby. The sense of the world as pure and virginal is one of her spells, so is the idea of dressing for life as if it were an endless party. She's there whenever we insist on seeing things just one way. Over-abundance and the wasteland are each ways she enchants and startles and challenges human imagination. Her half-ness calls for attention and completion. Change comes from the unfinished areas, not from pretensions of wholeness.

In her territory, whatever we deny of life, whatever we refuse to look at or experience holds the missing energy necessary for meaningful change. Though she stirs the cauldron of spells and enchantments, the Half-giantess turns out to be an essential force for emotional awakening and meaningful change. She can devour all the life in a person, in a relationship, in a family. She can drain a person, even lay waste a country. Yet when the area of concern receives enough attention, she calms down, rearranges herself, dresses up for a nice meal and enjoys life fully.

The giantess appears enormous and half at the same time. She shows both the enormity of life and its incompleteness. Like any compelling symbol, each person sees her half-ness in their own way. Like the wound given by the father in the story of the hunter and son, the image of the giantess depends on the inner conditions of each person's life. She's been seen as only the left half of a huge body; as a body whose right side is gigantic and whose left side is tiny; as just the top half of a body or only the lower half. She's been seen as a huge woman cut diagonally in half; as a big woman with only one breast; as a Cyclops in a dress; as a front half with no back or as just the back… always turned away. The idea of half of a giantess may seem ridiculous, yet each person's imagination quickly shapes an image that makes sense in their life, which brings them to an edge where the unfinished emotional body meets the greater world. Each person has their own giantess who waits at the edges of what is known and awakens whenever we seek to learn "what is in the world."

In many parts of Africa, half-beings wait at the border between the village and the bush. They prey on the irreverent and the unknowing. Many cultures have stories of a race of malformed beings that existed before humans. In Ireland they were known as the Formorians—giant women and men with one arm, one leg, and one eye apiece. They inhabited the land before humans arrived, and humans had to pay tribute to them in great quantities of grain and herd animals. Of course the Formorians, like the *Half-giantess*, made a big porridge out of everything that came their way. They claimed ownership of everything and were ready to go to war over the slightest issue. As soon as humans forgot the tribute or ignored them, they would become agitated and raise a big commotion. They had to be repeatedly calmed with gifts or else opposed in conflict.

Eventually the early humans defeated the race of giants through tricks and the use of magic. Before their defeat, however, the primeval giants intermarried with the human folk. To this day, their odd and singular characteristics appear in human descendants. In fact, they say that some traces of those primeval forces exist in each person born to this day.

Half-ness is a code for primeval, for things infantile and undeveloped, yet huge in their effect. "Individual" means un-divided; but until a person comes to know themselves fully, they will be divided within and will identify with only parts of themselves. Some people live in their heads while others experience life mostly in the viscera, as if only the lower half of the body has been activated. Some seem to be all chest, as they push forward whether a situation requires force or not. Under certain conditions, each person becomes an "emotional Cyclops," only able to see and feel things in one way. Such single-mindedness simply takes over and makes a person blind to anything other than how they see it.

The giantess in a person is strangely narrow and huge at the same time; it involves the areas where we can't see ourselves clearly at all, yet where we carry a huge charge of emotion. Under stress and particularly when life requires that we change, our half-ness becomes manifest along with our fears of facing the unseen in ourselves. The half-ness of the Half-giantess stands for the unfinished emotional state of each person, the undeveloped and incomplete persona carried over from childhood.

A compelling wholeness exists between mother and child and each must face some form of "halfness" when the time comes to separate and take up life individually. During her pregnancy with the son, the mother expands with the spirit of the Great Mother while the son races through stages of growth inside her. As a child, the boy cannot separate the Great Mother from the human mother. For years he feels close to wholeness when close to the mother, near the womb of his origins. Being near Mom substantiates attitudes he has absorbed unconsciously and activates feelings he has toward the world around them. For each of them, mother and child, the sense of where one begins and where the other leaves off remains unclear and increasingly distorted as the child approaches adulthood.

The child easily takes mother for granted, feeling entitled to drink from her pools as he did automatically in umbilical times. She feels he should understand her feelings and respect all she has done for him. She gave the very pulsing of her organs so that he could grow. He seems so much a part of her, yet will come to feel that his story gets entangled in hers, that his life might disappear in the intricate spells of mother-home-house.

While the curse of the father often has a piercing verbal component, the mother's spell has profound preverbal potency. It's hard to put our feelings about her into words, often difficult to discern how we feel at all when in her house or near the cauldron of her kitchen. As easily as a mother twines the hair of her offspring while thinking of something far away, an old spell can re-form around mother and child and entangle them both. One word from mother, or just a familiar/familial gesture can make one's head spin like a dizzy spell. They were so close at the beginning; they participated in the miracle of pregnancy and the intimate pain of birth. She will ever be mother, initiated to that role by the silent arrival of her child's soul. Yet her child will not know life fully if he remains within mother's spell.

Since spells involve both the physical as well as emotional bodies, they have a regional or geographic component. Usually a young person must move out of the house and go away from home to escape the family spells. Unless the spell between mother and child is broken, a person can't learn who they are in life or discover what the world requires of them. Spells exist between a person and the world around them. More specifically, spells reside near a person's genuine potential to give something to life. Since such spells keep particular feelings of incompleteness in place, they must be struggled with wherever life requires a genuine commitment or complete involvement.

Ancient peoples invented rites of passage in part to break the spell of childhood and move the initiate from mother's lap to the lap of the world. To this day, a person must dismantle the spells of childhood or fail to find their place in life.

When the inevitable issues of life cause the emotional pressure to rise, the inner cauldron heats up and old spells begin to simmer and emit steam and fog. What begins as a faint mist or a little cloud hanging over things can grow to become an enveloping atmosphere. Soon a person has slipped unwittingly into a mood. If left unattended, a mood can become a way of feeling about things in general, an unconscious attitude that affects how a person sees the whole world.

A man in his mood becomes like the Half-giantess. She doesn't mind; she doesn't scruple over gender. She's happy to wallow in anyone's sorrow, or get a good rave going. There's such a clearing of the air after a rampage that she may go off whistling to herself, all settled down, ready for dinner and a good sleep. But once the Half-giantess leaves the area and the mood has been dissipated, a man may feel as confused as the boy in the tree. Not understanding what has occurred, he may prefer to just get away and not talk about whatever happened. The old spells from childhood depend upon just such avoidances.

If emotions were a big problem in the original relationships of childhood, it can seem hopeless to be near them later in life. If the emotional territories of the psyche seem deeply disconcerting and dangerous, a man may try to avoid serious relationships in order not to stir the emotions and attract the attention of the Half-giantess. If he can stay away from the emotional areas within, he may slip past the giantess unnoticed. If he barely takes any sips at the pools of feeling and learns to forgo most forms of emotional nourishment, he just might get by with some tools and a dog.

Yet something hidden within life itself seems to provoke the exact type of trouble around which the spell originally formed.

One day, quite by accident, he sees a woman coming along. She is beautiful, remarkable; everything about her seems to fit. She looks whole, complete just as she is. They fall in love; they live together. He thinks, "She's all I want and all I need to be happy." Other people say she's his "better half." He agrees. Eventually, though, some things start to go wrong. He finds her too demanding and tires of trying to satisfy her needs in the relationship. She feels he's too distant, except when he wants comfort or sex. They begin to notice territories where they can easily trigger familiar disappointments and wild frustrations in each other.

If he's a young man, he's really in trouble. How could he have been so wrong? He feels caught, trapped, tricked. How could he not see the other side of her or of their relationship? He didn't see what was coming. She's either just like his mother in certain ways, or she's not at all like Mom; she can't compare, she's not half good enough. Either way, there's something missing: understanding, freedom, respect, faithfulness, support, erotic love, common interests, patience, passion—something. Soon the missing part becomes everything, just the way the Half-giantess feels at the lake bed or at the cauldron.

In the words "Something is missing in our relationship!" you can hear the footsteps of the Half-giantess. She has entered the spaces between the formerly happy couple. And she won't leave until she gets what she wants. And what she wants seems like the whole damn thing… it seems that way to each of them. It's no surprise if the man becomes less and less willing to talk about how he feels. Under the spell or inside the mood, he becomes less able to discern how he does feel. He begins to withdraw from her and from the "them" of the relationship.

She says that if it weren't for her, they'd never speak at all. He's always behind a newspaper, a book, a sales report. Or he's always in front of a TV, a ball game, or relating to a machine that needs tinkering with. There's less intimacy, less gentle talk, less touching. Secretly they take up residence on different sides of a lake of sorrow or on opposite sides of a cauldron that's in constant simmer, ready to boil over at any moment. They've entered the territory of the Half-giantess without knowing it.

With the slightest provocation, he either feels completely empty like the drained lake or about to boil over like the overwhelmed cauldron. Whatever words she might say, he hears as the howling mantra of the giantess saying: "Now, you've ruined everything, and it's all your fault." No matter what his partner may actually say, he hears an ancient howling in the tone of her voice. No matter what his physical stature might be, he feels smaller and smaller and that he is facing a huge woman. If she becomes more exact about the source of the trouble, he only feels more like a drop in a lake, about to drown or dissolve.

The Half-giantess has come out of her house inside the man, she intercepts anything that comes toward him and tears it in half. The more rational and calm his partner's statements are, the more they fill him with grief, rage, and helplessness, for the Half-giantess makes each statement sound like an impossible demand or a complete condemnation. He feels he's about to be smothered or torn into tiny pieces. If this situation goes on long enough, he will begin to see the Half-giantess in the face of his partner.

Relative size disappears as the presence of the Half-giantess distorts everything in sight. The grown man and his self-awareness have disappeared like the two drops of water in the story. His partner has become mixed up with the preverbal mother who was so large as to contain his entire life. An outside observer might see a scared, endangered woman; the man sees a terrifying giantess. Compared to his diminishing sense of self, she has become a giant.

If he has never dealt with this Half-giantess inside, he won't have any idea what is happening. Feeling overwhelmed and diminished, he'll be ready to flee for his life or fight for it. He's shrinking, disappearing, becoming an adolescent struggling to hold onto his identity, his sense of gender. He's a boy feeling overwhelmed and unable to do anything about it. He's an infant, a fetus, an embryo in fear of annihilation. Through the course of an argument a man may be many different psychological ages. If something touches the core areas of his mother complex he may lose it altogether—lose the various integrities of age and most aspects of self-awareness. In losing coherence he may become a giant himself, or a giantess; he may become the seething cauldron boiling with the bitter poison of raw resentment, or a threatened dog that barks and bites and snaps blindly at the world.

In attempting to "find what's in the world" a man enters a tremendous dilemma. On one side, the feminine appears as the womb from which all life comes, including his own. On the other side, it can drain the color out of life or devour him in a moment. Be it mother or Mother Nature, the feminine force manifests both as an image of awesome womb and of awful tomb. Part of the dilemma involves the basic dynamic of psychic projection. So that to learn how the feminine and the mother complex works within a person, it must be projected onto others in the world. Unless it can be encountered in relation to others, the feminine in a man remains unconscious and increasingly subject to exaggerated moods and mood swings like those of the Half-giantess.

If a man refuses to reflect upon times in childhood when mother's responses were way out of proportion or overly rejecting or devouring in some way, then he's still running like the boy at the end of the story. He may run back to father by clinging to principles, organizations, and abstractions that will keep the sorrowful lake and the seething cauldron at a distance. Or he may stay up in a tree, trying to remain above all the mess in the world and in his own psyche below. Either way the Half-giantess waits inside, waits for him to desire something forbidden or for him take just a little more than he should.

At each further step into the world, the Half-giantess can appear as a mood or an emotional block or a spell. She is an ancient image of the impossible size and strange shape of the emotional world which finds living form where people interact with the world. She represents a troublesome, eruptive, irascible side of life, which doesn't go away and repeatedly demands attention. She answers the question of "what's in the world," emotionally, irrationally, and by reflecting what's unconscious in each person's psychic realm. When a person steps further into what they fear or stumbles into frustration, the Half-giantess stirs and stretches. She watches to see how we drink at the waters of life and how we handle what we find in the world.

A man repeatedly faces a choice between living a lonely life in the treetops or dropping down into the disappointments, sorrows, rages and outrages of life. Becoming conscious of underlying moods and mood swings and reflecting upon genuine desires in one's life can give the Half-giantess *her due*. After the emotional situation becomes more conscious, she settles down. At that point the appetite, desire, or idea hidden within the mood or behind the storm can be found. Inevitably, what we find behind the mood or inside the spell turns out to be essential for becoming more balanced and whole in life. As the inner life becomes more conscious something shifts in the mother complex and something moves in mother as well as in her child.

THE LIZARD IN THE FIRE

A father told his son, "If you ever sleep with a maiden, you will die." Then the father hid his son in the bush. He let the boy grow up in the forest.

One day a maiden came into the bush. She saw the son. The boy saw her. The maiden said, "You live so alone. I'll come each day to visit you."

The youth said, "My father told me I would die if I ever lie side by side with a maiden, as if a sword would go through my heart."

The maiden said, "In that case, I'll not come again, for it is not my wish that you should die."

The young man said, "No. Please come again. I beg of you, please come anyway!"

The maiden said, "Good, then. I will come back, and if you die, maybe you will come to life again."

The next day the maiden came again. The youth and the maiden lay together. What happened? The youth died; he died. Just as the father said, the young man died.

What did the father do? What did the mother do? They wept.

What did the maiden do? She ran deep into the forest to the old hunter of the bush and told the hunter the whole story. The hunter said, "Why, that is no problem. All we need is a lizard and a fire."

The hunter went to get a lizard. The youth was brought to the village. Wood was gathered and piled high. The fire was lit. The people of the village all gathered round. When the flames were great, the lizard was set in the fire. The hunter said, "Now, here is the situation we are in: If the lizard burns on the funeral pyre, the young man will stay dead. But if someone pulls the lizard from the fire, the young man will return to life again."

The father tried to pull the lizard from the fire, but the flames were huge and hot, and he was driven back. The mother went forward, but she, too, was driven back by the raging flames.

The maiden? She jumped right into the center of the fire, pulled out the lizard, and brought it back alive. The young man? Well, he sprang back to life.

The hunter said, "Now, here is the situation: The young man is back in life again. He must do something. If he kills the lizard, the mother will die. But if he doesn't kill the lizard, the maiden will die." Kill the lizard, and the youth and the young woman will live. But the mother will die. Don't kill the lizard, and the mother and son will live on, but the maiden will die. The question is this: What would you do? What would you do?

CHAPTER 8

THE FIRE LIZARD IN THE FIRE

ONCE AGAIN THE SON of the village has been out in the forest of
life. In the previous adventure he barely made it back alive from
the cauldron of the giantess. This time he returns as a corpse. Will he die
completely or, through dying a little, enter life more fully? Or must someone
or something else die for life to continue? Nature depends upon the great
exchange between life and death; initiation involves a kind of death as well.

Consciously or not, the whole community becomes affected by the
burning issue of how young people leave childhood and attempt to enter life
fully. Like the youth in the story, young people have to do something. They
must throw themselves into the fires of life in some fashion, and the future
of the whole village is involved. An old saying reminds us that, "In initiation,
everyone suffers." The fires through which young men and young women
must pass affect everyone in their community. It was also said that youth
will either become a hearth that warms the community or else become a fire
that burns the village down. The questions regarding youth eventually burn
at the center of every culture.

I've told this story many times, to groups of men alone, to whole villages
of women and men, to people of all kinds and all classes. Each time the
story becomes like a fire thrown into the center of the room. People want to
answer the burning question: What would you do? Each one who answers
adds fuel to the fire because each answer sparks disagreement in others. The

discussion of the story becomes a ritual of disagreement as conflicts inherent in the listeners and in the society rise to the surface.

Suffering the heat of inherent conflicts can generate a glue able to convert a even a random group into a community. The troubles of youth provoke the burning issues that smolder unresolved in their cultural environment. Youth can't help but get into trouble; eventually everyone becomes involved, women and men, youth and elders alike.

A man says, "No problem. I'd kill the lizard." Silence. A woman responds, "That means killing the mother. Why doesn't the boy's father die instead? He started the trouble in the first place."

A young woman says, "If the lizard isn't sacrificed, the maiden will die, and there'll be no one to carry on the tribe." A young man adds, "She's the only one who actually entered the fire for him; he has to kill the lizard to be true to her."

Another woman laments, "I've already leapt into several fires for men and come out scarred and burned and it didn't change them at all." A man answers, "It's all or nothing. If the son doesn't kill the lizard completely, anyone who gets close to him will get burned over and over."

Someone protests, "Why does there have to be killing at all? Why can't everyone just live their own life, each doing his or her own thing?" Someone answers, "Doing your own thing can mean not doing anything, and not doing anything means the young woman dies. That's not right. She's the one who has risked the most. You can't suddenly say people are on their own! That's a cop-out."

Another voice pipes up: "I'd kill the old hunter. He's behind the whole setup. Who says killing a lizard will save the maiden? I don't trust him; I'd kill him." A woman agrees, " It's another patriarchal story: the father tells the son that the maiden is bad, then the old patriarch says the solution to everything is to kill the mothers. It's the same old story. Blame women. We need new stories that don't solve problems by killing women and animals. Kill the old patriarch."

Suddenly I feel I must jump into the fire to defend the story. "What new stories? All stories are old stories—how people see into them changes, how they appear changes, but the old tales keep surfacing like a lizard or chameleon. Call it *Romeo and Juliet* or *Westside Story*, it comes down to similar dilemmas whenever young people approach the flames of love. It affects everyone and troubles everyone because there's death in it. Besides, even a simple story is more complicated than it looks."

"Wait a minute!" Another woman is on her feet. "Who says the hunter was an old man? I thought she was an old woman who knew the forest and the nature of people. She knew where to find the right kind of lizard and intuited how people would react. Why couldn't it be a wise old woman stirring the pot?" Another argument breaks out: old man or old woman? Everyone looks at the storyteller.

What did I say? I don't know. The story isn't recited word for word. Each time it's part remembered and part created. The two aspects of memory and making go together like two streams rushing onto the tongue, each carrying words that become one river as they go over the cliff of the lip. Part of a story must be exact or the sense of it becomes confused; other parts invite interpretation or elaboration. So I don't know exactly what I said at the time; that's how I know that the story is old and new. Spontaneity in the telling and passionate involvement in the listener keep the story alive.

One woman remembers clearly: "It wasn't him or her; just the old hunter. It could be either a woman or a man."

Meanwhile, a group of young men has gathered on one side of the fire. They feel strongly that the lizard must die. The reasoning has become clear to them—each one desires to be with a young woman who loves them enough to face the flames for them, with them. They're excited by that. But, one young man disagrees; sadly he says he can't kill the lizard. He and his siblings have been raised solely by their mother; no way he could participate in harming her. He'd rather stay in limbo, stay out of the center of things. His manner brings a wave of sorrow into the room. The fire cools down a bit.

Each one present reflects on their mother or on their mothering. Eventually a mother states that the lizard must be sacrificed, no matter the feelings provoked. She has a son and knows that the time has come to let him go; what troubles her is the lack of wise, old elders, the lack of genuine communities, and the loss of meaningful rites which might make the struggles of love and life more meaningful. Most people agree with that.

Motherhood spreads a wide cloak through the psychic landscape. The spell that spins between mother and child may leave both spell-bound. The paradigm and paradox of mother may become a spell that stops growth, whereas formerly it nourished life. In order for the child to step fully into his or her own life something must sever the psychic umbilical chord and release both mother and child to another life-stage. The story of the lizard dramatizes the idea of "moving the mother" and thereby changing all the relationships in the psychic village.

The fire set in the center of the village presents a ritual moment in the life of family and community, a moment in which roles change for the good of everyone involved. The burning question arises when the son encounters a young woman whose feminine spirit comes between him and the image of mother. Will he continue to be her child, or will he die to that world and find a bigger life with a woman willing to love him as a man? The story makes a fire of the cultural, familial, and personal dilemmas and conflicts that arise where childhood must come to an end, where even a mother's love has limits.

Modern mass societies tend to obscure the subtle ties each individual has within their community life. As a result, people consider life changes to be mostly personal. Yet part of the human psyche remains tribal, and psychologically each person continues to be a member of the "psychic village." At that level the sense of initiation involves the idea that everyone must shift to some degree in order that the individual might change completely. The child of the psychic village doesn't simply grow into adulthood. Rather, the child must die in order that the whole person be born. In the depths of the psyche, change means death and rebirth to a new state in life. The "psychic death" or transformation of the child changes every relationship in the village.

Unless the *hood* of childhood be removed, the young man and young woman will not be able to sustain the gaze into each other's eyes. Unless everyone involved feels the intensity of the fire of change, the spells of childhood may dominate the next stage of life, as well. Going through the fire burns away the old skin and makes a new orientation to life possible.

The changes that inspire and afflict youth are natural at one level and *contra naturum*, or against nature, as well. Nature provides the patterns and energies for physical growth during childhood and generates a shift of instinctive drives and desires at the onset of youth. Yet the transition from child to adult involves more than natural instincts. The "second birth" involves psychological, spiritual, and sexual changes as the child becomes full born, psychically aware, and fully active in community life. Whereas the first birth was natural, the second birth is more cultural and used to involve a creative artifice, a symbolic process that delivers an independent psyche.

Ceremonies and rituals have been the age-old, creative effort through which human imagination combines the drives of nature with the arts of culture. The ceremony in the story places a lizard with its old, cold-blooded view in the center of a fire set in the midst of the cultural village. African cosmologies often equate Nature with change. While the element of earth stands for stability and continuity, nature means constant alteration as reflected in the watchfulness of animals and the subtle shifting of trees. Nature was the library through which tribal people studied the patterns of change in the world. Thus, the lizard in the fire becomes the symbol of how initiatory change moves through the village, touching everyone and altering all relationships. Thus, culture surrounds and includes nature, even warms it and heats it to the point where everything can change. For the change in each young person will come to affect both culture and nature as the human soul ever stands in the fire that burns between the two opposite and complementary realms.

On one hand, the son appears to be dead. He acted in ways that children do not act. As a result, he lies near the fire at the center of the village, the corpse of childhood laid to rest. The future life of the son sits in the fire in the symbolic form of the lizard. The son whom everyone knew lies there dead, yet he's also burning in the midst of life. He's betwixt and between life and death—the state of the initiate now represented as the fate of the lizard. If someone will enter the flames for him, with him, the son will enter life again and in a new way. He will be reborn from the flames of nature and from the heat of culture.

Placing the fire in the center of things makes clear that the fate of the son affects everyone else. Everyone will know that something has been born from a fire that tested how others view him and how they love him. For the implication is that the fire might kill him unless others sacrifice for him and love him enough to suffer pain for his sake. Not the pain of parents protecting their offspring, or even a village protecting its children; rather some suffering is required that helps release a new person from the corpse the child had become.

The old drama through which childhood must be left behind in order for the whole person to step fully into life becomes a ceremony which warms and involves and challenges everyone in the village to attend to the mystery of the essential changes required by life. Faced with the heat of this transformation happening to their child, both mother and father become helpless to protect or save him. Nor can the youth simply save himself. At a certain point, the one being initiated into the mysteries of life and death must suffer the conditions of radical change while others act on his behalf. The initiate acts a role, but also becomes the locus through which the forces of nature and arts of culture act.

In the ancient alchemy of the fires of youth, the parents become helpless to interfere with the fate of their child. The one to whom they gave life now appears as if dead and life must return from another source. The roles of the parents have reach a natural limit as their child enters a new stage and takes his or her own role in the next stage of life. A fire stands between one stage of life and another; it can't be negotiated away or simply grown into. The threshold of change must be traversed with a leap of soul. The maiden represents the spirit and courage and mystery of the new life burning in the youth. She leaps with a new love, as the soul leaps when it finds a new way to be in life.

Once the maiden leaps, the son comes back to life. The life and death circumstances shift: he has returned to life, but she faces a kind of death if he maintains childish attitudes. If he doesn't act in a new way, death will claim her and the youth will remain stuck in childhood patterns. The son must act decisively to change his own life and enter it more fully. If he doesn't slay the lizard, he may take on a cold-blooded view of life. He may lose the passion for life which caused him to disobey his father and risk death in order to know more of life. One form of love must replace another or the heat and warmth of loving may turn cold. If youth and maiden cannot find the iridescence in each other's eye, something of the future will go dim. For lack of sacrifice or because of the wrong sacrifice, the new life at the center of the village will die.

In order for the youth to leave childhood behind, he must end certain ways of being and relating. In a sense, he must kill off his childish dependencies in order to love life in new ways. Once the very image of life's abundance, the mother comes to represent what could stop life from changing. Whereas mother once sacrificed for her son's life, she now represents what must be sacrificed in his life. Unless the psychic umbilical is severed, mother and child will continue to share a psychic skin to the detriment of both.

The lizard first symbolized the condition of the son and then represented the plight of the maiden. Now lizard and mother become identified. Mother must move from caring for her child to the art of nourishing the community. Otherwise, what was once life-giving may turn cold-blooded and become a drain on life. The son suffers a little death in order to enter life more fully and more consciously. If something similar doesn't happen for the mother, she may experience a loss of life in some other way. Just like childhood, motherhood also has a limit. The end of motherhood also requires a conscious ceremony.

At the lizard's fire, clothes and cloaks and skins exchange as each character becomes nakedly human in order to feel the fire and be scarred a little, in order to learn where they have been and who they must become. No great change can occur, no birth of something new unless something else dies away. The lizard represents the shedding of dead skin where life would take a new cloak. Cultures with lizard totems say that lizards are the ancestors of all the land animals, that when lizards shed their tails they became the first people. In the heat of initiation, each person touches the animal ancestors again; being in touch with the very beginning allows everything to begin anew.

Traditionally, the cloak waiting on the other side of all the sacrifices required during motherhood is that of a tribal elder, often imaged as the wise old woman found in stories of all cultures. A specific problem arises where modern societies fail to imagine a meaningful role for women after the age and stage of motherhood. For mother to fully relinquish her children it helps to have another full role in life and a cloak that covers her with new meaning and respect. When a society doesn't offer women such a cloak, mother can become a stuck place because no meaningful next phase beckons.

The materialism and literalism of modern cultures intensifies the fixation of human mother with Great Mother. The loss of vital connections to Mother Nature and absence of rituals that indicate the psychic and mythic aspects of motherhood leave human mothers in a heavily conflicted place. Because mother and matter can be identified with each other, because mother matters so much, much can come to be the matter with mother. Without the sense that motherhood, like childhood, is a psychic, mythic cloak that can be removed to one degree or another, some women continue to mother, in the most literal ways, children who have grown into adults themselves. When this happens the spell between mother and child may envelop both from birth until death.

While the cloak of motherhood wraps everyone who enters life in its wide folds, it cannot be the only cloak a woman wears. Mother, too, must go through the fire and come out with a new psychic skin or she will cling and hold on to her children in ways that lose the warmth of life. In order to move the mother and the mother complex, there needs to be a place beyond the literal role of mother.

Where a culture cultivates a meaningful position of old wise woman or worldly crone, a woman may move from mothering children to mothering culture and caring for a community. She can find her place at the well of wisdom or near the cauldron of inspiration. Attending to the womb of culture allows a woman to mix lived experience with the lunar vision of inspiration. Seen metaphorically, mother becomes Grand-mother and moves from giving literal milk to actual children to dispensing the "milk of wisdom" to all of culture's children.

Another role typically associated with women and essential for conceiving the scope of the feminine energies is that of the midwife. In many traditions, midwives would attend the birth of each child as well as the death of each person. A midwife would be there to assist at birth, wash each newborn, and wrap it in swaddling clothes. At the other end of the road of life, it would be the midwife who washed clean each corpse and wrapped it in the death shroud. The midwife handled new life and held the newly dead, thus experiencing the two sides of the Great Mother: "she who giveth and taketh away." As midwife a woman would come to know the ceremonies of birth and death and the necessity for each in the course of life.

The title midwife referred to the role of marrying the soul trying to enter the world through the door of birth; but also marrying the soul as it departs for the *other side* through the door of death. The midwife stands for the Great Mother who participates in each birth and in every death. She represents both forms of wisdom, that which values life fully and that which knows the shadow of death that follows each step in life. She stands for the extended mother, the wise old woman who values life because she also knows the darker wisdom of death. In the old way of seeing, mother resides in both womb and tomb; she is there at the origin in life's teeming ocean and again in the living tomb of Mother Earth.

When a culture denies the presence of death in life, it loses the wisdom of this darker womb. In this loss, it tends to cut the road of mother short and force into biology what would live more mythically. A culture that refuses to study death soon comes to know less of life; what begins as a denial of death becomes a denial of life.

Modern troubles with "moving the mother" come partly from seeing the great mysteries of birth and death as practical and literal events. When the role of mother extends only to personal and practical aspects of family, a whole area of wisdom diminishes. When the image of the Great Mother as the womb of life and the tomb at death gets condensed into a literal mother, the personal mother becomes the focus of unreal expectations, surreal fears, and tragic disappointments. When the death-side of the Great Mother suffers denial, the human mother tends to be seen as more deadly. More than that, unconsciousness regarding the "tomb mother" converts to an increased fear of women in general and of strong women in particular.

Human mothers undergo an extended period of nurturing and nourishing their young—longer than most any mammal. On the other hand, a woman's period for childbearing comes to an explicit end with menopause. Mother Nature speaks in each instance, and speaks the language of death as well as that of birth. In the end, death is not the opposite of life; rather death is the opposite of birth and life includes both. Through the ancient role of midwife the relationship between birth and death could be studied and the role of mother and Great Mother could be better understood. Without such psychological perceptions and mythical impressions, mother and mothering gets stuck on the birth side of life. Without the sense of the Great Mother who operates through the process of birth-death-renewal, both the young and the old can become stuck in roles that can't hold the entire imagination of life.

Part of the cultural oppression of women derives from the cultural denial of the divine yet earthly feminine force in the world. As womb of abundance and birth, as old woman of wisdom and spinner of spells, and as the voracious tomb that awaits all forms of life, the feminine must remain a source of awe and mystery. Denying the scope of this mystery, from its underworld of roots and bones to its branch-ripened fruits suspended against the blue sky, forces individual women to bear the full weight of human projections and fears of the great feminine.

Moving the mother means not only moving huge projections off actual women, it also means facing the inherent powers that manifest through the feminine aspects of the world.

In the story many little sacrifices go into making the fire of community and clearing the way for change. The father's authority must be sacrificed in order that the son experience more of life. The idea that mother or father can and should save their child from the dangers and dramas of life must be sacrificed and must perish in the flames before the watchful eyes of the whole community. Meanwhile, when the son kills the lizard he sacrifices blind, infantile attachments to his mother. Yet any idea he might have of being completely independent or never needing help—that, too, becomes sacrificed when the maiden leaps into the fire to rescue him. The idea that a young woman could be helpless or superficial incinerates when the maiden turns out to be the only one who can stand the heat. The sense that a woman's value could be restricted to mothering also goes up in smoke. By the end, everyone has lost some skin; each has learned a new perspective and the lizard's old bones have been warmed.

The heat of conflict and the light of the symbolic fire generate an intense, dynamic exchange which releases an array of emotions and reveals hidden ideas. Rites and symbols of initiation poke at the mysteries of life while raising the psychic heat that makes meaningful change possible. Like any good symbol, a lizard can represent more than one thing. Lizards have a betwixt and between quality that reflects the condition of the initiates. They seem to live between one thing and another, between fish and mammal, between crocodile and snake. Lizards have been called fish on land, snakes with legs, little crocodiles, and miniature dinosaurs.

Lizards are brothers to snakes, for both shed dead skins and seem to pass from life to death and back again. Lizards live on a branch of the tree of animals that extends all the way back to dinosaurs in prehistory and to dragons in mythology. They were among the reptiles that left the mother ocean and found ways to move on solid land. They continue to move in every way possible—they swim and slither, they walk and jump, they even fly from tree to tree. Their ability to cling defies gravity. Grab the tail of some lizards, and they will leave it with you. What you hold will wriggle and remain alive for a while; but the lizard itself has escaped and already grown another tail. Symbols and stories work the same way. They leave a piece of living information with anyone who catches hold of them. Yet touch them again and something new will appear.

Whoever pays real attention to the story of Lizard in the Fire walks away with some "living philosophy" or a piece of symbolic knowledge that can shift something in their life, in their family. For a while such knowledge burns with life-warming spirit and soul. Eventually, it grows cold again and another lizard must be found, or another story.

CHAPTER 9

BREAKING SPELLS,
FINDING INSPIRATION

A N EMOTIONAL OR PSYCHIC SPELL keeps a person spinning around an area that remains mostly unconscious, yet holds hidden inspiration and essential life energy. We may try to avoid places where emotions erupt and confusions abound, yet will be secretly drawn to them like the boy entering the territory of the Half-giantess. Areas that become spell-bound turn out to be essential for emotional and spiritual growth. Spells tend to fall primarily on the body or else on the mind. For some the spell will fall over basic life instincts and they will struggle mightily with bodily issues of sex or food or health. Others will become spell-bound in the realm of ideas and images. They will hold "wrong-headed" ideas and be unable to think through things or intuitively find a way forward. People call it anxiety, worry, neurosis, addiction; yet it can be called a spell, as well.

The Half-giantess depicts the odd condition that a spell creates. Once activated, a spell becomes gigantic. It takes over everything, wraps us in it until we can't see anything except through its moody atmosphere or entranced attitude. Depression can be like that, or mania. A spell can seethe with blinding emotions or else cause life energy to drain and disappear. Spells cause one person to be recklessly impulsive and another compulsive to a confining degree. Or they can alternate between an insistent impulse and a fierce sense of guilt and restriction, which secretly feeds the impulsive side. Addictions work that way. So does the Half-giantess. She completely takes over, yet something remains missing at the same time. She appears gigantic in one sense, yet she remains only half.

Being half is like being unconscious. Part of what is missing where the spell falls or the addiction resides or the obsession commands is any conscious awareness. Under the spell certain things become huge and way out of proportion because proportion implies conscious awareness. Consciousness of what happens to us and why is the missing half of the spell-bound bind. In the proximity of the spell we become less present even as we become more filled with emotion or desire or fear. One aspect of psychic life becomes over-activated and overwhelms normal consciousness. We are swallowed by it as our ego functions and conscious attitudes succumb to something huge, yet lacking in self-awareness.

A psychological condition or emotional spell involves something other than who we truly are and keeps us less than who we might be. Avoiding the area that harbors the spell can secretly empower it further. Denying its presence simply increases its appetite, causing the Half-giantess to grow even more out of proportion. Breaking the spell involves entering the spell-bound area intentionally, rather than waiting until the spell falls again. The boy in the story watches the actions of the Half-giantess from the branches of a tree. In other words, he climbs above the uproar and observes the condition from a more conscious position. A spell or overwhelming complex must be looked into, seen from a clear place above where threads of the complications can be examined.

After seeing how the Half-giantess drains all the psychic water or life energy, the boy follows her closer to her dwelling place. In a sense, he tracks the spell to its source and looks into the spinning cauldron from where it continually rises up. In order to learn what is behind the spell or within the persistent symptom, it must be followed to its source, which means getting closer to the giant energies of the emotional realm of the psyche.

A spell can announce itself through physical symptoms or through psycho-somatic conditions, for a spell involves actual elements and substances of life, as well as unconscious psychological patterns. Yet a spell also contains a spiritual or mythical component, which must become more conscious if the condition is to be truly changed. The cauldron of the Half-giantess has rich psychic nourishment necessary for the almost impossible task of becoming fully alive and finding the right path through life. In the end, a person must face the spell or lose their way entirely.

Although two sips of the waters of the Half-giantess caused an unholy uproar, taking a third sip might change the entire equation. Mythical aspects are often the hidden key that unlock the complex lock formed by the concrete and psychological aspects of a fixed psychological condition. One secret of breaking spells involves going further into the spell-bound area intentionally. In stories meaningful things come in threes.

The third time can make the charm. The "mythical third" is often the missing half. The Half-giantess doesn't reveal the wholeness hiding behind her half-ness by putting two halves together; rather, the task involves finding a third aspect, a third side, or "third half" of the giantess and of the psychic condition she represents. Although a third half is truly odd and irrational in a certain way, in the territory of the Great Feminine three shapes a rhythm and a wholeness that can break the spells that bind.

Where *twos* tend to split into halves which become polarized, *threes* tend to shift things to another level altogether. In the geometry of the Great Feminine three halves make a whole. There needs be a third step, a third sip, a third bite at the apple. The missing third is the charm that can break the spell.

Behind the Half-giantess waits the Triple Goddess who likes to appear in triplicate form, as in the three phases of the moon or as the three Muses, the three Graces, and the three Fates. When a story repeats something three times, she is nearby. The Half-giantess may stomp and howl at two offenses, and the third sip has the danger of drawing her full attention. Yet it might loosen the spell as well. The third time can break the spell and reveal the charm hidden within it.

In old Celtic myths Cerridwen was the old goddess of nature and queen of inspired waters. Like the Half-giantess, she dwelt near a wide lake and she had a great cauldron. She was always cooking something up. Most of all she desired to brew a stew that would produce three drops of inspiration so powerful that they could transform her son. The problem that ate away at the old goddess involved her child, specifically the darkness that seemed to envelop him like a dense cloud.

Cerridwen was a powerful goddess. But the world is such that everything has some limitation; whatever exists is tinged with fateful limits. Being a queen of nature, she knew all the knowledge contained in all the seeds and all the rhythms of nature's great dance. Nonetheless, her very own son was a case where dullness of mind was matched with darkness of shape. His name was Morfran and he was neither wise nor handsome, and the old mother's natural knowledge perceived that he would not fare well nor marry well without one of those lights.

Knowing the secrets of nature as well as the nature of secrets, the old mother began to gather the items, which in due time and with proper attention could coalesce into three drops of inspiration that might make her dark son turn bright and radiant. She knew that whoever would taste those drops would all of a sudden know all there is to know about their life. One drop could open the past, another reveal the intelligence of the present, and the third release the shape of the future.

Cerridwen began to go around her lake and land collecting a bit of each herb, each blossom, and each root needed to cook the remarkable Milk of Inspiration. She took each item at just the right moment in its cycle, based on the phases of the moon and the rising of the life blood within it. It took a year to collect all that was needed, and it would take another year to cook and simmer and stir the stew. At the end three strong drops of inspiration would form and all else in the cauldron would be poisonous enough to cause death.

Soon a cauldron was brewing in the timeless cave of the old woman. It was a stew of the knowledge of life and of death. It needed to be stirred continuously for an entire year and someone was needed to do that task. A solitary boy happened to approach the lake at just the right time. His name was Gwion Bach and he was an orphan out to see what the world might hold for him and what he might have to give to it. Cerridwen quickly set the boy to stir the stew intended to brighten the brow of her ill-fated son.

Yet inspiration is a strange force, and, much like fate, it falls when and where it will. At the end of the year of turning and stewing, three potent drops coagulated in the cauldron. For reasons unknown to this day, the inspired drops boiled up from the cauldron and struck the thumb of little

Gwion Bach. Instinctively, the boy stuck his burning thumb into his mouth.

In that surprising painful moment the orphan tasted all three drops. As the moment opened to him he stood in a line of light and suddenly could see everything there was to know about the past, the present, and about his future in the world. One thing he knew quickly was that Cerridwen would fly into a rage at the realization that the three precious drops had fallen to an orphan of the world and not to her own son. He saw that she would howl and wail and try to devour him. He knew that he'd better flee right then and not appear as himself at all.

The boy became a hare and fled as the old woman arrived. Instantly, she knew that drops were gone. She ranted and she raged, then turned herself into a greyhound and pursued the hare that Gwion had become. He leapt into a river and became a fish. She chased him in the current as an otter. He became a wren and she a hawk. He turned into a grain of wheat among countless on the threshing floor. She became a black hen, found him out, and swallowed him on the spot.

For nine months she bore him inside. At birth, she planned to kill him for taking the drops intended for her son. But through the labors of birth he became her son and a beautiful child he was as well. Despite the fact that he was born of her rage and loss, she found herself unable to harm him. So she wrapped him in a leather bag and cast him on the mercy of the waters of the sea.

The child floated on the seas of chance until he was caught in a weir by a king's son, who was out fishing on a day he thought to be a day of luck. From the moment he arose from the waters, the child had the gift of inspired speech. For the luck of his arrival and for the beauty of his face, he received a new name: Taliesin, or "radiant brow." Soon the orphan became a poet who could speak the truth and do it with a touch of beauty.

His brow shone and his voice sang, and in the Celtic lands they say all poets descended from little Gwion Bach, who had been an orphan and had once stirred the spinning stew that held the drops of the Milk of Inspiration. It was also said that however gifted a person might be, to remain inspired a poet or an artist of any kind must practice speaking the truth. And the truth remains a difficult thing to find and to speak, for it must be drawn from a knowledge of the mixture of life and death, like the inspiration that leaps from the cauldron once things have been cooked so far that light comes from the darkness again.

The spell that prevents a person from knowing who they are in the world shatters with the surprising milk of inspiration. In a sudden break in the spell of time, the present moment opens to the past and the future. Once a drop of genuine awareness opens the thin skin of the present, time collapses before the presence of things eternal, as both past and future are revealed.

The youth found himself in a ritual that could break the linear march of time and alter the spell which held him in an orphan state. The heart of the ritual occurred when the all three drops were absorbed and he suddenly saw three ways into the world and into his own soul. It was the third drop that allowed the orphan son to see the world clearly and to know where he stood in it. The third sip awakened a knowing and self-knowledge that slept within. Yet, the moment of inspiration that deepened his knowledge and heightened his powers came only after a long period of stirring the pot.

Eventually, a person must stand in just that place that makes the head spin and the emotions boil. By staying near the center of the spell-making, spell-binding area, a moment of radical revelation can occur. The moment of inspiration involves a *poesis*, a poetry, a *making* that ever tries to come from behind the spinning of the daily world. Meaning hides in every moment, but only appears in the burning heat of inspiration.

Each person, in their own way, feels drawn to the cauldron of boiling and fretting and troubling over the inner brew of life. Automatically, unconsciously, and distractedly we worry over what we cannot simply fix or even cleanly grasp—what we cannot hold conscious for very long, yet which holds us as if in a spell. Yet "spell" means story, something "telling," a tale potent enough to be a charm or an enchantment. "Spellbound" means to be bound to a story that needs to be learned and told, which, if not told, will bind life's energy in a darkening spiral.

A man tells the story of how the first drink of whiskey he ever took opened his psyche to things he had never seen before. In that first sip his psyche soared; he felt a great weight lift from him. He saw and felt more in that moment than he had throughout his dull, dutiful life until that point.

In order to stay near the inspired feeling, he drank some more. Soon it took more and more to feel something of the feeling he felt in that one moment of sudden inspiration. In pursuit of what he no longer found, he became a drunk. For thirty years he stirred the cauldron of alcohol, taking drink after drink. What started with a sip of inspiration stopped just short of dying from alcohol poisoning.

After several years of drying out, he could see with some clarity again. He saw how he had been drinking poison while trying to taste inspiration again—thirty years spinning in a blind, drunken spell. He had confused the spirit of inspiration with the spirit in the bottle. He couldn't believe that the inspiration he had felt could come from something already within him. It was easier to treat the spirit of inspiration as a material substance outside himself.

Spells appear in important areas of one's life, in exact areas where meaning and purpose can be found. A spell gathers where a person's fate and destiny would be known. Avoiding the spellbound area means failing to learn where fate and grace have been woven into one's soul. Fate marks the spot not only where the limitations of a life insist on being known, but also where the deep imagination of that life resides. Breaking open a spell allows one to be touched by the grace of the world. Breaking the spell releases vital life energy and creative imagination; it releases an emotional blockage that makes all emotions more available and more serviceable to the self.

Young Gwion enters the cave of potential inspiration as an orphan. There's a suggestion that we must become as orphans in order to reach the place where inspiration and real knowledge wait to be tasted. In order to become oneself, a person must leave all that they know and come to stir the very trouble they fear to face.

Old Cerridwen is both the hag of the world and the Queen of Nature. She has two sons: Morfran, which means "utter darkness," and Taliesin, meaning "radiant brow." Though opposites in every way, they are each her child and they each dwell within us. Our radiant selves can only be found within a darkness we also carry. Becoming radiant also means suffering the condition of utter darkness, for the light of inspiration can be found nowhere except within the darkness a person already carries in their own orphan way.

In this world each person becomes an orphan until the tale already written in their soul is found. Whether seemingly successful or doomed to failure, each is a child of darkness until the milk of inspiration reveals the story contained within the cauldron of the psyche. Accepting that inspiration, requires facing and breaking whatever spells of self denial, self rejection, and self abuse might have formed within. The awakening only follows a moment of painful realization of what has held one so many years in the darkness of a spinning spell. The moment of inspiration also becomes a moment of initiation that opens the future as well as the past to the light of the present.

Gwion the orphan becomes Taliesin the found one, but only after a time stirring the inner cauldron with its darkness that can poison and its poesis which can remake life. It's the orphan in us, the part long abandoned and oft forgotten, that finds true inspiration. And the moment of illumination comes somewhat by accident, as if a mistake. Gwion worked for it, and it just happened to him.

The moment of awakening arrives after laboring near the spinning spell, yet it also comes as a surprise. And it is, in a sense, stolen as well. Gwion took what was intended for another and he received what was his all along. For the inspiration belongs to us, and again it doesn't. Even nature seems tricked by the surprise of inspired knowledge. What inspires us just comes, born out of utter darkness—a light that changes everything and yet simply reveals what was already there. When the spell that holds us bound to our own darkness breaks, a radiance that was obscured, but present all along, is revealed. From the dark cave of confused intentions and motivations come the luck and gift and destiny that the fated spell concealed.

The orphan had it in him to be a poet, a sooth-sayer and a truth-teller. Yet how can anyone tell the truth except by standing on the ground of who they already are, who they are in their own darkness and in the light of revelation. At the mythic, story-telling level, each person feels lost and abandoned, each suffers as a "motherless child," each is an orphan in search of a meaningful task. Mythically, the human mother never has enough milk or enough love or enough insight to take the darkness out of her child. In the depths of the cave of the self, each person must suffer a distillation of spirit, a stewing up that could turn poisonous. Only through touching the darkness and shadows within can the innate, inherent, and inspired sense of one's life come to be known. Such is the native intelligence of the myths of all the tribes of mankind.

The orphan in us seeks to be reborn to a mother with the milk of inspiration. A part of each person is mythic in nature and needs a "mythic mother" to be born into greater self-awareness. The second birth of the orphan son gives him a new life with a new name and a revealed gift of inspired speech that was his hidden inheritance all along. By suffering the spinning spell and laboring in utter darkness, the inner tale finally comes to be known and told, and the inner truth of the self becomes a story lived into the world. The harshness of the Old Queen of cauldrons turns out to be a thoroughness that chases us through all the shapes in which we might hide until the poetry hidden within becomes born to a world that needs just such inner truths to light the way again.

In the second birth, the mythic mother must be called upon and the darkness of the world must be faced if the milk of inspiration be found again.

The ancient Irish had the idea that the birth of each person involves three forces: the actual human parents who contribute life's passion and the necessary biological matter, now termed DNA. The second force involves unseen qualities and aspects of the parents, both their failings and their inner nobilities. The third level of influence at the time of birth comes from the gods, from the attention and involvement of certain deities who imbue the child with mythic and spiritual faculties and qualities. Thus, a human being becomes a complex arrangement of concrete, psychological, and mythical elements, each of which requires conscious attention to be fully real.

Seen in the light of that old idea, each person enters the world by virtue and labor of three mothers: the literal birth mother, who lends her body to the matter at hand; the psychological complex of mother, which forms between the psyches of human mother and child; and the spiritual or mythic mother, who stands behind the entire process of birth and growth and death. Taken together, the three levels of mother shape the mother complex and weave the great complexities of one's fate and one's potentials in life.

What we make of mother matters. It matters in terms what we make of our bodies, of the women in our lives, and of the world itself as it spins and cycles its endless way through the Milky Way. All relationships in life are affected by the mother complex, for it complicates how we see the world from the beginning, from even before we fully enter the world. At each important step along the road of life, the complexities associated with mother will come to matter again. The psychological and mythical levels of one's soul struggle to be born into this world each time a person attempts to enter life more fully.

A complex mystery resides at the core of the mother complex, an inbred story that only opens to our understanding in moments of inspiration. There's a dream at the core of life that ever tries to be born into the waking world. The dream that brought each soul to this time-bound world cannot be reduced to simple causality or to matters of genetics or social conditioning. There is a womb within the womb of mother, and by the time of youth something beyond both parents presses to be born. This second birth requires a double-womb that combines the rhythms of nature with the inspirations of memory and art.

Mother and child share an eternal bond. Yet the idea of initiation attempts to separate the threads of that bond so that the human elements as well as the mythic elements might be known. Initiation was a practice that put the child deeper in touch with the mythic mother while opening the complexities and spells that spin between human mother and her child.

Eventually a child grows too big to be held by mother and family, and he becomes a "temporary orphan." Another birth will be required if the child is to come to know the nature of the world and his or her place in the order of things. The orphan moves from mother to the Great Mother in nature and to the Mother of Inspiration, who presides over culture's well of memory and art.

Initiation introduces a second mother in the form of nature itself, with its great powers and inherent beauty, and reveals hidden aspects of one's inner nature as well. As the model for transformation and constant change, Nature becomes the "bigger mother" that can hold the child changing into adult form. Mother Nature becomes both the model for radical change and the background that changes very little as the ancient cycles and patterns rotate around each unique child. Where mother was once the "natural" source of comfort, Nature becomes the source of all medicines, the natural pharmacopoeia that secretly holds an antidote for each poison in the world. Initiatory exposure to the forces of nature helps to draw out innate qualities formerly hidden in the individual soul.

The other side of the second mother involves the "mother of memory" and the sudden milk of inspiration. Rites of passage typically involve an introduction to the inspired myths and spiritual practices of the community. Where the child once rested upon the internal waters of the mother's womb, the initiate enters the river of memory, which reaches back to the mythical beginnings and flows toward the future as well. Memory derives from *Mnemosyne*, the old Greek goddess who held the key to the knowledge of the past. She also was mother of the Muses, the spirits who give life its music and give each of us our style of musing upon the world and our place within it.

Ritual and art provide ways of entering and leaving areas of emotion and deep memory that could otherwise be overwhelming. The arts began as rituals that helped to break open the spell of literal time to reveal the deeper memory of life's sacred song. Part of the art of one's life involves awakening to what waits to be born from within. Everyone is an artist, not because of equal talents but because a creative cauldron simmers inside each soul. In the heat of darkness an inherent, inspired sense of life seeks to be known. From the place of inspiration, the individual life suddenly makes sense, as it seems aimed and purposeful. Under the unifying light of inspiration, culture and nature can become two ways of seeing and being in the world.

The imagination of initiation was one way in which ancient cultures sought to break the spells of childhood and open the life of each person to inspiration and meaning. Culture is like a mother who desires a child with a radiant brow, both for the success of that child in life and for the reflection upon her. Yet areas of utter darkness always appear between mother and child. Unless the second, psychic umbilical cord can be cut, mother and child can remain spell-bound, each unable to fully develop. Then the spells of childhood continue throughout life, leaving a culture without inspired guidance or a genuine sense of purpose.

Literalism is the great spell that binds and blinds the modern world. The literal view separates outer nature from inner nature in an exaggerated way. The lack of inspiration and loss of imagination that have become characteristic of modern societies stem in major part from the darkness and blindness caused by seeing the world as literal and time as linear. Exaggerating the perspectives offered by simple logic and literal perception has drawn a darkening spell over the earth and its inhabitants. In restricting the sense of the world to what can be measured and proven, people lose the greater sense of meaning that hides just below the surface of life. The dullness of facts and the dimness of information increasingly obscure the presence of imagination in the world and the human inheritance of the milk of inspiration.

Initiation means to begin and so once begun, conscious life becomes a long road of initiatory events. Sometimes the path winds through the fields of fathers, at other times it curves through the territory of the mothers. Back and forth the path of learning goes, as what has been wounded in the feminine must be healed through the feminine and what has been wounded in the masculine must be healed through the masculine. Only in that way can the sweet honey of life be found and the milk of inspiration be tasted again.

3

Ceremonies of Innocence

Tell a wise person, or else keep silent.
Because the mass man will mock it right away.
I praise what is truly alive, what longs to be burned to death.
FROM THE HOLY LONGING
BY JOHANN WOLFGANG VON GOETHE

CHAPTER 10

RECOVERING THE BOY,
UNCOVERING THE MAN

U P TO THIS POINT the stories we have followed have led to dilemmas and paths that mostly end in questions. They have been stories of incomplete initiations, adventures that don't fully reach a conclusion. They have also been village stories, old tales painted on a small canvas. With the next story, the Celtic tale of Prince Conn-Eda, we step into a big story, one that aims at a distant destination and winds all the way there. It carries many mythic tones and trappings and the particular sense of wonder characteristic of Celtic myths. Celtic stories insist on the presence of the "otherworld," the pulsing, inspired realm right next to the world of measurements and facts. The otherworld is also the inner-world and the underworld, alive with birds that speak and lakes with shining cities under the waves. This sense of an essential and nearby realm of living imagination is part of the old European and human heritage. Being imbued with the eternal, the otherworld remains in the depths of memory as certainly as the ancient paintings waited to be discovered in prehistoric caves.

Fairy tales are woven like intricate tribal carpets, the images spun of strong old threads of imagination that keep the otherworld near. Like old carpets they are made to survive and have many feet pass over them. They can be walked through or meditated upon. They can provide warmth and bring joy to the aesthetic senses. They can be used to cover the holes in reality. Old ideas were woven with the images in tribal carpets as the weavers sang the chords of old songs. Mythic and spiritual images were placed where people might walk upon them even if most forgot the old shapes that hold meaning for the human soul. Carpets, songs, and stories all hold old images that don't wear and, when viewed again, often carry a greater value than before.

Stories like Conn-Eda were used to teach a grammar of symbolic language and to sustain a study of life's innate rituals of change and growth. Bardic storytellers were itinerant teachers, carrying the old stories from place to place, reweaving the old threads, and spreading them out where people could step into the fabric of memory and find elements of renewal. Tales were told in gatherings at fires and hearths where the embers of ancient imagination were used to throw light upon contemporary issues. Irish tales were classified according to ritual aspects of life stages or adventures. There were stories for conceptions and births, for courtships, marriages and deaths, and others for voyages, cattle raids, and adventures. The story of Conn-Eda represents an initiatory adventure; a quest to determine if a son who happens to be born to royalty can awaken the genuine nobility of his own soul. He doesn't choose the adventure; rather, he is chosen by it as a kind of fate that must be entered if a destiny would be found.

Here the adventure divides into four parts that reflect aspects of initiation traditions, and a fifth chapter that considers similar elements in modern life. When a proper retreat can be arranged, I tell a story like this story over several days, offering a part each day. In that way the sense of each part sinks into the psyche of the listeners and mixes at night with their dreams, just as stories would have done in the past. Stories of this kind are not aimed at the front of the mind or the surface of the lake of the psyche. Rather, they aim at the back of the mind and the depths of the soul. They aim to awaken parts of the psyche that yearn for change and seek a true revelation of the meaning carried in the individual human soul.

CONN-EDA
Part I

Once upon a time, or below a time, in the time that was no time, that is our time or not, there was in Ireland a king named Conn Mor. He was powerful but just and good, and he was passionately loved by the people. Conn's wife was the good Queen Eda, equally loved and esteemed for her grace and wisdom. She was the counterpart to the king, and he the balance to her. Whatever quality was lacking in one was found in abundance in the other. It was clear that heaven approved of the royal couple, for the earth produced exuberant crops, trees gave ninefold their usual fruit, waters teemed with choice fish, bees made heaps of honey, and cows yielded such an abundance of rich milk that it rained in torrents on the fields and filled the furrows and ditches. In short, no one lacked for anything, and the people felt the sun of happiness upon them.

Conn Mor and Queen Eda were blessed with an only son. druids foretold at his birth that he would inherit the good qualities of both parents; hence they named him Conn-Eda. As the young prince grew, he manifested an admirable beauty, a ready strength, a noble bearing, and a bright mind. He became the idol of his family and the boast of the people. For a time things were perfect. But perfection occurs rarely on this earth, and when it does occur it does not last long. Good Queen Eda came down with a sudden, severe illness. In the course of it, she died, plunging the king, the son, and the people into sorrow and mourning for a year and a day. During that time, the crops began to decline, there seemed to be fewer fine trees, and people began to suffer lack and loss.

After the mourning period, Conn Mor yielded to the advice of his counselors and took as wife the daughter of the Archdruid. The new queen appeared to walk in the footsteps of good Queen Eda, until, in the course of time, and having had sons of her own, she perceived that Conn-Eda would always be the favorite of the king and the darling of the people, and that her sons would be excluded. This excited in her a jealousy and hatred for Conn-Eda, and she resolved to effect his exile or death.

She began by circulating evil reports about the prince. But as Conn-Eda was above suspicion, the king just laughed at the weakness of the queen, the people supported the prince, and the prince himself bore his trials with the utmost patience. He even repaid her malicious acts toward him with benevolent ones toward her. Soon her enmity knew no bounds, and she consulted a hen wife, an old hag who was known to be a witch.

"I cannot help you until I receive a reward," said the hen wife.

"What reward?" asked the impatient queen.

"That you fill the cavity I make with my arm with wool and the hole I bore with red wheat," said the old one.

"Granted," said the queen.

The hen wife stood in the doorway of her hut and bent her arm to form a circle with her side. Then she directed that the wool be stuffed through her arm into the hut, and she wouldn't let them stop until the house was full. Next she got on the roof of her brother's house, drilled a hole in it with her distaff, and directed that the red wheat be poured in until her brother's house was full. When these things had been done, the storage bins of the realm were much depleted of wool and of wheat.

"Now," said the queen, "tell me how to accomplish my purpose."

"Take this chess set and invite the prince to play. Propose that whoever may win can impose any condition on the soul of the loser. Because of the set's enchantment, you will win the first game. Once you win, order the prince to go into permanent exile or else procure for you, within a year and a day, the three golden apples that grow in the garden of Loug in Erne, as well as the great black steed and the extraordinary hound called Samer which are there. All are in the possession of the king who lives in the castle below the surface of the waters of Lough Erne. They are so precious, difficult to find, and so well guarded that Conn-Eda can never attain them of his own power, and he will surely die if he attempts the adventure."

The queen lost no time inviting Conn-Eda to play. He agreed that the winner could place conditions binding on the soul of the loser. The queen won the first game as was foretold. But she was so determined to have the prince completely in her power that she offered to play another game. To her great surprise, the prince won the second game. The queen announced her condition first: "Go right now into permanent exile, or procure for me within a year and a day the golden apples that grow in the garden of Lough Erne, the great black steed, and the supernatural hound of the king of Lough Erne."

After hearing that, Conn-Eda took his turn. "I bind you to sit on the pinnacle of that tower until my return," he said, "and to take no nourishment except what red wheat you can spear with the point of your bodkin. If I don't return, you are free in a year and a day."

The story of Conn-Eda begins in a period of abundance and a time of cultural unity. The king, queen, and little prince are perfect together, and the world reflects the coherence and fullness of the royal family. The child inherits the good qualities of both mother and father, and the prophecies at birth are promising. It is a seamless world of three-way perfection—mother, father, and child amidst abundance and mutual adoration. The flow of goodness is witnessed by heaven, earth, and all the people. But perfection, so fervently sought to this day, can only be temporary; it never lasts. Perfection is not only completion, but also a kind of death. The beautiful queen-mother dies, plunging everyone into a period of sorrow and loss. The perfections of the realm slip away. Eventually the king's counselors demand a new queen.

It's an old, familiar and familial story, the *good mother* dies and the *bad mother* appears, and she opens the door for the Old Hag of the World who is behind the whole thing. The birth mother must one day be succeeded by a death mother, for all stories happen on the road of life and death. The time comes when even the perfect son must fall from the privilege he inherits to seek a grace he may only find on his own. Whoever would rule wisely must come to know both the abundant garden and the road of loss and exile. It's not widely known anymore, but when abundance and wisdom disappear from this world they can only be sought in the Otherworld, in the inner- and under-world where all things fall whenever they fall from grace.

This part of the story reflects the universal human saga wherein the abundance of sweet milk and honey flowing through the Garden of Eden dries up and the child of life is driven out onto the dusty roads. The Garden and the fall from it are mythic inheritances within each human being. Each child inherits a sense of the garden of peace and fullness, each inherits an awareness of the fall from grace, and each is only ever one step from the wasteland outside the garden walls. The garden of abundance includes the idealized mother and father. This inner Eden is an inherited internal landscape, a magic circle of nourishment, loving attention, and protection remembered in the human soul. The Garden of Eden is the soul's reminiscence about the lost sense of home.

Each day includes a garden of promise as well as the chill wind of the roads of exile, for each person must one day be homeless in this world and a part of the soul always longs for a perfection that seems to reside in the past. The garden of abundance must be lost, longed for, and sought for again at a new level—that's the story of the human soul. Yet if a child becomes exposed to the harshness of the world too soon, it suffers wounds to its very essence. A serious lack of nourishment, love, or protection causes the garden walls to break too soon, exposing the child to a fall from grace before it can gather its own protection and incorporate enough love to make an inner garden.

A person exiled too soon from the sense of the garden of belonging feels deeply torn no matter what the road life offers to them. The initiatory circumstances inevitably encountered seem to deepen unhealed wounds and threaten both sanity and life itself. Conn-Eda represents the princely story in the soul wherein a "brush with death" creates initiatory circumstances. In modern times, a person may require a therapeutic return to the garden of abundance before attempting the dangers of initiatory paths. Modern psychology often attempts to strengthen the ties of the wounded individual to the culture while building internal strength for the rigors of life. Returning to shape again the garden of childhood may be a necessary step before the paths of initiation can be fully entered. In this context, the modern "recovery movement" is an attempt to go back and recover the child too soon exposed to the raw winds of life. Before they can benefit from the stripping down that initiation requires, some people must first recover from childhood wounds that cut too deeply into the fiber of their souls.

Conn-Eda represents the natural nobility of the soul nourished by ideal parents and surrounded by healthy community regard. If an ideal childhood state does occur, it can only be experienced temporarily as the story states. To become himself Conn-Eda must suffer a loss of innocence, a fall from grace. Childhood may follow a developmental curve, but the transitional stage of youth involves a series of shocks intended to awaken something hidden within the soul. Whatever the prince may receive by way of a fortunate birth will have to be risked on the rough roads where the individual soul is tested against the winds of fate.

Each fall from grace precipitates a loss of innocence, for innocence held too long becomes a danger and an obstacle to gaining knowledge of oneself and the world. The prince is too perfect and innocent of the ways of the world. This becomes evident in the way he treats the malicious acts of the new queen with benign superiority. The year and a day of grieving that casts a shadow over the entire realm failed to make him aware of the shadowy aspects in himself and others. Only when he faces the dilemma of exile or certain death does he begin to shed the innocence of his childhood and face the world where actions have distinct and often surprising consequences.

The second queen has other children, and the prince is not the apple of her eye. No longer is he the only apple in the garden. The loss of the perfect mother-queen and arrival of the "evil queen" or stepmother depict the loss of paradise as a child separates from the state of unity with its mother. This scene occurs in all families when a newborn child displaces the one who recently basked in the glow of mother's loving eyes. The psyche is quick to sense the new conditions; as soon as the mother turns her loving light away, the child sees the dark queen appear. Fairy tales contain many evil queens because all children struggle to reconcile the image of the perfect mother-queen with that of the mother who turns away and leaves them. Fairy tales allow a child to carry the images separately. But the day will come when a person must face this split inside their own life.

When the queen spreads rumors about him, Conn-Eda not only turns the other cheek but repays her with kindness. This kindness born of naïveté drives the new queen further into the shadowy land of envy and resentment, where the old "hen wife" waits to set the deeper game in motion. By holding to his innocence, the prince provokes an opposite energy that casts his fate before him. If he is to inherit the kingdom and reign consciously, he must learn the ways of the world where innocence can be a danger to one and all. The loss of innocence and naïveté sets the stage for initiation.

Once outside the garden of innocence, a person enters the path where initiation seeks to reveal the abundance of life hidden within the soul. Either a person accepts the challenge of searching for the garden inside the waters of the soul or they enter what could come to be a life-long exile from the meaning and purpose they secretly carry within. Once innocence has been betrayed, it's either self-exile or the long road of initiation and awakening of the self.

In tribal initiations and mythic tales like Conn-Eda the first steps of initiation are clearly indicated. In the modern world they are rarely as clear. Amidst the rapid changes in modern mass cultures, loss and pain and confusion are common experiences. Boundaries and borders can dissolve suddenly and images of violence and death increasingly prevail. As the future becomes more uncertain, lessons of the past are either forgotten or deemed not to apply. To be modern is to be disoriented—especially toward life and death. In the deep psyche such profound disorientation and intensity register as characteristics of initiatory ordeals. Entering the modern world can be like stepping into an initiation already under way.

When I tell the story of Conn-Eda, I usually stop at the point where each listener must choose to seek the golden apples or be exiled for life. Although the quest for the apples seems to mean certain death, many pick it right off. The sense of a heroic calling has a natural appeal. A quest may involve dangers, but the rewards are golden. On the road of life the point isn't simply to be heroic; it is rather to find an adventure and enter the ordeal of uncovering the soul's inner pattern. A genuine adventure does mean certain death—a little death changes one's whole life. Exile seems forbidding as well. Although, upon reflection, everyone admits to some familiarity with the roads of abandonment. In the end, exile is another form of death—especially exile from one's inherent purpose in life.

Although the story offers two options, often a third group appears consisting of those who refuse to choose either the road of exile or the dangerous quest. They claim they won't play the game because it is rigged from the beginning. One man says, "I'm not doing either one. I'm tired of being forced into bad choices. I'm not going. Fuck you." Several others join him. They are truly angry. They don't want to be in exile, they don't want to face an impossible task and they won't move from the center of the road.

They form a kind of "fuck you group."

Eventually their anger dissipates and they begin to feel vulnerable and isolated. The brush with life's dark cloak can be delayed but not avoided. Defiance held too long leads to a cynical, lonely place. Behind the wariness and angry defense waits a sadness that reveals that defiance constitutes another form of exile. Refusing to play or simply criticizing the game also has a cost. Like it or not, it is the "game of life" being offered. The game is rigged and always has been; it was rigged from the beginning. In order to win anything a person must lose something; in order to rise in life, a person must descend. For each person the rules are a little different and a person can only learns the rules by playing. Initiation makes life more compelling and meaningful; it shifts one's awareness from dreamy possibilities and sulking withdrawal to the immediacies of the present.

For lasting change to occur, the whole self must eventually become involved. In initiation a person becomes no one before becoming someone again. Initiation into the inherent drama of one's own life always involves more than one has bargained for. People who survive life-changing events often say, "Had I known what I was getting into, I would never have gone." Like most young people, Conn-Eda is in deep before he knows it. His life is on the line before he understands the nature of the game. Like most young men, he thought he would simply win; he didn't know how much loss the world could offer.

Conn-Eda awakens from the sleep of innocence when he accepts the conditions placed on his soul and in turn places some on the queen. He loses, he wins, and he accepts the nature of the game. If he must lose everything and enter the unknown, she'll at least have to be exposed as well. The prince walks away from childhood with its sense of innocence and perfection, but where does he turn when he turns away from all that he knows?

CONN-EDA
Part II

After playing the game Conn-Eda had conditions on his soul and trouble in his mind. He wandered about, uncertain of what to do or where to turn, until he happened to recall an old druid whom he considered a friend and a knowledgeable man. He went to the druid's abode. Immediately the druid asked the cause of the depression in the young man's spirit. The prince told him the entire history with the new queen and the chess game and the laying of conditions on the soul. The prince asked for help. The druid invited Conn-Eda into his hut and set before him the oldest of wines and the freshest of foods. The old man said that the morning was wiser than the evening. In the morning, he would go to his "green place" and consider the situation surrounding the prince.

The following day, the druid said, "My son, you are under an almost impossible *geis*, a condition of the soul which seems intended only for your destruction. No one could have advised the queen and provided the chess set except the Hag of Beara. She is the greatest druidess in all of Ireland and sister herself to the king of Lough Erne.

"It is not in my power to directly interfere on your behalf however. If you can find the ancient bird with the capacity for human speech, it may be able to advise you in this matter. In truth, that bird is difficult to find. It settles in the forest nearby, but does so for only three days in any year. The bird is difficult to find and troublesome to approach, but it knows all things past, present, and future."

"I cannot give much help in your search, but if you look out back you will find a little shaggy horse. If you mount that horse, it may lead you to where you need to go. If you are able to locate the ancient bird, present it with this precious stone. Then listen carefully, for it may tell you how to find the treasures you seek. That's all that I can offer you in this matter. If you do take the little shaggy horse, allow it lead you and follow where it goes."

CHAPTER 11

THE DRUID'S HUT

THE FALL OF THE PRINCE from innocence begins a descent that is also an education of the soul. For the first time he wanders the world on his own. The quest of his life is right before him, yet he does not know where to turn. He suffers a serious disorientation that separates him from all that he knew and counted upon. Thus, the story weaves aspects of initiation into the fabric of the narrative and shapes the condition that all youth face when the conditions of their soul become provoked by life. On the road that leads to revelations of the self, the things of childhood are of no help, nor are parents acting in their typical ways. Often youth become rebellious because they reach a point where the help of parents becomes a hindrance to their growth. Before the inherent orientation of one's life can be found, a thorough disorientation must be suffered.

Fully accepting the conditions on the soul and honestly facing the thorough disorientation in his life causes the prince to remember something. He recalls an old druid whom he knew to be wise in the ways of the world and somewhat friendly. The inevitable troubles of youth are intended to awaken young people to unusual perspectives on the world. Either the psyche will remember someone who can help, or a guide will suddenly appear. The trouble of the soul awakens a new awareness in the youth and he turns to someone with knowledge of these matters. In ancient times, druids were a kind of priest and healer and ceremonial leader. The druid offers a ceremonial meal and deepens the awareness of danger posed by conditions on the soul.

The druid plays the role of mentor to the prince. As such he doesn't simply ease the problem; rather, he confirms that the *geis* could destroy the youth. He takes care with the prince, but doesn't become a savior. He takes the "conditions on the soul" seriously. He welcomes the youth and listens to him. He nourishes him with what is truly old and what is most fresh.

A mentor is not simply a replacement for a missing father or a lost mother. A youth in trouble is no longer simply a child. A true mentor has the ability to listen and recognize the nature of the problem weighing on the soul of youth. He doesn't diminish the problem, reduce it to something else, or take it on his own trouble. He looks into the spirit of the youth and acknowledges the seriousness of the trouble and the limits of his help. It's more important that mentors act as elders than actually be significantly older. It's also important that mentors be familiar with exile and able to recognize how young people stumble into the great dramas of life.

The mentor can be any person or figure who comes to mind when a person realizes that they are in real trouble. Something in the mentor connects to the spirit in the youth—a spirit-soul connection. A mentor has an eye trained for young people in the "right trouble" and an interest in the spirit trying to awaken in youth. A mentor must be able to nourish youth who no longer can be fed by their family or treated as a child, while confirming the initiatory struggles that youth inevitably encounter. A mentor needs to know when to support and nourish, when to guide and challenge, and when the young person must go forward on their own. The druid's hut appears anywhere youth can find genuine guidance and become reoriented to the path of their own life.

It would be encouraging for everyone if druid huts existed at the edges of neighborhoods and barrios and towns. People in need of some advice—some food for the soul and some sense of direction—would know where to turn when the conditions of their soul required attention and a little guidance. The hut of the mentor is a way station on the roads the soul would take. In modern societies young people stumble into trouble. They break a law, violate a trust, have an accident, fall ill, lose a loved one. Something dangerous, foolish, or accidental happens and the druid's hut might have to be fabricated on the spot—at a neighbor's home, in a police station, a therapist's office, or a hospital.

Trouble makes a young person vulnerable and somewhat transparent. Tribal initiates often appear naked in order to indicate that the soul is exposed to those with the eye of a mentor or elder. That type of seeing— an eye trained for the spirit trying to awaken in youth—helps to reveal the exact conditions on the soul. "Real trouble" combines difficulties in the outside world with conditions already existing in the soul. The word "education" means to lead someone out, to draw something out of someone, to lead out what resides within a person and must become known to him or her. Meaningful education requires the presence of some difficulty or the right kind of trouble for that person to grow. True education takes place when the spirit and soul are engaged and involved in the genuine struggles of one's life. In the druid's hut the prince learns of the conditions within his soul and gathers surprising elements that can help in his struggle to become fully alive.

Stories display mythic backgrounds and ideal images that are the psychic inheritance of all people. Like the young prince, each individual needs to be and expects to be recognized and listened to while exposed to the conditions on their soul. Too frequently, this soulful expectation goes unfulfilled. In modern societies, people tend to focus on the trouble itself or the seeming causes of it. Lacking the eye for initiation, most people fail to take the troubles of youth seriously enough. Any sorting of soul conditions of youth tends to be haphazard or superficial. Yet without a clear separation from childhood and a genuine reorientation that includes the innate qualities of the youth, the inevitable ordeals of life seem chaotic, punishing, even meaningless.

The dynamics of initiation begin in youth, but recur at critical crossroads throughout the course of life. Initiation becomes the ruling archetype during the struggles that accompany the onset of each new life-stage. The psyche's sense of initiatory process also gets triggered whenever a person is unexpectedly thrown into circumstances of separation and disorientation. The psyche interprets any radical change as an initiatory adventure. From this perspective, any event that causes severe separation, a thorough disorientation, and a sense of life and death circumstances becomes initiatory. Whether others judge the events as positive or negative, legal or illegal, right or wrong, great or small does not matter. The conditions of one's soul and the change of life trying to occur are what matters. The feeling of life or death, or of life and death shifts the psyche to the sense of a complete change. In initiation a person becomes new, renewed, completely altered.

Without proper guidance, coherent rites, and timely ceremonies, initiatory events often remain incomplete and unfinished. What could have changed a person altogether and revealed something essential in their life becomes buried in the shadowy areas of the psyche. Instead of meaningful change and a greater sense of life's inherent meaning, there remains an incompleteness, a sense that something could have happened but did not. Narrowness and rigidity tend to grow where initiation would create conscious growth and flexibility. Yet events that had initiatory qualities continue to live in the psyche. To initiate means to begin, and what the soul begins waits to be continued and completed throughout life.

The druid and the druid's hut may have to be pieced together from bits of life, from brief "mentoring moments," and from vague memories of youthful exploits or sudden disasters. The druid's hut is a symbol of the space needed for reflecting upon and working through the conditions within one's life that can seem simply threatening, but ultimately can reorient a person to a meaningful path. The mentor is partly an inner aspect of a person and partly the actual people who have recognized, nourished, and offered guidance at the level of one's soul.

Each person carries an inner inheritance that includes aspects of the "wise old man" or "wise old woman." Each has an inner mentor, a capacity to know the purpose of his or her own spirit for life. A disturbance of the spirit awakens the mentor within and beckons to mentors in the world outside. No one can survive the struggles of life completely on their own. However slight or passing they might seem, each person experiences mentoring moments in which they feel seen and truly heard for who they are in this world.

On certain occasions the disturbance in our spirit became so evident that someone spoke to it and gave us something that helped us to bear it. Often, when we search our memories for these occasions, we look for something huge because our emotion at the time was huge. Instead we find that what was offered was often quite small. The true size of the "gifts of spirit" may only be revealed after it has been carried for long enough and far enough. Conn-Eda receives this nourishment, a small stone and a little shaggy horse. So when we search our memory for similar gifts we may have to look for brief moments when small things were given in the midst of a trouble that was great for us. The first mentor in the story teaches that there is no single, great gift that will solve all the problems of life. Rather, there are little things, often overlooked by others, that are enough to move us another step on the way that our souls must go if we are to fully enter the game of life.

While a sophomore in high school, I became wildly disappointed with the nature of school and the limited education it offered. I attended a Catholic boys' school where the instructors were religious Brothers. The situation could be seen as a potential druid's hut. The Brothers were older men who wore religious garments. They were there to teach, their roles being partly spiritual and partly practical. We arrived there in the usual condition of youth, walking out of childhood and more or less willing to learn. For me, heading off to high school created just enough separation to raise expectations in my soul. I felt a sense of adventure and so did my classmates. At times we each displayed the depressions in our spirits and revealed elements of the conditions on our souls. We couldn't help revealing ourselves—no youth can avoid that. Yet our teachers seemed not to notice as they tended to expound doctrine, recite established ideas, and hide behind fixed beliefs.

Youth suffers periods of desperation, and within me there was a spirit desperate to be recognized and led out. By sophomore year I felt torn between disappointment and desperation. I observed the same disappointment among my friends. At various times we each had to do something with the radical expectations innate to our young souls. In my case, I joined the troublemakers.

There was an unspoken division in school between the good boys who studied, were smart, and obeyed rules, and the bad boys who didn't obey, broke the rules, and couldn't or wouldn't study. The students knew that this separation was too simplistic, but complex issues were repeatedly reduced to simple oppositions.

In school, order and discipline took precedence over our clumsy efforts to become passionate disciples of something. One intrigue of the "bad boy attitude" involved the presence of a defiant spirit that rejected blind obedience and inspired creative responses to the overzealous discipline of the authorities. Defiance became our way of preserving our spirits amidst increasing disappointments with school and common life. We defied the system, broke the rules, disrupted the most boring classes, and studied the inadequacies and weaknesses of the teachers. Those who depended completely on control for keeping order, we provoked out of control. Those who were not really teachers at all and had no genuine reason for being there, we left their class. Those who secretly feared the students, we made more afraid.

Several in our group failed tests regularly. Some simply didn't study; others had difficulty learning, but received no help. So we devised ways of cheating in order to get everyone in the group to pass. Several times we were caught. We received physical punishment and attempts were made to break up our group. No one asked why we behaved the way we did, no one seemed to care what was behind our troubles or our troublesome behavior. We were warned and threatened repeatedly. But such warnings did not disturb us as deeply as the troubled conditions we already felt in our souls.

Eventually the school threatened several of our group with expulsion. I didn't know whether that included me. My situation was complicated by the fact that I maintained decent grades while presenting a disciplinary problem. The lines that usually divided good and bad, smart and ignorant became blurred and the teachers weren't sure what to do. While I waited to learn if I would be expelled, a little druid event or mentoring moment occurred.

One of our teachers was a Brother who came from Cuba to teach in New York City. He didn't speak English smoothly, and he was dark-skinned in a mostly white school. But the most noticeable thing about him was that he became strangely impassioned while teaching. He had a spirit that could not be hidden by the dark religious habit. Because he was passionate, he was easily provoked. Because he was new to the place and to the language, he was easy to make fun of. We couldn't help it; we imitated his speech and we mocked his great lips that seemed to grow larger when he became angry. We provoked his emotions so that the lesson of the day would be forgotten while he erupted into a mix of English and Spanish and angry sounds that were both terrifying and entertaining. We treated him badly. We assumed that he didn't care for us either.

While decisions about expulsion were under consideration, I acted up in his class. The Brother sent me out of class and followed me out into the hall. Usually that ceremony involved detention and often physical punishment. I was scared, but also angry. I wanted to direct the force of my anger somewhere. I was thinking, "If he touches me, if one more Brother lays a hand on me . . ." I didn't know what I would do, but I was ready to explode with the violence of my feelings.

In fact I was ready for anything except what actually occurred. He began yelling at me. I yelled back and cursed at him. I don't remember exactly what he said, for he had trouble getting the words out. We were both fuming. In the heat and confusion he mentioned loyalty. He acknowledged the loyalty we had in our troubled, troublemaking group, and he added something about loyalty to myself and to learning. He said the point wasn't to learn what was being taught but to learn how to learn. I was stunned. He was actually talking to me—not down to me, but right into me. He was talking to the loyalties in me, and he was challenging me. This strange Brother put his finger on a condition in my soul. He perceived that part of me wanted to study and learn, and that part of me could not resist joining the expression of the defiant group. He sensed something about my true spirit and my attempts to hold onto it through defiance. He saw the exile going on in me, and the greater exile I was heading for.

Looking back on that scene it becomes clear that he, too, was an exile—exiled from his own language, from his land, and exiled in the impassioned intensity of his emotional life. He was also exiled as a dark-skinned man amidst a rejecting "white culture." Somehow the exile in him spoke to the exile in me. It was no great thing. It was no remedy for the troubles of life, but he gave me little pieces of advice that temporarily ended my exile and made me more reflective. Instead of my wild disappointment with those who tried to teach, I had a genuine idea about "learning to learn." That reinforced my intrigue with mythology, something I had to learn that would never be taught in that school.

He broke the rules in speaking to me that way. He said that the board of teachers was inclined to expel me from school at the end of the term. In my case, the vote remained close simply because of some high grades. He said that with a few days of good behavior on my part, he could convince the board to keep me in school.

I don't recall whether I agreed with him right away, but the passion of his expression, his willingness to break the rules in giving me information, and his apparent interest in my welfare made me pay attention. It made me, in fact, thankful. That occasion made me decide to be more present in school. More importantly, it made me clear that my interest in learning was genuine even if the classes I attended were not so.

For this mentoring moment, for this piece of the druid's hut, for the gem of being acknowledged as a true student and for the honest bit of advice, I have to thank that Brother. I have to acknowledge that, suddenly, through him, the word Brother took on an expanded meaning. At least for that moment, it meant a true teacher, one interested in the spirit and passion of life. It also meant having the courage to speak genuinely, as oneself. He spoke with the insistence and desperation of an exile. He spoke as a *Cubano*, as an African in exile. He stood for a spirit willing to speak directly to the source of trouble. That small stone, that bit of giving, slipped past the defiant barriers I fiercely put up. That moment lived in my memory; it continued to grow inside me long after I left school.

Modern cultures tend to celebrate the inauthentic and offer abstract solutions to heartfelt problems. In such a wasteland, a person can fall into exile at any moment. One reason for men to risk a retreat together is to tell the stories of how they were seen and not seen while trying to grow in the world. The importance of being genuinely seen and truly heard cannot be overestimated, especially for youth. The soul grows through self-reflection and by being recognized by others. If a man has never been recognized at the soul level, he won't know who he is in times of crisis and will feel inauthentic more often than not. A person who has never been heard will have great difficulty truly listening to others. The soul grows by being seen, and a man must be truly seen by others in order to truly be a man.

Ultimately, what people have to offer each other is the stories they have lived, the adventures they have had, and the tragedies they have survived. Mythic stories offer a specifically shaped vessel into which people can pour their personal stories in order to learn how we each inhabit the eternal drama. The first piece of learning in this kind of shared story-telling involves opening the ears to the stories of others. It can be quite encouraging to hear a painfully familiar theme spoken out from another person's life, and it can be startling to hear how different another's life can be. Listening carefully leads to hearing with the "inner ear" and learning to respect what others might carry inside. Often the inner story stands in great contrast to the outer person. An African proverb suggests: A person is like a pepper—until you've tasted what's inside you don't know how hot it is.

The stories that people need to tell tend to go in one of two directions: either toward recovery of something from childhood, or toward revealing something initiatory. Some people must recover an aspect of childhood that tore them apart in some way. They were abused or severely mistreated. They were thrown into the fires of life too soon or rejected when they needed care. They can't fully risk further adventures unless they first recover something from the past. To the deeply betrayed child, initiation seems another form of abuse. To the abandoned child who has not found a way back into life, separation is not new but ever-present.

In a traditional community most people would know each other's origin and childhood stories; in modern life people often have to begin at the beginning. Often the first story needing to be told is a "recovery story," in which a person first uncovers some traumatic damage and tries to recover from it by making a story of it. Usually, such a story will be preceded by a description of the family and how it operated, so that the wound of the child can be understood in its original context. Sometimes the story drops out of the mouth of an adult as if a child were telling it. Sometimes a sense of shocked innocence remains, as stories of loss and helplessness in childhood lack the complicity of the child. What transpired happened to them not only without their consent, but before they were able to consent.

I have seen—standing in the same room and talking by turns—those severely debilitated by abuse in childhood and those who were initiated by similar forces. Each felt unseen and unrecognized by their communities and culture. Both groups seemed to stand in similar psychic pain: one turned with their backs to childhood as if still trying to gather themselves and find a way into the world, while the other was turned another way, and seemed to experience the pain with more conscious involvement.

An initiatory story sounds different; it resides in an area of the psyche separate from early childhood. There's a wound involved, but the person is more present to it and more genuinely responsible for it. Being of a different order, such stories have to be heard differently. Stories with initiatory aspects have to do with love and war, divorces and prisons, mental breakdowns, deaths, betrayals, addictions, sudden successes and life altering illnesses.

In some ways the teller was an active accomplice in the events. He entered a situation seeking something and was pulled to heights or depths beyond what he might otherwise have chosen. The teller was not simply a child, but contributed to the drama in some way and now cannot extricate himself from it. Critical things happened in some gray area between doing and being done to. If there was terror, there was also some sense of beauty. If there was great sorrow, it is now held with firmness, embedded in the voice in a way that says, "I'm not asking you to take this from me. It's mine to tell about." This type of story marks a person's life indelibly—take it from them and they won't be themselves. Something happened that changed them forever. They might not have experienced it by choice, but they have no choice but to carry it wherever they go. Even the finality of a lost limb can be told with a voice that holds together the limb, the cut, and the loss. This type of story has to be heard differently.

Initiatory stories don't tell of simple oppressions or unwanted weight dropped on a child before it could get out of the way. These stories reveal who a person has become, not just what happened to them. The weight of the events has been distributed throughout the whole person; it has become part of who they are and who they must be. The story continues to live in them; they lived through it and in some way continue to live by virtue of it.

These stories reveal the essence of the teller. Take away the pain, sorrow, wonder, or failure in it and you will erase their place in life. They don't offer the tale to be relieved of a burden; rather, they tell it in order to be confirmed in some way. Ultimately, initiatory tales indicate both the internal wounds and the inner gifts of a person. Take away the wounding that occurred and you might remove the gifts that were found. Initiatory wounds become a psychic womb that continues to give gravitas and meaning to a person's life. Only false innocence desires to remain unwounded; the initiated know that it is our wounds that keep us alive and seeking in this world. Hearing the speech of the genuine wounds of a person makes life more bearable for others and nourishes the soul of whoever has ears to listen.

Personal stories become enhanced and better understood when placed in proximity to myths and traditional tales. The point of a personal story isn't simply biography—"I am what these people and events make me to be." Rather, the point involves retelling meaningful episodes in order to stir the important themes hidden in each life. The inner instinct to reveal painful stories is essentially human and usually healthy. When something has been risked in the telling, if it isn't rehearsed and edited, you can see relief flood the body of the speaker. At the same time, each listener who meets the story with his or her own life feels somehow healed or enlivened by the occasion.

The personal story truly told becomes a communal story. The struggles and the gifts of each person belong to the community of souls as well. Sharing one's story in a genuine way can create a moment of community. Stories reduce everyone's feelings of isolation and hopelessness. Whereas false and self-serving stories drain the soul of a group, genuine stories make communities more authentic. Stories are a ceremony in their own way; through the telling healing can occur on both the individual and collective levels. Stories nourish the roots of community at the same time that they stimulate the branches of imagination.

One reason for the study of initiation lies in learning to separate psychic threads, distinguishing between those that lead back to unfinished pieces of childhood and those that can pull one across the threshold to a life more fulfilled. If too many threads tie a person back to childhood, that person is not able to fully cross the threshold to a conscious life. At some point a person must turn away from the stories of childhood in order to reorient the psyche and turn the head toward a possible destination and destiny in life. Rites of initiation were created to interrupt a person's life and arrest their vision, to stop their habitual ways of seeing life and open the psyche to a greater view of the world and their place in it. Unless a person gains some greater view of her or himself, they cannot see the world in a meaningful way. Unless a person comes to know who he or she truly is in this world, they are a nuisance and a danger to others. Either a person comes to some self-knowledge and thereby contributes something genuine to life, or they add to all that is inauthentic and distorted about life. For, no one can be neutral on the road of life and death.

The initiate is considered to be in a sacred condition. While they may be frightened and confused, their condition is considered a "holy confusion," which harbors more of desire for initiation than a need to be cared for. The desire for initiation arises from a place of destiny within a person, not simply from a need to be reassured and protected from pain. Initiation makes a crossroad between childhood and the rest of life. Childhood will live forever—forever and ever—just as a child imagines it. But it lives in a different area of the psychic forest from the place of the druid's hut and the crossroads of fate and destiny. The head of the initiate turns away from childhood and comes to see it differently because the adventure of life will change everything in some defining way. On an initiatory path, the individual finds surprising resources in the world and hidden values in themselves.

The initiate learns that something has carried them besides their parents and that there are teachers and helpers along the way. Once the real journey has begun a person must relinquish the control so favored by the ego. Once the possibility of greater life has awakened in a person, there is no turning back. The initiate must drop the reins and allow the horse of the psyche to lead the way.

CONN-EDA
Part III

Conn-Eda received the stone and thanked the druid. He mounted the shaggy little horse and turned away from all he knew. He let the reins hang loose, as he had been instructed, so that the animal could choose its own path.

After some difficulty, the shaggy horse managed to reach the hiding place of the Bird with Human Speech at just the right time. There in the dark forest stood the ancient bird. The prince placed the stone near the bird and asked how he could accomplish his task. The great bird took the gem, flew to an inaccessible rock, and addressed him in a loud, croaking voice: "Remove the stone from under your right foot, take the ball of iron and the cup you find there, mount your horse, cast the ball before you, follow it, and your horse will tell you all else you need to know." Having said this, the Bird with Human Speech flew out of sight.

Conn-Eda took the ball and cup, mounted the horse again, and cast the ball before him. The ball rolled and the horse followed until they came upon the shores of Lough Erne, where the ball disappeared into the water. Suddenly the little horse spoke: "Put your hand in my ear, take out the small bottle of all-heal and the little basket you find there, and remount with speed, for here your difficulties begin."

Conn-Eda did what he was told, and horse and rider quickly descended into the waters of the lake. The prince was amazed that they neither drowned nor suffocated. Where he expected to swallow water and lack for air, he found he could still breathe. They had entered the Otherworld. He saw the ball rolling along the bottom of the lake, and he clung tightly to his little steed.

They came upon a river there, a water among waters, guarded by three frightful serpents. A loud hissing filled the ears of the prince as he gazed into the serpents' great, yawning mouths with their formidable fangs. The horse spoke again: "Open the basket and cast a piece of the meat you find there into the mouth of each serpent; then hold on tight. If you cast accurately, I'll get us past them; if not, we are lost."

The prince cast the meat unerringly, and the little horse made a prodigious leap past the serpents and over the river. Once on the other side, the horse asked if the prince was still mounted, and the prince replied that it had taken only half his strength to stay on. The little horse commended him ,saying that while one danger was over, two more remained.

Again they followed the ball until they came to a burning mountain that filled the landscape and flamed with fire in all directions. "Prepare yourself for another leap," said the horse, and he sprang from the earth and flew like an arrow through the flames and over the mountain. "Are you still alive, Conn-Eda, son of Mor?"

"Just alive, and nothing more," the prince said, "for I am greatly scorched."

"You are a man of destiny after all," said the horse. "There is hope that we will overcome the last test."

The horse carried the ailing prince to a cool valley and told him to apply the all-heal from the bottle to his wounds. The all-heal soothed the wounds of the prince and healed his burns. In the green glade, the prince recovered his health and strength; in fact he was better than he had been before. Once recovered, he saw the iron ball rolling into a broad valley. The prince mounted the little horse once again and they followed the ball down into the plain below.

CHAPTER 12

THE LAND BELOW THE WATERS

THE DRUID CAN'T SOLVE the problem of the prince, but does offer him a little horse, a shaggy unwanted mount left out behind the hut. Little horses like this one often appear in stories. They are lame or hobbled, they can't go full speed, or else they go the wrong way. Typically, it's the only horse left in the stable after all the warriors have mounted the great war horses and ridden away. Symbolically, they represent the overlooked, left-behind, lowly aspects of a person—all that's left when we finally let go of our high opinion of ourselves.

At certain times the only way to proceed in a meaningful way requires that the ego let go of its stubborn ideas and fixed attitudes in order to allow something else to lead. For the ego, dropping the reins, means letting go, not being in charge, submitting, and even surrendering to change. Dropping the reins triggers the onset of further ordeals and precipitates a descent into the waters of uncertainty.

During initiation someone or something other than our usual self must take charge. The ego, the usual ruler in a person's life, must submit to some other force, an authority beyond, even below oneself. A person cannot remain in control and undergo change at the same time. Initiatory paths require a loosening of personal identity that allows hidden, undeveloped, and habitually denied aspects of the self to appear. The executive functions of the ego and fixed attitudes from childhood will ruin the timing and obscure the way forward. Unless he allows the shaggy little horse to lead, the prince may wander aimlessly on the surface of his life.

The ego tends to be like a prince or a king: used to giving orders and accustomed to being held in nigh esteem. The higher one tends to be regarded by others, the stronger the patterns of the superior ego and the more difficult it can be let go and descend to the common ground. The more responsible the ego feels, the harder it is to give responsibility over to another. The more in charge a person becomes, the harder it is to stop charging ahead and simply follow along. Of course, the last thing we will relinquish is our own high opinion of our self. There can be no real change, however, unless the ego bows low to the forces of change. If meaningful change were easy it would be more commonly seen.

The first conscious trial of the prince involves the question of whether he can let go of his station in life and his fixed opinions of himself. The little horse waits for just such an occasion in order to carry him further into life than he would go on his own. Initiation intends to awaken the whole person, especially the rejected and unknown aspects of oneself. Often the rejected, lowly parts of a person become the only way to survive and the keys to growth.

The shaggy little horse waits out back like the undeveloped, unkempt, and uncared for aspects of the prince's deep self. In a sense the horse has been there all along, just waiting for the princely ego to let go of the daily world in order to enter the deeper levels of life. Something neglected, rejected, and unkempt in a person carries a deeper inheritance than one's social status or family position. The ancient bird alone knows where the prince must go and it turns out that the shaggy horse part of him knows how to connect with that ancient creature and its unusual knowledge.

Dropping the reins means learning to trust the "inner horse" and the inner sense of one's life regardless of the judgments and opinions of others. It's clear that the horse cannot be made of a person's best features because it appears small and looks shaggy. The inner horse, with its unerring sense off direction, only becomes available when all else fails and all pretenses are dropped. Dropping the reins means trusting that something unseen and undervalued carries a person through life. Unless a person learns to trust the "shaggy-horse self," they can't really trust themselves. Those who don't trust themselves usually can't trust others either and during the ordeals of life a person must trust the *otherness* found inside as well as out in the world.

Getting off the high horse of self-control and of controlling others can be very difficult, especially for men who learn early that they must be in charge. How many wrong turns does it take, for example, before a man will stop charging ahead and ask for directions? Since finding the way without help is a form of succeeding, asking for directions seems a kind of defeat. Admitting to being lost and asking someone else the way usually comes as a last resort. It means accepting disorientation and admitting that we don't know where we are. Feeling disoriented and unknowing creates a sense of exposure that triggers old fears of being vulnerable and falling prey to unknown forces.

A man typically learns lessons about trusting himself and others within groups of boys while growing up. Friends will see what a man is made of and how you can trust him to be. Catching glimpses of the hidden horse that carries a person is often the basis of early friendships. Often friends can pick up where they left off, even after years of separation because their inner horses recognize each other and resume a conversation unaffected by superficial changes. Long before people became classmates youth would form deep friendships based upon mutual experiences during rites of passage. Initiatory circumstances make brothers of the inner horses of men regardless of the high or low positions the riders might have in daily life.

In traditional cultures men typically have times and ways to gather. Like horses meeting in a canyon, they sniff each other out, renew friendships and reflect on life experiences. In part, it's the horses within men that form teams, clubs, and gangs; it's true of political parties, and even of war parties. Men tend to have instincts for being part of the herd and inclinations for being as unreachable as a wild horse. Entering a group of men tends to awaken the inner horse with its memories and old feelings of trust and betrayal, of being a member of the gang and of having to go one's own way. Old fears and phobias, issues of trust and distrust, instincts to join or flee, to lead the pack or follow another's lead, arise where men gather and the inner horses become alert.

Proverbs can carry wisdom and genuine horse sense about life. At the beginning of a gathering of men I often offer a proverb to the restless inner horses. A favorite one came from an archaeologist who became completely lost on an expedition: "It is better to wander without a guide in uncharted lands than to follow a map made by tourists." Each serious gathering of men secretly invokes the territory of initiation and the attendant issues of trust and distrust. If it is clear where things are going, there's no real reason to depart. The little horse in a person's life continues to seek for uncharted lands regardless of one's social status or position.

The shaggy horse inside waits for the fearful, delightful occasions when being lost becomes the point and the shackles of an overly determined life can be cast aside. Hiking, hunting, and fishing are common lures for bringing men together. But the real expedition involves further initiatory steps where a man learns more of his inner nature, more of where the little horse within would lead him.

In working with men it is important to risk some uncharted land. Such a risk awakens the shaggy horse and evokes basic fears of fight or flight. Everyone is afraid at the beginning, and everyone should be. If you don't feel the fear, you won't feel anything else either. Everyone knows that groups of men are capable of great violence and cruelty. One fear that stalks the edges in a group of men is that someone might die. Someone might be sacrificed or exiled just to coalesce the group. It's an old history that lives in the bones and can be awakened by any serious issue or conflict. Men are particularly dangerous when they reach maturity without initiatory experiences that crack the ego and open the heart and mind to reveal the inner horses of passion and of compassion.

For a group of men to enter uncharted lands each must develop a sense of trust amidst feelings of danger and betrayal. The process feels similar to getting on the shaggy horse and letting go the reins. The fears don't disappear right away; but fear can be a guide to where the work must go.

One word for the fears among men is homophobia: fear or dread of what is similar or the same as oneself. Since American culture has a dread-love relationship to sex, homophobia usually means fear of love with those of the same sex. Yet homophobia has many other phobias inherent in it: because men fear each other in many ways. There are common fears of being physically harmed or defeated by another man; there are intense fears of being intellectually dominated, and of being spiritually damaged or misled by the vision and power of another man. There are fears of the bodies of other men, fears of the spirits of other men, and fears of the souls of other men.

At the bottom lies a fear that something in other men may be the same as something hidden in me, a shadowy something that I barely know of myself. At that level, homophobia is a fear of men based on not knowing my true self; in other words a fear of what may be hidden within me. It's not only a fear of the sexuality of other men and repressed sexual impulses in oneself, but also of fear of the power, intelligence, emotions, and spirit of others based on what I don't know about myself. It becomes increasingly difficult to trust others if I haven't learned what to trust within myself. Those who differ from me sexually, racially, and by physical type become the unwitting carriers of my inherent phobias, my fears of what I might be or could become. Excessive fears and phobias regarding others arise from a lack of self-knowledge and a blindness about who I am at heart and what the nature of my inner horse might be. Many fears are based in not knowing; we fear what we don't know and attack what we fear.

The lack of meaningful rites of passage leaves many men deeply unsure of who they are in essence and what their inner life might be. Sometimes during men's retreats we try to engage the fears and build trust directly through various exercises. Dropping the ego reins and allowing the inner horse to lead implies a kind of blindness on the part of the rider. Blindfold exercises can allow people to see things and learn things that otherwise might be overlooked.

An example: fifty men stand in a clearing in the middle of a wide wood. Each dons a blindfold. Standing still as trees, they must drop the reins of their lives as they wait to be led away. Another fifty men, not blindfolded, enter the clearing and each chooses a blind man randomly, instinctively. They lead the blind men off, each pair going its own way. Mostly they move in silence. The blind man doesn't see the path he takes and doesn't know who leads him on it. Even at the end the blind men do not meet their guides.

Later the blind and the sighted exchange roles so that each has a chance to be led by an unseen leader, and each leads a vulnerable man who can't see and must surrender to whomever takes his hand. It's a beautiful passage to observe, as the pairs of men move with incredible care all through the forest and over the landscape. A small man leads another almost twice his size. A timid man surrenders to someone who leads him faster and farther than he would choose to go on his own. Black leads white for a change. Young leads old, and old carefully guides the young. All kinds of unlikely pairings occur and each involves letting go on one hand and taking care on the other.

Things start out simply, with each pair working out silent communications and getting used to the horse aspects of each other. Gradually, though, it becomes very complicated and adventurous. What starts out clumsy and fearful becomes subtle and exhilarating. Blind men run through the forest at full speed, galloping like horses led on by the vision of other horses. Blind men climb trees, go up and down steep hills, and erupt into dance steps they never see themselves execute. Some go too far, as little accidents and jokes play out. Some become intricately involved in touching the striated bark of trees or the subtle bends of blades of grass.

The entire area becomes uncharted territory explored in great and careful detail. A multitude of fears arise only to be replaced with surprisingly deep feelings of trust and care. The forest becomes inhabited in new ways; the whole place feels more known than it ever could be through one pair of eyes. When it's over, there's a need to describe a surprising array off feelings. There's a gentle sense of being and a great deal of laughter, both of which bring tears to the eyes.

The experience has to be talked about. Each man has placed blind trust in another. There's no way to know the color, ethnicity, education, or social status of the guide. Trusting one man opens up the possibility of trusting any man and of gaining more trust in the inner man as well. Since the guide who shared this strange, intimate adventure was not seen, he could be any man at all. Men talk of feeling incredibly vulnerable and alone while waiting to be chosen. Some knew that they were among the last to be picked, and they felt as they had when not picked for games at school or even at dances. All felt great relief at the touch that indicated they had been chosen. The stages and subtleties of letting go are described in beautiful detail. Being led by another seems to release exuberant feelings of freedom that many didn't want to end. The gratefulness toward most of the guides is palpable and wonderfully deep.

Being blindfolded opens the inner eyes and forces a person to see life differently. It allows a person to sense how something mostly unseen guides us through life. Most men find leading to be more difficult and painful than being blind. Leading another with genuine care reveals inner qualities of leadership and gives a greater sense of what being in charge can mean.

A genuine ritual intends to evoke a meaningful change, and the outcome cannot be foreseeable. If the outcome can be foretold the change can only be minimal. Blindfolds were used in many initiatory ceremonies to suggest that we must go blind before we can learn to see what life has in store for us. Blinding tells the initiate that they can no longer see the world in the same old way; that they must learn to see in other ways.

Initiation requires that everyone see things in a new way. In some rites of passage the initiate is not only blind, but painted white, as if he had joined the spirits of the dead. Being blindfolded convinces the body and the imagination of the blinded person that he will not live forever, that someday the world will go dark. Death appears as the universal image of the end. Yet the death of one thing can also be the beginning of another. Initiation marks a little death, a dark walk that precedes the new way of being in the world. Common sight shifts to insight as the soul suffers a dark passage in search of greater knowledge and vision.

The ritual performances of tribal groups depict an elaboration of the inner steps that the psyche requires to effect real change in a person's life. In initiation, everyone goes a little blind. In initiation, everything and everyone changes in order that the world become bright again and the eyes learn to see the secret path the soul would take.

Conn-Eda became as a blind man led by the little horse into the presence of something ancient and wise. He offers the little stone to the bird and receives an iron ball in exchange. The ball was right below his foot. He was standing on it but didn't see it. The iron weight that will take him down into the waters of his life was right there, below his usual stance. After the prince accepted the conditions on his soul, each event continues his descent as he unwittingly approaches the deep waters of his life.

Once Conn-Eda drops the reins, the shaggy horse becomes the guide of the story and the vehicle that carries him through the ordeals. The story becomes a series of stations or tableaux that the prince and horse encounter together. The ancient bird represents the spirit world that brings sudden insight, visions and flights of imagination. In the presence of spirit, past, present, and future all become penetrable. The ancient bird of spirit opens the Otherworld to the youth and tells him to let go of all he knows and listen to the world in new ways. Although the eyes tend to dominate in modern culture, the ancient ways of wisdom involve listening, especially listening to the little voice represented by the horse with its grounded wisdom. The horse is the prince's menas of moving through the depths of change and the deep issues of life. The little horse is a metaphor for something innate and instinctive in him that typically has been overlooked and undervalued.

Meta-phor means to *carry beyond* and rites of initiation cause people to descend below and leap beyond what they know of themselves. People arrive at a place where they must sink or else swim with inner capacities and resources they didn't know they had. What happens cannot be simply explained or fully described in literal or rational terms. What a person learns in the ordeals of life defies definition and requires metaphorical images and poetic speech to tell. Whenever a person has been carried beyond what is commonly known, only metaphors can carry back the sense of mystery that accompanies meaningful change.

The soul conditions placed upon the prince as a result of the game of life provide the grain of sand that penetrates the shell of the oyster. Such a condition irritates the inner life, but eventually causes the formation and development of a pearl of great value. The process that creates the pearl remains hidden from sight. Similarly, initiatory experiences have a mysterious element that remains secret. At one level, the practice of ritual secrecy helps the initiate contain the changes occurring within. Another part of the secret involves elements so unique to each individual that they defy simple exposition. The soul grows around such a secret that continues to deliver information to its carrier. Beyond that, a meaningful change involves something ineffable that can't fully be captured by speech. Some things remain secret because they cannot fully be spoken. But metaphors are fashioned to point to the mysteries of change and to the secret exchanges of life and death in the soul.

The human soul, which itself defies definition, is a mighty beast capable of visionary flight, but also inclined to immerse in the timeless waters of the emotional world. A full initiation of the soul combines the confirmation of spirit's great heights with immersions in the emotionally soaked realms below the firm surfaces of the world. Initiations progress by way of spirit and soul, fire and water, and flights of confirmation followed by disturbing descents into realms where only feelings can find the way.

The next tableau occurs where the ball disappears into the waters of Lough Erne and the little horse stops at the edge between land and water. The edge where one thing turned into another fascinated Celtic imagination. Anything betwixt and between implied possibilities of radical change and magical potential. The edge, which is neither one thing nor the other, could become a magical line through which one thing can become another. The shaggy horse brings the prince to the point where immersion in the inner-world and otherworld of psyche becomes necessary for his life to change. Here, a rapid descent and full immersion is required. Once again the young prince must let go and descend inspite of his fears. If he is to become himself, the prince must come to know his inner life and the passions of his soul. He finds, to his surprise, he has an anatomy for breathing in the heavier atmosphere of the deep water where feelings and imagination overwhelm the surface world of hard facts and fixed measures.

The idea that men don't have feelings is deeply wrong. More often men don't have a way of immersing themselves in those feelings. Usually a man lacks the connection to an animal sense that can carry him to the depths of emotion. If a man doesn't know that something carries him in this world, he may shy away from the deep waters of the soul. He also may deny the inner pains if there isn't a promise of healing, a hint that some all-heal is near. Many a man carries a heart full of grief, but holds back a lifelong lake of tears. After years of not weeping, he fears he will drown if the dam breaks. After many years of not crying, I felt I that if I approached my own sorrow I would drown in my own tears or disappear in the sorrow of the world. Since I couldn't live with my own sorrow, I could not easily bear the sorrow of others.

Strangely, both culture and nature seem to conspire in building walls around the hearts of men. There is a complicated relationship among the water elements in a man—that is, among testosterone, sweat, and tears. Often a man finds it easier to offer sweat or blood instead of tears. Before birth an eruption of testosterone changes the embryo into a male. At puberty, however another eruption increases testosterone thirty times over. The flood of aggression and sexual drive that results from the increase of testosterone seems to occur at the expense of the tear ducts. Testosterone tends to inhibit weeping. Often a complicated psychic operation is needed to open the ducts of the eyes and the heart after puberty seals them off. Initiation matches changes in the body with changes in the soul.

Part of the function of youth initiation was to open the heart to the sorrow and beauty of being human, to release the fountain of emotion that is the human inheritance. At times the intensity of fire is needed, at other times the waters must flow or a person can't become fully alive.

The chorus of men has much to say about the descent into the fires and waters of the emotional realms within. Some gather along the edge of the water, others slip right into the lake to face the fears and fires within. One man says, "I didn't want to go any further. At the idea of going into the water, a wave of fear immediately rose in my chest like a welling up of old uncried tears." Another says, "I felt stuck. I felt that I couldn't go that next step into the water, couldn't follow the story either."

The next man says, "I was relieved, felt a permission to let go and drop right into the waters. I never cried at my mother's funeral and I've been weeping here and don't want to stop." Tears are a gift and often the tears of one man will pull the whole group into a descent into what matters for each person present. One man is right on the edge, the next plunges in, and the whole event changes shape and form and feeling. If one person trusts the sense of their inner horse, others are inclined to follow.

A man says, "I was delighted to be able to take the three pieces of meat and accurately throw one into the mouth of each dragon. It's something I've never been able to do in my life. But in the story I felt the exhilaration of hitting something accurately, with no time to spare and no wasted effort." Another man says, "I'm in the same place but without the same luck. I feel that earlier in my life I had opportunities, and if I had just been more skillful, more accurate, if I had cast things more carefully, I wouldn't be facing my second divorce as I am now. For me, the fire-breathing dragons are painful marriages that ended in ashes. As I look into the mouth of the third one, I seriously doubt that I'm going to make it past this river. I think that my story stops right here."

Another speaks, "I'm before that. To me the three fire-breathing dragons eat up my whole life. One is my marriage, the second my two children, and the third my job. To me they seem like mouths asking and demanding all the time, and I give them more and more and more. By now, I feel empty and stuck at the river of endless demands. Listening to the story makes me realize that if I could just cast a little bit of meat to each one rather than imagine I must feed them endlessly, I may be able to get by and go on. Meanwhile, I'm getting more and more angry as I wait here."

A younger man speaks up, "Listening to all the disasters in the world and hearing about marriages ending and all this brokenness, I don't even want to leap. I don't even want to look at those dragons. I'm discouraged. I don't even want to sit on the horse."

The next man says, "And I'm landed on the other side of the river and answering the question of the horse when he says "are you still there?" I say yes, and it only took half my strength, and I'm completely surprised to find myself at a place in life where I feel more grounded and more settled and still have a great amount of energy left. For a change I feel like it's time for me to move on and to deal with more issues in my life directly."

The iron ball rolls on, as if rolling down through the lives of those attending to the story. In true initiatory style, passing one test qualifies you for another; sorting out the devouring dragons qualifies a person for facing the mountain of flaming fire. In this area men seem to find a raw edge, an abyss of anguish that could destroy everything, including the themselves. An inner volcanic mountain forms part of the inheritance of many men. Although some push the volcanic impulses of anger and rage so deeply inside that it doesn't appear to be there at all, others explode with inner magma that can't be held back. Either way, most suffer dreams of beasts in basements, killers loose in the streets, or explosive worldwide catastrophes. Some simply have a massive heart attack instead. Eventually the mountain of feelings inside a person must be faced or it will destroy something. The little horse of the self encourages the effort by saying that surviving the turbulent emotional territories can lead to becoming a person of destiny. Meanwhile, a part of each person's fate includes their inner emotional state.

A man says, "The mountain before me is in the form of a serious illness. I know I have cancer. I don't expect I will live through it. It's bigger than I am and no doubt it will burn me up and destroy me. But it seems that I have to make the leap anyway and go through radiation treatments. Mostly I'm sitting here feeling that I can't move any further because of the size of the fire in front of me." Another says, "I'm in the same place, stuck here for twenty-five years. For me, the dragons were going to Vietnam and somehow getting out alive. But for twenty-five years I've been staring at a burning mountain of the dead bodies of those I served with who didn't ever come back. They are before me like a blinding mountain of smoke and fire. I feel that I have to carry them all with me. Every time I try to move my life along, I come up against that smoldering mountain." The weight of the sorrowful waters surrounds stirs around everyone, and feeling one's own feelings becomes the only way to breathe.

After a pause, someone speaks. "I did make the leap over the mountain, and I'm just now on the other side, clinging to life as the horse asks if I'm all right. Actually, I'm not sure how to answer. Years of drug and alcohol addiction have reduced me to ashes many times. I'm clean of that now. I'm on the other side of that fire, but am I really alive?"

"I'm there too," says another, "right with those words, 'barely alive.' It's not because I'm burned up, but because I think I'm burned out. I've had my career, been successful, leapt over many mountains, piled things up, raised my children. But if someone asked me where I am right now, I'd say—barely alive. I'm glad to be where I am, but I don't understand what I've done. I'm disoriented again… at my age."

In the architecture of the story, a green glade follows the mountainous issues that use people up and burn people out. There's a green glade where the wonder of all-heal can be found and life's burnouts and burnt bridges and burning questions can be eased, even healed. The skin of life can be renewed and those who have faced the fires of passion and the fire-fights and the dragons of life can become better even than before the flames. This is a promise that stories remember and remind about. The nature of this world includes the sense that there is a healing salve even for the worst illness and the most devastating blows. That's an old rule about life that echoes through folk myths and great spiritual traditions alike. Yet in contemporary times very few recognize and settle in this part of the story.

Once, out of a hundred men, only two made their way to the glade where healing happens. One was a young man and the other an elder. The elder was there because he had reached a place where he could finally let go of all the striving and trying and simply allow some healing into his life. He had begun to take care of himself, had begun to see himself as someone worth caring for, and had even let various things bless him. He was learning for the first time to count his blessings.

The younger man was quite surprised to be there. He said he was about to get married. Listening to the story caused him to confirm a little voice inside that whispered his desire to be married in a meadow on a hilltop. The image of standing among friends and family in the cool green of a high meadow kept appearing before him. Now he realized that the wedding was a healing of some sort. For years he feared that he would never marry. Suddenly he could feel a joy about going to his wedding; it began to feel real, as if he were headed for a place of beauty and promise. Everyone was surprised when the wedding scene appeared amidst the smoldering ranges of feeling, but everyone could feel the sense of promise it brought.

Stories remind us of the healing places and healing opportunities so often get missed in life; especially modern life which readily forgets what a ceremony tries to accomplish. If a person has no knowledge that there are healing places ahead, they may avoid the exact fires that can burn through to a new skin and a renewed sense of life. Without the occasional glade of healing the ordeals of life don't make any sense. For those who face many fires, there can be a tendency to overlook the moments when healing touches the skin. One of the keys to healing involves an awareness of when the psyche needs heat and when it requires cooling and quiet. It's helpful to know that a little all-heal can go a long way and that healing moments continue to live in the green glades of the soul.

The territories of fire and water, of burning and healing, must be visited over and over. Only by revisiting these places can a person develop the reflection of a true elder and glean the wisdom hidden in their own life wounds. Only from knowledge gained in the burning fires and the healing waters of the soul can a person gain the ability to help others through their fires and keep them from drowning in the their own lives. In that sense, initiation is not linear and direct; it winds back along paths that revisit the same river with its dragons, the same mountain with fire in all directions, and, hopefully, the same surprising glades of healing. Like a good story, the tempering of a person repeats the essential ordeals and themes.

In tribal life ordeals are condensed into formal rites of passage. Since the tribe returns to the same rites each time a group of youths come of age, the meaning of the ordeals can be revisited by all involved. An old saying says that initiation never ends. When the rites are ongoing a person can move from being guided through the emotions and spiritual ordeals, to preparing the rites, and to helping pull others through them. Each ceremony creates the opportunity to touch the core of one's life and reflect current issues against it. If a person doesn't take their inner life seriously, their outer life will lack meaning. The point isn't simply to rediscover the styles of initiation practiced by certain tribes, but to develop an eye for initiatory events, to enter into an initiatory style of perceiving and understanding suffering, and to heal the conditions life places on the soul.

The story lays out a series of surprising events in order to open certain territories of the soul. There are similar surprises in life, yet they may occur in seemingly random ways. One function of myth is to make life meaningful. Working within a story can lend a mythic order to random experiences, revealing hidden meaning in events that linger within. The complicated scenes woven into the story show the intricate ways in which the soul sees and feels dramatic experiences in the outer world. Each descent into the inner life of emotions and embodied thought stirs ancient ways of knowing and makes connecting to the web of the world possible again.

CONN-EDA
Part IV

The prince felt renewed and ready as he mounted the little shaggy horse again and followed where the rolling ball entered a broad field. Across the great plain before him, he could see a majestic city surrounded by high walls. There was only one entrance and it was guarded by two towers from which flames burst forth randomly. Anything passing between those fiery gates would be burnt to ash in a moment. As he watched, the prince saw the iron ball roll between the towers and disappear into the shining city.

"Stop here," said the horse. "Take from my ear the small knife, and with it kill and flay me. Then wrap yourself in my skin, and you will pass through that fiery gate unscathed. Once through, you can cross back and forth at your pleasure, entering and leaving as you wish. All I ask in return is that once inside the gates, you remember your little horse, come back, and drive away the birds of prey about my carcass. And if any drop of that all-heal may remain, pour it on my flesh. Then, if you can, dig a pit and bury my remains."

The prince was shocked! He said that he would never sacrifice friendship for personal gain. He said that what the horse asked went against his bearing as a man, his ethics as a prince, and his feelings as a friend. It went against all he believed in. Besides, how could he part with the one who had helped him through such great difficulties? The prince said he would rather face death itself than dishonor their friendship.

"Forget all that," said the horse. "Unless you follow my advice in this as you have before, we may both perish completely and never meet again. Besides, there are fates in this world worse than death."

Reluctantly, the prince took the knife from the ear of his little horse and, with faltering hand, he pointed it at the horse's throat. His eyes were blind with tears. The dagger, as if compelled by druidic power, leapt to the horse's throat. Before Conn-Eda knew it the deed was done and the horse fell at his feet. The prince fell, too, and wept until he lost consciousness. When he recovered, and with many misgivings, he flayed the skin off the horse. In the derangement of the moment, he covered himself with the skin and stumbled toward the flaming gate of the magnificent city. In this demented state, he passed through the flames unmolested.

Once inside the shining city the prince found himself in a busy marketplace filled with wonders and wealth. But Conn-Eda saw no charm there. As he stood in his daze, the last request of his faithful companion forced itself upon him and compelled him to go back. Returning to the plain of sacrifice, he found an appalling scene, for birds of prey were tearing and devouring the flesh of the little horse. The prince chased them off and poured the all-heal on the body of the shaggy steed.

No sooner had the all-heal touched the inanimate flesh than it changed before his eyes and assumed the form of a noble young man. Conn-Eda, awestruck, reached out and amid tears of joy and wonder embraced this fantastic brother. Then the marvelous youth spoke: "You are the best sight my sore eyes have seen, and I am most fortunate for having met you. Behold your shaggy steed, changed to his natural state! " He explained that he was brother to the king of the magnificent city, that a druid had enchanted him but was forced to release him by the honest request of the prince. He could only recover his natural state, however, when the prince performed the deep sacrifice. He also announced that the Hag of Beara was his sister and that she had not wished to destroy Conn-Eda, for she could have done that in a stroke. Rather, she wished to free the prince from future dangers and rescue him from his relentless enemies.

Together the young men entered the magnificent city and were received with great joy by the king of Lough Erne. A joyful feast began at which Conn-Eda received the powerful black steed, the hound of supernatural powers, and the three golden apples from the garden below the waves. By that time the year and a day were coming to a close. After saying many farewells and agreeing to return at regular intervals, Conn-Eda passed out through the flaming towers, over the mountain of fire, and past the three huge serpents. He was not harmed in any way, and his passage was swift on the great black steed.

Eventually the prince came in sight of his father's realm. The queen was still on the pinnacle, but she was joyful now because she was sure that this was the last day of her imprisonment. She was full of hope that the prince would not appear and that she would be done with him forever. Then she saw a movement on the horizon; she squinted her eyes and, after a moment, could make out a shape approaching. She looked as hard as she could. The shape grew into three shapes. Soon she could not deny that she saw the prince astride the black steed with the magnificent hound beside him. She raged in grief and anger, cast herself down off the pinnacle, and disappeared into a crevice in the ground.

Conn-Eda was welcomed by his father, who had mourned his son as lost forever. The prince planted the golden apples in the garden at the center of the realm. Instantly they produced a tree bearing similar fruit. The golden apples seemed to draw on all the splendor of the otherworld below, for soon the earth produced exuberant crops and the trees gave ninefold their usual fruit. The waters teemed with choice fish, the beehives overflowed with honey, and the cows yielded such an abundance of rich milk that it rained in torrents on the fields and filled the furrows and ditches of the earth. No one lacked for anything. In due time Conn-Eda succeeded his father as king. His reign was long and prosperous and even now the western province of Ireland is called Connacht after the royal son who descended to the waters of the land below and broke the spells binding both the worlds.

CHAPTER 13

BOUND FOR THE SACRED

THE GREATEST SURPRISE in the story comes when the prince must slay the little horse and envelop himself in the torn skin. This is the last ordeal, the mystery that the story has been aimed at all along. Like any true sacrifice, it defies simple explanation. After such close and careful work together, a conflict develops between the horse and the prince. After faithfully following the advice of the little steed, the prince suddenly refuses to be instructed. Something must be sacrificed in order for the transformation of the prince to continue and for the little horse to avoid a dark fate. But the prince has reached a deep place in the psyche where instincts become opposed and conflicting principles collide. The sacrifice defies all logic and most feelings, yet it must occur. Afterward, the prince enters yet another level of disorientation. This is the story's way of describing the mystery, ambiguity, and confusion present at the core of meaningful changes in the soul and in radical rites of all kinds.

A whirlwind of chaos and confusion swirls around the body of the shaggy little horse. Among the chorus arguments break out about what should happen and what it all means. The shock of the prince can be felt throughout the group. A man says, "I couldn't do it, couldn't carry it through. It's wrong. The horse has done everything faithfully. I wouldn't do it at all." This makes another man angry, "Your fondness for the horse doesn't go far enough, the horse itself is saying you have followed its advice until now, and if you don't follow this advice you will cause a fate worse than death. It's not your fondness for the horse stopping you; it's your fondness for counting on the horse and not wanting to be alone." Someone adds, "It's more like your fondness for your own ideas. The horse's instructions are as clear as ever."

People feel compelled to re-enact the conflict between the prince and the horse. It doesn't matter that everyone has heard the rest of the story and knows that the horse changes into a shining brother. What does matter is how each man felt and how each imagined the sacrifice. What does a modern person do with a scene in which someone must slay and flay what has faithfully carried them through trial after trial?

A man says that flaying the horse represents tearing off a marriage of fourteen years and standing in the shambles that result. He sounds torn and a little crazed. He stands in an unsteady silence. No one argues with him. Everyone begins to recall times when they had to pull away from something depended upon or someone loved. A man tears from his throat the exact words he cried while burying his dead child. No one knows what to say after that. Suddenly, another man states that he is the knife trying to cut through the darkness inside himself. He says it with such a cutting tone that no one dares to ask what darkness it might be. That causes a man near him to recall how he had set out one night to end his life, and was on the point of doing it when, through his tears and anguish, there burst a desire to live. He never understood that moment but never forgot it either. Another voice claims to be the horse, cut open and flayed. He has just been through a heart surgery and isn't sure if he's really alive. He still feels the cut of the knife and surges of dismembered feelings and thoughts that leave him in constant fear of his life.

In the story Conn-Eda must act in ways contrary to his opinion of himself and in contrast to all he has learned and been told about life. He reaches a depth where he must go against common belief and simple moral rules. In the exact tension of his soul, something arises from deep inside himself. A druidic force constellated by the close relationship between him and his horse cuts through all that he knows.

Some very painful internal cut will have to be made if the prince is to reach the place of inner resources that can return abundance to the wasteland above. Rather than being carried through the castle gates as a "prince" might expect, he enters unaware of what he is doing, stumbling, blind, and wrapped in torn skin and shadows. The prince winds up inside the very skin of what once seemed far below his station in life, inside that which has carried him beyond where he would go on his own.

Whatever a person's inner horse might be, it carries them to a place of sacrifice that cannot be guessed at, even by them. Who can name the mystery at the core of a person's soul? Who can say what it feels like to be that person, wrapped in that life, carrying whatever conflicts fate has dealt to them? People pass each other by with little hint exchanged of the internal struggles and sacrifices that their souls require.

A sacrifice turns everything around. From the same place that produced the healing oil, a knife appears; from what seems certain death, a greater life is born. The act of flaying the little horse creates a realignment of everything. The intensity of the image depicts the range of feelings required to completely change and fully initiate the inner life and the emotional and spiritual life of a person. A person carried by anger must learn to walk in sorrow. A person constant in their grief or complaint will have to learn the pain of others. One driven by fear will be required to find the blood of genuine courage. Where doubting was the skin of life, a deeper faith will be entered. A mean-spirited person will have to expand and stumble into generosity.

Each life grows around an inner opposition that escapes common notice. Each person carries an inner split that must be touched and suffered if moments of unity are to be found. Extreme life circumstances place a person up against it, between a rock and a hard place, in impossible circumstances where the rules no longer apply. Under the pressure to completely change a person either falls apart or else finds a hidden unity in the midst of the overwhelming conflict. What happens involves the depths of a persons soul; nothing could be more personal. Yet, as the story depicts, what happens has ramifications in the world above. If the fixed attitudes we carry cannot be slain, the connection to the hidden realm of soulful abundance won't be made. Without the life-generating resources of the inner-other-underworld, the wasteland of the outerworld will grow.

In the skin of raw emotions and unfamiliar attitudes, Conn-Eda passes through the fiery gates unscathed. Yet he is unable to enjoy the shining city or seek the gifts that are the goal of the quest. The prince feels compelled to return to the place of sacrifice, as if that were the real point of the entire adventure. The release of the "fantastic brother" shifts the relationship between death and life and releases the sources of abundance deep in the earth below the lake. Underworld and the upper world, inner world and outer world become realigned. Out of the sacrifice and suffering comes a radiant inner brother, the image of the awakened inner life.

Often in fairy tales breaking a spell releases an enchanted princess. When prince and princess embrace the world becomes whole again through the renewed union of feminine and the masculine energies. The tale of Conn-Eda points at another type of wholeness, another type of healing. One of the roles of initiation is to connect the initiate to an inner brother, a soul companion hidden within inferior aspects of the initiate. The radiant brother remains in the inner-underworld as a kind of "divine twin."

Conn-Eda agrees to return to the inner-under realm regularly as conscious relations now exist between inner realm and outer life. Because Conn-Eda releases his inner life from the spell, abundance returns to both worlds. Abundance returns when the trouble in each realm receives attention and healing. Initiation heals the wounds of this world and breaks spells in the otherworld. An old Celtic idea suggests that the two worlds open to each other in moments of initiation and at certain times of seasonal change. In those open moments healing can occur in both realms. In critical moments there seems to be just enough healing capacity, just enough all-heal, to make things whole again.

This old Irish story articulates and elucidates issues that arose in the African story of "The Hunter and His Son." That son had to sacrifice a great war horse in order to prove that he could be the son of a king. For a child of poverty and deprivation to sacrifice something of such great value, a radical shift of inner values must occur. The poor son must find inner nobility and sacrifice the outer trappings of royalty. For the son of a powerful king—for one born to be a prince—the shoe is on the other foot. A similar rite of passage is required, but the values are reversed. The prince must sacrifice every ounce of being special, of being especially noble, and of being above the fray or above the slaying and flaying that life requires for genuine transformation. The willingness to sacrifice the fixed and prevailing attitudes in one's persona makes the sacrifice.

Conn-Eda reaches the place where he loves the little horse more than anything he knew as a royal prince. He is in the world in a new and more vital way. He has relinquished his high horse and found some healing. But, on the road of initiation, this simply prepares him for an even greater revelation, one that requires a deeper sacrifice. Not only is the prince the son of a king in outerworld, he also has a place in the shining city of the otherworld. Wholeness means that the two realms unite through a deeply human sacrifice; that is the mystery. The willingness to fully let go of what we think defines us as a person allows the hidden sense of self to be fully present... at least for a moment.

The ritual of slaying horses deepens to reveal a divine connection hidden within life, be it the seemingly common life of a hunter's son or the seemingly glorious life of a royal child. The mysteries of initiation remove the outer coverings and even the inner attitudes to reveal a timeless connection that makes each human life sacred and valuable.

Something in the prince dies and is buried where the little horse was slain. He will never be the same again. He has survived a brush with death"and his sacrifices have regenerated life. Both innocence and arrogance have been sacrificed. The abundance at the beginning of the story returns with an important difference. The prince now knows that the source of life resides in the connection with the unseen world. He now knows that whatever shines in this world does so because the otherworld shines through it.

The story represents a radical reorganization of the prince's sense of himself; it points to the necessity for immersion in the inherent inner conflicts before having fruitful powers in the outer world. Those who would rule in this world should first learn to sacrifice the simplicities and fixations of their innerworld. The initiatory path was prepared by the Hag of Beara, who intended revelation of the inner life rather than destruction of the outer realm. The Old Hag was behind the whole thing, behind the good queen as well as the stepmother, behind the hen-wife and old druid. In many traditions even the male initiators are called mothers; the "male mothers" participate in the sacrifice which gives birth to the full emotional, spiritual, and imaginal lives of the youth. When the youth become conscious of who they are in their souls, abundance becomes available to the entire community.

Without formal rites of passage a modern person must look back over the arc of their life with an eye for initiatory moments. Since initiation remains an archetype in and an expectation of the soul, we can comb the surface of our lives for artifacts that can reveal unfinished rites still waiting for conscious attention. We can hunt for wounds and scars and extreme behaviors that mark the separations and ordeals that attempted to awaken us and broaden our lives. The eye of initiation sees things ceremonially and ritually. It looks for the iron ball that leads below the obvious levels of life in order to grow the connections with the otherworld, where an abundance of time and feeling and imagination waits to be reclaimed.

Initiatory experiences lay the groundwork for a person's life work and open inner territories that can be revisited over and over. As the story of Conn-Eda shows how perfection is always temporary; so is wholeness. And points of balance are just that—points between periods of imbalance. The Old Hag returns in another guise whenever a person needs to change and grow again. Each initiation qualifies a person for the next along-the life long road where the soul grows.

There is no certain ceremony that changes a boy into a man or without which manhood cannot be achieved. But the boy in a man's psyche may see it that way. When no clear or direct ceremonies mark the transitions through life's stages, a man can conclude that the opportunities of youth were completely wasted. Because life didn't change dramatically back then, it can't change now, and he will remain a boy forever. I've heard exactly that from many men who appear outwardly successful and mature but who state emphatically that they feel as a boy inside.

The psyche expects rites of passage that deepen the imagination, open the spiritual eyes, and expand emotional capacities. The inner life expects to be led out, to move from physical growth to sexual activity and learning of love, from naïveté to psychological savvy, from blind innocence to an awakened knowledge of life and death. When the expected rites don't occur, anything that effects a break from childhood and opens other ways of seeing and feeling becomes a substitute. Anything that burns like fire or that tears at life and stirs the shadows becomes a substitute rite of passage, and if parents, friends, and daily culture didn't perceive it as appropriate or meaningful at the time, all the better. What had to happen occurred in the depths of the soul in an unseen sacrifice that redeems the exact elements rejected by family and society.

It is not that the boy within missed the initiation. It is rather that at the time it wasn't seen as an initiation and so remains unfinished within him. Perhaps there was an accident, an illness, or a big mistake; rules or bones or hearts were broken. There was an outbreak of passion, foolishness, or violence. There was a mental breakdown or an emotional collapse. Things were never the same again and people never saw each other the same way as before.

Perhaps the event was overlooked, mistaken simply for a crime, or considered something the boy would outgrow instead of something he would grow from. As a result the event receded and was covered with layers of disappointment, cynicism, shame, or blame. Then it waited like a shaggy horse, out back behind all the successes of life. Each time a new obstacle appeared, the shaggy horse became restless, expecting to be recalled, expecting the unfinished journey of the soul to be undertaken again.

Somewhere in the strange events of youth lie the first stirrings of the little horse of the soul and the first cuts of the knife trying to lift the skin of childhood and reveal a hidden abundance within. Somewhere within, the first visions that opened the imagination to the genuine terror and genuine beauty of the world wait to be visited again. Somewhere are the words that carried wisdom through the ear of the child to the heart of the man. Somehow there was a touch that revealed the passionate intensity of a body capable of love and generating life. Neither the boy's expectations for radical awakening nor the pieces of unfinished initiation disappear completely. They lie hidden in the psyche of the adult, waiting to be uncovered and discovered again. They automatically stir, like the shaggy hair of the little horse, whenever the course of life offers a new obstacle or another opportunity to grow.

The eye of initiation can revalue each broken piece of life and fit into the story trying to live through a person. The eye for initiatory sense sees differently into divorces, wars, imprisonment, psychic breakdowns, sudden departures, depressions, and funerals. It collects psychic artifacts that can be reviewed and reworked to reveal initiations still waiting to be known. This eye sees with imagination; it sees the images trying to emerge from the events that have already marked us in unforgettable ways.

A tragedy becomes completely tragic if we remain blind to the part of ourselves that the tragedy makes sacred. Many cultures believe that the afflicted are sacred. The affliction in our lives is also the sacred trying to break through to greater awareness. A life trying to change wraps itself in afflictions; it smells and looks as bad as the flayed, shaggy hide of the little horse. A psyche trying to change will pour through any wound or break in life, whether it's physical, mental, emotional, moral, legal, or spiritual. The tragic events and glorious epiphanies in our lives offer opportunities for us to learn most accurately who we are and why we are in the world. The shocking nature of these events initiates the possibility of a sacrifice and conscious learning. Once initiated, such occurrences do not simply disappear; rather, they wait behind the clutter of life for us to seek them out again.

Conn-Eda faces death several times over, he suffers dementia, he thinks he has taken the life of the one being that helped him, and believes he has violated all principles of honor and reason. Yet the faithful horse tells him that it is "a fate worse than death" not to risk entering life fully, not to tear at the shadows, suffer the chaos, endure utter loss and loneliness. Why? Because each major obstacle, each tearing loss, and each stultifying defeat are there to create a sacrifice of what keeps us under spells and distant from the shining life of the soul. Life is truly a mystery—it has to be so—but it is a mystery trying to be solved. Any genuine solution involves a dissolution in the waters of the soul and a willingness to sacrifice superficial certainty for an embodied knowing in depth.

No single initiation gives a person status for the rest of his life. Initiation consists of the willingness to set out, to begin, to step into something fully aware that there can be no certain outcome. The initiate keeps being unmade and remade. All meaningful risks in life involve a brush with death, a sacrifice that makes a corpse of the former life, yet produces a vitality and abundance that spills over in to the lives of others. From the beginning the soul is bound for the sacred, and bound for a sacrifice that reveals a hidden abundance and gifts intended to be brought to the community.

CHAPTER 14

CONDITIONS ON THE SOUL

OTHER THAN THE IMPRINTS from one's family, initiatory events make a person who they are inside and open the ground for psychic growth after childhood. Yet events that leave indelible marks on an individual happen within the larger circumstances of a culture. Once a person separates from childhood and their role in the family, they enter the wider waters of culture and experience the great waves of historical events. Some events are both initiatory for the individual and critical for their culture. Some events indelibly imprint both the individual and their generation. There are dilemmas and obstacles that seem to require that a society also become initiated to a new cultural awareness. There exist conditions of the soul that are experienced as part of a generation.

Besides tempering the character of the individual, rites of passage attempt to make bridges for a meaningful exchange of knowledge between one generation and the next. Generations are not supposed to seal themselves off from one another. Rather, taken together, the generations become the living body of culture with the stages of life being places where everyone meets to consider the issues of life and death. The loss of meaningful cultural rites leads to an exaggerated separation between younger and older people. Modern American society has spawned the Lost Generation, the Depression Generation, the World War Generation and Generation X. Each generation seems to be carried further into the gap by waves of change rushing through a culture lacking internal cohesion and a genuine sense of meaning.

The generation gap represents a failure of one generation to engage the one following it in the gap where people struggle to find meaning and purpose. In the gap between generations, youth become increasingly disillusioned with culture, while older people become increasingly cynical about youth. Instead of the bridge of initiation there grows an increasing gap of understanding and a loss of wisdom regarding life's inevitable struggles.

The generation gap represents a betrayal of one generation by the other, a betrayal in which people try to substitute simple materialism and rampant indulgence for a genuine struggle for understanding and meaning. Simply winning or ruling or being dominant cannot produce either meaning or genuine caring about life. Each new generation must walk unwittingly toward the chessboard where the game of life gets played out. As in the story of Conn-Eda, the game is always rigged before it starts. The game is rigged because the point of being alive cannot be reduced to simply winning.

The word "win" arises from roots that mean "to strive" and "to desire." Those who win do so because they strive for something meaningful and desire something more than simple success or the appearance of a victory. When the meaningful sense of life becomes lost, death soon becomes meaningless as well.

By the time my generation came of age, the questions surrounding the meanings of life and death became heated to fevered pitch by the Vietnam War. Long-developing gaps in the culture became clear as generations, families, and social groups increasingly divided over issues of politics, race, oppression, and war. As increasing numbers of troops died in an undeclared war, growing numbers of young people felt that mainstream culture had no meaning for them. When the draft lottery became a mechanism for determining who would enter the burning fields of war, the way in which the game of life and death could be rigged became literally apparent. Soon an entire generation was faced with decisions about life and death, about privilege and disadvantage, about choosing between what could seem like certain and meaningless death or permanent exile, or even a fate worse than death.

By the time I entered the game of chance and fate, I already had questions about the Vietnam War. To me it was a questionable war at best. I was twenty years old, full of questions, and looking for a meaningful quest. In the midst of questioning my future and the future of the country, I received a draft notice. This was before the draft board offered the lottery that made clear that a game of chance was being played with an entire generation. Numbers had not yet been issued for each eligible male, but my number was up.

The draft notice came as a shock, saying, "Check. Your move." You may have been dreaming of where your life might go, but you have been part of a game already in progress. You are in check now, and it's your move. This type of message sets conditions on the soul; it requires a response. One response was gung-ho acceptance, to go for the gold, whether it meant a little death or big Death itself. Another possible response involved becoming an exile by going to Canada or hiding out somewhere.

I remembered that Odysseus went into hiding in order to avoid the Trojan War. He was called double-minded for his clever ability to see more than one side of any issue. Eventually he was found and forced to war. His long journey back from that battle still forms much of the metaphorical ground on which the Western World struggles with its hubris and its fate. In the Vietnam era there were other responses, each marking the soul indelibly in some way. A person could fake an illness or feign insanity. Some simply bought their way out. Whatever a person chose it simply deferred the underlying issues and raised questions other questions of how each might make their way home.

The draft notice included a deadline, a date by which I had to respond. I decided to respond in writing and wrote a letter back to the draft board saying that I objected to the war. If they had a war at some other time, one they were willing to declare as a war, one that had a purpose I could understand and to which I could fully commit, they could send another notice. As far as this war went, I wasn't ready to kill others or expose myself to death where the purpose was unclear and the meaning questionable. In my youthful way I was trying to say that I understood that circumstances could become conditions on my own soul; I knew that ordeals had to be faced, yet this game seemed rigged in the wrong way. I would wait for another game or a better conflict. Indirectly, I was also saying, "I have an arrogant, high-minded horse that's above this."

The draft board didn't accept my objection. They sent another letter requiring that I appear before them or be subject to arrest. I went at the appointed time and explained my position forthrightly to a strange panel of apparent war veterans. They conferred and gave me forms that detailed the nature of a conscientious objection and the rules under which such an exception could be sought. This gave me a new problem. In all honesty, I didn't qualify under rules that seemed to require a religious conviction and a lifelong practice of pacifism. My objection was more specific and my background more varied than the general notion of pacifism.

I couldn't say that all battles were wrong, or that I wouldn't show up for any of them. It was clear to me that if my family were attacked, I would defend them at all costs. My objection was that this was not a declared war; it was more of a military action, a kind of "optional war." It was also a questionable war, and to my eye, an unwise war. I objected to that and felt I had the option of declining to risk my life in that way. I had experienced the bizarre nature of battles in local gang wars. Wisdom seemed more possible before a fight, once shots were fired, everything could backfire.

Once I participated in a gang fight between rival neighborhoods. The reasons for that fight were highly questionable, as well. But there we were, trying to defend our turf even though little of it really belonged to us. As we faced off against the other gang, the guy next to me pulled out a zip gun and aimed it at them. Our rivals weren't far away and were about to charge forward, just as we were. He fired the clumsy zip gun and, before the bullet had gone very far, it turned in mid-air. Suddenly his bullet was coming right back at us. It went right between me and a guy on my other side. The cops came, we all ran, and I had to contemplate how a person could be killed by a misfire in the midst of a pointless battle.

At the draft board I considered the options. I even talked with a chaplain, who explained what it meant to invoke a conscientious objection. He stressed religious conviction as the clearest position. That didn't help me as I was struggling to separate from the religious doctrines I had been taught in Catholic school. The inconsistencies of the church, including its own history of violence and support of wars in the name of god, were part of my problem. In good conscience, I couldn't take refuge in a church I was trying to separate from. I left the draft board with a date certain for my induction into the army and an intrigue with pacifism as a philosophy that might explain my position. I decided to try being a pacifist during the time I had left before deciding between war and some form of exile.

At the time my friends and I hung out at a certain bar. We might go here or there in New York City, but we all met and usually wound up back at the neighborhood bar. It was 1964 and the war was a main topic of conversation even in the local pub. Some of the guys would return to the bar on leave from the Marine Corps and bring their new marine buddies. Other guys were waiting to be drafted and debating whether to go ahead and sign up. There weren't many long-term life plans under discussion. It was a blue collar, working-class bar and most of the older guys had been in military service at one time. The bar owner was a surly man, unfriendly to strangers and rough with young people. He would sing "Waltzing Matilda" when he was drunk and lead the older men in a tearful reminiscence about World War II.

There was a feeling, even in that place, that something about the war in Vietnam wasn't clear. The prevailing argument, however, was that if you were called, you had to go to war. If you wore a military uniform into the bar, you were not treated as a stranger; you would become a guest of honor and weren't allowed to pay for a drink.

One evening, sitting at the bar, I told some friends that I had decided I was a pacifist. A big argument ensued about pacifism and whether it wasn't cowardice dressed up in fancy words. I held that pacifism was a noble cause, but no one bought my argument. Not only was I the only pacifist in the bar, but no one there really believed that I was a pacifist either. I wasn't sure if I believed it myself.

In the midst of the discussion a friend asked me to step outside. I went out first, and he followed. I turned to ask what he wanted to talk about and suddenly found myself lying flat on the ground. He had sucker-punched me and knocked me down. Looming above me, he said, "If you're a pacifist, you'll stay right there." I was already getting up, saying, "What are you hitting me for?" when he hit me again. He repeated, "If you're a pacifist, you'll just stay there." I got up quick as I could and, before he could hit me again, I hit him. That stopped him from knocking me to the ground, but it gave me a new problem: I could no longer argue that I was a pacifist.

I wrote back to the draft board to restate my position: I wasn't objecting on general religious grounds and I wasn't objecting on the grounds of pacifism. I objected personally that this was not a just war, that it was not a wise war, and that it was not even a declared war. They responded with a clear set of options: either I appear for induction at the appointed date or I would be subject to arrest and would go to jail.

Like most families in the neighborhood, mine was influenced by World War II and held the feeling that when the call to war comes, you go in service of your country. They clearly felt I had to go whenever my country called. My father and uncles had served during the "great war" and I was simply next in line. Even my mother felt that way. Yet as the date of my induction approached, I felt increasingly isolated and torn by the burning question of whether this was my fight or not.

Most of the guys I knew claimed to be eager to show up and ready to do great damage when it came their turn. There were a couple of younger guys in the neighborhood who seemed to question things and a folksinger I worked with on a delivery truck understood my dilemma. But overall I felt alone and on my own. I went to the bar less often, preferring to walk the night streets, turning things this way and that in my mind, trying to reach a clear decision.

Should I just go into service and face the music? Could I leave and go to Canada, could I live that way? Could I simply stick to my guns and say no? "No" was clearly the strongest feeling, but I couldn't tell if it was an excuse not to fight or a meaningful place to make a stand. Eventually the day came. I went to the induction appointment with the questions still banging away within me. Inside, I was still picking up one position and laying it down for another. I was walking forward, but the voice within was still saying "no."

Everyone else who showed up that day seemed wrapped in their own shroud of silence. We were inducted in the midst of our confusions, each of us standing there for reasons we couldn't have articulated fully. Although we were each called as an individual, we were inducted as a group. The war didn't care who we were, what we thought, or how we felt. We shared a common age grouping, a common area of birth, and a date with fate—that was all.

Soon we were all on a train together. It was before dawn on a midwinter morning; it was dark and cold. The train rumbled out of the belly of New York, banging through the sleeping city, heading south in a hurry. After a few hours an announcement stated that the train would stop for half an hour. We could get off and stretch our legs. Someone suggested that there was enough time to make it to a liquor store, and a bunch of us headed off to find one. Sure enough, there was one nearby.

We rushed in there like madmen, hoping either to put out the fire inside or to fire up some courage. I bought a pint of Irish whiskey and joined the strange party that ensued back on the train. Bottles were passed around as voices grew louder and jokes were told. To the casual eye we looked like any bunch of young guys headed to a training camp or a sports event. A very different fate seemed to rattle up from the tracks below, but we preferred not to notice.

There was an African-American man sitting quietly by himself. I became curious about his continued silence. I went over, offered him a drink from my pint bottle, and asked what he was thinking about. He took a drink and handed the bottle back while looking me coolly in the eye. He said he was planning how to get out. I said I had been thinking about that too, but it seemed a little late now as the train moved rapidly into the passing day. I had no idea where we were by this point. It seemed way too late to get out or get off these tracks.

He said quietly, "I'm going to get out." I asked how he was going to do it. He said, "Two words." "What?" I asked. He repeated that he was going to use two words. He didn't say any more except, "You'll see. I'll get out of this with two words." We had another sip of the whiskey as I joined him in his silence. The word whiskey, I remembered, was an adaptation of two old Gaelic words, *Ouishque-bagh*, or water and life. Two words could say a lot, but I doubted that they could stop this train or get anyone off the tracks.

The train rattled along and plunged into the cold night that waited for us at the end of that day. We arrived at boot camp and were pushed off the train into the darkness. Disoriented and scared, we ran over loose gravel toward the lights of a distant building. I stayed near the quiet man with the two words. We entered a brightly lit orientation center and sat stiffly in cold chairs. A sergeant strode before us and began to tell us what was what. We were tired, disheveled, and confused. His uniform was perfectly pressed, and his posture erect. In the midst of our confusion and uncertainty, he was pretty impressive.

He had prepared his speech and he boomed it out with a big voice and very little hesitation. He looked strong. He had golden stripes on his sleeve, and he was laying down the law. When he finished, a captain stood in the bare silence and explained his position as an officer and a priest. He talked to us of religion and duty, of God and war. His religious faith in war made me look at the exit doors and recall language on the conscientious objection forms. Beyond simple fear, I felt wildly disoriented again.

Soon enough the sergeant began to read the roll call. At the calling of each name we were to snap to attention and answer, "Present, sir." A wave of nausea went over me. A voice inside wanted to say, "No, no, I won't jump to attention. No, I'm not present. No, sir. I'm here against my will, and against my better judgment. I'm here against everything that I know about living and even my hunches about dying." I began to worry about what I would do when he called my name. Eventually he did. I stood up slowly and nodded my head. The sergeant repeated my name more loudly and it echoed against the lonely night. I knew he was insisting that I answer with, "Present, sir." I felt myself shrinking, as if disappearing into the battle within myself. Suddenly I said, "Present." The "sir" wouldn't quite come out. He went on to the next name and I sat down.

Moments later a certain name was called. No one answered. The sergeant read it more loudly. No answer. As an electric tension bristled through the room, someone was ordered to check the head count. The full list was called again as soldiers watched us all and counted. Still no answer came for that name. The sergeant asked if anyone knew whose name it was. I knew right away that it was the man with whom I had shared the whiskey. He was sitting right there, as quiet as he had been on the train. I didn't say anything. He barely seemed to breathe. He didn't flinch or move as his name boomed through the room. Soon there were agitated soldiers in crisp uniforms going up and down the aisles trying to figure out whose name it was and why there was no answer to it.

We were instructed to look around and identify anyone near us who had not answered to the roll call. We hadn't even put on uniforms, but we were being commanded to point out anyone who was out of step or out of line. It was a critical little event. I learned later, that this kind of pressure to join the group would be applied anytime someone found themselves at odds with the collective or the orders being given.

Sure enough, someone sitting nearby gestured toward the quiet black man. The sergeant charged right over, veins popping out of his neck, his body stiffly at attention. Air puffed into his chest so that he seemed larger than before. He yelled for the man to stand up. He just sat there. The sergeant barked the order again. No answer. He insisted that the man stand and answer to the order. Slowly, as if he had plenty of time, as if the sergeant wasn't looming before him, the quiet man stood up. While every ear listened intently, he simply said, "Fuck you." Two words and he sat down.

An incredulous silence was followed by an explosion of orders. The sergeant was beside himself. He called for a captain—not the priest but a real officer. In came a fierce captain who fiercely fired off orders at the quiet man. Once more he slowly stood and said his two words. Repeatedly and from all direction orders were given to him; each time he answered with the two-word mantra: "Fuck you." After he was taken away roughly from the room, there was his empty chair that seemed to protest the forced unity of the stunned group of would-be soldiers. The sergeant pulled himself together and resumed to telling us what was what.

I realized that the quietness in the man had partly been his way of concentrating so that he could put everything he felt into those two words. There had to be nothing in them that could be interpreted as hesitation or holding back. There could be no hint of a tendency to agree or participate or reconsider. His two words had to be the complete antidote to "Present, sir."

The next day we were ordered to a strange barbershop where young men went in and lost their hair and came out like sheared sheep. Once our heads were shaved, we were taken outside, lined up in ranks, and made to double-time in place. Up until then I had an array of thick, long hair. Now the cold seemed to bite at my head. My new army hat bounced around my head as I angrily jogged up and down.

Just as I was cataloging the insults to my mind and body, I saw the quiet man. We were ordered to double-time back to our tents as he was marched in the opposite direction. He still wore civilian clothes and he walked silently between two armed soldiers. I broke ranks and ran to talk with him. I had to know what had happened. He said, "Up 'til now, I've only said two words. I'm on my way home. Good luck, man." I ran back to my position and double-timed along with the rest of the soldiers; somehow I was not so cold.

I felt a lot of respect for that man, for the clean simplicity of his plan and the way he stuck to it under great pressure. He achieved what he wanted with almost military precision. Like me, he had said yes when he meant no. Showing up implied an acceptance of the conditions of the game; in refusing to go any further, he set his own "conditions on the soul." He had stepped beyond the ambiguity that I still felt. To my eye he had converted the general conditions to specific circumstances. He had refused to become just a pawn in the game. Feeling estranged in my new uniform and bald head, I realized that he knew himself better than I knew myself at that point.

After boot camp I was sent on to jungle training in Panama. I enjoyed the physical training and the strange experience of a real jungle after so many years in the "concrete jungle" of New York. One day, everything changed for me as our entire battalion gathered in an outdoor amphitheater for a presentation on combat readiness. An officer showed us photos and maps of Vietnam. He described how the enemy would secure a hilltop, dig in, and aim various weapons down the hill. He said that in combat our job was to knock the "gooks" out of there and take over the hill. He emphasized that we would express our patriotism by running up such a hill.

I raised my hand and asked a question: "What is the value of that hill sir?" He said that wasn't the point. I said it was a point for me. If we were going to be asked to risk our lives for that hill, I wanted to know the value of it. He said he was teaching military technique and strategy; our job was to follow whatever orders were issued. I felt more conditions on the soul being laid on us. I tried another approach. I asked if it was possible to call in firepower or air strikes and take out the top of the hill with superior weaponry before we charged up there. He said, "Of course. The top could be blown off the hill. America has the most powerful weapons in the world. But that isn't the point. The point, soldier, is to follow orders and attack the hill."

Suddenly an inner voice needed to speak. I stood up and said, "No. I wouldn't do that. It doesn't make any sense." A big commotion broke out. Other soldiers started saying, "I'm not sure I would do it either. If there are other ways of taking the hill, why should everybody die like that?" Some argued back, "An order is an order." Sergeants and officers began to run around shouting orders for everyone to be quiet.

The officer teaching the class repeated that when the order was given it was our patriotic duty to charge up "that damn hill" together, regardless of the consequences. That was the meaning of patriotism and the essence of loyalty to the unit. We were soldiers and had taken an oath to obey. Once again the voice inside forced me to speak up, "No, I wouldn't do it." I was learning what the "no" inside me meant and that it spoke whether I liked it or not.

The next day I had to appear before the commander of my company. He advised me on the limits of my role as a soldier and warned me not to speak out again. I felt I had to restate my position: If I were given an order to do something as foolish as the example that was given, I would say no. The commander decided not to give me any more orders at that time and for a while, I was left alone.

The next training exercise put us in a "war game" out in the jungle. Each company had an objective and each platoon a specific role in accomplishing the objective, as well as a responsibility not to get captured by enemy platoons. The assignment for our squad involved locating and attacking a certain hill that was likely to be occupied by the enemy. Incredible, I thought, even more so when I learned that the assignment had nothing to do with my recent outburst about hills. The assignments were random.

Meanwhile someone decided that reverse-psychology might be a good way to deal with me. If I didn't want to follow blindly, I must want to lead instead! The fact that the replication of the hill issue was unintended and unconscious made more clear to me the notion that I was being asked to be unconscious of risking my life for a random goal. If they expected me to go up that hill unconsciously and die for no reason except obedience, well consciousness just might lie in the other direction.

I studied the mission and found a little valley near the hill that seemed to have a stream in it. As the new leader, I decided on a different objective and led the platoon to the stream, where we stayed cool and rested. When we returned late and unaccounted for, I was relieved of my new command and put on K.P. duties for an extended period. Following that incident, I found myself washing piles of dishes or doing an inordinate quantity of push-ups as sergeants and officers took turns giving me orders and punishments.

One day I received an order that seemed absurd. I don't recall whether it was to rewash something I had just cleaned or to do an impossible number of push-ups. Whatever it was I simply said, "No." I had reached a breaking point and it came down to just one word.

Saying no to one order caused everyone to give me orders of all kinds. Under this onslaught of orders, I found my attention focusing on the word "no." Meanwhile I received one company courts-martial after another. When not performing some punishment or other, I was confined to barracks. Either way, I was mostly alone and had time to figure out what was happening within myself. I realized that not only did I not want to be responsible for killing people in this war, but also I didn't want to die on some god-forsaken hill out of mindless obedience to an order not properly considered. My sudden reaction to blindly assaulting the hill had given me a glimpse of a meaningless death on a nameless hill. To me, dying a death that lacked meaning would also indicate a meaningless life. Something had shifted within me.

The conflict raging inside me had burned all the way to a conclusion. The inner voice saying "no" came from a place that knew there could be a "fate worse than death." Once I looked squarely at that death message, the doubts in my mind quieted down. At that point there was no turning back, the ball rolled before me and some unseen horse set the course. An imminent courts-martial offered a chance to articulate what had been stewing inside from the moment I received the draft notice. I began to write out my objections to the war and my refusal to take further part in it.

The day before facing the courts-martial I learned that the outcome of the trial had already been determined. The young officer who was theoretically responsible for my defense told me that the verdict and the sentence had been settled at the officers' club the night before. In a strange way that seemed to confirm the course I had set for myself.

When the time came to speak I stated as clearly as I could that coming onto the military was a big mistake. It was my fault, my mistake, and, since that was quite clear now, I would be going home. Of course, they didn't see it that way and they had already reached their own conclusion. I was sentenced to six months in the military stockade near Panama City, after which I would still have to serve my time in the army.

Once in prison I was subjected to an endless series of orders and punishments. Each guard and each officer I encountered seemed determined to be the one who would break my will. But, inside me the die was cast, the course was set, the iron ball was rolling before me and I was following on.

What began as an exile from family and friends, and from the world (as everyone in the army called back home) led me to a little prison near Panama City. Since I continued to refuse to take orders while there, I wound up in solitary confinement, alone in a cell at the back of an otherwise unused prison.

When it became clear that my words wouldn't convince the authorities that I really was finished with the service, I began to use sign language. I became silent. Eventually I refused to wear a uniform in case that seemed to indicate I was part of the service. One day, I was firmly struck with the idea of refusing to eat. That day I began a hunger strike. I refused all food and drank water only when I showered. My position wasn't that I was leaving, but that I was gone. It was as if I was saying, "If I can't leave, I'll disappear."

After I had fasted for many weeks of fasting, the decision was made to feed me by force. A device for force-feeding was procured from some kind of storage back in the states. The process involved a mouth brace that forced my teeth apart and a hand pump that drove ice cold liquids through a tube into my throat. This process went on for a time. I had entered the solitary cell weighing about 150 pounds and eventually left weighing no more than 87.

Wearing clothes that looked several sizes too big, I was placed on a military transport flying back to the United States. Everyone on the plane was in uniform, some on leave from duty in Panama, most returning from Vietnam. I sat between two guards, each handcuffed to me. They were the only armed soldiers on the plane; I was their prisoner. They wore Green Beret colors and were just returning from combat duty in Vietnam. They were curious about my emaciated condition, so I told them some of the story of how I reached my decision to leave and what had transpired in the prison.

Their interpretation completely surprised me. The more I told them, the more they insisted that I was fighting my own war in the midst of the one they had been fighting. They told me of their struggles to survive and maintain themselves under deadly and chaotic conditions. They spoke of the deaths they had witnessed and of their own devastation. Where I expected more grief—especially from them—they connected to the battle sense of my experience and seemed to feel that I had won a war myself.

Theirs was a minority opinion. Many of those on the plane knew who I was and the nature of my protest. I saw a sergeant from my original company. He was the first one to punish me for insubordination. He announced to the entire plane that I was a traitor and a coward escaping from the real punishment I deserved. He instigated others on board to curse and threaten me. At that point the two guards, just days from the fires of the war, stood up to speak. I had to stand as well because of the handcuffs.

As the three of us stood and the plane rocked, they announced that anyone who had anything to say to me would have to deal with them first. If anyone wanted to fight, they were ready, they were experienced, and they were the only ones armed. Was this clear? The plane quieted down. We returned to our conversation about battles and wars and survival.

The guards told me about fire-fights and the danger of being suddenly blown out like a flame on a candle. We talked in the heated images of fire most of the way back to the States. They reiterated that we were each trying to survive in different areas of the same raging fire. One of them had been drafted, the other volunteered. Now they were both battle-scarred and war-weary. They were clearly warriors but no longer sure of the war.

That remarkable conversation acted as a salve on my wounds. For the first time in a long time, I felt heard and understood and strangely protected. Their understanding of my battle helped me understand it better myself. We agreed that, in a certain sense, each person suffers their own solitary confinement once fate has evoked conditions on the soul. From those two heavy-hearted men I learned something about the role of older brothers when it comes to initiation by fire.

After several more obstacles, I was eventually released from the army and made my way home. My family welcomed me home, but everyone had to ask why I had stopped eating in the prison. At first I said it was just an instinct to refuse food. If I ate like normal and dressed as usual, how could I say that I wasn't present as a soldier? Not eating seemed a way to demonstrate that I wasn't really there. Years later I read a newspaper story about political prisoners in Ireland who went on hunger strikes to protest mistreatment. Some died of starvation while in solitary cells.

Their statements fully intrigued me and led me to research the history of hunger strikes. I was amazed to learn that it was an old practice in Ireland to involve fast against power. In this tradition, a citizen being forced by an authority to do something against his or her will would fast on the doorsteps of the authorities until the unjust and unequal use of power stopped.

Learning of the Irish tradition of fasting gave an ancestral quality to the instinct that arose within me. It was as if the little ancestral horse awakened as I struggled with my conscience and the burning questions of my generation. The sudden decision to fast was no longer simply personal. The personal struggle could be seen as part of an old tradition, remembered in the bones. I'm not saying that my own sense of justice should apply to everyone. I am saying that the conditions on my soul insisted on being recognized. I am saying that staying in the kind of fire that burns in the individual soul can erase differences that otherwise divide people.

At some point the fires of those exposed to combat and those opposed to combat become the same fire. I learned to call it the fire of initiation that, if it doesn't consume a person, leaves them connected to something ancient and ancestral. Ignoring the deeper sense of conflicts that erupt and threaten life can mean a kind of death in the individual soul, a loss of meaning for an entire generation, and a fate worse than death for the soul of a culture.

For me, the idea of men's work began in my struggle to find myself within the fires set by the Vietnam War. It was the tradition of men in my family that compelled me to appear for induction into the army. It was the radical action of the quiet man with two words that lit a pathway out of my darkness. Along the way I was insulted and assaulted by other men. Yet it was those men set to guard me who blessed the way I had to walk.

Many years later we held a conference where the affects of the war became a heated topic. More than one generation participated, but most were of the Vietnam era. As the discussion intensified, men began to represent the various positions taken during the war. Some identified themselves as "in-country" combat veterans. Others had been in the service, but not in actual battles. Some had served as medics, some had been conscientious objectors, several had returned from exile in Canada. Some avoided the battle through college deferments, while others used trickery to turn minor ailments into seemingly major medical problems. One had feigned insanity; another, homosexuality. Although the suffering of those exposed to the heat of battle was palpable, each position involved some fire, some burning, and some need for completion and healing.

The wounds of some men were still smoking; their words smoldered with sulphur and shrapnel. A vet told of paralyzing flashbacks and terrorizing nightmares, of constant efforts just to keep from exploding. Another said he chose the war as an adventure. He survived battles and won medals only to find himself in exile afterward. He found that he could live in civilization only half the time; the rest of the time he camped in forests and wandered the woods as if back on patrol. A man who left for Canada told of always thinking about the war and those who died while he had walked away It was as if something in him died as well. Another who had received a medical release told how that choice still burned in him. He needed to tell those carrying literal wounds how he had made a minor ailment his passport out of battle. Strangely enough, they had the forgiveness he needed. Their own wounds gave them sympathy for his wound and the exile it implied.

The room started to feel and smell like a field hospital or a gathering place for ghosts seeking a proper burial. Everyone knew someone who had not returned and probably had not been buried. The gathering evoked the presence of those still waiting in hospitals, those wandering the homeless streets, those unable to be close to loved ones for fear of hurting them, and those pouring liquor on inner fires that refuse to go out.

On that occasion the whole array of conditions on the soul of a generation became clear and palpable. Because those present decided to open and air out so many wounds, much healing occurred. Long-held tears flowed openly, loosening the gates of forgiveness and releasing smoldering corpses that were honored by all and given to the earth.

Men had gone into the flames of that war with idealistic attitudes and heroic beliefs. Many of those who did return were scarred and burned by the nature of the war as well as the rejection of the warriors that followed upon it. Some were still shocked from horrors they had seen, others unable to find a path back to what they had known. More than once we all had to leave the room as the ghosts and the suffering would become too much to bear.

It healed and cooled the combat vets to hear how those who had not gone to war had also suffered and held gratitude in their hearts for those who went right into the fire. Those who had not gone benefited greatly from hearing directly the suffering of those who had and from hearing their words of forgiveness. It was like finding the healing green glade after the burning mountain. Some all-heal was forged through all the different pains and losses and exiles being named and treated in the same room.

Those who burned from deadly combat were thrown back into homes and farms and cities. Call it cultural post-traumatic stress syndrome or a generation still burning—either way the flames continue to flicker and hiss inside the culture and erupt again each time someone thinks that the next war will quiet the demons.

Contemporary culture faces a "burning mountain" with flames shooting in all directions. When the fires of one generation are denied some all-heal, acrid embers smolder in the psychic forest waiting to erupt upon the next generation. If the severe burns and betrayals of one period are avoided, the shining city of inner resources sinks further into the waters of oblivion and the wasteland grows in the outer world.

4

The Land of Fire

You don't give a man a weapon
until you've taught him how to dance.
CELTIC PROVERB

THE FIREBIRD
Part I

Once upon a time, not this time but another time, in a certain place, not this place but another place where broad forests stood and many birds flew among the branches of ancient trees, there was a realm ruled by a mighty king. In the realm there was a young hunter who rode a horse that was a "horse of power." It was such a horse as belonged to the men of long ago, a swift steed with a broad chest, eyes like fire, and hoofs of iron. Nowadays no such horses are seen. They sleep deeply in the earth with the men who rode them, waiting for the time when the world has need of them again. At that time all the great horses will thunder up from under the ground and the valiant people of old will leap from their graves. Those men of old will ride the horses of power, and with a swinging of clubs and a thundering of hoofs they will sweep the earth clean of the enemies of God. At least that's what my grandfather said, and his grandfather said it before him, and if they don't know, well then, who does?

One day in the spring of the year a young hunter was riding through the forest on his horse of power. The leaves were growing green in the sun and little blue flowers sprouted under the trees. Squirrels ran in the branches, and hares worked through the undergrowth, yet it was strangely quiet. No birds sang. The young hunter listened for the birds, but the forest held silent except for the scratching of the four-footed beasts, the dropping of pine cones, and the heavy stamping of the horse of power.

"What has happened to the birds?" the young hunter mused aloud. He had scarcely uttered the words when he saw a big, curved feather lying on the path before him. The feather was larger than that of a swan, longer than that of an eagle. It lay there glittering like a flame of the sun, for it was a feather of gold. Then the youth knew why there was no singing in the forest; he knew that the Firebird had flown that way and the flame on the path was a feather from its burning breast.

Suddenly the horse of power spoke and said, "Leave the flaming feather where it lies. If you take it, you will know trouble and you will learn the meaning of fear."

The young hunter turned the matter over in his mind. Should he pick up the burning feather or not? He had no wish to learn fear, and who needs more trouble? On the other hand, if he picked the feather up and presented it to the king, the king would be pleased and might reward and honor him. For not even a king had a feather from the burning breast of the Firebird. The more he thought, the more he desired to carry the feather to the king. He knelt to the ground, picked up the feather, remounted the horse, and galloped back through the green forest directly to the palace of the king.

The young hunter entered the great hall of the palace, walked its length, bowed before the king, and offered the feather as a gift. "Thank you," said the king, "a shining feather from the burning breast of the Firebird is a thing of great wonder and value. At the same time, a single feather is not really a fit gift for a king. The whole bird held here before me—now, that would be a fitting gift. Since you have found the feather of the Firebird, you must be able to bring me the great bird itself. Either you present the whole bird here before me, or the edge of this sword will make a path between your head and your shoulders and your head will roll."

The young hunter bowed his threatened head and left the great hall weeping bitter tears, wiser now in the knowledge of what it meant to be afraid. The horse of power was waiting and asked why the youth was weeping. The hunter told that the king now required him to bring the whole Firebird. Since no man could do such a thing, he was weeping at the fate that awaited him—the certain and definitive loss of his head.

The horse did not console him, but said, "I told you so. I said if you took the feather you would learn fear. Well grieve no more. Go to the king and ask that a hundred sacks of maize be emptied and scattered in the open field near the palace. Ask him for three lengths of strong rope. Then rest well. Be ready when the sun wakes the world at dawn; for the trouble is not now—the trouble lies before you."

When the red glow of dawn burned the darkness from the sky, the young hunter rode out on the horse of power and came to the open field. The ground was covered with yellow maize. In the center of the field stood a great oak tree with spreading boughs. The hunter hid himself in the branches of the tree, while the horse wandered loose in the field. The sun rose higher, turning the sky golden. Suddenly there was a noise in the forest. The trees shook and swayed and seemed ready to fall. A violent wind blew across the sea nearby piling waves with crests of foam. Suddenly the Firebird came flying from the other side of the world—huge, golden, and flaming even in the light of the sun. It flew and then dropped with open wings onto the field and began to eat the maize.

The horse of power wandered closer and closer to the Firebird as it fed on the maize. All of a sudden the horse stepped on one of its fiery wings and pressed it heavily to the ground. As the great bird struggled the youth tied three ropes around it; he hefted it over his back and mounted the horse again. The horse carried the hunter as he in turn carried the great bird. In this fashion, the three rode to the palace of the king. As the youth carried the great bird into the great hall of the palace, broad shining wings hung on either side of him like fiery shields. As he moved through the hall, he left a trail of flaming feathers on the floor. The king gazed upon the bird with awe and delight. He thanked the youth for his services and raised him to a noble rank.

CHAPTER 15

THE BURNING FEATHER

W E ENTER THIS STORY on the thundering hoofs of a horse of power, as if the psyche has shifted from the prince in the story of Conneda to a hunter in a forest of surprise, as if the black steed that rose from below the lake now charges into the land of fire, and carryies the young hunter to his meeting with a fateful burning feather. Once again the horse can speak and knows which turns to take in the forest of burning beauty and sudden risk, along the paths of purpose and confusion. Two of the functions of initiation are to expose a man to the extremities of his emotions and to help him find true purpose in his life. Without purpose, a part of the soul turns bitter; without passion, the spirit can wither.

In this realm a single feather can ignite a purpose that will burn throughout a person's life. Yet it is also the realm where going one step too far can mean being burned to death. Here lie the great imaginations and ambitions of the human soul, the shining flames of love and beauty that can also leave one in the ashes. In order to survive the brush with the great bird of spirit, a man must learn ways of moving raw passions into forms that contain the heat yet keep the heart opening wider.

Like a great dream, this old Russian tale erupts from the forest of imagination. Nature is hushed when the bird of spirit wings toward this world and even the greatest king has nothing as valuable as a single feather from that burning breast. Both culture and nature must pause when the wondrous bird visits this time-bound world. There are echoes here of the Holy Spirit, of the magical Simurgh bird of the ancient East, and of the Phoenix, which repeatedly rises from the ashes of life.

Regardless of the continuing collapse of imagination into history and the spiritless materialism of Western cultures, each soul arrives on this earth with an expectation that the realm of spirit will one day open before it. Love is that expectation, as is ambition and the desire to serve something beyond oneself. This expectation lies not only in each individual soul, but also in the psyche of each generation through which the world must be fashioned again. The burning questions and issues in life generate a desire for the bird of spirit that might regenerate the world. Yet seeking answers to the burning questions, as the horse of power points out, becomes a task full of trouble and fear.

Before picking up the feather the youth has a sense of choice in the world. Once the burning feather has been accepted the path will be shaped by demands a person would not choose otherwise. In accepting such a burning feather a person gives up choice for being chosen." Picking up the burning feather is a symbol for risking the full-hearted, passionate presence of life. Telling youth that the next step brings trouble will act more as an incentive than a deterrent. Hearing of risks only intensifies desire, because the underlying instinct is to risk death in order to find a greater life. In youth the desire for risk is both a beauty and a danger, a failing and a strength, a dread and an expectation.

Young men in particular tend to risk everything in order to not miss having just one golden, burning moment. Much of competition, sports, and battle depend upon that inherent longing to stand out, to shine and burn like a flame against eternal darkness. The embers of love, which can only ignite through risking one's whole heart, dwell in the same area. The fires of great longing and of longing to be great intensifies as youth awaken to the inner dreams of life. In that sense, contemporary people are like the people of old, the people who burn with imagination and a need for beauty and purpose.

No one knows when an opening to spirit might come into their life. When it does the whole forest becomes still as a church, as if all of nature secretly watches the golden feather drop from the heart of the mythical bird into the heart of the young hunter and witness a flame of destiny falling like a wounded star into his life. For a moment he enters a sacred condition, and that open moment is enough to change the course of his life forever.

Telling the story of the Firebird at men's retreats is like tossing a burning feather into the middle of the group. For each, the flaming feather represents something right before him in life, or else it reminds of a past time when gold and fire fell upon him. There are many surprises as each man describes what the feather means for him. A glimpse of the passions and the purposes in each becomes illuminated. Some jump up to tell their story, just as they must have jumped to pick up the feather. Others recall backing away from what was before them and becoming cautious like the advice of the horse.

A man says the feather appeared before him when, at the age of nine, he suddenly knew he would be a writer. Another says that the first time he made love his world became golden, everything inside broke apart and he felt a new form of knowing. The light touch of love opened a hidden heart he didn't know was there. That was the feather for him. The next man says he never held a flaming feather until his hand picked up his divorce papers and he found himself devastated and seeking for a king who could confirm that his life still had meaning. Another offers that a golden moment occurred when he decided to have children. Although it seemed a bright joyful occasion, it also gave him trouble, which forced him to open his heart and surrender his life.

Someone speaks with pained certainty about the flaming feather in his life; how it ignited the moment he began to play music as a teenager and joined a pick-up band. That band took soaring flight, leading to golden records that allowed the entire group to live like kings. As one of the hottest bands in the world, they flew on the wings until one of them burned up in flames and died. The speaker survived the soaring flight, but spent years trying to discover the purpose of it and the meaning within him. For many the feather appears through the haze of drugs and alcohol. A man tells of trying a "little line of cocaine, light as a feather," which soon became a burning habit. The first hit sent him "high, flying like a bird," but it led to a hell of addiction for years.

People don't necessarily understand each other's image of the golden feather. For one it appears as religious fervor, for another as the lure of actual gold. The burning feather is a symbolic piece of the heart of spirit, one touch of which heats up the core of a life and opens a fateful road. Each feather is an entry pass to one of many realms, each realm ruled by a different king or queen. Some are huge feathers from the beginning while others start as little tail feathers that grow. The flame of spirit may burn as a vocation that calls clearly, or a talent that must be shown; or it may disguise itself as a seemingly small choice that creates bigger and bigger consequences.

For some the feather is clearly golden and shimmering bright; others experience the burning aspects with little of the gold. Some pick up anything that might be a feather; others need to be reassured that something in their life actually involved something golden. The feathers of spirit tend to drop into the breaks of life, where we finally get a break and where we become broken; wherever a life breaks open, breaks out, or breaks down.

Getting to the imaginal, emotional, and spiritual heart of a person requires something extreme. Ancient people instinctively created elaborate rites of revelation in the caves of Lascaux and Altimira. There, in the solitary depths and absolute stillness, lights would suddenly flare and those being initiated would see a hidden realm of spirit and imagination. Images of soaring birds and powerful horses would appear deep inside the earth, along with bird-men and animals as spirits, as if to demonstrate the depth of power and imagination inside each person. All that can be seen upon the ancient walls may also be found in the hearts of mankind, for the human heart is extravagant and has always carried mysteries capable of erupting with beauty as well as danger.

Paintings and carvings on hidden walls and bold cliffs have survived the passing of ages and the rise and fall of many cultures. It required extreme imagination and determination to go deep into the core of the earth, and extreme care went into the creation of radical visions as the otherworld suddenly appeared from the dead darkness. A sense of the elaborate relationships between light and dark, life and death, art and ritual appears in structures like New Grange in Ireland. The old stone structure was built so exactly that the light of the sun at the reach of the Winter Solstice pours through a hole, and travels along a narrow walkway to flood the ancient sanctuary with the first light of a new year and light up ancient designs on the walls. All at once the sun speaks with new light from its point of farthest decline and sends its message of renewal directly into the hearts of people waiting in the darkness, which can be felt as both tomb and womb.

There is no simple explanation for this event even now. It is a heart mystery that connects the inner expectations of people with the extreme motions of the earth and the sun. Something extreme must occur in order to deepen one's connection to life, warmth, and beauty. That remains true for the human heart, which was ancient to begin with. Each young person carries a preconscious expectation of such a sudden, extreme awakening to imagination and spirit, just as animals anticipate the dawn.

A feather is a light thing, its hollow core filled with air and wind. But a burning feather comes with the impact of an arrow. It penetrates a person and opens a crack between the worlds. The moment when the feather falls is like a flame of spirit entering the common world. Typically, some voice nearby warns against picking up that feather, that aspiration, that career, that lover, that ambition, that gift, that draft notice, that weapon, that plane ticket— for it will only deepen the trouble and increase fear. Usually the warnings confirm the attraction to whatever it might be that glows and shines.

Youth become driven to seek outer experiences to match the increase of inner heat as biological, emotional, and spiritual flames intensify within them. They will drive horses and horse-powered cars as fast as possible to break through to a place of radical opening in the world. They will explore the depths of the earth and fall into great depressions in order to enter the cave of the heart. They will climb trees and mountains or break sound and light barriers in order to touch one feather of the Firebird in its flight. They will fall disastrously into the depths of love and lose all contact with the everyday world in order to feel the inner fires that can suddenly enlighten the heart. In this land of fire and sudden inspiration, the first step is not to grow up and take more responsibility. Rather, the point is to open up, break out, and feel the feathers of the heart burn with flight.

In traditional cultures initiation rites may take the shape of a quest for a spirit vision. It may involve austerities and meditations that help precipitate a breakthrough of spirit. There may be herbs, drugs, strange foods, or lack of food—all used to break past the initiate's usual sense of self. A youth may be thrown into a competition or struggle that forces him to reach deeper, get smarter, or try harder than ever before. As a result the initiate becomes flooded with sensations, feelings, dreams, and visions as knowing voices confirm that he or she is blessed with luck, courage, wisdom, strength, love, and magic.

Later the experiences are told to a chief or a healer, a spiritual man or a wise woman who fixes the blessing in the heart of the initiate and sets them on the road of learning to live with that piece of spirit, that beginning vision, that way of being or making in this world.

For a modern person the rites—with their preparations, encouragements, admonishments, and acknowledgments—won't be there. Extreme events will happen, but not in the context of a ritual. The opening of the heart to spirit may be interrupted; it may close too soon to reveal its secret or stay open to a person so much that they become unstable instead of enabled. There will be life-defining episodes, but no shape to contain them. The life-informing message of the spirit may go unconfirmed or even be dismissed as foolish, too dangerous or anti-social.

The feather of spirit is intended to magnify the presence of a deep inner self and a core imagination that holds the essence of the life trying to live its way into the world. In these moments the mundane becomes mysterious. Everything falls into place, or some unusual capacity breaks through. Inner legends grow around the sudden courage that one displayed at certain times. Surprising insights came just when everyone else was stuck; strength arrived that seemed superhuman; sublime nuances of feeling became a song whispered in a lovely ear; persistent effort persevered while painfully alone and against all odds.

It can be as simple as a youth making the winning basket. He may not even be a great athlete, and may have a limited career. But, for one moment he rose in the air as if on invisible wings and released the ball at just the right time, making a basket as the buzzer went off. Everyone saw what was happening. They were all drawn to their feet as a golden, exploding moment occurred. Something broke out of him and some collective attention fell on him. Afterward, he takes up this or that career, but frequently reads news accounts of games and watches tournaments where similar conditions occur again. He re-visions that moment in which it became clear that something unusual and golden lived within him.

Once I heard a man tell, with exquisite detail, of the intricacies of kicking a soccer ball into a net to win a game. He became completely aware of everything that happened within that moment—how his body lifted off the ground and turned in mid-air, pivoting exactly so that his foot could meet the ball flying toward him. He felt, and could almost see, the little bones and ligatures of his leg align themselves to meet the ball, change its direction, and drive it toward the goal. He could also see, through peripheral vision, the place of everyone on the field, and beyond that he saw his father sitting in the stands.

He could recall the feeling imbued in him in that moment and, as he spoke of it, you could feel it in the room as well. He's never forgotten the goal or the sense of all eyes being upon him. Strangely enough that was the end of his soccer career. Neither his father nor teammates could understand of why he decided not to play anymore. He struggled with his own understanding that decision for years. Eventually he began to study physical therapies and became a body-worker. In the course of his practice he learned that the golden moment had been a glimpse of a genuine vocation, not the career of an athlete, but a calling to study and work with the intricate movements of bodies at rest and in motion.

Another, a man told of being beaten almost every day by his mother and father throughout childhood. He described the torment of knowing another beating was coming, yet also knowing that the mistreatment would be the only time he would get their full attention. Eventually schoolmates began to taunt and beat him as well, as if he wore a sign that everyone could see. Somewhere in the midst of the torture he struck out in a blind, crazy rage. To his surprise, this caught everyone's attention. In the red frenzy of the moment he saw the fear in everyone's eyes and felt the effect of the power of his rage.

Unfortunately for those around him, he experienced burning moments while when he pounded on them. He reveled in the attention and feelings of power after being powerless for so long. For years he lived the dark, shadow side of that fire, raging out of control. Only after two stints in prison for assault did he begin to figure out what drove him to such brutal rages. When he noticed the same desperate look in the eyes of youth in his neighborhood he understood the cry for attention behind it. He began to work with the most desperate and fearsome youth. They had to respect him because of where he had been and what he knew. He could give them proper attention and he benefited from receiving their admiration.

If the flame of life isn't shaped in ways that create meaning and wholeness, it will burn in the shadow areas of life. If the inner heat of life cannot illuminate something, it will reduce things to ash. Either way, the light and heat of the inner fire blazes during youth in order to be seen, recognized, and blessed. Through rites of initiation the fire of each youth can be revealed and contained while connecting to mythic stories and spiritual symbols.

The feather of the divine bird touches a spark of the divine within the young hunter. Finding the feather makes the youth momentarily whole and holy. In touching the feather, he touches the *numen*, the spirit in himself and in the world. *Mana* or "holy heat" falls upon him as part of the hidden spiritual inheritance of mankind. When the spirit has entered someone, they are said to be *on fire* with it. In ancient India, *tapas* named the inner heat or creative sweating caused by a communication from the spirit world. This infusion of spirit and heat from the breast of the Firebird places the young hunter in a sacred condition. His imagination turns toward the king. He wants to be seen at the center of the realm, as the center of attention holding the golden feather. He rushes there full of *enthusiasm*, and the center of the word enthusiasm is "theus," or god. He is "god-struck" and bound for the sacred, seeking a confirmation of the spirit in his life.

The horse of power warns that the feather is spiritually hot, glowing with *mana*, dangerous with taboo. That which is taboo can heal and make whole, but can also burn and destroy. The feather radiates both light and heat. The one who holds it can receive honor and rewards, or may just as easily lose his head. Negotiating the ambiguities of spirit requires an increase of knowledge and some wise guidance. Hordes of people have confused the power they feel in holding gold or a gun or a needle or a bottle with the sacred condition their soul seeks to know.

Picking up a golden feather from the bird of spirit represents a breakthrough to the place where the hidden genius of a person resides and the sense of life purpose dwells. The genius aspects of a person are not exactly human: the word genius comes from "genie," which refers to the spirit of a place. Genius indicates the "spirit already there." It is not the measure of a person's rational intelligence, but the resident spirit in a person, the inner flame that can light the way through a dark world. In that sense, everyone has a unique "genius" in them. Like a genie, one's genius can generate a kind of magic or it can wreck everything.

In the Arabian story of "Aladdin and the Lamp," a genie—or genius— is suddenly released after being bottled up for too long a time. The genie explains that at first he was ready to thank and serve whoever released him, but as time passed, he grew angry and vowed to destroy whoever set him free and rain destruction on the world as well. Aladdin must have his wits about him and quickly learn the trick of dealing with the intensity of the genius he has found. He must learn to bargain with a spirit bigger than life and learn how to trick it back into the lamp and contain it. If he learns the way of this spirit he gets what he wishes for; if not, more destructive spirits enter the world. As they say: "be careful what you wish for," and be ready for how tricky things of the spirit can become.

In a European version of this story, "The Spirit in the Bottle," the genie resides in a tiny bottle at the root of a great oak tree. A young student finds it while wandering in the woods looking for signs of birds in the tops of trees. He hears a tiny voice coming from the roots of the huge, ominous oak. There is no horse to warn of the trouble to come, so the youth casually opens the bottle and a huge spirit rushes out. The spirit describes how it will crush every bone in the body of whoever has released him from his prison. Like Aladdin, the youth learns to trick the spirit.

The student pretends not to believe that something so huge could come from something so small. The spirit re-enters the bottle to prove the point. The youth quickly closes the bottle. In order to be released again, the spirit offers the youth a special cloth that can turn anything it touches to silver and, with its other side, can heal any wound. The youth accepts the cloth, saves his father from poverty, and becomes a great healer. So, the spirit that would crush whoever goes near it and set fire to the world also has the capacity to grant abundance and heal any wound. The big mistake comes from ignoring it, rejecting it, or bottling it up too tight or for too long. That's the case with the "spirit in the bottle" and it's the case with the spirit of the youth of any culture.

Young people pick up burning feathers regardless of the warning of their elders; they rub the lamps and pop open the bottles of spirit. That's the job of youth: to get into trouble with the spirits of life. In doing so they become exposed to great dangers and to shining gifts. The gifts include the capacity to create abundance and the ability to heal wounds. The dangers include becoming caught in ancient rages of the spirit and confusing the spirit in the bottle with substances that simply get a person *high*. There are no guarantees, no insurance plans, and no turning back once we touch the place of genius. Trouble, fear, and the heat of passions are signs that some spirit is near and warnings that the time has come to learn the tricks and skills required to handle the resident genies of our lives.

In terms of the Firebird story, picking up the feather at the edge awakens the king at the center of the psychic realm. The king's command for a greater exposure to the Firebird is also a demand that the youth embrace his genius fully. When the young hunter carries the burning feather into the hall of the king, he enters a rite of passage that will send him back and forth between the demands of the king and the guidance and resources of the horse. He will be torn by desire and power, by the contraries and dualities of the spirit.

From the king at the center comes extravagant desires, demands, and threats of death if the hunter doesn't rise to fulfill the longings of life. From the horse comes advice that limits the emotions stirred up by the king and strategies to keep the young hunter from losing his head altogether.

The king sits in the place of expanding desire, while the horse holds the place of deepening skills and resources. They can also be seen as the hot and the cool poles of the youth's psyche. The king keeps firing up the hunter with ambition and driving him to further extremes, while the horse awakens innate instincts and strategies for survival. The king makes it now or never and all or nothing, "Either bring me the entire bird, the whole thing, or your head will come off." The horse advises, "One step at a time," for "the trouble is not now, the trouble is before you."

While the king gives orders, the horse gives a sense of order. The horse part of the psyche has been through all this before and gleaned knowledge from the experience. The horse of many powers can see trouble coming and provide strategies to meet each ordeal the young hunter encounters. The horse also helps contain the torrent of emotions released each time the hunter finds himself in a seemingly impossible situation. The horse has its own powers and resources. Its horse sense and instinctive wisdom represents another aspect of spirit: both one's inner spirit and the helping spirit of the world. Mythic tales are populated by symbolic animals that help shape the raw emotions and guide the energies of life. The horse has a mentoring sense of how to use genius and the inner gifts it brings.

The horse carries the sense that the whole situation and the whole psyche needs to become more grounded and capable of withstanding the intensity and longing inherent in the human soul. One initiation simply qualifies a person for another; each step on the paths of spirit opens a greater and deeper test.

CHAPTER 16

LITIMA: THE INNER HEAT

O N THE STREET CORNER where my friends and I hung out for hours and days and years, a volatile energy would accumulate around us like an atmosphere. Being on the corner made instinctive sense to us. It was a crossroads where the parade of life passed before us and it reflected our need to find direction in life. You could feel the intensity but you couldn't predict the which direction it might take. Everything could change at any moment, fired up by the smallest incident or even by a single word spoken.

Sometimes we were all readiness and edges; at other moments we became strangely dependent on an accident or a sudden inspiration in order to move. If nothing moved us, we simply hung out, like a crew on a becalmed ship waiting for a wind to rise. It was as though we were waiting for the arrival of the Firebird or instructions from the horse of power or commands from a king.

The inner heat might turn us into an a cappella singing group, and we would look for a subway or hallway to serve as a resonating chamber. The dark stairs leading to the underground were irresistible. There, between the ear-tearing, mind-wrenching passage of subway trains, we sang harmonies, bringing a kind of light to that underworld. We would become lost in the harmonies of songs and the little dreams they evoked, singing our way through the images and emotions in one song after another. Love songs expressed losses and longings we felt but could not understand. Early rock and roll and bluesy jazz allowed us to sing out inner conflicts and announce rebellious drives. At times we made harmonies of our conflicts, at other times we made conflicts where life seemed too dull or predictable.

We felt separate from the mundane march of life through the subways and the streets. We were at the crossroads and on the edge, yet we needed to be seen by the people passing by. We were posing, singing in public, and we were dressed to draw attention. We became heated and volatile if anyone questioned us, yet we needed to get something out of us and into the cultural air. Hanging out on the corner was like being on the edge of the village; singing in the subway was a way to visit the underworld; and roaming the streets was an unconscious and ongoing experiment with the spirits of life.

Our outer cool was a covering for an ongoing inner dance of constantly changing emotions and sudden crises of the spirit. Someone would arrive at the casual gathering on the corner angry at a parent, a cop, a store owner, or some rival, and ignite everyone's anger. The corner would turn red with activity. Boasting, cursing, and threatening would erupt. We would push each physically and emotionally like a football team before a game. Lethargy would turn into a frenetic dance. The outcome might be a simple show of anger that overthrew garbage cans or broke some windows, or become a fight with outsiders, or even a battle within the group.

If we had worn red cloth, or had painted intricate, black patterns on our limbs and woven feathers into our hair, if we had been standing on one leg and leaning on tall spears, like initiates in Uganda, we would have looked even more like how we felt. The feathers and painted designs would have expressed our affinity with the Firebird's song and flight. The spears would have shown our instinctive willingness to fight or defend something.

For us the corner was a place of song and battle. Without knowing it, we stood like the youthful warriors of the Red Branch in Ireland, who were set along the borders of a province. When a stranger came along, they were offered a choice: Would you like a poem or a battle? In the intensity of youthful spirits things can go either way—burst into song or break into battle. The beauty of the song and the edge of the spear are forged in the same place.

Without knowing why, we found and made ambiguous, asocial places in which to display ourselves. We explored the edges of our culture and found marginal areas within the landscape of the city. We blindly enacted the inevitable fight and flight experiment of youth criss-crossing the borders of the unknown.

The desire, courage, and recklessness required for seeking the gifts of spirit are an inheritance of the human soul. Wherever young people gather, innate longings also gather and intensify. The Gisu tribe in Uganda calls the awakening spirit in young people *Litima*. To them, Litima is the inner, eruptive emotion peculiar to the masculine part of things that can be the source of quarrels, ruthless competition, possessiveness, power-driveness, and brutality. Yet it also can be the source of independence, courage, upstandingness, protection, and meaningful ideals.

Litima names and describes the willful and natural emotional force that fuels the process of becoming an individual. It is the source of the desire for initiation and the aggression necessary to undergo radical change. Like the burning, golden feather, Litima is ambiguous. Like the feather, it has two sides, for when left unguided, the source of independence and high ideals can also become a conflagration of ruthlessness and brutality.

The inner force that expects to be initiated is both powerful and undetermined. Seen through this lens, it appears as masculine in tone and eruptive in style. The Firebird depicts such an ambiguous eruption: when it approaches the waves crash, the very trees shake and tremble. There's violence about and everything else falls to silence. Similarly, societies that attended to the initiation of youth often required that everything else come to a halt as the time of the rites approached. Important questions hang in the air: Will this generation of youth find a connection to spiritual meaning and beauty that can lift the flames of Litima to the high emotions and ideals needed to keep the light at the center of the tribe burning? Or will they become a lost generation of competitive, greedy, power-driven people? They knew that when the vital questions and burning issues are denied or avoided, the eruptive inner forces automatically move toward disrespect for life, egotism, possessiveness, violence and brutality.

Cultures that provide initiations offer forms within which the raw emotions and sudden spirits of youth can find channels for meaningful expression. In each individual case, the emotional body and raw Litima characteristic of youth must be revealed, tested, and educated. As we saw earlier, to educate means to lead out, to educe, to elicit, even to extract something. Litima is an ancient reference to that something—both the capacity to erupt in violence and the capacity to courageously defend others, the aggression that destroys things and the force that can create and protect life.

Litima describes a spirit characteristic of youthful exploits as well as a vital energy regenerated during the challenges and disasters of later life. It is volatile and asocial. It can disrupt, create friction, throw sparks, and blow smoke. Litima intensifies everything it touches and lights up what hides in the shadow areas of the individual, the family, and society. The red and black colors often worn during rites of passage seem to indicate that the road of self-revelation begins in flames and shadows, continues amidst tears and smoke, and can produce illumination or ashes.

All the old tribes realized this and knew that the arts of life had to be used to contain the wild energies of youth and the urge to battle. Many traditions developed dances that intentionally provoked the emotions and inspirations moving through the youth. Feathers and fire and leaping into the air were common elements of the displays. Initiates would dance for longer and longer periods, leaping higher and higher and falling into ecstasies and exhaustion. The steps from childhood to adulthood were danced out while the emotions and spirits of the youth were encouraged and indulged, just as those of infants are.

Adolescence involves a return to the womb before entering the great road of life—not the physical womb of the mother but the creative womb of culture and of nature. The transitional period called adolescence incites a wondering and wandering as youth encounter the mysteries of both culture and nature in new ways. The word adolescence derives from *ado*, adult, and *lescere*, to nourish. Adolescents become adults by absorbing whatever the culture happens to be digesting as well as the shadow issues that are being denied conscious attention. Although it has become common to dismiss the acting out of young people, they tend to be feeding back the unresolved and unwanted issues of cultural life.

If their deep conflicts are ignored and left unresolved, they become adults who are not ready for the crises they encounter in life. What modern societies try to dismiss as a stage or phase that youth will outgrow is actually a crucible in which the continuity of culture must be forged.

Left on their own youth will find conflicts and invent reckless ways of altering consciousness. Hanging out on the corner or the edge of town, seeking the extremes of life where beauty and danger meet, and pushing everything right to the edge are all part of the impulse in youth to reach the margins of individual and cultural life and dance in the fires of change.

Take away the attention of an interested community, which sees beauty and value in the extreme dances of the initiates, and youth appear to be wasting time. Take away the sense of experimentation, in which youth learn about human nature and the unifying images of spirit and myth, and youth become simply a troublesome source of fear and disruption of daily life.

On our corner every aspect of life was dealt with in some fashion. We approached the edges of legality, morality, sexuality, and spirituality as young people must, but we crossed the lines randomly, being either unguided or misguided. Life-altering events occurred without the focus or relative safety provided by genuine rituals of learning. Where the accidental knowledge of the group came to an end, fear, ignorance, and reckless bravado took over. Our internal conflicts were pushed onto other people and attacked outside instead of being suffered within. We had to act out and emote or become depressed, but our actions lacked real guidance and vital forms within which to encounter our own spirits.

Our loyalty to each other was essential. Through it we felt a shared spirit and sense of belonging. Yet blind loyalty could be proven simply by attacking anyone different: anyone too gay or even too straight; people who talked differently or simply had different colored skin or just different colored jackets.

Looking back at those days on the corner, I can see how the conflicts we acted out existed in the culture as well as in our over-heated psyches. We absorbed and expressed back the sexual, racial, and class conflicts waiting in the shadows of the culture. If you hang on the corner long enough, you can see every conflict in a culture go by. If you don't find a way to greater understanding, the marginal period can easily become a marginal life.

In tribal cultures, youth become the marginal ones who leave the village and enter the wilderness in order to experience their own wildness directly.

This old tradition was practiced by the Maasai in Africa, the Indians in America, and the Celts in old Europe where the Fianna used to roam the wilds of Ireland for half the year. The same instinct captures the spirit of aboriginal people in Australia, when they feel the call to walk out of society and go on "walkabout."

For them, the features of nature hold a piece of mythic story. Walking about in nature means encountering myth and spirit. In old cultures, the separation from ordinary activities and from the previous stage of life was both literal and mythical. It was lived out, carried out, worn on the body, made evident to everyone. In order to become a new person, the young ones had to visit all the ancient places.

In modern youth, the "walkabout" happens, but mythic narrations and guidance of elders tend to be missing. The urge to separate, decorate, and be in the extremes of life still occurs to modern youth. It happens both as a natural instinct and as a sudden inspiration. Displays of long hair or baldness, body piercing and tattoos, or strange clothing or nakedness are all typical initiatory styles that continue to arise spontaneously in youth. Earrings were used universally to mark the shift of attention and feelings in both girls and boys. A ring would mark the organ of hearing to indicate that the holder was beginning to hear in a new way. Through a little rite of wounding, the ear becomes extended toward wisdom and beauty. Later the entire head and body would be marked, decorated, and treated differently to indicate the sweeping changes occurring inside the one being initiated to a greater life. What occurs randomly among modern young folks used to be initiated intentionally as youth became a living display of the arts and traditions of a culture.

Among the Maasai youth indicate the end of childhood by giving away all their possessions, ornaments, and toys. The long hair of childhood is shaved off and replaced with ashes. The search for purpose and self-knowledge must begin with the loss of the previous identity. They leave the village, join the band of seekers, and wrap themselves with black cloth symbolizing the emptiness and darkness that precedes the fires of initiation.

Everyone becomes involved in the initiation of the youth. Older people assist in and insist on the procedures. On one hand, the youth empty themselves of childhood in order to open themselves to manhood. On the other hand, the culture strips them of their positions as children. In this way each youth lets go of the previous stage of life and has it taken from him. He participates in giving it away, and he suffers the loss of it. The death of one stage creates the full momentum for the birth of the next stage.

If a contemporary youth begins to give away valuable possessions it can be seen as a sign of potential suicide. In an initiatory culture, this would not be a signal of quitting life altogether; rather, it would mark the beginning of a ritual departure, a little death intended to increase life. It is the responsibility of elders to demonstrate to youth the difference between little deaths and the big death that waits for everyone at the end of the road of life.

Psychologically, youth naturally become both manic and depressive. They suffer emotional and spiritual extremes, even become torn apart in order to be remade with a greater awareness. Among the Maasai, initiates wear red and black cloth to indicate their natural exposure to internal extremes and oppositions. Outer decorations and displays indicate the bright hopes and depths of despair common to the inner lives of youth.

Since the primary ideas and images of one's life will erupt during youth, the head is often a focus for initiatory displays. The implication is that the initiate's head is also a nest in which the bird of imagination can grow. Maasai initiates are expected to hunt and capture a multitude of birds in order to make a proper headdress. Birds of all colors and habits are sought. The seeking itself causes the youth to imitate and learn the wide wanderings of birds. Lovebirds, songbirds, and water birds are hunted, as if to replicate the intense and diverse flights of imagination, beauty, wonder, and spiritual delicacy of the psyche. Eventually the youth become moving works of art, dancing symbols of the spirit of the tribe.

These *Morani*, or seekers after spirit, become bird-headed and bird-like. They join Horus, the bird-headed god of Egypt, and the bird-cloaked shamans of Siberia. They walk with the feathered braves of the American plains and the hunter in the story when he appears enveloped by the great wings of the Firebird.

The Morani not only wear their hearts on their sleeves but also their psyches on the top of their heads. During this nesting period, the youth cannot touch weapons, nor can anyone attack them. They have entered a state of radical vulnerability, like newborn chicks in a psychic nest. Even enemies of the tribe see and respect this; they believe spiritual danger will follow any who would harm them. During this period they must be nourished as birds about to take their first flight.

In the temporary nest, the psyche of the initiate broods on the elements of *Litima*, the ferocity required for hunting, the artistry essential to singing, and the gentleness required for loving and healing. At this point the initiate is a small bird, gathering the force necessary to begin the fights, flights, and long dances of one confirmed in the spirit. Later, when he is confirmed and wrapped all in red, he will become like someone turned inside out.

The brilliance of the Maasai tradition is evident. Inside the nest will grow the new hair of the confirmed initiates and the dreams, ideas, and ambitions that will be the songs of their adult life. Their inner emotions and indwelling spirit become conscious by being exposed through their appearance, movements, and songs. In terms of our story they are moving through the great hall toward the king. They are dancing within the Firebird and dropping flaming feathers on the cultural ground as they dance.

Imagine if modern youth wore self-made crowns that symbolically adorned them and indicated on the outside what was going on inside—or even if adults learned to recognize in the spiked hairdos, Cardinal baseball caps and radical hairstyles, the mythic and psychic states of their children.

For the Morani, the nesting stage precedes immersion into a decade or more that will be spent "reddening" the psyche. When the nest comes off, the head is blessed by elders using water mixed with honey or milk and then encased in a thick paint of red ocher. The hair is braided, plaited into dreadlocks, and turned red like the burning feathers of the Firebird. Many rituals are worked up for these initiates, who perform leaping dances that grow longer and longer in duration. During the dances they spend more and more time in the air. In a sense, they take flight as the psychic heat intensifies.

During the stage of "reddening the psyche," the Morani describe themselves as emotionally volatile. They make no attempt to hide or control their feelings. Whatever emotion arises in them, they pour it out into the environment. They resist being restrained and insist that they are angry and want to assert themselves as individuals and as a group.

They often wander about free from responsibility. They raid other people's cattle; they steal food for their feasts, and fight among themselves in public. They dress flamboyantly and paint their bodies with dramatic designs in order to attract the attention of both the elders and the young women. They are promiscuous with young women their age, and fight among themselves to impress them. They avoid all commitments so that they can wander and dance and engage in their conflicts. They make up songs, sing whenever people look at them, and decorate each other as if they were moving art projects. They are not, however, just irresponsible or unaware. They also do the heavy work of the tribe and protect the herds and villages.

As the reddening increases, quarrels and displays of competition occur. Fights break out among the initiates, and the young women encourage the fighting. Older initiates monitor the goings-on so that the initiates don't seriously injure others or themselves. The eruptive, aggressive behavior of the young males is carefully observed for its brutal and artful qualities, just as modern people observe sports heroes. The ritual attention modern people tend to give to a specialized group of performers is, among the Maasai, given to the entire group of initiates.

The point is to learn the strengths and faults of their individual characters as well as the style of their generation. Eventually the burning youth will become the tribal elders. Since they are writing the story of the tribe's future, everyone wants to read it and see who the new authors of culture might be.

In contemporary societies we pretend that this behavior should not happen, in spite of overwhelming evidence that it is happening, has always happened, and will happen again. Adults pretend to be innocent of the vagaries of their own youth, while blaming young people for the turmoil of their emotions and the presence of irrational desires and impulsive actions. Instead of rites that invite and recognize the intense emotions and imaginings erupting in youth, an increasing gap of alienation grows. Suppressing the passions of youth does not reduce the intensity of their inner fires, but it does incline what could be a great source of imagination, idealism, and beauty to become seemingly mindless involvements in violent games, fantasy worlds, rude behavior, and addictive numbing.

The concept of Litima suggests that in order to get to the part of the flame that burns with beauty and idealism, the part of the fire that has the capacity for brutality and rage must be risked as well. Too strong a restriction on the eruptive and disruptive energies of youth also restricts their imagination and spiritual capacities. Not allowing messy outbreaks of the fires of youth can narrow their ambitions. When the forceful energies of the young men of a culture are not accepted, those aggressions will become directed at the culture that rejected them.

CHAPTER 17

THOSE WHO ARE BURNING

T HE WORLD is made in such a way that fire must be experienced symbolically as well as literally. People become inflamed with passions, burn with undying love, turn red with humiliation, and rage against injustice. Automobile makers, insurance agents, weapons manufacturers, cigarette companies, and many others count upon the willingness of men to play with fire. Young men repeatedly answer the call to war and willingly walk into the fires of battle and of hell because of a sense that they will come out of the flames with shining colors.

The call to battle can appear like a shining feather from the Firebird. For the chance to go for the gold, to burn brightly even for one moment, to be blessed by a king, or a general, to be admired by women, to stand for something, men will answer the call. The soul carries an ancient expectation to be called to serve something that transcends one's little self.

Even when war stops being an arena for individual battle and becomes a massive and blind exchange of firepower, the secret allure of the burning feather still causes most to answer when called upon. While for some the call to battle leads to a greater life, modern wars increasingly leave a wake of scorched earth and destroyed lives. Fewer heroes emerge and many more carry indelible scars of ongoing traumatic stress.

During the Vietnam War, some charged directly onto the battlefield only to be consumed, literally, in the many fires there—in the torching of flamethrowers and napalm storms, in clouds of Agent Orange and hails of burning metal, in firefights, and even in friendly fire. Others went through those fires and came out—some barely alive, some half burned, many still on fire—just surviving. Others found a protest feather, taking their fire directly against the war, channeling inflamed emotions and ideas into political movements. The war was like a huge bird tearing through the land, touching everyone, and leaving a wake of burning feathers from the United States all the way to Asia and back again. The heated issues raised at that time continue to ignite basic oppositions within the culture, which continue to smolder inside political parties and within the walls of family homes throughout the land.

After entering the military I found myself increasingly at odds with the blind obedience that was expected of me. Questioning orders and commands led to more orders and commands and eventually landed me in a military stockade in Panama. My enforced education in the fires of Litima continued behind the walls of the prison.

I arrived at the prison midmorning on a Saturday, during the time when prisoners had access to the prison yard. I saw a basketball court, so I immediately went to play. As I dribbled down court, looking to pass the ball, and thinking that prison wasn't as bad as I'd expected, everything went suddenly dark. I found myself lying on the concrete looking up at the biggest, blackest man in the place, who asked me if I wanted more. He had blindsided me and almost knocked me out. He did knock the fantasy that this wasn't so bad right out of my mind.

This was his yard—I could accept that or I could fight him for it. It was clear that I had no chance in a fight with him, so I said, "I just wanted to play some ball." He walked away. The guards all seemed to be looking the other way. I got up and played ball, still unsteady from my introduction to the little prison. If the horse of power had been there he would have said, "Don't weep too much. The trouble is not now; the trouble is before you."

Once the gate slams closed, a prison quickly becomes a world unto itself, not simply a separate place, but an underworld. Entry to it involves certain rites that indicate the nature of the realm. Upon entering the prison I had to strip down completely, bend over, and have all bodily orifices inspected by guards. From then on, each passage out of or back into the cells involved the same procedure. Anyone can imagine the practical reasons for this daily routine, but the experience of it has a different effect. The daily exposure was also a ritual humiliation. On one level it distinguished guards from prisoners, and on another level it made clear that you had lost the most fundamental human rights. In a strange way, you were stripped down to who you were essentially. In a prison if you have something to hide, it must be well-hidden.

About thirty of us lived in a large cell with concrete walls that reached to a high ceiling. We slept on metal platforms suspended from a cluster of low walls in the middle of the room. There were few private possessions and no private areas. We lived continually exposed to each other and to the guards. During the night, guards would pass through the open cell every half hour to make sure everyone remained in their bunks. There was a predictable rhythm as the guard came down one hall, opened the gate to the cell block, walked all through the cell with his flashlight, and departed out the opposite gate. After each check there was a period of quiet and uninterrupted darkness.

During the intervening period, the prisoners would sometimes work feverishly, often focused on building a fire. I learned that the primary ritual of the prisoners involved the setting of fires just beyond the gates to our cell. After a guard passed through, prisoners would scramble to gather enough paper and matches to start a fire. Paper would be piled in the hallway outside the steel bars as far as a man's arm could reach. Then matches were lit and tossed at the pile until a fire started.

Once the guards smelled smoke and saw flames flickering against the walls, they came on the run to stamp out the fire. Afterward they would charge into the cell block, throw on the lights, and act as if they were going to catch someone with a burning match in his hand. We would all pretend to be innocently sleeping on our bunks. It was a kind of game and a kind of ritual—another form of literally and symbolically "playing with fire."

The fire ritual had been well established before I arrived. Both guards and prisoners knew their roles. I couldn't help but notice that paper and matches were also key elements of the limited economy within the prison, which comprised paper, matches and cigarettes. If you were caught setting a fire or breaking another rule, you would lose smoking privileges and you could lose writing privileges. The privileged items were the very things used to make the fire.

In the ongoing power struggle within the prison, the guards knew that fires would be set by the prisoners. They also knew that these fires could not damage the concrete and steel box of the prison. Yet they had to rush and put out the flames or be seen as losing control. The fires were mostly symbolic, but prisons make clear how real symbols can be. The guards felt frustrated by the untimely fires, while the prisoners experienced a momentary release from the feeling of being powerless. The fires were also acts of revenge for the daily humiliation and dehumanizing experience of stripping and being exposed to the sadism of certain guards.

Each fire made a symbolic statement that those imprisoned still had some fire in them. Since the primary paper used for fuel was letter-writing paper, two basic discoveries or gifts that define human beings—fire and language—were brought together in a nightly ritual of defiance. I couldn't help but think of Prometheus stealing fire from the gods for the sake of humanity. Despite the diminutive size of the fires, there remained something Promethean in creating them, something of defying the gods as well as the guards. The group that worked together to set the fire by the cell door enacted a old rite insisting that, "We are human."

People become prison guards for various reasons. For some the opportunities for sadism hold the primary attraction. One of the guards clearly fit that bill and everyone in the cell block knew it. Although we had many differences amongst ourselves, there was unity in our dislike of the guard who never missed an opportunity to humiliate a prisoner. Fires flared up more consistently on his watch than on any other. His presence virtually ensured another fire and guaranteed that we would suffer some subsequent punishment. In this vein, a small war ensued that was most intense between that guard and the prisoners.

As wars tend to do, the situation escalated. He would find some contraband somewhere in the cell. Someone would be blamed and lose privileges. More and bigger fires would be set. Eventually everyone lost smoking privileges and all cigarettes and matches were taken away. This stopped the little fires in the hallway, but it increased the fires that burned inside the inmates and within the walls of the prison.

We had become used to getting up at night to make the fire. Now we would all wake up and have twenty-minute intervals with nothing to do. By this time I had made some friends and we began to gather and talk about alternatives to the practice of making the fire, partially to provide some variety and partially to regain smoking privileges. Other groups existed within the cell as well. Some gathered around the big man who acted as king of the yard. Others stuck close with a Jewish fellow from New York who somehow managed to smuggle drugs into the prison on a weekly basis.

When the other groups saw that we were meeting at night, they feared we were planning something against them. Strangely, they insisted on joining us. Soon, what started as a few gathered around one bunk became the entire group gathered in a kind of midnight congress.

The primary question could be clearly stated: Could we find something to do other than set fires in the hallway? Just by considering the question together we had entered the next practice of our group. At least twice each night we would gather for twenty-minute sessions between the passing of the guards with their flashlights. We would have an open discussion in which each man could state what he wanted.

It was an odd congress, held in the dark; yet it was mostly democratic and strangely human. The guards knew something different was going on, but had no idea what it might be. We had found a new form of power: the unifying force of secrecy. Mostly the guards left good enough alone, but the sadistic guard had to know. He would come in at odd times flashing his light to catch us out of our bunks. This felt like a new form of humiliation because it tended to make us feel like children. It enraged everyone and ensured that revenge against that guard became the main topic of discussion.

One faction within the group wanted very much to lay a trap to assault and even kill that guard. They weren't joking; even the "king of the yard" was willing to work for that and less inclined to randomly pound on the rest of us. Many seemed to find a justified target for lifelong feelings of humiliation, shame, frustration, anger, and hatred. They felt if they could kill that guard, they would have a moment of freedom worth whatever consequences might follow.

I was shocked to see our nightly meetings heading in that direction. Many became adamant about the plan. There was no question that some of these men would do it. Several were inside for assaulting other soldiers. One had assaulted an officer and another would occasionally take on all the guards. Another man had swallowed a handful of nuts and bolts in order to be taken to a hospital for an operation that would keep him out of the prison for a while. Once the authorities learned that his intestinal pains came from swallowing army-issue nuts and bolts, they refused him any medical treatment. There he sat each night, his stomach growling with assorted hardware and a burning desire to do damage to someone.

For several evenings the faction committed to killing the guard presented plans to the group. They were as zealous as a new political party with one chance of being elected. In their zeal they split over methods of doing the deed. One group preferred pounding and kicking the man senseless—that way everyone could have a piece of the action—while another preferred smuggling in weapons to do the job.

I argued for some alternative, feeling like a lawyer presenting a capital punishment case before the commission of the crime. I pointed out that none of us had a long term in there, but that everyone would receive a long sentence if they continued with the plan. I argued that removing that guard could just cause the arrival of more punishing guards. I argued that it was wrong as well as unwise; that it was as damaging to the soul of a man to kill as it was to the life of the man who was killed. Just like the officers at my recent courts-martial, those prisoners wouldn't listen.

Not only was I losing the argument, I was losing some respect with the men committed to the revenge plan. It became clear that we might soon lose the unity that otherwise made our lives more even and peaceful. If there wasn't some alternative to which everyone could agree, our strange congress would break into factions again. The primary faction would be those planning to kill the guard.

One inmate who joined me in the arguments against the murder plot was a guy from Puerto Rico. He felt it was morally wrong to do such a thing. He and I talked at length about what else could be done. One night he proposed the idea of planning a prison-break instead. He described how we could steal a boat and set sail for Puerto Rico. I asked if he knew how to handle a ship and navigate to Puerto Rico. He said it must be somewhere to the north.

I thought the idea was off the wall and nothing would come of it, so I was surprised when many of the other prisoners became acutely interested in breaking out and sailing away. It turned out that within the idea of killing the guard was a hidden desire for freedom.

A heated discussion began about the feasibility of actually breaking out of the prison. The walls were examined carefully. Measurements of time and distance were calculated. For a while the plot to kill the guard was forgotten as everyone became intrigued with the idea of a mass prison break. Even those who were most determined about the murder plot would agree to the escape plan if the guard could be killed as well. That was as close to consensus as the group could come.

The new plan became designing a collective prison break, with a few committed to disposing of the sadistic guard and everyone sailing off on the general's yacht. The only practical detail in the escape fantasy seemed to be the timing—the breakout had to occur on the watch of the cruel guard.

I didn't think anything would come of the plan, but rather expected that it would be a distraction from the murder plot and a way to preserve our newfound unity. The plan to kill the guard was put aside as the nightly meetings revolved around the escape plan. When it developed that the Jewish fellow with the drug connections also had experience making explosives, the centerpiece of the plan became a bomb that would blow out the long wall across from our bunks. Once the purpose was set and agreed upon, the ingenuity, dedication, and skills of the group became apparent. Previously unfocused men went to great lengths to acquire just those little bits of material that, pieced together, could fashion a bomb.

Everything had to be stolen while on work details under the scrutiny of the guards. Since we were stripped and our orifices examined upon return to the prison, we could only carry elements of the bomb inside the cavities of our bodies. Once the group began to work on the plan, a whole new hierarchy of capacities became evident. Some men were capable of bringing large objects in without anyone detecting them; others struggled to contain small things. Once the implements were in the cell, they had to be carefully hidden or else everything would be ruined. Some of our evening sessions were spent with one man holding matches while another taped some item in a crack and covered the spot with toothpaste.

To my amazement and growing concern, many actual ingredients for a bomb were soon hidden throughout the general cell. It seemed that the cell was becoming a symbolic bomb that might explode. I think everyone knew that as far as plans went, this wasn't a good one. Yet it incited a surprising level of invention and a palpable sense of camaraderie. Strangely, we seemed to reflect a core idea of the army itself: that of destroying an enemy position or taking a hill against all odds.

I don't know what might have happened if the authorities had not learned of the plan under way in the general cell. One of the men in the cell told the guards about the bomb and the plan to blow out the prison wall. If one extreme of the human soul shows men to be sadistic and brutally cruel, another shadowy edge reveals those willing to betray any group for some slight personal advantage.

The authorities took this information very seriously. While we stood at attention out in the yard, they searched every square inch of the general cell. It wasn't long before they found all the pieces intended for the bomb. Next they began to determine where to place the blame and what the punishments should be. While they worked on that, we returned to the cell having lost once again the privileges of having matches, cigarettes and paper.

For a while we were in there without the ability either to set fires in the hallway or to work on our plan for blowing out the wall. We also had the problem of a betrayal in our midst. The murder-plot faction immediately switched its obsession with killing the guard to a determination to kill the traitor as soon as we could figure out who it was. Actually, some of us already knew who it was. Only one man in there was hard to read. He participated, yet withheld something all the time. It didn't take much reflection to determine that he betrayed everyone; the question was what to do about it.

Someone had violated the fragile unity of the group; we felt the need to re-establish that unity. After arguments, long discussions, filibusters, and delays of all kinds, it was decided that he would be beaten but not killed. It would be, in a sense, a ritual beating. As part of the rite, each prisoner had to give a blow or the authorities would blame and punish only a few. At the appropriate time the man was awakened, brought to the farthest corner of the cell, and each of the other men delivered a blow. He was left right there until a guard came through on the regular inspection and found him. Although knocked around, he wasn't seriously hurt. With this done, our bizarre unity had been re-established.

The prison authorities and guards remained very disturbed and the palpable sense of impending trouble filled the air. As the horse of power said, "The trouble is not now; the trouble is before you."

The unity of our group was founded upon the hope of escaping the humiliating aspects of prison, the focus of rage at the guard, and the surprising feelings of working together in secret. As crazy and as bound for its own destruction as the group seemed, the fact that someone would violate this unity caused a great sadness. In the midst of the awkward sadness, a new plan developed.

In the course of the nighttime meetings, it became clear that the violations that each man felt and the violence that everyone held toward the prison generated intense expressions. There were repeated orations describing the cruelty of that one guard. Elaborate descriptions of the feeling of being trapped inside those walls were offered, even reveries for old times and lost freedoms. The fires that had burned night after night had become heated discussions and inflamed orations.

I don't recall exactly how the idea arose, but we had focused on the wall opposite our bunks for so long that it still seemed to represent something. Somehow I became struck by the idea of using the same practice of smuggling in pieces of the bomb to accumulate magic markers. It wasn't that much of a stretch to bring in markers and write on the wall the feelings that surfaced after the betrayal and when all the wild plots had failed.

Things had to happen quickly before someone told the authorities that we were now stockpiling magic markers. There weren't many places to hide them and it was certain that the authorities planned to disrupt the momentum that had developed in the general cell. The same men who had shown a capacity to bring in bomb parts now began delivering markers of all kinds. We all went on good behavior in order to maintain opportunities to accumulate markers and to regain smoking privileges. We would have to work in the dark, using the markers in the twenty-minute periods between inspections by the guards, and we needed a batch of matches to create enough light in order to write.

Just when we had accumulated a quantity of markers, we were informed that there was to be a general's inspection of the prison. The boat we had been planning to steal for the sail to Puerto Rico was the general's boat, which on occasion we were released to clean. The same general, it turned out, was coming the next day to conduct a formal inspection of the prison. The general, some top brass, and their staffs were due to arrive the following morning. It became clear that between the passing of the guards that night each of us would write what we felt on the wall we had planned to break through.

In the darkness we began to write on the wall with the markers. At the beginning men stood and wrote at eye level, each working with a marker and a match for light. Everyone had to write quickly in the intervals between the bunk checks. As that level of the wall filled up, men began to crouch down or sit down and write in the space below. There was a consistency to what was being written. Mostly it was "Fuck you," and "Fuck yours," and "Up yours," and "Up your mother," and suck this or eat that—curses of every variety written with great intensity. The writing was as furious as the curses. Legibility wasn't very good, given the semidarkness and the intensity of what was being said. But most of the words were familiar and had been seen on other walls at other times, so it was easy to get the message.

Periodically the guard came through and all of us would scramble to our beds. The whole place would become quiet, like a church during silent prayer. After a while, the lower levels of the wall were fully inscribed and most ways of cursing had been thoroughly explored. In order to continue writing, we had to reach up to a higher area. The cursing become more elaborate—you could even say creative. Images not typical of bathroom walls began to appear.

As words climbed up the wall, the cursing disappeared, and men began to write what they wanted and longed for. They described what they missed in life and what had been lost to them. In the flickering light some began to weep. A deep quiet settled over the men and the wall as some held matches to help others see. Some began to thank people as others began to write verse. Spontaneous poetry, which had apparently waited behind the curses, began to be scripted on the upper wall. Eventually one man would have to lift another man up to write. Finally men stood on the backs and shoulders of others, writing with fervor at the top of the wall.

Eventually the markers started running out, words ran out, the matches burned out, and everyone cleaned up quietly.

There was one more thing. We all knew that in the morning we would receive the grandest punishment the authorities could think up. We knew that what had happened had come from all of us and that it had surprised us all. We knew that there would be an attempt to lay blame on certain prisoners. We couldn't allow the sense of what happened at the wall to be broken by the typical pettiness and divide-to-conquer methods. So before the ink ran out each man bent over while another man wrote across his two cheeks the first two words that had been put on the wall: Fuck you!

We went to sleep knowing that in the morning when everyone went out for the ritual of inspection, the guards would see our shared feelings written on the backside of each man. In a sense we became the wall ourselves. We were as solid as a wall and we found a way to speak back from a vulnerable place. One by one each prisoner dropped his pants, bent over, and delivered the same message. Since the general and his entourage were due to arrive in a short time, the guards preferred not to deal with this affront. They simply marched everyone straight out to the yard.

By the time they went into the cell block to see if everything was clean and orderly, it was way too late. The arrival of the general was imminent. There was no time to erase what had been written. The inspection by the general and staff would include the thoughts and feelings of the men in the general cell.

It was a long inspection. The general, two colonels and their staff, the captain of the prison, and the prison guards had to read everything on the hundred-foot-long wall. It was too compelling to ignore. For a time there was a reversal of the usual conditions. The authorities stood inside the cell, unable to leave. They fumed with outrage and anger as the prisoners stood outside, breathing the air, knowing that something essential had been expressed. For us it was a moment of liberation—not an escape, not even a rebellion—more of an expression of freedom.

We were all punished. Everyone lost smoking privileges and matches were confiscated. I was immediately singled out and placed in solitary confinement. But that didn't matter nearly as much as the image of the men standing on each others' shoulders, beginning to write poetry that no one knew they had in them. That's when I learned of the hidden connections between violence, rage, beauty, and truth. It wasn't that profound poetry had been created and the wall needed to be preserved, but that deeper sentiments and even ideas existed below and behind the common levels of rage and insult. Once all the outrage and injured feelings came out, what remained were more gentle, even noble expressions. Behind the hell of rage and violence another level could be found, a release that brought a sense of freedom, an expression that brought water to the fires and tears to the eyes. No punishment could remove what had been seen and felt as we worked at that wall. Any tour of the underworld would be incomplete without that.

Since I never saw that wall again, it remains in my imagination as it was, a strange monument that began in a murderous rage and moved unevenly through sorrow into expressions of gratitude and affection, finally taking the shapes of poetry and prayer. That was the radical ritual that the nightly fires were burning toward. The defiant fires in the hallway became the pieces of the firebomb that were hidden in the walls. When the possibility of the bomb was taken away, the explosion that would have blown out the wall went inside the men and came out mixed with hidden feelings and art.

The wall turned out to be both in the prison and within our selves. The little prison was part of a big war, and we were each prisoners within our own inner conflicts. We were prisoners of war in some way, each suffering the human struggle to make a genuine expression and find moments of peace.

For a short time everything went upside down and everyone had an opportunity to see and feel further than before. The guards were momentarily caught in their own game of humiliation and power as they viewed the parade of asses talking back to them. The prisoners had found an unusual unity and had expressed the full range of human emotions and dreams. In that sense walls had been broken down. Officially, the officers were outraged, but they also read certain parts of the wall again. I assume that those parts spoke directly to them and perhaps for them. When the general came to my solitary cell, he readily abandoned the formal dressing down. Instead, he quoted something he had read on the wall and asked how such a thing had come to be.

For a memorable moment, the Firebird flew across that wall and even the eagles on the shoulders of the officers had to pause and attend to that burning message. It's not that everyone in a prison burns with elegant inspiration. But each time a fire starts burning in an individual or in a group, there is also an opportunity for everyone to escape the prison of raw emotions, blind reactions, and vengeful ideas.

In my mind's eye I continue to see that wall in its different phases of prison wall, wailing wall and poetic mural. I've felt the wall rise up inside myself when I need to break through something painful. I've also felt it nearby each time another war starts. I've seen the wall in cracked buildings covered with graffiti, heard it screaming through the broken bottles and broken dreams of city streets. And I've seen the wall steadily spreading through the culture in the rapid growth of prisons, in the increasing number of buildings that require security systems, and in the use of armed guards at school entrances.

The African concept of Litima helped me understand the levels of expression at the prison wall. The fire within each person is an ambiguous flame, it can burn things down or burn through to a deeper expression waiting in the soul. The living heat within people can become emotionally explosive, in frustrations and outbursts of rage, and it can become literalized through the forging of weapons and bombs. Or the same internal heat can become more of a light, an illumination capable of revealing meaning in a dark and conflicted world.

When the inner fire— in an individual or an entire culture—does not find a symbolic imagination such as the Firebird, it burns toward raw emotions and literal expressions of brutality. When Prometheus stole fire from the gods and gave it to humans, people became as the gods, and the gods are capable of creating and also destroying what they create. Each time a person or a nation picks up a burning feather the dual possibilities of the flame of Litima is lit once again.

THE FIREBIRD
Part II

After the young hunter brought the entire firebird to the center of the realm, the king immediately charged him with another task. "Since you have known how to bring me this wondrous bird, you will also know how to bring the bride I have long desired. In the Land of Never, at the very edge of the world, where the red sun rises in flame from behind the blue sea, lives the beautiful Vasilisa. It is she whom I desire most. If you bring her to me, I will reward you with silver and gold. If not, well, my sword will pass between your head and shoulders like a wind that tears through a forest taking off the tops of trees. Is this all clear?"

The young hunter walked out weeping bitter tears that fell to the floor of the great hall. He descended the steps and went to where the horse of power was waiting in the courtyard.

"Why do you weep now, master?" asked the horse.

"Because the king has ordered me to go to the Land of Never and bring back the beautiful Vasilisa, or he'll take off my head."

"Didn't I tell you that you would know trouble and learn fear? Well, weep no more; grieve not. The trouble is not now; the trouble lies before you. Go to the king and ask for a silver tent with a golden roof and all kinds of food and drink to take on the journey."

The youth asked for a silver tent with a gold embroidered roof, bottles of old wine, and the finest of foods. The youth mounted the horse of power, and they rode many days and many nights. They came at last to the edge of the world, where the red sun rises in flame from behind the deep sea.

The young hunter looked out onto the blue sea and saw a beautiful woman floating in a silver boat with golden oars. The youth let the horse loose to wander and feed on green grass. As for himself, he pitched the silver tent with the golden roof at the edge of the world where the shore of desire met the waters of uncertainty. He set out a great variety of food and drink, dressed himself in the finest clothes, and sat down to wait for the beautiful woman.

Vasilisa spied the embroidered tent where it stood in the sand between the green grass and the blue sea, and she admired it. She came to the shore in her silver boat. From there she could see scenes from old stories embroidered on the sides of the tent. She saw the open door of the tent and, within it, the hunter, who sat silently in the center of the scene.

Vasilisa left her boat, went to door of the tent and looked inside. The hunter welcomed her and offered her old wine and fine foods. She accepted, and they ate and talked and toasted each other. The wine was heavy and foreign to her, and her eyes closed as if the night itself had perched upon them. She fell into a deep sleep. Quickly, the youth folded the tent, lifted up the beautiful Vasilisa, and mounted the horse of power. She lay as light as a feather in his arms and was not awakened by the thundering of the iron hoofs on the ground as the three of them rode back to the palace of the king.

CHAPTER 18

COOLING THE FIRES

O NE TASK FOLLOWS ANOTHER as the psyche heats up and follows the innate drive for wholeness. Bringing the entire Firebird simply qualifies the young hunter to seek for beauty at the edge of the world. The psyche seeks one impossible thing after another as each initiatory event qualifies the seeker for the next trial. The great bird of spirit has been carried to the center of the realm, holy feathers fall everywhere, and the king reveals that he longs for Vasilisa, the most beautiful woman in the world and symbol of the soul. The king, who might seem to have everything, lacked any contact with the great bird of spirit and secretly longed for beauty.

The presence of genuine spirit evokes a longing for soul. In a sense, the Firebird descends into the waters of the psyche, where a vision of beauty arises. The power and heat of the bird of spirit generate a vision that was sleeping in the heart. The quest of the young hunter must shift from fire to water, from the heights of spirit to the depths of the soul.

Having wrestled with the bird of spirit, some nourishing of the soul must now occur. A person can't dwell with the intensity of spirit for very long without some cooling in the waters of life. A person is like the earth, which has a great fire burning at the center and needs to be covered with the waters of oceans and river and seas. Once the spirit of a person has been released it must be tempered with immersions in the waters of the soul.

In the story the beautiful Vasilisa waits at the edge of the world. She rides on the sea in her silver vessel. She dips her golden oars in the waters of life and waits to become known again. Her name suggests "sovereignty;" as she is the counterpoint to the king. Mythically, she is connected to Aphrodite who was born of the sea; Isis, Mother of the Nile and source of new life; and Mary, Mother of the Christ who's name "mare" means sea.

The Russian tale requires that the hero shift from being enveloped in the flames and intensity of the Firebird to sitting in quiet meditation amidst the fineries of art and culture. Since these stories have no timetables in them (they depict the eternal dram that lives in the human heart and soul). Many years could have passed between the flight of the Firebird and the time when the young hunter settles down at the edge of the shining ocean. The tale doesn't tell what settled the youth, only that he wept profusely and felt despair again.

Although any form of extreme behavior might qualify as being caught in the flames of spirit, the image of the embattled warrior inhabits most heroic sagas. Similarly, most tribal groups have required young men to experience the sense of warrior energy, with its capacities for competition, aggression, and defense and protection. Yet cooling the warrior's fury, turning his heat toward beauty and intimacy, has always been a difficult task. One form of trouble occurs when a man fails to fully awaken to the spirit in his life; the next form of trouble results when a man cannot escape the territory where his psyche fiercely burns.

When modern military forces release those who have been in battle back into regular society without reducing the warrior fury burning in them, they violate ancient rules of humanity and unwittingly turn the fire intended for enemies back on their own people. Warriors enter a state of battle frenzy subject to recurrent outbreak unless cooled and thoroughly treated. The fury of the warrior takes a person beyond human limits and past the borders of common humanity. Unless fully cooled and properly contained, the frenzy of battle will rise again when tension and stress reawaken the warrior heat. Cooling requires a reorienting of the psyche at a level equal to the ferocity of the frenzy evoked by battle.

Although modern military groups lack genuine ideas of how to treat the overheated psyches of soldiers, images and ideas for the "reduction of the warrior" can be found in the myths of many lands. The old idea was that those who intentionally expose young people to the frenzy of battle must also learn practices for cooling that heat. If the individual is required to forgo the bounds of common humanity, they must be reintroduced to those limits once they have served the collective purpose.

In Irish mythology the warrior spirit reaches its extreme in Cuchulain (pronounced Coo-hoo-lin), who leapt into a battle frenzy while still a boy. His story depicts the wild condition of the young hero, both the powers evoked by battle as well as the trouble of taking the war out of the warrior.

On a certain day, Cuchulain overheard a druid telling older lads that whoever took arms on that fortuitous day would die young, but would win eternal fame as a warrior. Cuchulain went to the king and demanded arms. People tried to dissuade him, but he would not be turned from his purpose. He took a chariot and horses, spears and a sword, and headed for the borders where he might find a battle. Eventually he encountered three brothers, enemies of his people from an ongoing feud. Each was a hero and a full-grown warrior. The first brother couldn't be wounded by the points or edges of any weapon, the second would never be defeated if he wasn't defeated by the first blow in a battle, and the third was swifter than a swallow crossing the sea. Young Cuchulain slew them each and all.

He turned his chariot toward home. On the way he saw a flock of wild swans in flight. Sixteen of them he stunned with his slingshot and brought them down alive. He tied them to his chariot with ropes and continued homeward. The wild swans flew above his chariot as it raced across the plain. He saw a herd of wild red deer that his horses could not overtake. Cuchulain leapt from the chariot and ran them down on foot. He caught two great stags and harnessed them to each side of his chariot and continued on.

As he approached his own village a report was brought to the king: There is a solitary chariot approaching at great speed; wild white swans fly above it; great red stags run alongside its charging black horses; and it is bedecked with the bleeding heads of three enemies. The king knew it was Cuchulain in the throes of his battle frenzy and that the entire tribe was now in danger. The women of the village gathered together and went to meet the frenzied youth. They went out naked to the waist, their breasts exposed to him. That caused the youth to slow down and lower his head, allowing the men to grab him and plunge him into a huge vat of cold water.

The water boiled from the heat of his frenzy and the vat burst apart. They plunged him into a second vat. It, too, boiled and burst. They put him into a third, which came only to a simmer and then cooled down.

The fury of Cuchulain subsided, and he regained a normal appearance. He was then dressed in fine clothes and placed at the foot of the throne of the king, where he rested. After a time he was taken by the sight of a beautiful woman, Emer of the Fine Skin. Though she set riddles for him to solve and tasks for him to accomplish, they eventually married.

The myth depicts the sudden eruption of the warrior spirit that prefers a famous death in battle to a long but unheralded life. The same spirit for battle and attitude toward death was the original meaning of the Aztec word "macho." The saying, attributed to Native American braves, "Today is a good day to die," also announces the presence of this spirit that would know life by facing death. Because it involves a spirit, the battle frenzy cannot be commanded and it describes a different attitude than the obedience of the soldier.

The braves who know "a good day to die" distinguish that day and that battle from other occasions when they might simply refuse to do battle. The ir bravery comes from the spirit invoked in them. They become willing to die because they are carried by spirit, touched by forces of the otherworld. Those who honored the powerful presence of the warrior spirit also honored its absence. Irish warriors and the Knights of Round Table refused challenges and battles if the warrior spirit did enter into them.

Everything changed when war became a massing of soldiers forced to obey and an onslaught generated through mechanical means and modern machines. And while the methods of war have changed radically, the effect of battle frenzy on those who experience it has changed very little. Once it is evoked, the fury of the warrior becomes a danger to everyone including himself.

The myth of Cuchulain describes the necessary reduction of the warrior through ritual methods for the safety of the very people whom he would serve and protect. In order to enter the battle frenzy the warrior departs from common human conditions. Those who go to battle are considered heroes because their service requires them to become both less than and more than human. When Cuchulain arrives he is on fire and his spirit is soaring like the wild swans over his head. But he is also caught in the "jaws of death" symbolized by the skulls hanging on his chariot. Unless his fury is reduced and his fervor cooled, he will not regain a fully human condition and he will remain a danger to himself and his community.

When the women appear bare-breasted, it implies that they remind the warrior that he was once a human child who suckled at the breast of his mother. The white milk of mother is used to dispel the red haze of the gods of war. One archetypal image and energy is used to subdue and alter another. The slogan "Make love not war" also shows how one potent ritual can be substituted for another. One of the few powers strong enough to alter the blind course of battle fury is the love of a woman. The concept of "women who take the war out of men" connects to age-old methods of shifting the psyche from one archetypal orientation to another.

Water also dampens the flames of war. As soon as the warrior's head drops from the height of its fury, skilled men take hold of the youth and immerse him in water. The three immersions indicate a ceremonial process through which the heat of battle is taken out of the man. Once reduced to human scale, the warrior receives symbolic clothes that replace his battle gear. In his changed condition, much like the hunter in the story of the firebird, the young warrior is placed near the king at the center of the realm.

Several ceremonies are required to bring the warrior back from the war and to bring his psyche back from the state of fury and frenzy. Only after that can he dwell safely among his own people and know the beauty of his own soul. Only after that can he solve the puzzles of love and seek the hand of a woman in a way that perceives the beauty of her soul.

Warrior initiations such as Cuchulain's took advantage of the capacity to enter the battle frenzy yet also developed responsible techniques for limiting it, for the benefit of both the individual and the community. Among many warrior groups, stepping across the line into battle involved both discipline and practice. The warrior only crossed the line when absolutely necessary—that was part of the discipline. It is by crossing the line that the killing and maiming in war escalates so quickly. The same person who can be calm and helpful on this side can quickly do great damage once across that line.

Crossing the "frenzy line" is a psychic risk that which involves the entire community and deserves as much attention as the decision to go to war.

In another famous passage, Cuchulain's wrath and fury are described as a fearsome distortion, causing every part of him to shiver. His calves and feet turn in reverse position; one eye bulges out and the other recedes into his skull. His hair becomes a tangle as a jet of blood erupts straight up from his head and causes the surrounding atmosphere to fill with a red mist. In this condition he's almost impossible to defeat and he has no fear of death. Unfortunately, in this condition he can not discern friend from foe.

Battle frenzy, going berserk, and warrior fury, are all ways of describing inner psychic heat that crosses the line from common anger to utter rage. Rage is a blind territory that exists beyond the borders of anger. On the anger side of the line the fire has eyes, for anger looks piercingly at its object. An angry person will often point specifically to what was said or done to stir their ire. Although anger has a punishing tone when expressed, it generally has a point to make and it seeks to clarify and continue feelings between those involved. Once the point has been made, the fire of anger begins to diminish and the emotion can dissipate like steam.

Anger can maintain its focus up to a certain temperature, which varies in each individual. When the heat goes beyond a certain borderline, a person's focus begins to fragment as the eyes of anger turn darkly into blind rage. It's as if the spear point of anger has been replaced with a fragmentation bomb. Once a person goes over the line the ego structure melts and the fire itself takes over. Most people would rather not cross the line into blind rage; yet, unless a person crosses the line, they don't really know where it lies.

Many would like to avoid the problems that accompany the psyche's capacity for anger. But anger arises when and where a person needs protection. Not going out to the borderlines where anger can be learned leaves a person feeling a bit unprotected and uncertain of their own boundaries. Anger senses when an invasion of personal territory begins and can raise a heat put a stop to the invasion. Healthy anger can work like the immune system and which musters just enough forces to protect the integrity of the body.

Anger can muster protection and can even be a light that clarifies the borders between people. Not having enough capacity and experience with personal anger can leave a person unprotected and can leave a coolness in all a person's relationships. When a relationship cools too much, you can guess that anger is not being expressed. Where anger crosses too readily to rage, the heat can destroy the respect necessary for sustaining a relationship.

A relationship can end from having no borders or from having too many borders. At the emotional borders between people, if one person feels angry and won't express it, the other person sharing the border feels it. The person who feels anger but won't give expression to it is called passive-aggressive. They aren't non-aggressive, rather they are passive and aggressive at the same time; they are passive about their aggression. Nevertheless their anger leaks over their borders and increases the aggressive flames of the people they relate to and live near.

In the old parts of the psyche, there is an expectation that the land of rage will be visited and that the skills of anger will be learned. Each person carries some sense of the archaic warrior spirit within them, despite the lack of direct attention to it in modern life. In fact, the density of population in urban centers, the extended periods of work required just to make a living, and the alienation caused by huge institutions increases the frustration in people while reducing opportunities to express anger, rage, and outrage.

The capacity that could protect the home often becomes a rage within the home. The rage individuals erupts at home and the collective rage pours over the national borders onto other countries. Without mythic images that can give shape and direction to human life and ceremonies that can contain the heat of raw emotions, both individuals and societies become subject to rages and frenzies that consume the landscape and obscure the soul's great longing for beauty.

On the other side of initiation, in the territories of fire, waits the image of the most beautiful woman riding in her silver vessel with her golden oars on the endless expanse of the blue ocean. To know love and find beauty is the other great risk of the psyche.

After his dance in the flaming wings of the Firebird, the hunter sits within the reflective circle of the silver, lunar tent. After his adventures with the flights of spirit and the fiery emotions, the hunter comes down to the ground and sits by the water. By being at the shore, he enters a place betwixt and between the land and the sea, the earth and the water. The soul attends all betwixt and between places: the evening when the light softens and lovers meet; the gentle places between one heart and another; the edge of never where simple passion shifts toward the mysteries of love. Vasilisa, as the embodiment of the soul, is drawn to the tent set betwixt one thing and another.

The representative of the soul's innate beauty comes from the sea drawn by the appearance of the hunter, who has wrapped himself in the fabric of art. He greets her kindly and invites her to taste the food and wines. Surrounded by beauty, they toast one another. The wine has a strong effect on Vasilisa, and her eyelids become heavy as if the night itself weighs them down. Soon she falls asleep and the hunter lifts her onto the horse where she lies in his arms, light and curved as a feather. A single feather became the entire bird of spirit. Now the Firebird is replaced by a gentle, sleeping image of silver-gold beauty.

The "most beautiful woman" has found the young hunter, silver has been woven with the gold, and all should be well with the world. Yet we know from the refrain of the horse that more trouble waits ahead. The youth must bring the beauty he has just found to the king or lose his head completely. What does he lose if he relinquishes her? Why doesn't the king seek his own connection to beauty? What did happen in the embroidered tent? Was Vasilisa misled and mistreated? Are both the king and the hunter treating Vasilisa as an object? Are they equally guilty of dominating and using her? What is going on?

The patterns in old stories crash against the sensibilities current in modern cultures. In telling this tale to contemporary listeners some respond with anger at the idea of the seduction of the beautiful woman. Why doesn't she have a choice in what happens? Isn't it simply another example of the patriarchal dominance with both hunter and king taking advantage of a woman? Why can't there be a meeting of equals and more straightforward proceedings? The old images stir up current conflicts that keep both women and men from finding the betwixt and between places where the soul touches some essential beauty.

Clearly there is something wrong in the way women and men encounter each other in modern cultures. The feminine qualities essential to both individual and collective life have been devalued just as the earth has been exploited. The accumulation of suffering and harm amongst women reflects the loss of an essential connection to the feminine side of the world. In the frequent distances that result between women and men, fear and resentment of men and the masculine grows.

In the terms of the old Russian story, contemporary cultures blindly ignite the elemental fires of life, but thoroughly lack the cooling water of life needed to temper them. Meanwhile, the elegant and creative shapes needed to contain and protect both the young women and the young men have all but disappeared.

There is a magnetic logic in the old tales that can pull one's deepest feelings up to consciousness and reveal ancient imaginations trying to live again through the human psyche. There are old mysteries here, and the old stories tend to say: This has happened before. What threatens the world and causes human suffering has always been there, depicted in various ways in old stories, and struggled with in the ceremonial practices of many societies.

This sense of mythic logic inhabits ancient stories from all cultures and can also be found in many tribal ceremonies and teachings in which the inner psyche becomes acted out.

Let's look again at the concept of Litima and the attention to the masculine fires of emotion. The Gisu people of Uganda place an importance upon awakening feminine qualities and awareness in men. The Gisu value individuality and the development of independence, as people do in the West. But they know that opening the emotional channels of Litima in men presents a danger to women. The rites of passage for young men, therefore, include an initiation into the mysterious powers of the feminine and a distinct, nonsexual bonding with women.

Kinship bonds are woven between men and women and the essential value of each gender becomes demonstrated during crucial ritual events. In particular, the young men enter into complex relationships that include connections to the ancestral as well as to the current society of women.

At a critical point in the initiation process the male initiates wear adornments that are typically associated with women. Each initiate receives strings of beads to be made into girdles and worn diagonally across the chest and over his heart. The beads are tokens of affection from women intended to give the young man the strength needed to endure his initiation ordeals. The number of strings worn indicates the number of his female kin and the quality of their affection for him.

Since the women of the tribe wear similar bead girdles over their wombs, the beads represent a metaphorical intimacy. As a decoration and honoring of the womb, ovum, and genitals of the women, they represent the generativity, creativity, power, and sacredness of the feminine. When worn by women the beads both cover and draw attention to the womb of the tribe, the source of all its people. When worn over the heart of the young initiate, the beads indicate another type of womb, a "heart womb" through which the male can conceive and give birth to life.

The womb of the man is shown to be within his chest, in his heart. As a symbol, the girdle of beads combines the identification of the initiate with the women of his group and with ancient feminine images. In addition, the beads remind him of the rules of etiquette in sexual life. The identification of the males with inner feminine aspects and with actual women happens concretely, psychologically, and mythically all at once, through the bead ornaments.

A young man can receive symbolic strings of beads from two different feminine lines of connection. Initiated women may confer the beads. They have child-bearing status and are considered the mothers in the tribe. They are not the biological mothers of the initiates but rather the ritual mothers of the new generation of men. As ritual mothers, they cover the initiates with the fruitfulness and power of their own wombs, conferring strength and generativity upon them. Other beads come from cousins and female kin who become the ritual sisters of the initiate. Being of the initiates' own generation, they provide side-by-side connections to women and the feminine as the boys pass from childhood to manhood.

The ceremonial beads are an important symbol that indicate both uniqueness of the individual and unity of the people. The beads remind women that they are the creative womb of the people—each a source of endurance and strength, and each one a bead of beauty in the strand that winds all the way back to the original ancestors. The beads remind the men that each was a boy whose heart opened through the eruptions of his own spirit, but with the support and affections of his mothers and sisters.

The initiates do not enter adult life through a simple elaboration of maleness, but through a combination of masculine and feminine powers. The process makes clear that more than male strength is necessary to complete the initiation into manhood. For the Gisu, an initiated man must have feminine strengths and a sense of beauty as well.

Among the Gisu, breaking the beads of a girl or woman is a great violation equal to a rape. Only a woman can remove the beads that decorate and protect both her virginity and her fertility. Rape also becomes a desecration of a man's own spirit, a violation of his own heart, over which he wore the girdle of the womb during initiation. Thus, many aspects of the psychological conditions shared by women and men become visible through the beads.

The initiates receive their beads just as they begin a series of dances that will lead to a public ritual of circumcision. On that day they will stand before the entire tribe. They will be admonished and not flinch, despite the pain, in order to demonstrate their ability to contain fear and maintain self-control. Days and days of dancing will increase the inner heat of Litima before they face circumcision. While the initiate loses some male covering in the rite of circumcision, he gains a feminine adornment over his heart.

As the initiates stand before the older men and the knife that cuts away the boyhood covering of their maleness, they stand within the ornaments from their ritual mothers and ritual sisters. They are held in the protection and affection of their female supporters.

Among the Gisu, circumcision must be requested by the initiates. It is not done at birth; it is only accomplished with the young man's awareness and conscious preparation. His penis becomes uncovered before all, so that even that private part does not belong only to him. A stoic attitude is maintained, in marked contrast to the emotions stored by dancing. The pain is anticipated, not denied, for it mimics the pain of a woman in childbirth. The initiate stands before the tribe representing the ancestors, male and female; the living kin, both women and men; and the masculine and feminine aspects of his own heart and soul.

All elements of the individual soul entering life are fully displayed in his adorned appearance, in his emotional dancing, and finally in his stoic stance during the circumcision. His ability to withstand the ordeals of adulthood derives from this combination of intense emotionality and stoic containment. The ritual makes clear that he is made of the elements of male and female and must embody both to be in the community as a man.

The stoic attitude does not represent a simple repression of pain or numbing of emotions. Initiates are encouraged to express the full range of emotions before and after the circumcision. The stoic moment marks the birth of the elder within the initiate. By demonstrating control of fear, anger, shame, and grief, he acts as elders act. In relation to the fires of Litima, he becomes cool. Coolness is an essential quality of the elders. During this initiation process, the youth learns the oppositional and complementary roles of fire and coolness. He is initiated as both a fiery young man and an cool-headed elder-to-be.

Modern psychology might describe this decoration of the youth as an expression of the inner feminine. The feminine aspects of the *anima* or soul are displayed in the eruptions of emotion engendered by dancing, drinking beer, and singing. Later the initiate wears the feminine symbols over his heart. This makes an extended display of the inside-out quality typical of tribal rites in which the inner life becomes displayed on the outside. Through the creative use of decorations, tattooing, piercing, and painting, the heart and soul of the initiate becomes known to all who pay attention.

The pain experienced during initiation ensures that the initiate consciously knows pain in himself, and, as a result he won't need to put others in pain in order to learn about it. Awakening the elder in a young man's heart helps to establish compassion for the suffering experienced by both genders.

Although the women of the tribe have watched the boys grow up and know much about them, they must now learn who they are as men. The elder women brew the beer that fuels the dancing and eruptions of the emotion among the initiates. In this manner the women fuel the expression of the youths' emotions and also cool them with beads across their hearts. Meanwhile, the elder men ritually clean the ancestral groves, repair the shrines of the village, and make preparatory offerings. The elder men make the outside world ready for the ritual birth of the next group of men. They demonstrate the spiritual attention and ritual care that men must undertake for the ancestors and the living community.

Modern societies have almost completely lost the knowledge of rituals that can weave a sense of shared respect between women and men and bless the importance of both feminine and masculine qualities in their souls. To be modern is to be lost and to suffer the loss of meaningful traditions that would reveal the natural strengths of the feminine and open the innate qualities of the masculine heart.

In the story of the Firebird, the young hunter must convert the intensity of spirit that he experiences into a display of beauty and nourishment in order to attract the feminine qualities that seem to be missing at the center of the realm. Since a mythic story has no sense of linear time, the youth may wait for a long time before his heart fully opens and the soul of the world comes toward him. He can't simply have an involvement with surface beauty. It must be an opening of his connection to the beauty that lives in his own dream of life as well as the beauty he finds in the world.

In order for the hunter to sit in the tent long enough and still enough to attract the beauty of the soul, the intense passion he has been living through must be converted to compassion for his own struggle and for the struggles of others. What the Firebird awakens in the soul of a man cannot be simply for the benefit of one person. Like the heart of the tribal initiate, the heart of the hunter must continue to open.

Vasilisa arrives when the seeker is wrapped in song or in rapt contemplation. Someone asks, "Is she a woman? Is she a part of him? Is she a goddess?" And the answer is, yes. For the sense of living beauty can be found in another person, in creative arts, in the depths of meditation, or in the dance of nature. The woman of gold and silver is the beauty that's in the eye of the beholder. She is the wonder within each soul. She comes from the sea like Aphrodite, the goddess of love. She comes from silver like the moon sailing across the sea of the night sky. And she also comes from the womb of his own heart. Whatever she is to an individual, she is equal to the Firebird, for she replaces the presence of the Firebird in the story.

Where the hunter once carried the flaming, golden-winged bird, he now holds Vasilisa's silver presence. For a moment, the place where fire and water meet in the heart of man opens fully. The change is overwhelming and neither Vasilisa nor the hunter are used to the strong wine of the heart. She loses consciousness and he recalls the errand the old king sent him on. The horse of power has been waiting patiently to carry them both to the center of the realm where it seems likely that there will be more trouble before them.

THE FIREBIRD
Part III

The horse of power carried the young hunter again and the youth carried Vasilisa and all three arrived at the great hall of the king who was overjoyed at the success of the quest. He thanked the hunter, rewarded him with silver and gold, and raised him in rank. Meanwhile, Vasilisa awoke and, discovering that she was far from the blue sea, she began to weep and grieve over her situation. The king tried to comfort her, describing the forthcoming marriage that would make her queen of the realm. But his efforts were in vain, for she longed to be in her realm and riding in her boat on the blue sea.

When the king insisted on the marriage, she finally spoke, "In the middle of the deep sea there lies a great stone, and hidden under that stone are my wedding clothes. Unless I wear those garments, I will marry no one at all. Let him who brought me here return to that land and find the gown." The king ordered the hunter to go at once, saying that if he brought the garments back, he would be rewarded; if he did not, his head would roll into the sea.

The young hunter walked out weeping as before and, again, the horse asked him the cause of the grieving. He said, "The king has ordered me to return to the edge of the world and retrieve wedding garments from beneath a great stone at the very bottom of the sea. I'll surely die attempting it, and if I don't die from that, my head will roll anyway. But there is new trouble as well. Even if I should manage to bring the wedding clothes, I'll be helping the king marry the beautiful Vasilisa, and I would rather die than see that!"

"I told you," said the horse of power, "if you picked up that flaming feather, you would learn fear and find trouble. Well, grieve not. The trouble is not yet; the trouble lies before you. Now mount up and we'll go back to the sea."

After a short time or a long time, they arrived at the edge of the world and stopped at the shore of the sea. The horse of power saw a huge crab crawling on the sand. The horse approached and suddenly stepped on the crab with its heavy hoof. The crab cried out, "Don't give me death; but give me life, and I will do whatever you ask."

The horse spoke, "In the middle of the deep sea, under a great stone lies the wedding gown of the beautiful Vasilisa. Bring that gown to us."

The crab called in a voice heard over the wide sea. The water became agitated, and from all directions came crustaceans of all forms and sizes. The shore became covered with the crabs and lobsters that gathered together. The old crab was a chief amongst crustaceans, and he directed them to move the stone at the bottom of the sea and bring up the wedding gown. The horde of crustaceans disappeared into the sea. After a time the water was disturbed again, and out of it came thousands of crustaceans carrying the gold casket that contained the wedding gown.

The horse of power carried the young hunter, and the hunter carried the casket and gown just as he had carried Vasilisa and the Firebird before. Soon they arrived at the palace and the hunter once more walked the length of the great hall.

Vasilisa however, still refused to marry the king unless the young hunter was put to bathe in rapidly boiling water. The king ordered some servants to gather wood and make a great fire in the hall. They placed a large cauldron on the fire and tended it until the water boiled fully. The rest of the servants were busy preparing the palace for the royal wedding. As the water in the cauldron boiled, a great feast was prepared and all the people of the realm gathered.

Everything was ready at once; the water came to a seething boil just as the wedding feast was ready. The hunter said to himself, "Now this is trouble. Why did I ever pick up the flaming feather of the Firebird? Why did I not heed my horse?" Remembering the horse of power, he said to the king, "Presently I shall die in the heat of the fire. I only request that I may see my horse once more before my death." Because of deeds accomplished, the king granted his last wish.

Once again the young hunter left the palace weeping tears that fell to the ground of the great hall. He descended the steps to where the horse was waiting in the courtyard. "Why do you weep now?" asked the horse.

"I weep because the king has ordered that I be boiled to death in a cauldron already heated and ready. I weep because you and I will never more see the green trees pass above us and the ground disappearing beneath our feet as we race between earth and sky."

"Fear not, weep not," said the horse. "When they take you to the cauldron, do not hesitate; for if you hesitate you will be lost. Rather, run forward and leap into the water yourself!"

The hunter ascended the stairs and entered the hall. When the servants came for him, he ran forward and leapt into the seething cauldron. Twice he disappeared under the boiling waters. Then, suddenly, he leapt from the seething cauldron. All stood amazed at the sight, for not only had the youth survived but he stood before them more handsome than before and imbued with a beautiful glow.

The king thought it a miracle and, seeing the beauty of the hunter, he wanted to bathe in the cauldron himself. He plunged into the seething waters and was boiled to death in a moment. Afterward he was buried. In the meantime, the wedding feast was waiting and all the people remained gathered at the center of the realm. The great hall was prepared for the wedding of a queen and a king. What else could happen? The beautiful Vasilisa celebrated the wedding ceremony with the hunter. They became the new rulers of the realm and they lived long and brought beauty and love to the land and a sense of meaning and nobility to the people.

CHAPTER 19

LEAPING INTO THE CAULDRON

V ASILISA FINDING HERSELF AT THE CENTER of the realm and
expected to marry the king, laments the loss of the freedom she
knew when she rode in her silver ship unbounded and unrestricted. She will
only marry and cease her lament when her wedding gown has been brought
from the depths of the sea. She will ride in a silver boat with golden oars
or wrap herself in a gown of gold and silver. But she won't remain without
symbols of her sovereignty.

From the moment when the hunter becomes aware of the passion and
compassion in his own heart, a revolution begins that will overturn the ruler
of the realm. Although the king continues to give orders, an essential shift
has occurred that makes the woman of the soul the ruling force of the story.
Vasilisa replaces the king, yet her desires and commands are just as extreme
as his once were. For the human soul seeks to unite the opposites whether
they appear as the heights and depths, the masculine and the feminine or
the birds and the crustaceans. An uncommon longing inhabits the heart of
each person's heart.

The gown cannot be a common wedding dress, but one woven of the
silver threads of the moon and golden threads of the sun. It must be brought
from where it has fallen in the deepest depths of the waters of the soul.
When symbols of sovereignty and unity become lost, they are often found
in the lowest place. In some stories, a golden crown has fallen to the bottom

of a lake, or a gold ring representing union surfaces in the mouth of a fish. The realm had lacked the renewing energy of the Firebird, but behind that lack was the deeper-down longing for symbols of unity lost in the oceans of time. Just as the golden feather turned the realm in a new direction, the gown is necessary for the transformation of the realm to continue.

If the king demanded one extreme, Vasilisa required the other. If the hunter became a man made by fire. Can he also be made through water? If he has been touched by the source of the sun, can he also embody the moon? Once the psyche opens to the task of fully becoming oneself, it would go all the way. The soul, being a microcosm of the great cosmic song, would know the heights as well as the depths. Once the path of initiating the self has been undertaken, there is not turning back, for the soul would go all the way and know the way completely.

The hunter has become a seeker after wholeness. He has worn his passions on the outside in the burning cloak of the firebird. He has gone directly into the fire and brought a radiant heat to the center of the great hall. Can he now move sideways like the crab and learn to descend to the depths of the psyche where darkness and pressure grow? Can he learn the slowness of deep waters? Can he tolerate great pressure and shape a shell that will protect others from his otherwise-burning passions? Or can he find another way?

In the architecture of the story, the garment of fiery feathers must be matched by the silver and gold gown from the dark waters; the lowly crab must be seen as ruler of its realm just as the Firebird rules above the earth. The soaring of the Firebird is balanced by the depth and stillness of the very bottom of the sea. For the realm to be remade through the tests of spirit, the symbols of both masculinity and femininity must be brought to the center and made conscious. The hunter must carry the gown of sovereignty to the court at the center of the realm, just as the Gisu initiate must stand in the midst of his community wearing womb-beads woven by women over his heart.

This common world is ruled by time. Yet it is often out of touch with eternity, time's uncommon source. The gown of sovereignty and the Firebird cloak keep getting lost in the narrowing circles of time's dull rule. The old people knew that each generation had to search for and find again meaningful symbols of the great energies of life. The rituals intended to carry boys and girls into adulthood were a means of reweaving the mantles of sovereignty, thereby awakening and shaping the nobility of the next generation, the new rulers of society.

The royal wedding involves a symbolic union through which the entire world becomes remade and regenerated symbolically through fire and water, sun and moon, male and female. Each wedding ceremony reflects the reuniting of the opposites of life and symbolizes the potential unity within an individual, between a woman and a man and between the gender groups as carriers of the creative and procreative energies of life ongoing.

In many ways the uneasy distances between women and men so characteristic in modern societies can be viewed as the separation and ordeal stages of a lengthy collective initiation, a prelude to a reunion that requires the rediscovery of the ancient symbols of sovereignty. That which can heal and make whole must be searched for again and again. What's lost at the center can only be found at the edges of what is currently known and in the depths beyond common opinions. If separation and loss can be seen as initiatory openings, then unions and reunions become more possible as the underlying longing for the marriage of genders grows again.

Once, at a conference with approximately fifty women and fifty men in attendance, the idea arose to separate the women and men into different camps. There was a camp across the lake from where we first gathered, and enough canoes to carry half the group in a single crossing. Once the opportunity for such an experiment became clear, the question became who should go and who should stay?

If the men took the canoes and left, would that not simply repeat the usual pattern of men leaving, once again going off to work, off to war, off to hunt, while the women were left at home? Would women feel abandoned and rejected all over again? On the other hand, if the women had the canoes and left the men behind, would they feel better? Should the men experience that, for a change? Would the men benefit from such a reversal of common patterns or simply worry about the women on the unknown side of the lake?

In trying to decide, the members of the group expressed an almost endless array of opinions and interpretations. In the end the women decided to stay at the first camp. They liked it and didn't want to spend valuable time traveling. So the men pushed off in canoes, forming random groups, learning to paddle in rhythm with each other, and heading toward the unknown.

The separation lasted several days, during which time each group worked on issues pertinent to its gender. Even before the time came to reunite, both groups had realized that the separation had increased everyone's sense of loneliness and loss. The waters between seemed to carry a sense of longing as sad waves lapped against the shores of each camp. Yet each had also experienced some of the joys of being separate. All had noticed that language became more direct and more certain in groups of all one gender. Certain issues became more readily focused and more thoroughly explored in the absence of the other gender.

On both sides, a desire for some ceremony of reunion and sharing had been growing like an undertow below the separate camps. Once the groups met on the ground of the original camp someone suggested forming concentric circles, with all the members of one gender in the center and the other group in rings around them. The inner group could speak while the outer group listened and then the positions could be reversed.

Of course, we had to discuss the issue of which group should speak first and which should listen. Each side found both positive and negative aspects to going first. Eventually it was decided that the men would speak first and the women would listen—or that the women would listen first while the men spoke. For a while it was like that; everything had to be said twice, as if two languages were required.

The men sat on the floor in a cluster of concentric circles and the women sat in larger rings around them. There was to be no dialogue, but those in the center would speak out what they felt while those on the outer rings simply listened and reflected within themselves. The men began to speak into the fragile silence. The separation and the separate work brought out many thoughts and feelings. Concerns and complaints were expressed, some deeply personal, some more collective in nature.

At times there was weeping which seeped through all the surrounding rings. But there was also screaming rage—rages that went all the way back to childhood as mothers seemed to attend as an invisible ring around the groups. In contrast, a man expressed careful, heartfelt gratitude to a wife who stuck with him through dark times and was present somewhere in the ring of women. There was deep anguish over what children and particularly daughters would experience in the current chaos of the world. As the sense of deep feelings grew, many women began to weep, pushed to tears by the emotions arising from the men. As the telling continued, the weeping grew in both groups as some shared wound was delicately being opened between. Throughout the entire presentation, not one woman spoke. When a long silence eventually prevailed, it became time to change places.

The women moved to the center and sat in close circles, their knees touching. The men readily gathered around them; clearly everyone felt closer together. As the women began to express their feelings about men and make statements to them, a completely different thing happened. The men could not stop themselves from answering. Men blurted out corrections or elaborated upon what women said. It was shocking.

In order for the women to continue, the men actually had to keep each other from bursting out with some statement of disagreement or even of agreement. The event was almost broken by the inability of many men to simply remain still and listen to what each woman had to say. Had the men not locked arms and held onto each other, becoming as one encircling body, the women would have stopped speaking altogether.

The men held each other in check, and the women were able to say all they wished to say. Things that an individual man had great difficulty hearing from a woman had to be listened to as part of the group. Once again, a wide range of emotions—from anger to rage, from great fears to soft tenderness—arose from the central group. Caring things were said about specific individuals, and about the men as a group.

Afterward it was clear that the men were more shocked by their inability to listen quietly than women were. Many women said they frequently experienced exactly that reaction in private with a man. Some men tried to explain that they just couldn't help themselves; words came bursting from their mouths before they knew they were going to speak. Several men said that although they tended to silence in their private relationships, suddenly they found themselves impulsively speaking out in this group.

In the end everyone found it valuable to hear what the other side had to say. It wasn't that everything expressed had been accurate, meaningful, beautiful, or even absolutely truthful. The importance of the event came from the careful listening happening within the atmosphere of charged emotions and mutual risk. The ritual of listening opened another ear inside, an inner ear intrigued by what the other gender group might feel and know and say.

The reunion required a full expression from each group as both women and men contributed fire and water to the invisible cauldron at the center. Desire, demands, accusations, grief, and losses came from both sides. Eventually the fearful feelings diminished, the angers were soothed by being heard, and gentle feelings began to grow.

In order to shape a genuine reunion both fire and water—inherent intensities of the genders as well as the innate ways of caring—must be used. At this conference we used art and little rituals to form connections within and across genders. We sang and danced and talked. Stories were told and interpreted in many different ways. Without artful connections to others of the same gender, it becomes more difficult to open the inner ear of sympathy.

When honestly connected side-by-side, men can act as the horse of power for one another. Without that kind of connection, men tend to feel isolated and overly threatened when women have the need to vent their frustrations about life. With a steadying presence nearby, a man can more readily hear what's being said in the circle of women and can also hear what's being called for by the woman in his soul.

If a man hasn't learned to sit within the tent of his own heart, he won't hear the struggles of others with his inner ear. If a man can't imagine a connection to "the most beautiful woman" floating in her silver and gold boat on the sea of his soul, he won't be able to sense the soulful longings in a woman and won't understand her demands for sovereignty. The feminine doesn't fully enter until the fiery passions of the soul have been evoked and survived; but the feminine won't remain unless a radical immersion in the waters of the soul occurs. Initiation can't be complete until the entire person submits to and undergoes radical change.

By the time the hunter returns with the wedding gown, the order of the realm has already begun to change. Part of the realm prepares for a wedding, while the other part prepares the fire to heat the water. In the great hall, at the center of the realm, the cauldron of death and rebirth heats up. The old order, with the old king at its center, is about to end and everything seems possible at once.

The cauldron that appeared earlier in the story of the Half-giantess returns, but at a deeper level where its function as an instrument of change can be better seen. In contrast to cauldron of the giantess, which devours any form of life that happens by, this stew of possibilities could become the great feast that can renew the culture, reunite the feminine and the masculine, and realign the inner realm with the outer world.

As in the critical moments of an initiation rite, what happens to the young hunter at this point is sudden and surprising. Where he expects to suffer death, he finds a greater fullness of life. Where he expects loss and isolation, he finds a grand marriage. Where he expects great sorrow, great joy becomes possible for everyone.

Instead of waiting to be ordered and commanded to enter the next stage of life, the motion for change arises in him. Like the initiates in ancient rituals, he reaches a point of awakening in which he consciously seeks to completely change. Before life can catch him in one or another spell of confusion and uncertainty, he makes the leap himself.

Of course the old king demands it, the new queen requires it, the horse advises it, and all the people wait for it; yet the actual leap of faith must come from the initiate himself. In the heat and confusion of the moment, the initiate becomes the embodiment of life's radical ability to change completely, to shed one condition for another, to dive and die into the moment and thus be reborn from it.

In one sense, he has no choice about his actions, since now every aspect of his life has become focused on the cauldron in the center of the hall. But, as the horse of power points out, within these dire and narrow circumstances, he can still find a choice: to leap into the sacrifice before he is dragged to it. The difference between pain and suffering lies in that willing leap. Pain comes to everyone, but suffering requires an awakened participation that opens pain's hidden relationship with the capacity to truly change. Eventually the one being initiated by life comes to see the essential role of pain like the labor required to give birth to all life in this world.

The cauldron combines the feminine powers of the womb and the tomb. For the one who lets everything go and dives in as if it were a tomb, it becomes a womb from which he emerges better than before. A genuine leap of faith, and any adventure that would produce it, cannot conform to rational patterns or to simple expectations. When the old king leaps into the cauldron a completely different outcome results. At the point of radical change the cauldron holds both the waters of death and the waters of life. Only an act of complete submission can generate a renewal in the face of death.

The story doesn't describe what happens in the depths of the boiling waters of the cauldron of death and rebirth. During an initiation, something always remains secret. What happens in a life that gives it renewed motion and change remains a mystery only captured through metaphors and symbols. Each initiate's experience is unique to them and symbols are the signs which speak both the unique and the universal at the same time.

Since the young hunter came out ready to be a king, he must have integrated the qualities of kingliness into himself. His willingness to sacrifice allows him to take his place next to Vasilisa. In the end, king means sacrifice. When the old king ceases to sacrifice for the benefit of the realm, another ruler must be sought. When the story says that they rule the realm together, it also means that the hunter has learned how to be near the beauty and power of the feminine in his soul without falling unconscious and without losing his head. He has learned to burn with the fires of genuine emotion and has learned to love and respect the feminine powers and women. That also makes him a king able to rule the whole psychic realm.

At the beginning of the road through the land of fire, it's important to ignore the warnings of the horse so the heart can learn to sing its fiercest and brightest songs. There's no telling how far is far enough until one goes too far. Eventually the words of the calming, guiding inner horse echo with sense and steady truth, and the seeker comes to know the meaning of fear and the size of the trouble that can plague life.

In the great hall of the old kingdom, where the hunter has come and gone between the king and the horse, the wild dance of symbols culminates in the wedding of the hunter of the Firebird and the queen of the seas. That which soars above all, rivals the sun, and quiets the forest now communes with that which stretches from shore to shore, reaches to the depths, and comes and goes like the moon. In the midst of turbulent emotions, both the height and the depth of the spirit are revealed, and the realm is remade through fire and water.

The dramas encountered in modern life rarely follow the patterns of an ancient tribe or the sequences found in mythic stories. A modern person may have to gather episodes from various times in life and review them in order to see the changes trying to become conscious in their life. But what seeks to be known and waits to be born from the inner life of a person is at once ancient and immediate. It will risk many scorching fires for its heights and depths to become known. Once revealed and confirmed, the fiery heart can learn a gentler song, one that keeps some soul water near the core.

5

Water of Life

Today is the day for crying in the kingdom.
Today my destiny is too much for me.

PABLO NERUDA

THE WATER OF LIFE
Part I

There once was a king who became sick and no one thought he would live. He had three sons who were very sad. They went down to the palace garden and wept. An old man heard them and asked why they wept in the center of the realm. They told him their father was sick and sure to die, for nothing seemed to cure him. The old man said, "I know of one remarkable remedy: the Water of Life. Anyone who drinks of those waters will get well. But the Water of Life is a thing hard to find."

"I'll manage to find it," said the eldest brother, and he went to the sick king and begged to be allowed to go in search of the Water of Life.

"No," said the king, "the danger is too great. I would rather die myself."

The eldest son begged and pleaded until the king gave permission. In his heart, the eldest thought, "If I bring the Water of Life, my father will love me best, and I shall inherit the kingdom and become the king."

The gates of the castle swung open and the eldest son rode out on his horse. He galloped right down the road, looking straight ahead. He had not gone far when he came upon a dwarf standing on the side of the road. The dwarf called up to him, "Where are you going so fast, looking neither to the right nor to the left?"

"What does it matter to you, stupid runt, little next-to-nothing?" said the prince. And he rode rapidly on.

The dwarf grew furious. He fixed his anger on the oldest brother and cursed him; he thought hard on him and befuddled him. Soon the prince rode into a ravine. The farther he rode, the closer the mountains on either side came together and the narrower his path became. Still he kept going until his horse couldn't go another step forward. Nor could the prince turn the horse around, or dismount, or back out. The horse was stuck and so was he. He might as well have been in a prison.

The sick king waited in vain for the return of the oldest son. One day the second brother said, "Father, allow me to go look for the Water of Life." He thought to himself, "If my brother is dead and I succeed, the kingdom will fall to me."

Eventually the king gave his permission. The gates of the palace swung open, and the second son rode out on his great horse, charging straight down the road. He looked neither left nor right but only straight ahead, much like his elder brother. He encountered the same dwarf at the side of the road. The dwarf asked where he was going so fast. "You little runt," said the second brother, "what business is it of yours?" He rode on without bothering to look back. The dwarf grew furious, fixed his anger on the second brother, and cursed him. Soon this brother rode into a ravine that became more and more narrow. He kept going until his horse couldn't turn around. He might as well have been in a prison.

The sick king waited in vain for the return of the second son. One day the youngest son asked permission to search for the Water of Life. The king said it was too dangerous. Besides, if his two older brothers hadn't returned, how could he hope to succeed? How could one as foolish as he expect to do what his betters had not? But the youngest implored and eventually the king gave his permission. The gates of the castle swung open, and out rode the youngest son, charging down the same road as his brothers. Once again, the dwarf appeared and asked where this brother was going in such a hurry.

The youngest brother stopped, looked at the dwarf, got down from his horse, and said, "I'm seeking the Water of Life because my father is sick unto death."

"Do you know where to find it?" asked the dwarf.

"No, I have no idea," said the youngest.

"Since you've spoken well and have not been haughty like your false brothers, I'll tell you where the Water of Life can be found. It springs from a fountain in the courtyard of an enchanted castle. But you'll never make your way through the gates of the castle unless I give you an iron rod and two loaves of bread. If you strike the iron gates three times with the iron rod, they will open. Inside await two lions with gaping jaws. If you accurately cast a loaf to each of them, they will calm down and not devour you. Then you must hasten and fetch the Water of Life before the clock strikes twelve, or the gates will close again and you will be imprisoned."

The youngest brother thanked the dwarf, took the rod and loaves of bread, and set out for the castle with the Water of Life.

CHAPTER 20

THE TERRITORY OF BROTHERS

STORIES ARE LIKE DREAMS and working with stories can be like waking over and over again in a compelling new dream. The psyche wanders from place to place and, from story to story, like Ulysses trying to find home. The orientation of the psyche shifts this way and that, and the flow of life pours into a riverbed that had been dry. We must follow that flow or else become stuck in life. Initiation works that way as well, with the initiate repeatedly becoming disoriented as seemingly solid ground erodes, the landscape changes, and new problems and ordeals must be faced, for, finding one's way requires being lost again and again.

At the beginning of this story life has become stuck and energy drains from the very center of the realm. The father-king is dying from a lack of the essential Water of Life, and the realm is drying up as the life force of the king diminishes. The only water flowing comes from the tears of the sons as they contemplate loss of the king. Reconnecting to grief and sorrow and the sense of loss within life are main tasks of an initiation by water. Within an individual, the fountain represents the source of the waters of the soul, the natural and essential flow of emotions at the center of one's life. The tears of sorrow wash away what otherwise can become stuck and block all life-flow.

Modern societies tend to be overheated, on fire, and driven to consume life in search of external achievements and material goals. Grief flows another way and slows down the driving horses of accomplishment. Often losses are covered over, grief is denied, and sorrow is suppressed. Economic depressions may be avoided, but depression falls upon the soul where the accounts of sorrow are kept, even if they do not rise all the way to wash the eyes.

Such a "soul sickness" eventually causes a person and a society to become deeply stuck; the unattended losses at the center of life become stones that can harden into despair. Weeping, on the other hand, cleanses the soul and starts a flow to a new direction where a cure might be found.

When sickness reigns at the center, when the king or the ruler of the moment has lost genuine vision and vitality, the realm can have no clear direction. Every light casts a shadow, and in the shadows of the bright, burning stories of accomplishment lie the waters of self-reflection. A person can't soar forever. Every ascent must eventually lead to a descent that touches the life-giving fountain of the soul. Initiations by water involve an awareness of loss and sorrow as the world of water dissolves and wears away established patterns and common achievements. Where there had been an abundance of life, the wasteland begins to grow.

Stuckness at the center is a sign to stop and descend to where the waters of the psyche wait to bubble forth again. Although there are exceptions, the sequence of initiation by fire and then by water is common. Traditional initiations took this shape by first heating the spirit, then tempering it in the waters of the soul. Once it has been lost, the Water of Life can only be found by wandering off the beaten path, by letting go of the usual standards, and by following voices foreign to the mainstreams of life.

Fire, sight, and heated vision all go together. Water, listening, and going without a clear view mark this initiation. The powers at work here appear smaller and lower down; they involve things more easily overlooked or left unheard and frequently dismissed. When a golden feather from the burning breast of the great Firebird falls directly in front of a man, there are plenty of compelling reasons to stop. But when a small voice calls out or questions what normally goes on in one's life, it's easy to charge right on, even if the old aims and purposes no longer move the soul.

When the daily world becomes truly stuck the tasks shift from simply taking outer risks to healing within. No longer can one climb to higher and greater encounters with spirit. Instead the path begins with stopping and descending to the waters of the soul. The issue here involves the flow of the psyche and any attempt to force change will be blunted, softened, and slowed by the dense elements of the inner-underworld. Stopping and listening become essential. Without the ability to hear the whispers of the soul and the voices of the body, life becomes more profoundly stuck, like the older brothers locked in the rocks. Everything appears bleak and empty, as if a whole kingdom were wasting away.

Someone with a fire in their head won't hear the subtle voices, won't find the right questions, and won't see the byways, meandering paths, and the empty places where soul now waits to be found. The passport to adventure is no longer a golden feather but the memory of things lost, of sicknesses endured, of collapses and sorrows, of depressions and times alone. Usually all the other pathways and escape routes must become blocked before a person will stop long enough to catch the little inner voices that question the ruling attitudes and carry knowledge of alternative ways of making life. Even though the feelings of sorrow and loss may be overlooked for a long time, there comes a day when there is crying in the kingdom and no place left to go but down.

The opening scene makes clear that this is not the territory of heroic conquering it is rather the land of loss, longing for a change of direction and a new flow of ideas and feelings. Some weeping is always going on in the soul. This is a reflection of the old saying: Every increase of knowledge is an increase of sorrow. Knowledge and tears flow together and tears become a creative force for releasing whatever is blocked in the psyche and in the heart. Tears stir the Waters of Life just as the weeping of the sons draws the old man to them and opens the doors to the knowledge of a cure. If people refuse to acknowledge the losses and sorrow at the center of life, the old wise ones simply pass by unnoticed.

The road to the Water of Life feels crooked and dark, its direction uncertain. To follow it we must take time away from the regular pursuits of life. The story can't even get under way until the older brothers are properly stuck and the youngest one stops willingly. On the way to the Water of Life, acceptance is more valuable than will, and surrender more meaningful than force. Stopping, letting go, and dropping down to suffer inner conflicts are necessary on this road.

The older brothers represent the existing order in the psyche, in a family, in a society. As long as things are in order, just as they should be, and as everyone expects things to be, it is their realm. The older brothers are committed to the system as it stands. The more one stands to inherit from the system, the more it appears to be the only alternative to chaos. Those who stand to benefit from the status quo don't want to change. Even to say quietly, "I don't know where I'm going," can seem like the loss of all order and the onset of pure chaos. From the fearful and hardened point of view of the dominant ego or the dominant class of society, the youngest brother or youngest sister can appear to be a complete lost soul with nothing to offer except confusion.

Psychologically, the youngest represents the inferior function, a seemingly undeveloped aspect of a person that carries unusual and necessary but rarely used qualities. Unless we slow down enough to allow our seemingly foolish parts to catch up to us, we act foolishly where we could become wise.

But the youngest brother has a view from behind the family patterns. He can see the expectations that were placed on the older brothers. He can feel the sadness that the older ones think they can't afford to feel. The youngest brother can see what the older brothers and the ruling attitudes repress, deny, and avoid. Because he has been left out and left behind the others, he sees the issues people are encouraged to just "put behind" them in order to move on in the willful pursuit of outer life. And it's precisely the weight of all that's been pushed into the shadows and put behind that drains life from the psyche, from the family, and from the culture.

Family can be a storehouse of love and inherited riches. It can also be a source of sorrow and a prison made of fixed attitudes and positions. When politicians and preachers call for a return to "family values," the heart may fill with warmth, but the skeletons in the closet dance with the irony of it. Which family? Which values? For family is also the locus of tragedy, as ancient Greek drama cycles demonstrated. Oedipus was one of many father-kings whose blind spots about both family and state resulted in disaster. Family is the birthplace of human affection and nourishment, as well as a nest of symptoms and fate. Families carry curses as well as blessings, spells as well as potentials. Families involve fixed attitudes, inherited illnesses, and fateful shapes that resist change and can cause everything to get thoroughly stuck.

Rivalries between brothers are famous and infamous; they form the basis for key family dramas in Judeo-Christian source stories. Part of the psychic inheritance of any man includes the stories of Cain and Abel, Jacob and Esau, and young Joseph sold into slavery by his envious brothers. Brother dramas are re-enacted daily in schoolyards, in halls of academia, and in corporate boardrooms. As soon as brothers are mentioned, the seeds of struggle and betrayal stir in the psyche. Cain and Abel are never far away. They move closer when men gather together.

Men working through this story feel compelled to consider actual brothers and their position in their families. Of course eldest brothers are quite willing to speak first, and they can say a lot about being the oldest. "The oldest receives adulation for no real reason," says one. "Not for me," says another, "I had to be super-responsible and achieve at a high level or the whole family would be let down." "For me it was like being a front-line soldier. I had to take all my parents' shit. My little brother could just duck and get by. I got hit by everything" "In my case, I was the point man. I went first into everything, and that made it easier for my brothers." "Well, I went first because if I didn't one of my brothers would have taken over. I was sure I'd lose out if I didn't go first. I still act that way. I'm driven through everything I do, and I'm afraid to look back." "I always envied my youngest brother because he was carefree. He got to enjoy his childhood." "The strange thing for me is that my younger brother reveres me, treats me with adulation. I don't know why, and I don't return the feeling or the affection."

Middle brothers begin to chime in, "I adored my older brother. He would barely talk to me, but that added to the feeling. There's still a distance and awe between us." "My older brother was a father figure. Later, I acted as a father to my younger brother. I still do; we can't talk any other way." "I was the middle one and had to be the good boy. Being the good boy meant being the scapegoat for the whole family." "For me, being stuck between my brothers meant being the go-between. I became the mediator for the entire family." "For me, it meant being most connected to my mother. In our family, the oldest brother went out into the world; the middle one was supposed to be Mama's priest." "In my family, I was expected to be the therapist; I don't know why, but I had to hear everyone's problems and not talk about my own." "I only got to deal with little things. My older brother was the big shot, and my younger brother was the baby. The older one had already done everything I tried; I merely followed him. And my baby brother was so young he needed everyone's help. I just filled the space between them."

Finally youngest brothers begin to tell their stories. "I was the youngest son and the favorite. Compared with my brothers, I was spoiled and indulged, and I feel guilty about it." "Being the youngest of many brothers, I had to be tricky and quick or else I would be beaten by the older ones." "It was the opposite for me. I was the most held and the most held onto. Everyone wanted me to stay at home. I was supposed to stay innocent of the world and care for my parents." "In my family, being the youngest was like being the last victim, the last hostage, the last one caught in a crazy household." "I always felt like a serf, like I would never get anything. My parents were old, and it was as if everything was used up when I got there." "I was just left alone a lot. It was as if I were handicapped, or too small, or too young to be part of things. I didn't like being seen that way, but it made me free to do what I wanted to, unobserved." "Exactly the opposite for me. I was expected to undo my brother's failures. I was the last hope. It was as if I had to rescue the family name." "My father died when I was young. As the youngest, it was clear that I would survive everyone else. I always felt lonely and had a constant awareness of death. It was like I was left in the shadows of my family." "What if you're no one's brother? I was an only child. The expectations that an older brother gets were put on me, but I had the feelings of a youngest brother. To my father, I was an oldest son; to my mother, I was a youngest. I've never been convincing as either one."

Each man has all three brothers in their psyche, and in daily life men often unconsciously arrange themselves in positions that reflect this inner sense of oldest, middle, and youngest brothers. In that sense, men act as "unconscious siblings" to each other and often re-enact family dramas through one another.

A man tells of having abdicated his role as oldest brother and heir to the family expectations. He finds repeatedly himself in work situations where a younger man is chosen over him, while he feels senior and more qualified. Men who were bullied or ignored by actual older brothers also experienced that with other men. Meanwhile, an older brother's protective spirit readily awakens around a younger-brother type, even if the younger brother is older in actual years.

When men work closely together, the sense of each one's position as brother can have a stronger influence on relationships than actual age or practical experience. Through the psychic brother roles, the disappointments and jealousies, protections and betrayals, and generosities and treacheries are repeated in friendships and in work situations.

As the territory of brothers extends beyond the family, it enters the area of initiatory brotherhoods that form the archetypal background for male bonding. Whether it be blood brothers, brethren of the spirit, or brothers in arms; the Fraternal Order of Eagles, the Christian brothers, or fraternity brothers; class mates, team mates, or band mates; crew members, gang members or brothers in crime; men are "brothers under the skin."

These groups have conscious and unconscious initiatory aspects that extend brotherhood beyond biology into emotional, ritual, and spiritual relationships. Whatever the intentions and values of the band, brotherhoods share tendencies to form hierarchies, to shape rituals for entering and maintaining the group, and to find symbols to represent and unify the group.

In many initiation patterns, the initiate is assigned two elder brothers who have already been through the stage of initiation he is about to enter. The older brothers are there to protect, encourage, contain, and inspire him. Their role is to keep him from hurting himself or others while he lets go of who he has been. He is temporarilythe little brother, regardless of age or social status. Youth initiations are made for the little brother or little sister within a person.

The initiate connects sideways to the brothers who are his fellow initiates, as well as to the elder brothers. They form the rings of initiation that expand from the little brothers at the center, through the elder brothers who have recently passed through initiation, to those who are about to step into the ring of the elders. The elders themselves are held by the ring of the ancestors. Each ring contains the next group within it and looks out toward the groups beyond.

The shapes of initiatory rings and fraternal hierarchies lie dormant in the human psyche like empty containers waiting to be filled. Some variation on the rings of initiation underlies most learning systems. They follow the form of initiation unconsciously and include either hazing or honor ceremonies between grades. Modern systems of education adopt the ancient forms, but use them unconsciously or superficially, so that those who participate don't fully benefit. The structures of high schools and universities use the forms common to old initiations, usually without attention to the transcendent purpose within them.

"Freshman" names the novice, the new initiate taking his or her first steps into another stage of life. The "sophomore" has moved further along and stands at the next ring, still an underclassman but looking ahead more than looking back. From the view of the entering freshman, the sophomore seems wise (*sophos* means wisdom in Greek), but from the point of view of the upperclassmen, the sophomore is still wet behind the ears and foolish (*moros* from the Greek implying moron). A junior holds the lower position of the upper-class, while the senior inhabits the outer ring, about to graduate completely.

For the most part we get to experience these initiatory rings in a deteriorated state. Entry rituals deteriorate into hazings, which are often hazardous and unconscious of the underlying dynamics that would initiate instead of simply humiliate. Some of the elements that belong to initiations are present, but the purpose is forgotten and the depths of feeling are avoided in favor of exercises of control and dominance.

The ancient patterns and instincts don't disappear simply because they are no longer understood. Clumsy ceremonies persist because the need for an initiation is indelible in young men and tends to arise whenever there is evidence of a transition or change. Ignoring the inherent need for initiatory experiences simply leaves the door open for further harm where healing and learning might occur.

Gangs of boys will continually form, whether they consist of Boy Scout troops or old-boy networks. Entry rituals and graduated steps or rings will develop with or without societal approval. There will be ringleaders, big brothers, and veterans whenever a group forms around a common interest or a common need. The question regarding groups of males is whether the group will be self-initiatory or self-revelatory. Will it be street gangs or initiatory brotherhoods, old-boy networks that preserve the self-interests of the old boys, or radical fraternities of the spirit that foster and protect the interests of others? It is not the form that perpetuates anguish and tragedy; it's the absence of the outer rings of ancestors and elders and the lack of conscious understanding of the eternal youth and little brother inside.

At one level men carry an innate sense of graduation, an internal ladder of masculinity. The fact that the ladders can be used to descend as well as to climb upward is usually overlooked, just the way the older brothers in the story overlook the importance of the dwarf. The "hier-" in hierarchies does not refer to "higher," it comes from *hieros*, an old Greek root meaning sacred. Any genuine hierarchy forms around something sacred. Sacred means sacrifice and often what needs to be sacrificed is an unconscious sense of hierarchy as simple entitlement. A genuine hierarchy includes a lower-archy through which the waters of the soul remain present.

One of the purposes of gathering grown men together is to revive and reconsider each man's memories and feelings about his brothers. A man who has never felt that he was protected by another man will not trust any man and will not be very trustworthy himself. If a man can't imagine being protected by a brother during a time of vulnerability, he will feel a sense of threat and danger from all men. He will have an exaggerated fear of letting go, a dislike of little people, and no knowledge of where to look for the Water of Life.

The source of what truly troubles a family, a culture, or an individual psyche cannot be reached by the older-brother parts of the psyche. They have too much at stake in the status quo. Families, businesses, and entire cultures get stuck in the ways of the older brothers and sickly, old kings who cling to power even as it drains away. The youngest brother and youngest sister are a bit out of it. As such, they are able to sense what's really wrong and remain open to what would be unimaginable and unthinkable by the status quo. The youngest brother is the part of a generation or an individual that is closest to the source of the core problems and most able to find healing and change.

The older brothers may want some healing but still wish to hold to fixed positions. They want to inherit the familiar, familial castle with its ghosts intact. The youngest brother, on the other hand, inherits the full weight of the family trouble. The third child comes to know the sickness in the family, in the society, in the realm. That is their inheritance. They have been at home when the family skeletons were being aired out and heard them rattling in the troubled dreams of parents when the older brothers were fast asleep. The gates of denial that close over family secrets cannot open until the youngest brother has broken out.

The youngest brother is the part of a person or of a culture willing to try any direction that may lead to healing of long-standing wounds. Walking in the wake of the older brothers, he sees and hears what they fail to perceive. On the yardstick of success in the outer world, the youngest brother may come up short, may himself be a dwarf of sorts. He is not the glorified young son but the one left behind, the one of whom no one expects much. Since no one knows what to expect from him, he doesn't know what to expect either. He is more able to accept what's actually there and take what comes. The youngest part of the psyche is willing to be at the beginning again and able to say, "I don't know."

The youngest brother or sister in the psyche only comes out when all the usual attitudes and predictable ideas have failed. There's nothing left to try and so there's no reason to hold back. The little brother may appear as slow, foolish, dumb, weak, overly emotional, underdeveloped, highly intuitive, or poorly prepared. The longer the little brother has been kept inside, the stranger and more foolish he looks when he comes out. Yet the initiatory road is intended for the youngest part of the psyche, for the eternal youth, the genuine seeker and the "beginner's mind" harbored in the soul.

Initiation requires that the whole psyche enter the troubles with nothing left out or held back. In initiation restrictions are loosened and the stiff-necked ego submits to what it considers below itself. Initiation changes the shape of the psyche so that what appeared foolish, retarded, or despicable is brought forward, reconsidered, and given a new value.

The oldest brother part of the psyche tends to be a fundamentalist. He feels higher than others, elected, or entitled. He has a fundamental interest in inheriting the realm by right of the law of succession. His success seems predetermined by his primary position. He can't afford to deviate much to the left or right because the straight line of succession leads to him. For him, "straight is the path and narrow the gate." Eventually, he becomes such a fundamentalist that he is imprisoned in rock-hard attitudes and superior opinions of himself that turn his imagination and feelings to stone. His exaggerated spirit of certainty leads him to a place where change can't occur at all. He may as well be in a prison.

The middle brother in the psyche shares the older brother's sense of entitlement. He believes that if he stays in line, everything will fall to him by default. He becomes a follower, practicing the same steps, taking his turn, and getting caught in the same fundamental mistakes as the oldest brother. While the first brother is a man of facts, a hands-on, straight-ahead, no-detours son of the status quo, the second doesn't have the conviction of the first. Although he has an affinity for the attitudes of the oldest brother, the middle brother also has some of the foolishness of the youngest. Thus, the second brother can be fooled. He's more carried along by events and by the hope that the eldest will fall out of the picture one day. He may be more resigned than determined; he may be fond of saying, "It's always been this way." He may imitate the oldest brother or compete with him, but he won't step far out of the line of direct inheritance, for one day he expects that it will all fall to him.

Everyone has the two older brothers or two older sisters within. Remember Cinderella? They represent aspects of the ego that are usually the first to respond when something needs doing. They are capable, in their own ways, and even necessary. They keep things going the way they are going already. They manage and repair things. They defend and accept the comfort and order of the psyche or the society, just as it exists now. They keep the main roads clear and oil the machinery of the status quo.

Yet the older-brother attitudes ignore or exclude inclinations to deviate from the most obvious route. As a result they always wind up in the same hole. They attack and insult anything that lies off the beaten path and they can't hear certain basic questions because they are so certain that things will go their way. They keep going even when life closes in from both sides. They are the "ego brothers," the CEO and middle management levels of the psyche. They represent the fixed attitudes and ideas of the psyche or of a society. They won't make basic changes and must become completely stuck before the youngest and seemingly foolish aspects can slip through the gates of denial.

In one sense, the strenuous ordeals and impossible tasks found in stories and suffered in initiatory experiences are used to confound and wear down the older brothers. After we have failed twice at something, the soul knows that this is not another developmental task to be managed properly. The sickness of the king and of the older brothers lies partly in their exclusiveness. The cure begins with the inclusion of what seems foolish as the entire psyche becomes engaged and all of its hidden resources released. Only when we are at the end of our wits do we turn to the deeper wit of the youngest brother.

CHAPTER 21

PERMISSION, SUBMISSION, SURRENDER

T HE OLDER BROTHERS make the mistake of being certain that they have all they need to go straight out and find the Water of Life. The idea that a cure exists is mistaken for actual knowledge of the way to find it. The ego brothers have a sense of entitlement and the wrong-headed idea that being direct and in-charge will always win the day. While it may be necessary to build a strong ego in order to grow and survive in a competitive world, healing the effects of being ego-driven requires a less haughty manner and a more indirect approach.

Whereas most men relate quickly to the idea of picking up a burning feather, contemporary men may balk at the idea that permission must be sought before an adventure. Reactions to this kind of story often include questions about permission: "Why should the brothers ask permission from an old king? What's the point? I'll do what I want. If I want to go after something in life, I'll just go. I don't need anyone's permission." "It's my choice whether I do something or not. I don't have to ask permission, it's my choice." "Why can't I just initiate myself? It's my life to live."

That's the hard-headed older brothers talking their way into another place between the rocks. It's easy to miss the point that water is the missing ingredient, that the situation lacks fluidity and natural flow. Once the ego is strong enough to function it tends to go on ego trips. Following the ego will just create more ego. Genuine change requires a loosening of the ego, a softening of the hard hold the ego comes to have on life. Healing involves a reorientation to the flow of life and initiation requires a disorientation that opens the ego to the unknown. The ego brothers may convince themselves that they can self-initiate, but it's just a matter of time before they find themselves between the rocks and their own hard-headedness or hard-heartedness.

One form of trouble comes when a person does not have enough ego to get going on the main roads of life. The other trouble comes when a person's ego won't relinquish the reins and won't give up control for fear of being out of control. Once established, the ego doesn't want to admit that sometimes it knows nothing. The ego aspect of the self comes to believe that only it is capable of keeping chaos at bay and making a way through life. What feels appropriately humbling to the little brother feels humiliating to the ego brothers. The ego feels humiliated when it is not in charge and crazy when it is disoriented. But for lasting change to occur, the ego brothers must step aside.

Seeking permission indicates a willingness to change; bowing our head acknowledges that something is greater than ourselves. Once the soul becomes involved, humility becomes more possible and the sense of needing a blessing soon follows. The more we allow the soul's vulnerability to be present, the more we seek permission and a blessing for what we are about to risk. The ego may deny it, but the soul knows how often we fail in life. Unless we invoke something greater, we simply make the usual ego choices and soon, the older brothers are back in charge and we're heading for the usual rocks.

The ego doesn't like to admit it, but people seek permission all the time. When we know something is missing in our lives there is an instinct to ask permission in order to seek for it. We find someone to play queen or king and bless the way for us. We present someone with a sketch of something we desire, but don't call it asking for permission. If that person approves and encourages us, we're off. We secretly use their authority to get going. But let them miss the point of our plan or dismiss it as too foolish and we behead them, throw them down from the throne on which we had just installed them, and defame them to others in the bargain. Or else we feel crushed, dispirited, full of shame that we ever mentioned it, certain that they are so far above us that they know better and we'd best retreat to our room in the basement of the castle.

Some forms of hero-worship are also means of seeking permission. We see a potential of our own soul in greater measure in someone else and we study that person. We carry him or her in our minds, even in our hearts. We imagine how that person would act in our predicament and secretly receive their blessing to try. The role model becomes a guide and gives permission without knowing it.

Without permission there can be no real mission. Many mission statements forget that permission precedes any real mission. After permission comes the necessary step of submission through which the ego allows the unknown to be present and the path of the soul to open.

The story indicates that submitting to the presence of the dwarf is far more difficult than receiving permission from the king. Bowing to the king may be humbling, but stopping and submitting to the dwarf feels positively humiliating to the ego. The ego, like the older brothers, likes to be on its high horse and the dwarf seems lowly, weird, and of no account. The youngest brother in the psyche doesn't mind bowing to a greater spirit. He knows that a genuine mission will require unusual help. He can admit to not knowing the way and doesn't mind seeking advice and directions.

Submission involves leaving the high horse of certainty aside. The loss of horsepower can leave a person feeling a bit powerless. But when the daylight world and surface aspects of life become stuck, vitality and change must be sought on the side tracks and winding paths where the oft-ignored small voices of intuition and instinct wait to have their say and indicate surprising ways to turn.

During my struggles with the military I developed a strong willpower as well as an increased distrust of authority. I felt a need to defend myself against an uncaring world. The experience of solitary confinement left me inclined to self-sufficiency. In times of trouble a voice inside would say, "Well, I don't owe anybody anything. I can take care of myself." To me, owing others meant some kind of subservience and a loss of freedom. Admitting to not knowing what to do brought up fears of having to submit to some unknown person or process. So I learned things on my own and felt that I didn't owe anyone anything, although I often felt stiff and had headaches at the back of my neck, right where one might bow the head.

In a sense, I tried to keep the youngest brother in the inner castle where he would be protected, since he had been clobbered for sticking his head out a couple of times. I managed to get married, become a father, and undertake numerous occupations. But something in me did not fully submit to anyone. Meanwhile the internal king was not feeling well. Mostly, he felt the increasing weight of the responsibilities of life, of being a father more than a daddy, and of earning a living for the new family. While the two older brothers were gainfully employed and keeping things going, the inner world was wasting away and the youngest brother hadn't been heard from for a long time.

When the king inside gets sick unto dying, a lament grows in the interior castle—be it heard or not. Most times I tuned out the lament. But one evening I happened to be listening to it, and it brought some good fortune, the kind of luck that happens when the youngest brother gets loose and permission and submission are not only possible but necessary.

It was evening as I walked through the city, wrapped tightly inside myself, listening to a lament. My newborn daughter and first child were quite sick and the doctors couldn't determine the cause. I felt helpless, powerless, and desperately afraid of what might happen. After a while I lost any sense of where I was; I simply followed my feet. The rhythm of walking helped to dislodge the stuck feelings inside.

I happened by a storefront from which music seemed to pour forth. The windows were painted over and the door closed, but music seeped out under the door and through other unseen openings. I couldn't help but stop. I was listening hard anyway, and the music fell right into the place that was listening inside me.

As I moved closer, I recognized in the flood of marimbas and songs cascading onto the street, the music of Zimbabwe. I stood in the doorway and listened for quite a while. Finally my hand tried the door. It wasn't locked. I slipped quietly inside and saw a remarkable scene taking place behind the dull, painted windows. Some people were working on dance steps in a line while others played marimbas and a few played drums. In the center of the musical whirlwind a small African man kept everything going. He showed a little step to the dancers, taught a technique to the marimba players, and encouraged everyone to participate fully.

I moved to a place beside the drums and watched in amazement. I had stepped from my lonely, aimless walking, right into the water and flow of the ancient music. After a while the African man came over to me. In a playful and inviting way, he said, "If you can walk, you can dance. If you can talk, you can sing. If you can clap, you can drum. Now what is it going to be? Are you coming out here to dance? Are you going over there to learn a melody? Or will you play on the drum?" His warmth and charm disarmed me.

On almost any other day I would have said, "No, thank you. I'm too busy. No, thank you. I'm too arrogant. No, I'm too determined to keep pushing on. No, if I were going to learn those things, I would have learned them when I was younger." I would have had an endless number of ways to say no. But on that night I stood in the midst of my own loneliness, torn by the lament I carried inside. Having no idea what to do with the trouble I felt, I couldn't refuse the choices he offered me. I had to submit to his grace and charm. I had to surrender to the music.

Since the drums were nearby, I said, "I'll drum." With delight in his eyes and playful movements of his body, he showed me a pattern on the drum. The youngest brother had already begun to take over within me—after all, it was his foolishness that had led me to try the door to that place—so I had little resistance to the rhythm. Soon enough my hands were playing and, instead of watching the dance or listening blindly from outside the painted windows, I became part of the music. I played and sweated and laughed and listened as hard as I could to all of the instructions until the session ended.

It was a stroke of luck. I had gone from feeling the sickness in my inner world—an aloneness that had been brewing there for a long time—to being part of a joyful, expressive group. I had entered unwittingly and was given a part in the community of sound and rhythm. The youngest brother inside had been invited to come out and I felt a renewed sense of life. On the way home I considered how my tiny daughter loved me to hold her and sing along with the music and dance gently around the house. We were connected through a music that seemed to heal both of us. I was struck by the idea that the cure for her illness might be found behind the doors of another culture and that turned out to be the case.

It would be great to tell that that African man became my teacher, that I learned everything I could about drumming and music from him, and that I went on to greater things. But that wasn't to be the case. As is often the way in encounters with mentors—or dwarves—that occasion represented the opening of just one little door into a big world. That night I learned something about bowing my head and stepping into the foolish place of knowing nothing and gratefully accepting what was being offered. I submitted to that man's teaching because I felt lost. For once feeling foolish did not stop me. The ego brothers were worn out and not paying much attention. The youngest brother heard the music, he wanted to drum, and he knew a teacher when he saw one.

For me the man from Zimbabwe appeared like a dwarf putting a question before me that I had to answer with a hidden part of my life. Had he challenged me in a way that wasn't playful or, had he insisted on something, I would have left. But his joy and playfulness in the face of the sorrow and fears I carried that night allowed me to bow my head and surrender. In that realm, I did not fear that the youngest brother would be tricked or mistreated. He freely handed me gifts and tools, a place to put my hands, and a way to release my heavy load; a place where I could begin to learn and learn as a beginner.

Opening that door opened me to the world of the dwarf. It's difficult to learn about the dwarf inside ourselves and the gifts in his hands without getting near the dwarf in someone else. Dwarves can't be seen from a distance or heard from above; only at close range do they hand over what they have to offer. Permission may be obtained from a distance, but submission requires proximity.

After that, I had several drum teachers. Some were generous, others were harsh. Some I could learn from, others I could only learn about. But to each of them I had to submit. To learn drumming means to bow to the drum and to bow to the teacher of the drum. In order to follow the path of the music, I had to surrender repeatedly.

Healing and learning require getting down, and drawing close to the source of the problem and the source of the cure. In terms of deep change and any real learning, the youngest brother or youngest sister inside must become involved. That part of the psyche knows when to stop, how to submit to the music and the dance, and how to surrender to a greater sense of life. That only happens when the ego becomes completely stuck and the hidden inner brother appears again.

The dwarf is anything in life that slows things down and teaches us through the doors of submission and surrender. Since issues of authority and submission are continuous problems for men, the dwarf likes to provoke authority issues. He'll enter a situation with the rod and the bread or other tools to test people's attitudes toward submission and to open the surprising doors of creativity.

The path to the Water of Life is also the path to finding one's inner authority. But awakening inner authority requires submitting to genuine authority in others. Authority issues can only be solved through developing genuine inner authority. "Authentic authority" and submission go together; there is no learning one without the other.

Working with men and doing men's work inevitably leads to facing issues of authority and submission. If the issues of authority remain unclear, the work will stagnate. When authority issues are squarely faced remarkable creativity can result. Once we held a series of conferences in a towering redwood forest. Each event lasted seven days, with about a hundred men in attendance. Most did not know each other. We came together to delve into issues of the soul and found we were mostly aware of our individual problems. At the beginning everyone agreed there would be no physical violence, and all agreed to seriously engage whatever else came up. The agreement to avoid physical violence removes one great danger among any group of men. But the issues of power and authority don't simply disappear.

Each man was randomly assigned to a small group with six or seven others. Each group was expected to contribute a sense of what they were experiencing to the community at-large through a presentation or display of some kind. The displays served as a kind of ritual designed to arrest everyone's attention and reveal inner states of struggle and creative expression.

One of the groups was being led by a teacher of Aikido, the Japanese martial art that studies the point where force and grace meet. The entire group had been getting up at 5:00 A.M. to learn a practice of working with sticks. You could hear the rattle of their staffs through the quiet of the camp each morning. The psychological side of their focus involved the need for boundaries and limits in their personal lives and in community experiences. They studied the traditional issues of warrior training: protection, force, commitment, purpose, and service. They addressed whatever questions arose. If there was to be no physical violence, then what was the point of martial skills? How do you hold a boundary without the use of force? What purpose does a skilled warrior serve?

They wrestled with these questions and with the techniques of stick work. In the midst of their discussion and martial exercises a little idea struck them—you could call it a "dwarf idea." The group got the notion to place themselves between the other men at the event and the next meal being served. It was a simple idea, yet it set one thing against another and it clearly evoked some basic instincts and an area where private needs and community issues encounter each other.

Meals were served in an old log lodge at the center of the camp. There was no other food available, and everyone had great appetites because of the intense work going on. Each time the lunch bell rang everyone would converge on the old hall, ready to eat, relax, and socialize. It came as a great shock when no one was allowed to enter the hall despite the compelling aromas coming from within. Guards holding staffs and wearing masks or painted faces blocked all four doors. It was announced that we could enter the lodge and eat only after we had offered a poem at the central doors. The poem couldn't simply be read from a book, but had to be made up on the spot or drawn from memory. It could be a song, a prayer, a rap, or a blessing, but it had to have some poetry in it and a breath of inspiration.

After announcing the rules the guards remained silent in their places. It was a simple display, a clear request, and it had the dwarf in it. Everyone slowed down and everything stopped except the consideration of boundaries and the poems.

For most the situation became disconcerting. People felt surprised, trapped, provoked. The cleverness of the display unfolded slowly. We had already agreed there would be no physical violence. So what did it mean that the doors were blocked by armed guards? If we couldn't use force, neither could they, so what was to stop us from going through? They were counting on everyone keeping the agreement and not muscling their way in. But we knew they had been training and they looked ready to use their sticks. Their masks and silence were also effective barriers that seemed to suggest that they represented another world and an otherworldly commitment. We were stuck unless they made a false move, and they weren't moving at all.

I went to a side door where there was a single sentry. I thought I could slip in and watch the drama from inside. After all I was part of the teaching staff and we sometimes had to go to the front of the food line because of a meeting or some pressing demand. I suggested to the silent, masked guard that he could let me slip by. He didn't answer. I tried to pull rank, saying I had to get in. No answer. I tried to distract him and duck through. I tried to think of a bribe. The masked face didn't respond. On one level, I knew every man in the camp; on another level, I didn't know who this man was at all. One of the effects of radical rituals is a reordering of hierarchies so that the status quo no longer exists. Getting to the front of the line in this case meant giving a poem, not being officious or in a hurry.

Back at the front of the lodge there was an extraordinary commotion, a storm of disbelief and dismay. Men couldn't believe they were being denied food with no warning and no chance to appeal. Some shouted that they had paid for the damned food, they weren't about to pay again. Some became outraged. "We have rights to that food," they claimed. "This is ridiculous, it's childish, it's fascistic, it's abusive, it's illegal," they said. Men were threatening to leave, to attack, to go to town and eat burgers.

In the midst of the tumult and confusion, some began to give poems at the entrance. After each recitation the guards would pull back their staffs, and the man would disappear into the hall. The way through was clear if one would submit to a demand for poetry. While some continued to argue and work at refining and sharpening the point of their protest, others composed and practiced songs and poems. It became clear that the warrior group had shifted everyone's awareness with their disciplined demeanor and disconcerting request. Whatever had been rushing through the minds of the hundred men had stopped. All became focused at the entrance to the hall, and everyone either formed a poem or fumed in protest.

It takes a long time for each one of a hundred men to compose a poem and tell it out. Rituals alter time and shift space. The rush for food was replaced with listening carefully. Even those who made it inside returned to hear the words of others. Our appetite for food had been transformed into an appetite for hearing what poetry each man had to offer. And poetry is, after all, another form of food, a nutrition the soul requires.

While waiting in line someone picked up a stone and placed it by the entrance while giving his poem. There was something about that action that felt right, so everyone started putting a stone at the entrance. Now a kind of grace entered into the event as each stood in line, which was advancing slowly up the stairs, and listened as men we could hardly see gave a poem, or the semblance of one, each of us trying to hold onto the thread of our own verse while hearing the attempts of others. One man made a soft prayer because he had realized it was the anniversary of his mother's death. That was a real bowing of the head that took the edge off the remaining protest. Some converted their protests into poems that rhymed and thereby killed two birds with one stone.

Some of the verse was good, some was bad, but it was not poetry or prayer by rote. Most of it had never been said before. The ritual couldn't be explained or dismissed. And it wasn't finished when all the poems had been said. There was a mysterious quality to the event that affected the entire meal and made it a continuance of the ritual. No one who was there will ever forget it. And we never did it again.

That night everyone gathered together for a community meeting and the entire display had to be revisited. Each of us carried a little piece of what had happened and when we reconvened, the emotions of the event recurred. The feelings provoked were undiminished by the time that had passed. Some were still outraged. We had submitted to something we didn't understand. We were still chewing on it; it was still working on us. We argued and fought about it, praised it and defamed it. We couldn't let it go.

The blocked doors and armed guards had stirred painful memories of past outrages. In the 1960s some had faced off with National Guard and police during protests over the Vietnam War and civil rights. Others had been through military battles, incarcerations, and union lockouts. Men had been locked out of houses, kept out of jobs, and forced to submit to endless rules and regulations. Any number of doors had been slammed in their faces and this event brought all the memories rushing back, complete with the confusing emotions involved. The guardian group was accused of everything from a desire to bully to conspiring with the military-industrial complex.

When the group that staged the display finally spoke, it became clear that they were as astonished as everyone else. It had seemed a simple idea at first, and they were amazed at their own emotions during the process. Fear, sympathy, anger, and boredom, had all coursed through them as well. They had been caught up in it as well, surprised by the other men's intense reactions but committed to seeing things through. Some defended the outpouring of poetry and the value of being made to slow down. Others wanted to repeat the entire thing at every meal.

Even after everything was said the life of the ritual continued, for the stones still lay by the central door, piled like pillars marking the entrance to a ceremonial house. Everyone approached meals with more awareness, with a keen eye for changes, and with some attention for the beginning of a poem.

The warrior display had the dwarf in it, for it forced the issues of submission out into the open. The other side of the warrior's ability to defend and do battle involves a practice of genuine submission to a purpose beyond the individual. Remember the question of the young border guards in ancient Ireland: Would you prefer a battle or a poem? At various times in his life a man must surrender, bow his head, and give a poem or something else that displays the language living in his heart. If he does not, his life will consist only of battles, of offense and defense, and of keeping his guard up. Without submitting to something greater than himself, a man cannot locate the flow of the Water of Life, or contribute to the poetry of life.

Submission is not the same as blind obedience, although the original meaning of "obey" includes bowing in respect or service. The true warrior willingly submits to serve a higher purpose, while a soldier can be commanded to obey any purpose his superiors may chose. Too often people are forced to obey rules that humiliate them rather than be invited to humble themselves before a transcendent goal. Besides the drive for success and recognition, men naturally feel a desire to play a part in something meaningful beyond themselves. Yet many people resist acts of submission because of mistreatment at the hands of a parent or authority figure early on. Some kind of obedience was required that was excessive for the spirit of that person. As a result, defiance, toughness, strong defenses, and reactionary attitudes form as a protection around the wounded spiritual core.

Those who don't become directly defiant often respond to early abuses of authority with trickery and humor. Like the wise guys in school, some men keep their wounded spirits alive and protected by converting issues of power into jokes. Joking and fooling helps to deflect the effects of the power of others, and sharpened wits directed at authority figures can reveal their weaknesses. Some internal integrity is maintained by pointing out the lack of integrity in outside authorities. And the need to submit is avoided. The trouble with this trickster defense appears when the trickster grows tired or begins to age; the wellspring of wit begins to dry up or becomes poisonous. What was once a biting irony becomes bitterly sarcastic. What was sharply witty becomes darkly cynical.

The defenses necessary to preserve the integrity of one's spirit during early stages of life tend to become life-threatening later on. An overly defended person eventually begins to suffer feelings of emptiness and paranoia, like a besieged town. The sword that could cut through any outer force also keeps allies away. The inner resources become consumed or dried up, but the habit of not accepting help remains in place. The head that is so capable of scanning the surroundings for enemies can't allow itself to bend to any blessing, even when the body and soul suffer increasing pain. Strong defenses eventually keep one isolated from the flow of life and poison the inner waters of the soul.

Another defense against submitting to any authority is to become an authority oneself. In my attempts to avoid having to submit at the front door of the dining hall, I tried all three of these defenses at the side door. Once it became clear that I couldn't force or trick my way into the hall and couldn't simply use the authority of my position to get through the side door, I began to give up, slow down, and bow my head to the circumstances.

While waiting to give my poem at the central door, I held a stone in my hand like everyone else. As I held the stone I began to think about my father and recall his funeral and burial. The stone became a little weight pulling me toward my father's grave. In my hand the stone became the sorrow I had felt at that time but had been unable to express completely.

I was living on the opposite side of the country when I received word that my father had gone into a deep coma back home. I had been writing a letter to him, inviting him to visit so we could spend time together. It was a lonely, broken time for me. My marriage was ending and I was separated from my children. I felt an inexplicable gratitude toward and a sympathy for my father. In the letter I suggested that we find a boat and go fishing, though neither of us fished. The letter was interrupted by the news of his impending death.

By the time I reached his bedside it was clear that his soul was leaving this life. It was clear that he would not return to life in any meaningful way. As the oldest brother in the family, I wound up negotiating with doctors to remove the life support machinery. As the oldest brother, I made the funeral and burial arrangements. I also tried to help my mother and brothers and sisters cope with the shock and loss. But as the oldest brother standing at the grave site, I was dry of tears. There was a gap between the well of sorrow inside and the determination necessary to carry things through on the outside.

As I stood in line to give my poem to the masked guards I felt as if I were standing at my father's grave again. I made a small prayer that carried some of my sorrow at my father's death; I said it quietly and placed the stone at the entrance to the hall. During that prayer tears that had not been able to flow at the grave site began to come. Once they started there was a gushing of sorrow, a flow of tears that went all the way back through childhood, picking up rages and angers along the way. The prayer awakened the sense of loss and even anger at my father for dying before I could make contact with him at a time when I needed his strength myself. The tears washed over those feelings and over the humiliation and guilt of not having finished and sent the letter to him before his death.

The submission that I had tried at first to avoid opened a well of feeling within me, and the flow of water moved obstacles that had been sitting like stones inside, blocking sorrow as well as other feelings.

Sometime later I finished writing the letter to my father. I also began speaking to him in small ways. One night he came in a dream. He was dressed in fine Sunday clothes, wearing a brand new fedora hat, something he would have relished in life. He stepped from behind some trees, tipped his hat, and smiled at me; then he turned and walked off to a lake beyond us. That was his letter back to me. It was his way of saying he had received my letters and my tears. Had I not submitted to the request for a poem I might not have felt the quiet message of the stone in my hand, I might not have felt the prayer waiting in my heart, and I might have missed the well of waiting tears. If the head can't learn to bow and bend, the heart won't open; as they used to say: Grief held too long can make a stone of the heart.

The story of the search for the Water of Life is guided by the dwarf who has an affinity for the youngest brother in the psyche. Like other inherent helpers of the soul, he waits for us to attempt something creative in our lives. He inhabits the details of life and sees hidden values that others would miss. He's small, like the beginning of a feeling or an intuition. He's not ponderous or obvious. He appears and disappears, cultivating invisibility. In many stories the dwarf is crafty; often an actual craftsman. He can mine gems in the earth and work as a smith forging minerals into tools. He knows the veins that run through the earth and what treasures lie therein. But he practices and teaches other skills; he bakes and sews and makes shoes. He has a great interest in footwear and heels and how the foot touches the ground; he also can be a dancing master. Because he is constantly in touch with the elements and the patterns of things, a dwarf can predict the weather and foretell the future.

In many ways a dwarf is the opposite of a giant. Giants are huge, clumsy, oafish, stupid, and committed to hoarding. In stories, giants hold things of great value that they don't use and usually don't understand. Like big corporations giants concentrate on their appetites and hoarding things. They consume great quantities, sleep heavily, and are oblivious to the destruction they cause. They step on people and don't even notice it. They act like the big psychological complexes that block change and waste huge amounts of energy.

Dwarves, on the other hand, present a different kind of complexity. In stories a dwarf is like condensed matter and condensed time. He's appears small like a child, yet old at the same time. He's a carrier of old knowledge and he's completely unpredictable. He's both explosive and generous. His ambiguity is disturbing to our usual frame of mind.

Dwarves are experts in the connections between things; they see what holds things together. They are deeply connected to the earth and what's in it and of it. They are old like the earth and know the time it takes for metals and ores to form. They have the basic interests of children: where are we going, why do you do that, what is that for, do you want to know what I know? But they also have the wisdom of the age-old earth, and so their questions don't spring from ignorance or innocence. Like children, dwarves don't like to be talked down to. Unlike children, dwarves can do something about it.

The appearance of the dwarf represents an interview between inner need and outer circumstances. The dwarf dwells within the circumstances of our lives, where the practical details come to represent the elemental situation in our soul. The dwarf tests the qualities that are essential for a person to travel his or her road in life. His connection to shoes lets him see how a person walks, and from that he sizes up the person's motivation and true destination. If you don't exhibit the humility and awareness essential for that road, he'll send you back, turn you astray, or plague you with difficulties.

In the story he knows where the healing waters can be found and what instruments and timing are needed to effect the change from sickness to a healthy flow of life. Unlike the general knowledge of the first old man, the dwarf's guidance is specific and insistent. In daily life, the voice of the dwarf can be an inner whisper that questions one's habitual attitudes and assumptions. When it comes time to deal with a malaise at the center of a person's life, the voice of the dwarf can speak as guidance. If ignored he will seize a person's attention by tripping them on their usual path. He can be seen in things that keep going wrong and at times when there are dead ends no matter where we turn. When he's overlooked the world becomes narrow and hard. And the longer he's overlooked, the harder we fall.

In one three-month period I encountered three middle-aged men, each of whom had fallen from a rooftop and broken numerous bones. Each became incapacitated, stuck in bed, knocked right out of the flow of life. Two of them volunteered that they had been resisting a voice telling them that they needed a change of career or a complete life change. They had known that a change was being called for but they couldn't stop themselves from marching forward anyway. They only recognized what was happening when their lives came crashing down.

Down is where the dwarf would have us go whenever we get above ourselves or stuck up on our high horse. He represents a force in the life of a person, a group, or a culture that will cause gridlock, engineer an accident, or deepen an illness in order to force a necessary change of direction. If the ego brothers block out the inner voice of guidance something becomes seriously the matter with us, or something that matters a lot may be taken from us.

THE WATER OF LIFE
Part II

By following the instructions from the dwarf the youngest brother arrived at the castle with the great iron gates. After striking three times with the iron rod, the gates swung open and the youngest brother faced two ferocious lions. He tossed a loaf of bread into the gaping maw of each lion and appeased them. He entered the castle before him, and he soon found himself in a large, splendid hall. Wherever he looked he saw men standing, but they were very still. He touched them and found that each had turned to stone. He passed among them and instinctively drew a gold ring from the hand of each stone man. As he was leaving the hall he found a sword and another loaf of bread and he took those as well.

The youngest brother continued on and came upon a room in which a beautiful woman was quietly standing. When she saw him she rejoiced. She embraced him and declared that he had set her free. "My whole realm will be yours and all the enchantments here will be broken," she said, "if you return in a year's time. If you return we shall celebrate our wedding." The beautiful woman told him where to find the fountain with the Water of Life deeper within the castle. She encouraged him to hasten and be certain to draw the water before the clock struck twelve.

The youngest brother felt encouraged and went on until he came upon a room with a newly made bed. The bed was covered with quilts that were finely embroidered with scenes from old stories. He was tired and thought he might rest a while. As soon as he lay down he fell into a deep sleep and didn't stir at all until something suddenly awakened him at a quarter to twelve. He jumped up, ran to the courtyard nearby, and found the fountain with the Water of Life. Quickly, he drew some water into a cup he found, and hastened to return the way he had come. He rushed along until he could see the huge iron gates. They were already swinging shut. The clock struck twelve just as he went between the gates. They closed with such force that they cut off a piece of his heel as he left the castle of the fountain.

Wounded in the heel and limping a bit, the youngest brother still rejoiced at having found the Water of Life. Carrying the healing water, he started toward home. As he was going along he heard a voice from the side of the road. It was the dwarf, who said, "Those are great treasures you've come by. With that sword you can defeat whole armies, and that loaf will always be the same no matter how many eat from it."

The youngest son did not want to return to his father's realm without his brothers. He said, "Dear dwarf, can you tell me where my two brothers are? They set out for the Water of Life before I did and never came back."

"Don't worry about them—they're safe and secure," said the dwarf. "They are contained in a place well suited to their narrow views and haughty ways."

The prince pleaded and at length the dwarf released them. "Beware of them," the dwarf warned, "They have wicked hearts."

When his brothers appeared the youngest brother rejoiced and told them all about his adventures. He told how he had found the Water of Life and brought away a cup full of it. He told how he had rescued a beautiful queen and how she was going to wait a year for him and then they would be married and would reign together. The three brothers then set off for home. They came upon a country where war and famine were raging and where the misery was so great that the king and the people thought that they must all perish. The youngest brother gave the loaf of bread to the king, who was able to feed all the people until they were satisfied. Then he gave the king his sword and the king destroyed the armies that were oppressing his people. The land was returned to peace. The brothers entered two more countries where war raged and famine made misery and each time the youngest gave the loaf and the sword. Each time peace and abundance were restored to the land.

CHAPTER 22

MEN OF STONE

THE DWARF WAITS outside the gates of both realms. He can be in either realm and he reminds humans that they have the same capacity. The dwarf is an intermediary who helps the youngest brother as he goes to and comes from the otherworld. The Irish, who kept sight of the little people, had the idea that a person could step into the otherworld at any time. Any moment in this world could suddenly loosen and reveal a door or gate that opens to the "second realm" where deep feeling and great imagination rule. Once in the otherworld, each person sees and feels more fully whatever condition of the soul they carry through that doorway. Each person experiences the otherworld as a reflection of and an elaboration upon the current state of their heart and soul.

The spell or enchantment that has fallen over the second realm mirrors the sickness of the king in the first realm. The hall filled with men of stone elaborates the hardness and stuckness of the older brothers trapped between rocks. The first realm lacks water and flow. In the second realm things have turned to stone. What happens in the daily world has unseen consequences in other realms and levels of life. In effect, we live in two worlds at once and the human soul connects the outer, measurable world with the inner-other-underworld. The common world of facts and measures increasingly diminishes the value of the individual as merely one among the untold masses. But at the level of the soul each person has the ability to unlock the gates of imagination, find inner beauty, and touch the essential waters of life.

When the world becomes stuck and hard to bear, the flow of feelings, ideas, and images must be found where they originate, on the other side of the gates of imagination. The cure for what ails this world can only be found in the otherworld. Conversely, what becomes stuck in the otherworld can only be healed from this world. The youngest brother and youngest sister in the soul may seem foolish to those who swear by the facts and believe only in simple logic, but they become the go-betweens who open the wells of compassion and release the living waters of imagination.

To find the Water of Life, we must pay a price exacted by the lions: we must open our eyes when most are sleeping; we must look past the gates of reason and beyond the usual reasons people have for doing things. Striking at the gates of the otherworld awakens the sleeping lions that must be fed with the bread of attention to one's inner life. Like the great stone lions outside temples and museums, the inner lions guard that which is sacred and precious in the soul. They require a taste of something substantial, an accurate attention to what really matters in a person's life, or they shut the gates of knowing.

The lions that guard the soul sleep with their eyes open. They represent the reversal of values that occurs at the gates of the soul. They desire something of meaning and substance to chew on. The distinct troubles in one's life bang at the gates of the soul. If we deny genuine attention to what ails us, we rattle and rouse the lions without nourishing them. Not getting to the specific trouble that rattles at the threshold between inner and outer realms creates a general sense of anxiety that causes the daily world to take on this uneasy, rattling quality. The lions represent a test of whether the seeker has truly awakened to meaningful life issues or is simply disturbed.

Paying attention to dreams will often oil the gates between the worlds. When we attend to the images and feelings that arise in dreams, we feed the inner lions and can bring back to life something that was missing. Denying the realm of dreams and imagination offends the lions of the psyche and can turn them into demons that are impossible to satisfy.

Addictions often develop where the doors between the worlds partially opened but the person was not ready or able to deal with the intensity of what was released. Something substantial became damaged and the inner lions became enraged. The mechanism for closing the gates was broken and one or another addictive substance is used to plug the hole and quiet the lions. They can be bought off with substitutes for the bread and wine that feeds the soul, but the cost of keeping them at bay becomes higher and higher. Addictions and compulsive habits are substitutes for the painful learning of more genuine rituals that can open and close the gates that lead the way to the fountain of the Water of Life.

Denying the importance of one's inner life and the emotions that flow through it tend to numb a person in this world and begin to turn everything in the inner world to stone. The pain inherent in one's life may no longer be fully felt, but neither does the Water of Life flow. The pain remains but becomes buried in the soul, encased in stone. Life continues but meaning drains from it and the inner lions rage from lack of nourishment. The Water of Life waits in the garden at the center of the soul, but a person must pass through an emotional zone to reach it.

The inner realm includes painful places and joyous possibilities. The sword that defeats armies and the bread that feeds everyone are ever nearby—that's a rule in this world and a promise from the otherworld. But between each man and the healing waters within there stands a stone brother encased in a spell. Each passage to the Water of Life requires breaking through something that has become fixated in the mind or has hardened in the heart. Unless he touches this brother and allows the hard story to come out, life will remain stuck and he might as well be in a prison.

What a person cannot bear alone can often be suffered in a group where others admit to similar pains. A person can take heart from another's struggle to be present to the pain of living. Many traditions use some form of collective ritual to help each person suffer what they need to suffer but lack the courage to endure on their own. When a group of people arrive at the gates of the soul together there can be an increase of courage as well as a deepening of determination. Honest, uninhibited emotions are part of banging at the gates. Although each person gets through the gates in their own way, as soon as one person cracks the gates of emotion fully open, others can more readily find ways to get through to their own essential issues.

When a group of men begins working at the gates of the inner life no one knows where the opening will occur, or who will crack and release the necessary flow of emotions. Each time is necessarily different and what opened the gates before may clang dully the next time around. Before things crack open, there's often an increase of tension and an edge of fear.

Once, while we worked within this story, a man stood up to say that he was carrying the corpse of his wife; he had been carrying her for years. He struggled to find words and even more to find feelings as everyone listen carefully and tried to follow where he was going. He told of shutting down and turning numb when she died of a sudden illness. His anguish was palpable but cold. As he continued to speak, he told of her beauty and the way she brought an ease and grace to his life. He stumbled over words until something cracked and he began to cry. The flood gates opened and you could feel inner rocks crack apart and fall.

Soon another man began to speak, barely leaving room for the grieving one to gather himself. If he didn't speak right away he said, an old silence would grab him again. His life had come to feel old and cold. He used to have friends; he used to have dreams. But now he feels isolated, as if standing outside his own life. He has held his feelings in check for so long that people can't get to him; they sense the coldness and leave him alone. At one time he wanted to be left alone. But now he feels like he's a small voice locked way inside his house where no one can hear him.

Another man says the he's stuck in a marriage that is going nowhere. "There's no passion in it," he says. At first he said it didn't matter, he had plenty to do; now it's killing him, yet he rarely speaks of the pain of it. Another man says he is frozen with fear that if he leaves his marriage, he'll die old and alone. If he doesn't leave, he'll die of loneliness within it. The next feels that somewhere he lost the purpose he had early in life. Now he's just going through the motions; there's no point to what he's doing, and he's not going anywhere.

A man tells how losing his job slowly led to completely shutting down inside as depression settled all around him. Other men who still hold powerful positions and have experienced outward success also speak of the loss of real passion and a hardening inside themselves. The room grows heavy with the weight of sorrows that were there all along but not seen or felt clearly until the first man broke his silence about the death of his wife. His sorrow cracked the gates open and soon everyone followed on through.

There's a huge and growing weight of grief inside American men. When the heart knows sorrow but never weeps, when loss is present but not accepted, things turn cold and hard. Often the outside world must be left far behind before men can crack the inner gates and move the stones over the heart. Often there's heavy lifting to do, as the weight of sorrow grows when it is denied. People suffer through wars and divorces, tragic deaths and other losses, yet the common lack of rituals for truly grieving leaves most people carrying corpses inside their lives.

When a group of men discovered in talking that they were all veterans of the war in Vietnam, they each found many corpses and unfinished funerals. They felt eventually a need to stand together and speak of the sorrows they had come to know. They stood side by side, as if stuck together, as if the only way to move the weight buried within each one was to become like a squad again. They spoke from the other side of war, from the side that leaves bodies on battlefields and leaves souls bereft of hope. As each told of carrying the weight of dead bodies and dead dreams for many years, the room dropped and their words rolled on the floor like stones that could break a heart. Some inner funerals that had been stuck in time began to move and carried the entire group to the doors of grief.

Another time in another hall, five Latino men found themselves in a sudden funeral that involved both the loss of friends left cold on the battle fields and others lost to the ongoing war in the streets of the barrios. The storm of grief shook them hard and they had to do something to avoid hardening any further. They erected an altar and lit a candle for each friend lost to the battle between life and death. Each stood at the altar and addressed their lost friends with a passion that broke everyone down to tears. They poured out anger and anguish, sorrow and grief in burning words and wordless sounds at the altar. They banged at that altar with rage and outrage. They fed it the bread of their sorrow and the room felt like an ancient battlefield after a bloody battle. That night they stayed up until dawn making dead bread in the deep Mexican tradition of offering the bread of life to those in the land of the dead. In the morning they placed the bread on the altar with prayers and fed it to the entire group as we stood in a silent communion with all those who have passed.

The dedication and artistry of those men pushed the gates between the world wide apart and unlocked sorrows long carried by other men. Those of older generations began to unload even older stones of grief. The Korean War arose from cold forgotten ashes and the Second World War spoke again with a voice of grief that history and films do not convey. Soon it was difficult to tell which war was being grieved, but it was evident that everyone in the room felt as if they had been through a war. It was too much for words, so we began to sing an old lament, giving both words and tears a place to flow and keeping the weight moving lest it crush someone.

We sang an old Irish dirge that lamented the loss of life and limb through war. Some vehicle was needed to carry the weight of the grief. Often the lack of a vehicle is what stops men from grieving—that, and the belief that they are alone, that other people's grief is not like their own.

In the midst of the lament a man stood and angrily protested, "Not everyone dies in a war; not every loss comes because men are soldiers and street fighters. Other things kill. Other things take life and limb and leave gaping wounds." It came as a shock. The song quieted and everyone listened. This man worked with people dying of AIDS and had buried many of them. He feared that the attention to those lost through war excluded the grief that burdened him and the sorrows of so many he knew. He was afraid that the gates were closed to gay men, that the tragedy of AIDS would be denied here as it was so often elsewhere. He worried that women might also be excluded from this opportunity to lament and grieve as a community. A small argument started, as some felt that their grief was being intruded upon.

Finally someone said, "Listen, this whole thing is a war. Whenever great numbers of people are dying, no matter what they're dying of, there's a war going on. No one is excluded from war and no one is outside the grief it causes." The truth of this struck everyone. The weeping increased. The song rose up again. And it went on until the weight was so heavy it seemed we would never get out of that room. Someone suggested that we carry the lament outside to the trees and the entire group went out among the huge redwood trees where the lamenting and weeping continued. The flood of tears had cleansed our eyes and the trees stood clear before us and around us as if the things that separate people from living nature had simply been washed away.

We were on the other side of the gates and we were there altogether.

When someone picked up a stone it made evident sense for each of us to bring a stone back into the hall. We piled the stones carefully, shaping a cairn, a monument to the sorrow of being in a world of loss and grief. For days we passed back and forth among the stones of our grief. Later we carried all the stones down to a stream and placed them amidst those already lying where the water flowed.

The instinct for making ceremonies and shaping rituals lives inside the bones of people. When the walls of denial break apart and the soul waters flow, the bones ache to be in the kind of rituals that reconnect people to the forests and trees, to the rivers and streams that quietly enact the rites of life day and night. In losing the sense of a living connection to nature and the immediate presence of spirit, modern life can become a death march and a funeral that has no end.

The Water of Life includes the tears shaped within each heart. Shedding them moves the soul, softens the boundaries between people, and heals the separation from the living realm of nature. Once, after weeping like that, a man said that he felt that his friends long left dead on foreign battlefields could still see into this world when he released his tears. Human tears flow between the worlds and allow us to see more clearly what happens in each realm. It used to be better known that the world weeps and that people inherit the "sorrow of the world." To be alive at this time means to witness and feel an ongoing funeral, a huge shedding of life that includes human atrocities as well as great losses in the natural world.

The increasing hopelessness felt over the loss of forests and animal species can become another stone that hardens in the heart. The anguish seeping from lives lost and wasted on harsh city streets secretly pile within the soul. When the heart knows sorrow but never weeps, grief gets locked like a storm inside the heart. When the storm can't pour out, it turns solemn and gains weight. Grieving clears the heart and keeps it open. There is an old saying: "Too much grieving makes a stone of the heart." But you could also say that too little grieving surrounds the heart with stones and turns it cold.

Until modern times men have consciously participated in the sorrow and lament of the world. Most traditional cultures had rituals through which men learned the importance of grieving. Participating in funerals and grief rituals was an essential part of the life of initiated men. Frequently men have lamented as a group, for men can draw the sorrow out of each other. "You don't fully know a man until you've seen his sorrow," they used to say. Men of one race or culture are often surprised at the depth of sorrow in those of another culture. Seeing another through his tears can create sympathy and empathy more effectively than ideas or beliefs about peace and unity. When tears are shared, the stones that might have been thrown at each other become part of the cairns of grief instead.

Most cultures had specific, shared songs and chants for opening and carrying the grief of both individuals and the collective group. The sounds and rhythm of certain songs can set the stream of sorrow flowing. They can also wash away differences that keep people on opposite sides of the rivers of life. Once we held a conference that brought together Asian American, Native American, African American, Latino American, and European American men all in one place. Right at the outset a fierce conflict interrupted over race and class issues. Things became overheated very quickly, even before we could establish ground rules and a sense of trust. As many feared that the fires of conflict would burn out of control, someone began to sing an old gospel song: "Wade in the waters. Wade in the waters. God's gonna trouble the waters."

Fierce angers had entered that room, born of a culture divided against itself and closed to the persistent suffering of many. Those angers had to be heard or justice would fail to be served again. There were rages that burned a fiery path back through colonial history and across oceans of inherited suffering. There needed to be room for the rages to storm and there needed to be a place for sorrow to carry away the bitterness and fear.

The song started just as we reached the point where things would move toward battle or else shift toward sorrow over all the battles of the past. Fortunately the singer had a true voice and it was a legitimate call, a lament that had its own heat and didn't deny the depth of the trouble. It didn't separate God from the trouble either. For God is implicated in all the suffering and the old song places everyone and God in the same troubled waters.

The song had an edge to it, a growl that seemed to carry both conflict and sorrow; it carried things that had just been said in anger; it carried echoes of things said and done before our time that continue to torture and trouble us nonetheless. Eventually everyone gave in and poured all the anger and fear and confusion into the waters of the song. "Wade in the waters. Wade in the waters, all God's trouble in the water." The flow of the feelings moved from conflict into sorrow as tears mixed with the flowing song. We sang for a long time, adding harmonies and variations, tolerating all kinds of false notes and broken rhythms. The waves of sound grew and grew as if we were washing ancient wounds in a river made fresh with tears.

As the song grew a swelling of joy began. What had begun in confusion began to gather a wave of hidden joy as the song flowed to surprising heights. "Wade in the waters. Wade in the waters. All God's children in the water." We are all god's children when the waters of grief are allowed to flow and cleanse the wounds and wash away the hardened attitudes that otherwise divide people.

That's what people are supposed to do: enter the waters of life in such a way that one emotion leads to another, in such a way that the fountain of the Water of Life erupts beyond anyone's control, and in such a way that everyone becomes washed in the waters of forgiveness and healing. Then a radical change occurs within each person and throughout the group. The flow of life increases and everyone gets nourished by the hidden abundance of life.

Men in particular need to authentically enter the waters of life or else fall into isolation and hard-hearted battle with the world. Singing and weeping opens the heart. It joins a person to both the sorrow and the joy of the world. It cools the fires of rage and calms any excess of aggression. Excess heat pours out through the tears while the sounds of sorrow clear the heart and mind. But the opposite can happen as well. If a man has become too cold within or frozen in life, weeping cracks things open and a heart-song can soften the stone.

The Water of Life, the treasure sought by the youngest brother and a substance sorely missing from the modern world, has a general healing effect. It cools the excessive heat of an individual or group while it heats up those who are passive. In both individual and group, the split into violence or passivity, or excessive aggression or excessive lethargy can be brought into balance by deep grieving. Weeping can raise the temperature of one psyche and cool the overheated psyche in another at the same time. Water is the inherent reconciling force in this world. Those who enter it too hot will cool and calm. Their water becomes more stable. Those stuck in some passivity or numb to the whole inner world become flushed with feeling and capable of meaningful action again.

Contemporary studies in human biology have come to see the balancing effects of weeping in men through studies of those in prison for violent crimes. Some research indicates that deep, convulsive weeping alters the testosterone levels in a man's system. Those who are excessively aggressive and violent often have elevated levels of testosterone, making them not only "testy," but prone to violent outbursts. If weeping can be induced, the level of testosterone diminishes and so does the impulse to violence. The opposite also holds true. Men with low testosterone will experience an increase through weeping. The more extreme the levels of testosterone beforehand, the more radical the change. If a man has not wept in a long time, the missing passions of his life can return, or the excessive passions can be cooled for some time. Tears balance the emotional realm and cleanse both mind and heart.

On another level, activating one's own sorrow makes a person part of an inclusive, fully human community. The Water of Life makes a community from below where ancestors nod wordlessly to each other. A change occurs below the level of language and culture. When a group has gone through the gates, calmed the devouring lions, and cracked the stones of sorrow together, it becomes very difficult for those who have shared the deep waters of the psyche to attack one another.

Men learn how to grieve most easily when they are in a group with other men. When a man reveals the incredible sorrow that he has hidden all his life, other men perceive him differently and begin to look at themselves differently. Recognizing his sorrow gives other men the courage to recognize their own. Having the grief shaped into a song, made into an altar, or put into some artful form moves the sorrow from a stuck place within to a flowing connection to other people and to the world around us. When the Water of Life begins to flow back into the world it changes everything it touches. Water is the element in this world that can lead to a grand solution or else can cause greater dissolution.

As the youngest brother in the story moves through the hall in the inner-other realm, he takes a gold ring from each man of stone. Is he stealing from the dead? The story doesn't say. The gold rings are never mentioned again. Yet the young brother only finds the magical sword and loaf of abundance after he takes the gold rings from the stone men. Gold rings often symbolize loyalty, commitment, and shared faith. These rings seem to be a symbol to remind the brother of the men turned to stone, a reminder of the healing purpose that caused him to seek the Water of Life for the benefit of others. In order not to become stuck in this hall himself, he must remain married to his greater purpose. The stories of how people turn hard-hearted and stony often involve a loss of purpose in life and a loss of faith in the presence of meaning of their lives. The rings remind us that each soul holds an inner purpose that, even when denied or forgotten, dwells close to the source of the Water of Life. What turns to stone is the living connection to a sense of gold, of beauty, and of value inherent in the deeper levels of the self.

Once the youngest brother has collected the gold rings he finds the sword that cannot be defeated and the loaf of abundance. In other words, after passing through the alchemy of the hall of stone, the iron rod has becomes a sword that can defeat all armies. The two loaves required to feed the lions reappear as a single unified loaf, as if something that was split has now been unified and imbued with limitless abundance. Such is the promise of the otherworld, that whoever is willing to be torn apart and struggle in an honest way will find a unity of purpose and meaning that was already in their soul.

Learning to feed his own inner life enables the youngest brother to nourish others. Learning to open wide the gates to the imagination inherent in the soul makes available a sword that can defeat any army. The process of feeding the inner life and facing the sorrow that has turned a man to stone returns abundance to the outer world. The sword that protects and the bread that nourishes can't come from simple good intentions or wishful thinking. Rather they are made from the release of benumbed emotions and the rediscovery of passionate purpose and great imagination buried in the heart.

When the spell of stone begins to break, the lady of the fountain is also released. She represents the sudden appearance of beauty and joy to eyes that have been washed with true emotion. She awakens after the prince passes through the stone hall and approaches the central source of life's healing and renewing waters. She is part of the beauty and healing that the soul ever longs to find. She raises the sound of joy and directs him to the Water of Life. If a man doesn't get far enough into the genuine suffering of his soul, he'll forget that this source of joy and beauty even exists. If he loses all sight of her, he won't be able to recognize the sorrows and joys in other people. He will be deaf, dumb, and blind to both the suffering and the beauty of the world.

In the realm of the lady of the fountain, heroic battles accomplish nothing. This lady doesn't need to be rescued from a tower or saved from a villainous king. Getting through the stone-making spells are what's required. Acquiring the Water of Life is not about heroic effort. The youngest brother falls asleep once he reaches the area of the fountain. In this realm of water and feelings and imagination, falling asleep doesn't deprive the hero of opportunities. It prepares him to find the healing water in the right way, at the right time.

The youngest brother continues to act in ways that might disturb the older ego brothers. When he's almost at the goal, he falls asleep; he rests and dreams. Instinctively, he seems to know the difference between stopping in time and being stuck. At the last moment he awakens, pulled by unseen rhythms of intuition. He collects the Water of Life and unceremoniously heads back through the gates to the realm above. In the psyche, change occurs at what seems like, or feels like the last possible moment. It's always the last chance and just in the nick of time. He makes it all the way there and back, his only injury a nick on the heel as he passes back through the gates.

On the way into the otherworld, bread was enough to pay the price of admission. On the way out the price becomes a piece of the man himself. The wounded heel is a part of the sacrifice necessary for any who would aspire to handle the healing waters, the sword that can't be defeated, or the bread of abundance. The little brother knows more about loss now, and losing a piece of himself will keep him in touch with the realm of healing. Part of the youngest brother is left behind in the underworld with the stone men and the lady of the fountain, making him partly of them. Initiation leaves certain wounds and scars that mark a person specifically as who they are and where in life they have been.

The price for carrying some of the water that flows in the depths of the inner-underworld is to bear a wound at the lowest point of the body. While the youngest brother's hands are full of the water and bread of life and the sword that can defend them, his foot carries the mark of the underworld. The wound marks him in the backward, downward place, opposite of and far from the glories of the head. Some knowledge is deposited in the foot as a reminder of where the brother has walked, and of what he has felt. It's a funeral scar, a limp that becomes part of every step he takes, a reminder of the spell of stone that still grips the otherworld.

Of the three brothers only the one who has sacrificed himself to the otherworld can help others. It is not his wholeness or lack of being wounded that creates healing; rather, the healing potential lies in his conscious wound, in his knowledge of loss that he now carries every step of the way. He may be able to cover the wounded heel, but every baring of his soul will reveal it again. Ultimately, the wound that makes him limp a bit is also his passport for crossing between the daily world and the otherworld.

As with any genuine initiation, a "little death" is required. A piece of the youngest brother remains behind in the otherworld as he has been initiated and claimed by that realm. His life has changed completely and he has the scar to prove it. The youngest brother limps out of the second realm, bearer of an underworld wound that will affect his stance and all his movements in life. His hands and heart are full—he carries the cup of the Water of Life, the sword, and the loaf—but he also carries more knowledge of stones and sorrow. The little brother has been deepened and darkened; he knows what wounds a person in this world and what heals in the other.

THE WATER OF LIFE
PART III

After the kingdoms were restored through the use of the magical sword and loaf of bread, all three brothers boarded a ship and sailed for home across the sea. During the voyage the older brothers considered the situation, saying, "Our younger brother has found the Water of Life and we haven't found anything. Our father will reward him by giving him the kingdom that should we should inherit. He will rob us of our birthright." They began to seek revenge and plotted to destroy the youngest brother. They waited until he fell fast asleep and took the Water of Life and refilled the cup with bitter seawater.

When the three arrived home, the youngest took his cup of water straight to the ailing king, fully expecting that he would drink the water and be quickly cured. But the king had barely tasted the seawater when he fell sicker than ever before. As the king was lamenting his state, the older brothers came in and accused the youngest of trying to poison their father. They brought the true Water of Life and gave it to the king. At the first drink of that holy water, the king felt his sickness leaving him. Soon he was healthy and as strong as in his youth.

In private, the older brothers mocked the youngest, saying, "You certainly found the Water of Life, but much good it has done you—you have the pain and we have the gain. You get the hardship and we get the reward. You should have been more clever and kept your eyes open. We took it from you while you were sleeping on the ship, and in a year we will go and claim the beautiful queen as well. Even if you tell the king about this, he will never believe you, and you'll likely lose your life as well. But if you keep silent, we will let you live."

Believing he had plotted against his life, the old king was bitterly angry with the youngest son. He summoned the royal council and had them secretly sentence the youngest to be killed.

One day, the youngest brother, suspecting no evil, went hunting. The king's old huntsman was ordered to go with him. Once they were alone in the forest, the huntsman looked so sorrowful that the youngest brother asked, "Dear huntsman, what ails you?"

The huntsman answered, "I can't tell you, yet I ought to tell."

"Speak openly," said the brother. "Whatever it is, I'll forgive you."

"Alas," the huntsman said, "I'm supposed to kill you. The king ordered it so."

The youngest brother was shocked. "Dear huntsman, let me live. I'll give you my royal garments. Give me your common ones in their place. Pretend that I am dead and that you have taken my clothes."

"I'll willingly do that," said the hunter. "For I couldn't find it in my heart to kill you."

The old hunter and the youngest brother exchanged clothes. The hunter went back to the castle and the prince, dressed in the hunter's common garments, went deeper into the forest, his head hanging down and his eyes looking nowhere except into himself.

Sometime later three wagon-loads of gold and precious stones arrived at the king's castle. They had been sent to the youngest son as tokens of gratitude from the kings who had defeated their enemies and sustained their people with the sword and the loaf. The old king began to consider, "Can my son have been innocent?" Aloud he said, "If only he were alive. Oh, how can I forgive myself for having him killed."

At that moment the huntsman spoke up, "He is alive. I couldn't find it in my heart to carry out the command." He told the king what had happened and a stone weight fell from the king's heart. He had a royal edict proclaim in all lands that his son was free to return and would be welcomed with open arms.

Meantime, it had come to the end of the year since the youngest brother had found the Water of Life. The Lady of the Fountain overlaid the road to her castle with gold. She set guards at the entrance and told them, "If a man comes straight down the middle of the road, he will be the one awaited here. Anyone who comes along either side will not be welcome and should be refused entry."

As the time was close at hand, the eldest brother set out for the castle of the Lady of the Fountain, intending to pass himself off as savior of that realm. He fully expected to wed the lady and to rule with her there. When he came near the castle he saw the road covered with gold. He thought, "It would be a pity to ride on such a beautiful surface." So he turned aside and went along the right side of the road. When he reached the gates, the guards reviled him and sent him away.

Soon after the second brother started out and eventually came to the golden road. His horse had put one hoof on the path when he thought, "It would be a sin and a shame to ride over that. What if I were to break it?" So he turned aside and went along the left side of the road. When he reached the gates, the guards reviled him, too, and sent him away.

At the very end of the year, the youngest brother turned toward the castle of the Water of Life in hopes of at least glimpsing the beautiful lady of the realm. As he went along he thought of her beauty and all that he felt in her presence. Between the sorrows brought by betrayal and his desire to be with the lady again, he didn't see where he was going. He walked right down the middle of the golden road, and when he reached the gates they opened without the need of the iron rod. The lady of the castle welcomed him with joy, announcing that he had saved the realm and broken the enchantment over it.

The Lady of the Fountain and the youngest brother celebrated their marriage with great joy. The lady told him of the message of forgiveness from his father. So the youngest brother returned to his father's realm. The old king welcomed him, and the youngest brother told the whole story of his betrayal at the hands of his older brothers and how he had kept his silence. Although the king wanted to punish the older brothers severely, the youngest brother had them put to sea again and they never came back as long as they lived.

CHAPTER 23

THE PATH OF BETRAYAL
AND THE GOLDEN ROAD

A S BEFORE, THE DWARF waits by the gates for the youngest brother to come out into the world. The little fellow explains the purpose of the sword and value of the wondrous loaf and he warns against the wicked hearts of the older brothers. But the youngest son, imbued with the essential flow of life, will not be deterred in his determination to restore everything. Whereas in his first meeting with the dwarf he submitted readily and fully, now he won't submit at all. Whereas before he didn't know where he was going, he now feels certain that he must save his brothers. Feeling the true abundance of life, he imagines everyone will welcome him and embrace the life curing waters in the same way as he did.

A transforming event or a genuine initiation changes a person completely and alters all relationships radically. When a person truly changes, all connected to them changes as well. Under the powerful influence of the healing waters, even the dwarf must bow to the desires of the little brother. But those who have no idea of their own true gifts can be troubled by the appearance of meaningful gifts in others. The abundant gifts gained by the youngest provoke a deep envy in the older brothers. The king also reacts treacherously to the powerful presence of gifts from the otherworld. He receives the cure, but condemns the one who found it and brought it to him. The connection to the otherworld and the radical potency of the Water of Life can make a person an exile in the common world where self-involvement rules and selfish motives abound.

The youngest brother can't refuse the expansive feeling caused by contact with the healing waters of the otherworld, even if it means exposure to what remains wicked-hearted in this world. He can't contain his experiences on the other side of the gates and must tell the story. On the one hand, it's a naïve thing to do; on the other, it's impossible to resist. What he holds in his hands and heart overflows any caution or fear. Besides, the gifts and cures he carries are not simply for himself. Even the dwarf must bow his head to that.

The youngest brother has exchanged the iron rod for the sword that protects people against injustice. He has the loaf that can feed all who are besieged with hunger. But while he is able to defend and feed so many, the youngest brother cannot protect himself. Self-interest and self-protection are older brother tactics. In his newfound state of fulfillment the youngest brother has only the strategy of giving freely. The Water of Life is both bitter and sweet medicine; in its presence things get worse before they get better. Sometimes the remedy is harder to take than the illness.

Just as entering the otherworld enhances the conditions existing in a person, bringing the Water of Life to this world has the effect of deepening what already exists. Bringing water from the fountain of life means deepening the passions of all who are touched by its presence. When the older brothers touch the water of the otherworld, their greed, envy, and drive for power increases. Their sense of entitlement and self-importance expands and their mutual support of their false selves fosters new forms of treachery. In the act of handing the cure to their father, they poison his heart toward the youngest brother. Even in recovery the king is quick to judge and hasty to condemn. While receiving the healing he needs, the king's ear remains open to the poison of the older brothers, and his counselors emulate his vindictive traits. As Goethe said, "Great passions are incurable, their very remedies make them worse."

An African proverb offers this: "What the heart loves is the cure." But if the heart harbors envy, revenge, and vindictive notions it doesn't know what it loves and can only respond to love and care with resentment. The heart that doesn't know itself can do nothing but betray itself. The youngest son has something to learn about the terrible territory of betrayal. He becomes stuck, trapped not by the narrowness in his heart but by the pettiness in the hearts of others and his own naïveté.

The changes effected in the otherworld will be sorely tested in the bitter waters of this world. The youngest brother has taken on the common clothes of betrayal and even the harsh cloth of self-betrayal and must wander in the stunned exile of the solitary heart.

The chorus of men stirs again, pushed by an anguish of life's many betrayals. A man says sternly, "He should have listened to the dwarf the second time as well. The youngest brother started all the betrayals when he refused to follow the dwarf's advice." Another man disagrees completely, "It was the dwarf who betrayed him. The dwarf should have insisted on keeping the wicked brothers frozen in the rocks. The dwarf knew what would happen and allowed the wickedness to take over." Another says, "The youngest brother betrayed his own mission. He was naïve and foolish and full of himself. He should have known not to tell the brothers about the Water of Life and about the beautiful queen at the fountain. By telling them he betrayed his mission and the queen herself." The next man says, "It was the queen who betrayed him. She should have told him what would happen when he returned to the daily world. She knew that the Water of Life would have the opposite effect of healing on some people. It's her fault, she should have told him."

"If he hadn't fallen asleep, the betrayals wouldn't have started at all. It's his own fault. He betrayed himself by sleeping," says another. "Everyone has to sleep," says the next man. "It was the older brothers with their wicked envy who switched the real water with the salt water. They betrayed their own brother, as well as their father and the whole realm." "It's the betrayal by the father that's killing me," says a pained voice. "Once again, the father betrays the son. He should have seen through the tricks of the older brothers. He should have been more curious about how the water got there. He should have been more observant. He should have known his sons better." Someone else says, "Even Christ ends questioning, "Father, why hast thou forsaken me?" How could this father be expected to know more than God, the Father?"

Yet another says, "It was the youngest brother who betrayed himself by not defending himself. He had the sword that could defeat all enemies; he could have defeated all of them. He had the bread that could feed endlessly, and he could have made a show of the power of that bread. Then it would have been obvious who brought the Water of Life. He could have defeated the brothers and counselors and proved to the king that he was the right one. He betrayed himself." Someone else says, "He betrayed himself from the very beginning when he came out of the gates and did not talk about the wound in his heel but only talked about the glorious things he had seen. He betrayed himself and his own wound, and he betrayed the stone men in the underworld."

There's plenty of blame to go around, for each person has their own stories of betrayal buried in their heart. Betrayal first occurs early in life. It hits the heart like a stone and can cause a great fear of being wounded that same way again. The young hero can help entire realms besieged by enemies and famine, but he can't defend himself against those closest to him. "You're always betrayed by your own!" That's the old saying. Betrayal can only come where trust has been placed. It's the love in one's heart that gets betrayed; the innate magnanimity and bestowing nature of one's soul are inevitably crushed by the harshness of this world.

Once a person has been betrayed, each further betrayal is also a self-betrayal. "I should have known better," says the too-trusting heart. There are early signs of the presence of betrayal, but most prefer not to notice. Betrayal marks a deep, forbidding place in the heart. I've never met a man who hasn't been betrayed. More than that, anyone being fully honest with themselves can tell how they have also betrayed others.

The Water of Life and an open heart, the wounded heel and betrayal, all go together. The word betray comes from two roots, one pointing to misleading people and the other refering to handing over oneself. Betrayal involves a loss of innocence and a participation in the world where people only find what truly sustains them after all expectations have been betrayed. Betrayal is one of the most common garments people wear in this world. After a certain age, anyone still playing at innocence is either asking to be betrayed or setting up the betrayal of others. Eventually most protests of innocence become another form of betrayal.

Sometimes a person must simply give up the claim of innocence, hand themselves over, and walk the broken ground of betrayal. When he faces the depths of betrayal at the hands of those he trusted, the youngest brother joins the common human condition. At some point, a person either hands over the overly innocent view of life and walks on the common ground of the betrayed, or joins the bitter and betraying brothers in their guise of innocence.

Betrayal is often the cause of a heart turned to stone. They used to say that what's left after a betrayal is truly one's own. What truly belongs to a person cannot be completely lost or given away. What belongs to us comes back to us again. It's easier to blame oneself or blame others when the nature of one's soul has been betrayed. Only after betrayal can a person sort out what truly belongs to them. Before a person can walk down the golden road where the soul is ever welcome, they must first wander in the forests of exile and the haunts of betrayal. Otherwise we would never know how to value and protect the inner fountain where life renews, where the hard-hearted learn to forgive.

Although he began the quest for the Water of Life with a true desire to heal his father and return the realm to abundance, the youngest brother eventually enters the path of his own healing. What he would do for others he must learn to do for himself. He has held and seemingly lost that which can rescue life from the hands of death. He has stepped onto the path of the "wounded healer" where a person can only bring to others the quality and quantity of healing they find in themselves. Although he is considered a savior in some lands, he is exiled from his own land and thought to be dead and deservedly so.

The old hunter knows the pathways in the forest of the psyche and recognizes the twist of fate in the suffering of the youngest son. He knows too much of life and of death to carry out the wrongful sentence. He recognizes the limping of the youngest son and reveals his own sorrow about the inequities of the world. While others are quick to condemn, the old hunter hands the brother over to his wounded heel and gives him a cover that allows him to dwell in the common ground of lost innocence.

The exchange of royal garments for common clothes begins a series of reversals and radical changes at all levels of the story. While the youngest son begins a descent in the forest of exile, caravans of gold and gifts from the once-famished kingdoms begin to arrive at the center of the realm. Recognition that could not come from the father comes from the rulers of the other lands. The effect of work done in the otherworld flows toward this world regardless of whether people understand the economics of the soul. Exchanges between the two worlds can only be understood when people remain open to both.

Eventually the sick king realizes his own role in the poisonous condition of the family and the punishing quality of the realm. He has a change of heart that allows the old hunter to reveal the secrets he knows about the youngest son. In his moment of realization, the king sends forgiveness across the land. In a sense, the son he thought was dead becomes reborn and joy and forgiveness become possible throughout the land.

Meanwhile, the older brothers have departed in hopes of exploiting the resources of the otherworld and cannot be part of the great changes and healing of the ailing realm. Forgiveness can't occur for the ego brothers, for they are still going for the gold. They become even more rational and thoughtful in the wrong way. They have finally encountered something that exceeds their estimations of their own self-worth: an entire road covered with gold. They exercise a sympathy for the gold road that they don't have for people, especially those close to them. This time the dwarf doesn't have to stop them, for their own distorted values lead them away from what they desire. While they are once again sure that they know how to proceed, they completely miss the goal and wind up out of luck in both worlds.

The youngest brother, lost in the interior of his own suffering, doesn't see the golden road at all. Yet his deep practice of reflection and contemplation opens the gates again. He doesn't arrive as the conquering hero or the rightful heir or the dutiful groom. He arrives without even knowing it. It is as if by being at the center of himself he arrives at the center of the otherworld, as if those two centers secretly coincide. This time he enters the gates, not as a prince on nobly seeking a cure for others, but as someone needing healing himself. By attending to the healing of his inner life, he arrives in the right way and at the right time. He doesn't manage it, direct it, command it, regulate it, or empower it. It happens through hunting inside and limping along.

The lady of the fountain waits for just such an approach; that turns out to be the key to breaking the spell on the otherworld. The deep healing of the individual becomes the lever through which both realms renew. Suffering in a way that is deeply and uniquely human not only reunites the two realms, it also heals what ails the otherworld. Both realms were lacking something that could only be provided by the conscious suffering of the human soul.

Each time the Water of Life and the garden of the soul must be found by way of a different approach. This point it is the lonely road of betrayal that leads to the heart's golden road. It is a secret that eludes many people, even those who follow religious and spiritual paths, if they follow those paths with attitudes similar to the older brothers. The ego brothers can't see the true nature of this transformation. The unforgiving remain blind to it and those who would rule the world by force ever miss where the source of true sovereignty can be found.

When the youngest brother comes out of his deep reverie, everything has changed. The grieving road turns out to be the golden road. The spell on the realm of the lady of the soul has been broken and all becomes quickly ready for the wedding feast that joins the two realms again. News arrives from the father's kingdom and forgiveness and joy flow back and forth. Both realms are revived and the state of abundance returns to the world. Nature is renewed and culture is revivified by the Water of Life.

The road between the daily world and the otherworld is never obvious. It appears as a side road, a wrong road, or a lonely road; as an in-road, a narrow road, or a golden road. It's never a highway or a freeway, not the main-way or the only way. It's neither reasonable nor practical. It wanders the byways and traverses the less popular paths. Sometimes grieving and loss and betrayal are the only signs along the way. Often the healing waters that can return the flow of life can only be found along that dark, uncertain road. Only the youngest brother and youngest sister who dwell in the heart of hearts are able to find that road and suffer it fully.

What ails the ruler in anyone's psyche longs for just one taste of those waters of healing and renewal. Yet, most people avoid going there and many deny that renewal is possible at all. The old stories try to keep the sense of little redemptions present in the midst of a loss of imagination that plagues the entire world.

There are three areas involved whenever healing is attempted. The first is the daily world where often those in power are themselves sick in the soul, where the ego brothers tend to dominate, and where the imagination required for love and healing are far away. The first realm is also the ongoing, dog-eat-dog, everyday world. It's the world of facts and matter-of-factness; the place of simple survival and the realm of common oppression. In the first realm healing is hard to find, and truth and meaning are rare commodities.

The other realm, or otherworld, holds the healing waters, the fountain of renewal, the queen of life and, and the beauty and truths of the soul. The other realm includes the haunts of the muses, the groves of inspiration, and the gardens of love. Everyone desires to be in the ecstatic conditions created by proximity to the all-healing waters of the eternal soul. But the only way to travel from the restrictions and afflictions of the daily world to the revelations and healing of the second realm involves repeated expeditions through the heart-torn territory that lies between. The territory betwixt and between the two realms includes the fury and spells of the dwarf, the angry lions at the gates, the haunted paths where betrayals gnaw, and the lonely places where a person feels condemned to exile and death.

The trouble lies in this: Each passage from the hard-as-fact limits of the daily world to the flowing waters of the otherworld requires that a person be willing to sacrifice a part of themselves. Passing through the gates between the worlds requires some pain and suffering. There needs to be enough ferocity in a person's inner life to bang the gates open. The lions must be fed the food of real issues and genuine emotions. Otherwise it's business as usual, with sick kings inheriting power or being elected to it and with the misguided ego brothers running the whole show.

In order to heal we must be willing to limp our limp, because the inner wounds connect us to the fountain of healing waters. Finding the Waters of Life again means suffering a kind of exile from the world of common expectations. We must become a bit lost like the youngest brother. Then, unawares and limping our limp, we come upon the golden road to the center of the psyche. It is as if for a time everything seems right in the world, and then it all shifts again and the path to the otherworld must be sought again.

Even when someone does succeed in opening the gates of imagination and releasing the flow of life again, not everyone can benefit from the renewing waters. Those stuck in fixed attitudes like the older brothers cannot imagine a different world. They prefer to steal and manipulate and will do anything to avoid facing their own pain. Their power can only come from inheritance or theft, from treachery and betrayal.

There is something incurable in this world that makes the soul long for the healing and beauty of the otherworld. Each visit to the other realm requires stopping the business and busy-ness of the daily world in order to listen to the questions being asked from the inner-under-other sides of life. The more people ignore the little voices of the soul, the less often golden caravans arrive from the other realms. Unless the inner voice and the little people are heard from again, the world will continue to drain of meaning and will keep turning a cold heart to the immensity of human suffering.

6

The Companions

The other refuses to disappear: it subsists, it
persists... in what might be the incurable
otherness from which oneness must always suffer.
ANTONIO MACHADO

THE STRANGE COMPANIONS
Part I

In the old times, not long ago but way before anything else, there lived an aged queen, who was also a sorceress, and her daughter, who was simply the most beautiful maiden under the sun. The Old Queen, however, had no thought but to lure mankind to the edge of destruction. When a man would appear and seek the hand of the beautiful princess, the Old Queen would require that he complete a difficult task or die. Many had been drawn by the beauty of the daughter and had taken the risk, but they never could accomplish what the old woman required. Then, no mercy would be shown. They had to kneel on the ground and a blade would sing in the air between their heads and their bodies.

A certain king's son heard of the maiden's incomparable beauty and said to his father, "Give me your permission to seek the daughter of the Old Queen and ask for her hand in marriage."

"Never," said the king. "If you go in that direction, you go to your death."

Hearing this, the son fell into a sickness and began to waste away entirely. For seven long years the youth lay ill. Physicians of all kinds examined the youth, but none could cure him. The king perceived that there could be no simple cure, and grasped that this was not in his control. Finally, with a heavy heart, he said to his son, "Go and try your luck, for I know of no other means of curing you."

Hearing this, the prince rose from his bed and was well again. No sooner had he arisen than he joyfully set out on his way.

Once on the way, he came across a field and saw a huge mound rising from the ground like a heap of hay. As he drew closer, he could see that it was the stomach of a man who had laid himself down, but it was a stomach that looked like a small mountain. The prince walked all the way around the side of the mound until he encountered a head. The huge man turned toward him and asked, "Where are you going? Where are you headed these days?"

The prince said, "I'm seeking the beautiful daughter of the Old Queen."

The Stout One rose slowly, saying, "If you're in need of company and would like assistance, take me with you."

The prince replied, "No offense, but what can I do in the company of a clumsy man that I couldn't do better on my own? How could it improve my condition to be in the company of such an oversized person?"

The Stout One said, "Oh, this is nothing; when I really expand and puff myself out, I'm three hundred times this size."

"If that's the case," said the prince, "you're welcome to come along."

So the Stout One and the prince went on, and after a time they came upon another man lying on the ground with his ear held close to the turf.

"What are you doing down there?" asked the prince.

"I am listening," answered the man.

"What is it that you listen to so attentively?"

"I am listening to what is just now going on in the world. Nothing escapes my ears. I even hear the grass growing out of the ground."

"Tell me, then, what do you hear at the court of the ancient queen who has the beautiful daughter?"

"I hear the whizzing of the air sharply divided by the sword that is descending upon the neck of a youth who tried to woo the beautiful maiden."

The prince said, "With ears like that, you are welcome to travel the way with us."

The three went on. After a time they saw a pair of feet lying on the ground and saw behind the feet a pair of legs. But they could not see the rest of the body because a forest got in the way of their looking. They walked on a great distance and saw how the body continued; finally, after another extended hike, they encountered a head.

"You are a tall rascal," said the prince.

"This isn't the full extent of the story," said the Tall One. "When I consciously stretch out my bones and limbs, I am three hundred times as tall as this—taller than the highest mountain on this earth."

"If you have an interest in travel, you are more than welcome to go the way with us," said the prince, and the four traveled on.

After a time they came upon a man standing by a tree at the side of the road. His eyes were bound and bandaged like one who had wandered off a battlefield. The prince asked him, "Have you weak eyes that you cannot look at the light?"

"No, but I must not remove the bandages, for whatever I look at with my eyes shatters into pieces because of the power of my glance. If you are going somewhere, I should be glad enough to go along with you."

"You are welcome to travel the way with us," the prince replied.

And on they went. After a time they came upon a man standing in the direct light of the sun in the intense heat of the day. Despite the heat, he was trembling and shivering all over.

"How can you shiver when the warm sun is striking your body?" asked the prince.

"Alas," said the man, "I am of a different nature. The hotter it is, the colder I am, and the frost pierces through my bones. Now, the contrary is also the case: the colder it is, the hotter I am. In the midst of ice, I cannot escape the heat; in the midst of fire, the cold assails me."

"You are a strange fellow," said the prince, "but you are welcome to travel the way with us." And they all traveled onward.

After a time they came upon a man standing and stretching out his neck, squinting his eye, looking all about him, and searching to a great distance.

"What are you looking at so eagerly?" asked the son of the king.

The man replied, "I am exercising my sight and polishing my vision. I have such sharp eyes that I can see into every hill and valley throughout the world."

"What do you see at the court of the Old Queen?" asked the prince.

"I see the bits of dust in the air being divided by the edge of a sword that is descending on the neck of a man foolish enough to court the beautiful daughter of the queen," the man said.

"You are welcome to come along, then," said the prince. "We can use such a man as yourself." And they went along together.

After a time they came to the realm where the Old Queen had her dwelling. The son of the king went directly before the fearsome queen. He did not say who he was, but he spoke out, "I have come seeking your beautiful daughter. I will perform whatever tasks you require of me."

The Old Queen was glad to have the handsome youth caught there in her net, and she said, "I will set you three little tasks; that is all I require, no more or less. If you are able to perform them all, you shall become the husband of my daughter. If you should fail, well, don't hold it against me, but your head must come off."

"I agree to the terms. What is the first task?"

"First you must fetch me my ring, for I have dropped it somewhere. I haven't been able to find it for years. It may be in the depths of the Red Sea, though."

The king's son went to his companions. "The first task is not easy. The Old Queen's ring must be retrieved from the bottom of the Red Sea. How can we do it? Can anyone help in this matter?"

The Man of Great Vision said he could readily see where the ring lay. He gazed into the deepest waters and said, "The ring hangs there in the depths, caught on a pointed stone."

The Tall One said he would readily snatch up that ring with his long arm, but he could not see clearly through the water.

"Is that the only problem?" asked the Stout One, and he lay down, put his mouth to the water, and began to drink. The waves formed and moved toward his great mouth and fell into him as if he were a whirlpool. In a short time, he drank up the entire sea, leaving but a dry plain. Then the Tall One reached down and plucked the ring from the stone.

The prince rejoiced and carried the ring directly to the Old Queen, who was quite astonished. "Yes, it is the right ring," she said. "You have done it, and you are safe into the bargain. Well, then, you have qualified for the next task."

CHAPTER 24

INCURABLE WOUNDS, DARK TIMES

ONCE AGAIN, the young prince of the psyche follows the initiatory pattern of separating from all he knows and entering a series of ordeals and unusual events. This time he must endure seven years of breaking down before his incurable condition becomes recognized and accepted. This time the sickness that drains life from the bones has fallen upon the young prince rather than the old king. This time the seeker after the beauty and mysteries of life will not go the long road by himself. This time he will take hardly a step along the way by himself, but will encounter the Strange Companions who seem to rise up from the earth once the incurable nature of the "soul disease" becomes understood.

This story appears in most cultures and under many guises. It is called "The Six Servants," "The Six Who Went Through the World," or something else altogether. I call it "The Companions" in order to focus on the company of ancient helpers who awaken once the real source of the illness of the soul has been allowed to surface. The Companions are connected to what seems incurable in the prince, and they connect him to the cure he seeks. They appear when a certain depth of desire becomes set in the heart and when there is nowhere else to go. The Companions are part of the human heritage; they are ancestral forces that become available at the last hour and in the darkest times.

The opening scene lays out the story's major themes. There are two realms and two rulers, and each has a problem. The ruler of the first realm won't admit the loss of beauty in the world and won't allow the heart sickness to seek its own cure. The ruler of the second realm won't relinquish beauty to the world without wild tests and ordeals that cause most to quickly lose their heads. The king suffers from an overdependence on what seems rational, while the Old Queen seems far too irrational. She, too, is incurable like the ancient ache in the human heart.

On one side the deepest longings of the soul are denied, on the other the beauty of the world is imprisoned. The dilemma of the human soul stretches between that which seems incurable and that which appears impossible. The tension between the two realms grows until it becomes clear that the heir to the realm will die unless he is released to seek the beauty his soul longs to know. The Old Queen insists that the king of earthly powers bow his head in the direction of her realm in the otherworld. Head after head will blindly roll until the Old Queen's power over life and death becomes acknowledged.

In this world what is young and compelling and indelibly connected to beauty will waste away unless people accept again the strange and ancient powers of the soul. Only then will the weird old helpers of the psyche awaken from their sleep in the earth.

Only after all superficial cures have failed do we accept the incurability of what ails the soul. What struck the young prince was an old story, not some new symptom.

He heard what the soul listens to hear: That which is most beautiful does exist and she can only be found in a distant place and must be approached through impossible tasks. Many have tried the adventure, but they have all lost their heads in the attempt.

The young prince hears the "call to the soul" that awakens its longing for a greater life. Somewhere something of overwhelming beauty is imprisoned, that seeking it means fear and great danger. It's the old story that ever hits the heart of mankind anew. The news of beauty and danger falls all the way through the labyrinth of the ear to awaken the sense of destiny buried in the heart. From there it works its way all through the bones and organs until the prince of life has become sick in body and in soul.

The call to beauty and danger speaks directly to an ancient, ancestral, and imaginative place within. This is what life must be about; this is something worth risking life for. This is the eternal drama, the story constantly being recreated in the soul of each person and in the soul of each generation. The object of desire may vary, but the soul retains its ancient and extreme longing for the presence of the beautiful and its willingness to face death for glimpse of it. The son of the psyche knows that the sense of danger and death must be part of it. The road of greater life and certain death appear together. He heard it all at once—beauty and the danger of death lie in the same direction. This is the point—the exact initiatory point—the release of essential beauty and an encounter with the realm of death and things ancient in the human soul. That adventure can change a life completely.

What he hears holds both sickness and cure, both beauty and terror, both immediate and ancient conditions. The prince has become weirdly sick; he has become sick and weird. No amount of rest can cure this illness and all the physicians together can't manage to heal it. It doesn't respond to less tension or to more pressure. Hearing that his desire is impossible to achieve won't change a thing. Self-medication won't help. Improved self-esteem won't help. Being the child of powerful parents doesn't matter. There's nothing for it in the end except for him to seek exactly that which creates both longing and fear. He has contracted the initiatory disease: If he goes, he'll face death. If he doesn't go, he will surely die.

As long as the longing of the soul is denied, life wastes regardless of one's position or estate. The soul is sick and the situation remains incurable at the level of abstract theories and common expectations. The seven years of incurability signifies whatever length of time it takes strip away the trappings of life and shed anything that obscures the vision that struck the center of the soul. The only way to treat the condition involves getting all else out of the way and allowing the soul sickness to speak for itself. It can only be heard when all the possible cures have been eliminated and its incurability has been admitted. The soul sickness needs permission to be the strange story that it declares itself to be.

Most people have within them a chamber of the heart where an essential and noble part of them lies incurably ill. The inner sickness comes from being separated from beauty and denied the full range of life that the soul imagines. The ideas of life one has been handed and the ego attitudes one has constructed argue that we will lose our heads and go mad if we follow the extreme longings harbored within. Yet repressing the longings of the soul drives us crazy in another direction even if the mask of normality is carefully maintained. In the end there can be no normal people, for each person contains something of the other, something otherworldly and inherently weird.

To be human means to inherit the extreme nature of the original ancestors and the "incurable wound" that places longing deep in the heart and desire strong in the soul. To be human means to suffer that which is incurable while longing for what seems impossible. Like our ancestors we are nailed to the cross of impossibility where heaven and earth conspire to hold us until imagination is allowed to shape a radical redemptive path. Each soul suffers its own incurability and each must find its own radical cure.

No description of the sick prince is offered because he is the sick child of the nobility native to each person. No description of the "most beautiful woman" is needed because she represents the hidden beauty in every living soul. He is sick and weird with longing and she is beautiful beyond belief. The prince of the soul is incurably ill and the daughter of the Old Queen of life is incurably beautiful. Both conditions sleep and stir within each person and trouble each epoch.

Any real movement towards a cure begins with acceptance of the incurability of the condition. The youth knows that beauty, terror, and death are all calling from the other side of the door. He has no way to heal the conditions of his soul except to cross the threshold to the adventure that calls to him. Yet the king, representing the status quo, maintains a great resistance to the opening of that particular door. He'd rather have a sick son than risk opening up to otherness and the unknown. It's as if the king were actually resisting something else, not just the son's passing through the door but the unveiling of the path that leads to the weird, ancient companions of the soul. For beyond the forbidden door waits what has been repressed in the family and in the culture. "Not that," says the father or the king or the president. Many stories carry the warning, "You can go anywhere you wish, but don't open that door." Everything else must be tried, but "not that."

The human psyche carries an inheritance of a most conservative king as well as an indelible cast of radical characters aching to live again. One day, whether through incurable illness or unquenchable desire, we must open the forbidden door or else waste life away. Simply opening the door to the forbidden road changes the nature of the sickness of the soul. For a cure is first of all an exposure, an airing out. What gets cured first gets exposed to the light and fresh air. The king's son has been a curator of his ailing soul; now he begins to air it out.

The prince has contracted a creative illness. Nothing can help except he become more imaginative about his life and more creative in how he handles the longings within him. Sure enough, the first task will be to find and return the lost ring—the gold hoop of unity and sovereignty—that has fallen to the very bottom of the sea. The unifying symbols continually become lost and must again be found or the problems of the world will remain incurable and impossible to resolve.

Despite the modern fascination with the surface of life and the sense of entitlement and enlightenment, what has been lost to the world can only be found below. The powers of beauty and healing lost in the day-bright world have fallen into the dark and forbidding places beyond the light of day, otherwise they would be plain to see and easy to find again. The eye of normality and rationality seeks the cure everywhere except off the beaten path where it must be found. Things become darker and weirder until a person turns toward the weird on their own.

The incurable condition of the soul appears as a dark time, as a dark night of the soul, that can envelop an individual, a community, an era. The incurable condition of the son of the realm can also represent the condition of modern life beset by incurable diseases in the realm of culture and radical disturbances and losses in nature itself.

In the incurable area of the psyche, the real matter at hand is always an issue of life or death. It's always the dark time when everything is about to change. It's always the last hour, always the end of one stage and the beginning of another. It's always the millennium come round again. When the structures have broken down in a culture, that which has been denied and repressed can return. This return brings with it new potentials, energies that were long held back and that have a capacity to burst through old disabilities. The results can be both terrible and beautiful.

Curing the soul sickness means learning to see despite the increase of darkness. The Strange Companions seem to wait just beyond the reach of the enlightenment, on the outskirts of modernity in the darkening light at the close of the modern era. City lights glow twenty-four hours, day and night, as if everyone secretly knows it's a truly dark time. The morning papers and nightly news repeat a litany of loss and destruction, and a rant of conflict and confusion. Meanwhile, the trees and forests weep.

The trees, which once stood as reminders of the Tree of Life and often represented the ancestors as well, now stand like empty icons amidst the endangered species of life. A thousand years ago the forests were wide and impenetrable and news traveled slowly. Now the news eats the forest in order to print itself, it speaks on lines that cross through the trees, and it leaps over them with the ease of a fire driven by a heedless wind. As the life force drains out of forests it also drains out of the institutions of culture. Losses in nature are paralleled by losses of vitality in the patterns of culture. As the wind of the rapid-fire events whips through the world, actual forests and the forest of imagination grow smaller each day.

It is partly the nature of the end of a life stage or the end of a historical age that some aspects wind down and some collapse. Loss is an integral part of any major change. The modern world stands at the threshold that ends one age and begins another. The dying age sees the history of the past thousand years pass before its eyes, just as a person who is dying may see his or her life flash by. As we struggle at the threshold of change, we face the question asked at the end of each age and each stage of life: Is this the end of reality, or is it a metaphorical ending that is occurring? Is it the shedding, breaking down, and falling off of old forms so that the threshold can be crossed into another stage of culture, another age of life? Or is this the final curtain?

That has been the question hanging on the threshold of life since World War II and the dawning of our capacity to destroy the greater world by exploding the smallest pieces of it. At the threshold the facts of life, the inner truths of psychology, and the timeless wisdom of myth begin to merge. Outerworld, innerworld, and otherworld coincide briefly. The actual, the incurable, and the impossible meet. The end of an age or a stage is like a near-death experience. Is it necessary actually to die, or is this cultural brush with the great wing of death the prelude to a new era? This serious and mysterious question can only be answered in the minds and hearts and imaginations of people who find themselves standing at the threshold in times of radical change.

On the threshold of an age, time seems to flow backward and forward at the same time. Old battlefields are revisited. Old kingdoms try to resurface. Nations form and reform more quickly than even instant news can travel. Money changes value faster than it changes hands. The "new order" is both disorder and many orders at once. We witness the return of the incurable, of the sins of the fathers visited on the sons, and of the old wounds and conflicts refusing to be covered over or treated symptomatically.

Old battles for sovereignty, struggles among religions, and surges of tribal revenge resurface from their hiding places just below the ground cover of modern times. The incurable returns in the form of issues that won't go away, won't stay buried, and won't allow themselves to be put behind us. Once again the great question of a woman's right to choose abortion lies on the legislative tables and in the courtrooms of America. Once again the death penalty is in question in state after state. Once again the demand for civil rights flares up throughout the country. Again, the question of racism in America demands attention. Meanwhile, the great questions that divide the genders rattle within houses and institutions throughout the country.

Can there be female and male faces in positions of authority and, if so, what is the nature of the authority enacted by each? Can the multiple faces of the diverse cultures that are thrown into the great sea of America surface and be seen? As the number of incidents of violence increases in city after city, can America survive only as an armed camp? Can a country founded in colonial wars, indentured servitude, and slavery and, therefore, dreaming of freedom and democracy survive a return to the roots of its own origins? Does the right to bear arms ultimately mean that we have to live under siege? Will the experiment in democracy end in a democratic shoot-out or through holes shot in the ozone?

Entire cultures now pass through periods of initiatory ordeals, as a shedding of forms leaves hordes of people stripped of even basic aspects of life and everyone becomes exposed to the radical changes erupting from nature and culture alike. The changes are so sweeping and rapid that they are quicker than the eye of the television camera. Film has to be slowed down in order for us to see what has actually happened and, even then, there are as many interpretations as there are viewers. The same questions are asked over and over, the same incurable scenes broadcast again and again, the same old battlefields revisited, and the same religious issues fan the flames and overheat the conflicts. This is not history repeating itself but history defeating itself while something essential remains hidden from common sight. What repeats and repeatedly seeks for genuine attention are the great symbols of the psyche, the crucial images of a culture, the startling forms of nature, and the incurable dilemmas of life.

Allowing the incurability of life to be a felt presence can feel like a great loss, especially to those who would claim to save everyone. Admitting the incurable wound adds gravity to each person and gravitas to each situation. If there is no miracle cure just around the corner, things become heavier in the present and things must slow down. What's the sense of rushing forward if the same dilemmas await everyone in the future? And why rush ahead if the real path begins right here in the shadows of uncertainty, in the darkness at the edge of common awareness?

Like the golden ring of the Old Queen, the missing key that might unlock the door to a cure lies in the shadows of the present. When everyone has lost their way, the way must be found again in the darkness and unconsciousness that waits right at the edge of the overly bright lights of the anxious daily world. "We can only go as far forward as we reach back," they used to say, back when people could hold the future together with the past. Some old golden ring that holds things altogether has been lost and can only be recovered from the deep waters of the psyche, from the refuse of old traditions, and from the residue of ancient wisdom thoughtlessly tossed out of sight and into the darkness.

In a dark time the repressed tries to return through incurable diseases and impossible tasks. In the darkness of modern life what seems most repressed are the instinct for authenticity and the powers of imagination that connect living people to the strange old companions of the soul with their weird ways of surviving and creating life anew.

The road of the Strange Companions involves the return of that which has been repressed in the individual and in culture. The Companions are the "radicals of the soul," each as radical as the tasks are impossible. Each embodies capacities and powers beyond the normal. They are bizarre and exaggerated, ridiculous and extreme to the normal eye. But on the road of destiny their strange capacities become remarkable and necessary gifts. They are the strange guardians and curators of the soul and they are equal to the wild imagination of the Old Queen who's behind the whole thing. Each represents a connection to the *wyrrdd*, the Welsh word that gives us "weird" and carries meanings and intimations of both fate and destiny.

Young people quickly perceive any essential strangeness in a person and to this day label it weird. Typically, such qualities are both attractive and repulsive; they distinguish a person from everyone else and indicate something decidedly abnormal in them. Nicknaming tries to name the otherness and weirdness in a person. Often this can be the actual point around which friendships form and the place where friends remain timelessly connected. Denying the strange extremes and the deeply different aspects of people can turn their strangeness into something damaging to themselves and others. The strangeness and otherness of the soul does not leave a person. It seeks ways to live into the world. It's the weird and otherworldly aspects of a person that make unusual contributions to life possible. The weirdness in one person can help another move closer to their purpose and can remind each of the uniqueness of each human soul.

The Companions are not literal people. They represent the extremes of imagination, purpose, and capacity that can awaken when the psyche reaches the edge of the unknown and faces the impossible. Secretly connected to the genius in a person, the Companions awaken when a person finds a genuine calling in life. If the soul is bound to have troubles and symptoms, it is also bound to have strange helpers. They tend to show up once the road of fate and destiny has been accepted. The Companions of the soul can appear as animals, strange beings, the spirit of trees, or wise old souls who wait along the paths our souls were destined to walk. They are made of the same otherworldly stuff as the dwarf, the horse of power, the little shaggy horse, and the lizard in the fire. Being connected to the soul's indelible and unique purpose, they run counter to what has been suppressed and repressed by fixed attitudes and abstract standards for living.

The Strange Companions of the soul underlie our personal and cultural symptoms. In one sense, the Companions are the symptoms carried to the extreme. But once engaged they become ready to reveal how to move toward a cure. The huge man can be seen as an eating disorder personified, yet his unlimited appetite clears the way to the ring that represents unity and wholeness. Once aligned with a meaningful purpose the symptom becomes part of the solution. Remove his unlimited appetite and you lose his limitless capacity to absorb and digest and contain.

The symptoms of personal and cultural sickness are aimed at something; they are purposeful. On the surface a symptom seems to be the problem. Yet treating only the symptom makes the underlying trouble worse. Purpose hides within the symptom. Wisdom seeks not simply the cause of the symptom in the past, but the purpose hidden within it, the goal that the symptom secretly points to and aims at.

Wisdom is attained by going to the depths, finding meaning below in the dark tangle of emotions and repressions that appear as illness above. It's important not to take the darkness out of wisdom, for wisdom begins in the half-light where the upper-world meets the underworld. Those who try to be wise without descending to the deeper levels of meaning turn out to be just clever. Under pressure, they easily lose their heads. What's missing and needed, what has been repressed and has fallen below common awareness, must be sought in the exact extremities of the psyche, at the edges of knowledge and in the depths of awareness.

The prince doesn't do the tasks, yet he's not above them. He suffers the tests of the Old Queen and her daughter, but the weird Companions carry them out. The Companions involve extreme, usually hidden capacities of body and soul that awaken when the search for the unity of life is genuinely undertaken. A part of the soul can withstand extremes of heat or cold, like a yogi able to practice under any conditions. Another aspect can eat and drink huge quantities and have an even greater appetite for whatever else life has to offer. The soul has an inner ear that can listen to anything, as if the capacity to hear and understand can be extended to the farthest extremes of sympathy and empathy. The awakened psyche can also cast a glance that shatters all illusions and cracks the hardest case of fixed ideas.

The psyche carries extreme capacities that mostly go unused, especially where a person lacks knowledge of their own inherent purpose in life. Once awakened, however, the psyche can release even opposing powers in ways that cooperate with the innate sense of that life. The Companions cooperate strangely; they relieve each other's symptoms and reveal the purpose in each other. What the Man of Great Vision sees at a great distance can be grasped by the Tall One; what blocks his ability to reach can be absorbed in the endless appetite of the Stout One. All are radical aspects of an individual and of the ancestral psyche, each able to assist the other once the entire psyche becomes committed to the task of seeking beauty, healing, and finding a sense of wholeness.

The first test of the Old Queen requires and inspires the cooperation of several extreme capacities. Finding and retrieving the lost symbol of unity and faithfulness can only be done when the latent powers of the soul become fully engaged. The gold ring falls where it always falls... to the depths. Those who are single-minded, simply heroic, or working from an abstract theory will be easily overwhelmed at such depths. Those who approach the problem with simple logic or rationality will lose their heads in such deep waters. But the weird and often repressed appetites and energies of the deep self, strangely working together, can bring the whole psyche together long enough to return a symbol of unity to the world.

Considered from the view of the otherworld, the Old Queen is teaching the "wisdom of the weird." Like Mother Nature, she resists giving up the secrets of life and the mysteries of beauty and being. Yet she too can be moved by the weird elements of individual destiny. Like the kings of the world she can resist and be possessive, but she must offer dilemmas that can be solved. Although her tests seem impossible, they must be passable. Those are the rules of the weird, and even the Old Queen must bow to the limits of fate and the secret connection between the human and the eternal.

Each individual soul inherits radical roots that can tap the family tree and reach beyond it to ancestral resources containing all the ancient passions and abilities known to human memory. No matter how long they have been suppressed or ignored, the Strange Companions represent radical aspects of the soul that won't be fully repressed. On one hand they are the extreme passions that only worsen when repressed; on the other hand they are radical capacities equal to the "almost impossible task" of becoming oneself, fully alive in the world.

Humans are radical by nature. Radicals are those things that cannot be eradicated, the elements in the individual soul that run so deep that they draw nourishment from ethnic root systems that outlive history and from even deeper roots universal to all human life. The "radicals of the soul" are our ancient, imaginal roots, the eternal, indelible qualities that secretly connect us to the otherworld. They can neither be fully repressed nor pulled up by the roots. Knowing oneself at the root level awakens an inner connection to the ancestral helpers. A person's originality comes from the radical roots that connect them to the mythic origins of life. That's where the wise elder in a person originates, that's where the purpose in a life is rooted, and that's where the passion for living can be located when lost and desperately needed again.

The meeting with the huge man appears as a test of the initiate's ability to tolerate and value the extreme appetites and passions of the ancestral world. The conversation between the prince and the Stout Man is like a psychological interview through which the huge being explains himself and the nature of this strange territory. He makes clear that he is not simply a fat man who can't control his appetite and eats himself to a standstill. He's not lying on the ground because he can't get up. Rather, he waits—as the dwarf waited—until someone recognizes the need for his insatiable appetite for life. If you think he should be ashamed of himself for overeating, you're mistaken. If you think that pointing to his excessive weight and awkward state will get him out of the way, you've got the wrong man. He isn't moving and he isn't ashamed of himself. In fact, he points out, "This is nothing. When I puff myself up, I'm three hundred times this size." He knows who he is and how he's valuable. He's an aspect of the soul's insatiable desire and appetite for life in this incarnated world. "Deal with it," he seems to say.

The prince cannot be cured of his desire to seek what is most beautiful. The huge man can't be talked into a diet or shamed into another form; he is the possessor of and is possessed by a huge appetite for the immediacy of life. If you are going to take him along, you have to take the radical appetite as well. He isn't asking for the usual sympathy or for good advice or for support for his problem. He is beyond help, beyond any cure. He has fallen below the symptom to the ground of its origin.

The huge man seems to be the other side of the wasting sickness of the king's son. He appears after seven years of wasting away, as if when the prince finds his appetite again he finds the very essence desire. He encounters appetite personified, an unquenchable thirst and hunger for life finally released from the imposed limits of the father and king representing family and society. The huge man is like a symptom released and allowed to reach its full extension. The word "symptom" means to fall together with. *Ptoma* is the Greek root indicating a falling body, or something that falls upon a person and comes to inhabit their body. A symptom appears where something essential to that life becomes ignored or rejected. Being part and parcel of the body-soul of that person, it cannot simply disappear. So it falls into the body where it continues to live unconsciously. From there it aches or itches as it tries to draw attention to life energies that need to be attended to and released.

The huge man turns our usual perspective upside down: In contrast to the idea that inside every fat person there is a skinny person trying to get out, the huge man says that inside every fat person struggles an even bigger person trying to get out. From the point of view of the huge man, the cure for his overeating isn't dieting; the cure lies in falling further into the source of our appetites. Beneath the overeating of daily bread or junk food lies an appetite for life that is not being recognized, much less satisfied. "You can never get enough of what you don't really want," people used to say when people used to consider more thoroughly what the soul really wants, lacks and desires. Below simple hunger for food is an indelible appetite for participating in the great dramas of the psyche and being at the great feast where everyone is fed what they truly need. Behind the doors of bodily shame and pangs of guilt lies an even bigger person with a huge appetite for the spiritual quest that can return the senses to the living beauty of the world.

The Old Queen wants the desire for beauty and wholeness to be felt at the depths where it originates. If it cannot be experienced in depth, then it must be lived unconsciously and compulsively at the surface of life. If a person or a culture won't seek to learn life's genuine meanings and purposes, then symptoms that mimic desire will be lived literally. Appetite will manifest itself in overeating. Desire for beauty and wholeness will become simple greed stuck at the literal level of accumulating and hoarding goods and gold. Ambition will keep conquering the same plots of ground and never look to discover why those grounds are fought over again and again. When the symptom is taken literally, the voices that are trying to speak through the symptom are missed and dismissed.

The huge man teaches the son of the realm what kind of imagination is needed on the road of "almost impossible tasks." As they encounter more strange fellows, the prince becomes increasingly alert to how the seeming symptom of each companion can also be a huge help. He speaks directly to the symptomatic place in each companion. The excessive, obsessive listening of the man with his ear to the ground would be considered paranoid if in the daily world. On the road of awakened longing, however the obsession with listening becomes hearing all the way into the ground of things and anticipating dangers. The Listening One is like a dream interpreter who hears every voice speaking in the soul. The prince needs him because moving on the ground of destiny is like following the dream of life and learning the languages that the inner dream speaks.

By suffering his own incurable condition long enough, the son of the king attracts and is attracted to others with extreme conditions. Each seems to suffer alone until they align with the great dream of freeing beauty and returning it to the world. They recognize in each other not sufferers of the same disease but sufferers experiencing the same intensity of dis-ease. They see into each other's trouble in a way that permits them to go along together, forming a group based on having suffered something to its very roots and, being no longer stuck with the weakness of it, finding the radical power hidden in it.

The Companions represent capacities that surface and can be glimpsed during "life-defining" moments that are also the steps of initiation in a person's life. For a moment a person had a huge appetite, felt insatiable desire and an unlimited imagination. On that occasion one or more of the Strange Companions and capacities of the soul entered the world through them. Faced with what felt like "life and death circumstances," a person suddenly could see far ahead or hear the whisperings of fate, understand the language of birds or withstand tremendous heat and pressure. The huge man's appetite for life was present and the heights and depths of feeling and imagination were experienced. The ear of the Listener opened and heard all the way into the ground of being and a whisper of destiny was revealed. Another person suddenly looks within with a penetrating vision that shatters the walls of denial and opens an inner world that had gone dark with pain and numbness.

Unfortunately, experiences with the radical Companions of the soul do not fit well into daily life. Often the capacity to be present at that level lasts just long enough for a person to make an important turn—one that saves a life, or gives meaning to it, or leads it to find love. The Stout One disturbs everyone with his insatiability and complaints about the inadequacy of the common daily fare. People feel uneasy at his lack of boundaries and limits. The Man of Shattering Vision is invaluable when turned loose on a problem or when attacking false arguments or bitter enemies. But after he's looked things over most points of view are torn apart, things are shattered, and deconstructed.

The fierce and extravagant Companions of the soul are too much to bear all the time. As with most of the radical figures in the psyche, the point is not to become one of them but to develop conscious relations with them. The prince of the psyche must continue to focus on the purpose that once afflicted him severely in order to be a unifying force amidst the radical and overwhelming energies harbored in the depths of the soul. After death, a person goes to join these ancestral forces. Until then, the idea is to remain human while opening the soul to the eternal forces of life.

THE STRANGE COMPANIONS
Part II

Once the first test had been passed, the Old Queen directed the young prince to look out the palace window. "Do you see that meadow stretching out beyond my castle? Do you see those three hundred fat oxen feeding back and forth there? Those you must eat. The skin, the hair, the bones, the horns, the flesh, the entire heft and hoof of each one of the three hundred must be eaten. That may cause you a thirst or a dryness in the mouth, so in the cellar below lie three hundred casks of wine. Those you must drink as well. If one hair of one ox remains in that field, if one drop of wine remains in the corner of one of those barrels, then your life is forfeited and your head must leave your body."

"Well," said the prince, "a dinner, whatever its size, is a poor thing if it is taken without company. Can I not invite guests?"

The old woman laughed with malice, "For the sake of companionship, you may invite one to join you, that is all."

The king's son went to the Companions and called the Stout One, saying, "You shall be my guest today, and you shall eat your fill." The Stout One was ready for this event. He first puffed himself up and then began to capture oxen. Some he pounced on, others he caught on the hoof as they ran by, and still others he rolled over as he went about. Whatever way he caught them, he treated them all similarly, devouring each one, skin, flesh, bones, and marrow, down to the last organ, to the last hair. After finishing the three-hundredth ox, he began to complain that it was unfair, false advertising, seriously misleading to invite someone to a meal and provide nothing but little snacks.

The complaining engendered a thirst, and the Stout One was glad enough to enter the cellar and drink the wine that was there. He drank it by opening the spigot of each wooden barrel and drawing the wine out, until there was no moisture at all, until the barrel was as dry as old bones and completely collapsed. He treated all three hundred barrels of wine in that fashion, and berated the keepers of the cellar for the paucity of their stock, saying that it was a crime of another order to have such a limited supply that a man, just as he was beginning to appreciate the fine qualities of the grapes, should find himself already at the bottom of the barrel.

When the meal was over, the prince went to the old woman and told her that the second task was completed. She was amazed and said that no one had ever gotten this far before. "Still," she said, "one task remains." And to herself she thought, "You shall not escape me, nor will you keep your head connected to your shoulders after this night!"

"Tonight," she said out loud, "I will bring my daughter to you in your chamber, and you shall put your arms around her. But you must keep your arms about her and beware of falling asleep. When the clock is striking twelve, the last hour, I will come. If she is no longer in your arms, you are lost forever."

The prince thought, "This task is easy and pleasurable. I will keep my eyes open gladly." Nevertheless he called the Companions and told them of the task, saying, "Who knows what treachery may lurk behind this. Let everyone take care that once the maiden is in my room, she does not leave it again."

Night fell and the Old Queen brought her daughter and gave her over into the prince's arms. Then the Tall One wound his arms around the two of them, and the Stout One placed himself in front of the door so that no living creature could gain entrance past him. The rest of the Companions arranged themselves around the room. In the middle sat the prince and the daughter of the Old Queen. The maiden never spoke a word, but the moon shone through the window on her face and the prince beheld her wondrous beauty in that soft silver light. He did nothing but gaze upon her. His heart filled with love and his eyes did not weary for all he looked. He held her in his gaze and in his embrace until eleven o'clock. At that time, the old woman cast such a spell over all of them that they fell sound asleep, and in the same moment the maiden was carried away. They slept a deep sleep until a quarter to twelve, when the spell reached its limit and lost its power.

"She is gone and I am lost," cried the prince. The Companions all began to lament the loss of the whole thing.

Finally the Listener called for quiet. "No more noise, I want to listen… she is stranded on a rock far from here, bewailing her fate and isolation. Only you can reach her quickly, Tall One, with your long strides."

"I'm off," said the Tall One, "but the One with Piercing Eyes must go with me, that we may destroy the rock." The Tall One took the one with bandaged eyes on his back and, quick as an eye can blink, they reached the enchanted rock. The Tall One took the bandages from the head of Piercing Eyes and turned him toward the rock. One piercing look shattered the huge rock into a thousand pieces. The Tall One caught the maiden in his arms and carried her back in no time, turned her over to the prince, and returned and fetched his Companion. In short order all were sitting exactly as they had been before.

The clock struck twelve and the Old Queen abruptly came in, certain that the maiden was stuck on the enchanted rock and that the prince was in her power. What a shock when she beheld her daughter gazing into the eyes of the prince and the prince raptly gazing back on her as the moonlight bathed them both! "Here is one who knows more than I do," she said in alarm. She feared to set up any further opposition to him, and she promised her daughter to him.

But she whispered one little thing into the sweetly formed ear of the beautiful maiden: "Isn't it a disgrace and a shameful thing that you have to obey common people, to give yourself over to a common man and not even be allowed to choose a husband equal in quality to you and suited to your own liking?"

The daughter of that old and powerful queen began to think about what had been said. She knew nothing of this man; he appeared to be common enough. What if he meant harm to her, and what was one to make of all those Strange Companions? Soon she was cooking up a test of her own.

CHAPTER 25

SACRED AND AFFLICTED

THE STORY IS VERY SPECIFIC when it says that the Old Queen has no purpose other than to bring mankind to the edge of destruction. But she also would continually bring mankind to the edge of creation. In many old stories the grandmother or Grand Mother of the people waits in her cave at the end of the road of life. She offers the simple fate of death or an encounter with destiny—that is, with one's hidden destination. At the entrance to the cave she conducts an interview and administers a test. The old grandmother draws half of a design in the dirt; the soul poised at the edge of life and death must fill in the missing half so that it fits the design of life she has drawn. If the visitor is able to match her design with an equal design learned through living, he touches his destiny; if not, his head rolls. . . again.

The old woman never tires of such encounters, nor does her daughter. Each time a different design appears, for each soul carries a unique shape. Losing one's head in such encounters is not the worst thing that can happen; it is much worse to never glimpse the other side of the design, to never have the insight of the dream woven into one's own life. That is a fate worse than death.

One meaning of the word "symbol" is to throw or fit pieces together. The old grandmother draws a part of the symbol of a life and the one trying to be fully alive must find the other part of the design in how they have lived and loved in the world. When drawn together the two halves symbolize who that person must be. Being and becoming who we already are means accepting certain incurable things and finding certain indelible qualities within. The idea of the "elder" includes the sense of a person who has survived the struggles with life and brushes with death enough to extract knowledge of their own place in the great design. The elder has studied both sides of the web of life and found a foothold in each world.

The "old woman of the soul" is an essential image that waits at the end of many roads, handling the destinies of people and the fate of cultures. She is one of the radical images that moves in the depths of both the individual and the collective psyche. She has a hand in every birth and a hand in every death. She waits at the fountain of life, at the shores of the river Styx, and at the well of healing and inspiration. She often presents herself with the horrid face of death. But behind her waits the daughter of renewed life and inspired beauty. Sometimes all she requires is a kiss that shows a certain courage for all of life and an acceptance of aging and death; more often she also requires the accomplishment of seemingly impossible tasks.

She may appear as the hag at the well, the old mother at the cave, or simply an old woman asking for food. An individual or a culture can be destroyed by not handling the initiatory fires of youth, but can also become unraveled by neglecting to shape elders from the trials of life. The beautiful princess, who represents new life waiting to be seen, is nourished at the old hag's well. The Water of Life is returned to a culture through that well. The elders of a culture, both women and men, sip at the well. The Old Queen will abide the foolishness of youth as long as the imagination of beauty remains in the world. But she doesn't tolerate arrogance or blindness where vision is required, and she'll take the head of any who lack the courage to handle the tension and conflict necessary to fully awaken the dream of life.

The loss of mythic imagination that plagues and severely limits modern understanding of both problems and cures also limits the sense of the ancestors. With the meaning of death narrowed to a biological condition and a literal end, the door to the ancestors and otherworldly helpers closes and the inner resources connected to human origins are cut off. "Original"

comes to mean new, newly invented rather than created again from the living depths of origin. The soul cannot shed its innate connections to things old and ancient because each person has an old soul. Yet delusions of a future divorced from the past and obsessions with things that seem new under the sun have become the common view. Under the obsession with progress and a life-saving future, old has come to suggest worn out and useless, while elder indicates one soon to be over the hill.

In old cultures what mattered in the end was that which was old enough to be ancient and, therefore, in touch with the realm of origins from which all things originate. Under that world view the elders become those who survive their own incurable wounds and learn to work with what ails the community. The elders are old enough to know better than to fall for the latest scam or the promise of simple retirement from life. They are old enough to know that death comes to everyone. Though hard of hearing in terms of this world, the elders learn to commune with the ancestors who guide from the other side of the grave.

An old proverb says, "The elders are wise because they know more dead people." In this way, the land of the dead or the territory of the ancestors and wisdom can be seen as being connected. Knowing more dead people means knowing more of the otherworld as well as the inner-underworld. In the old view, dead people are still people in some ways. Dying makes one an ancestor, not simply a corpse. The body dies and decomposes but the soul returns to the ancestors and it retains an interest in life.

The ancestors are those from whom we are derived; they are our forefathers, foremothers, and forerunners. We have descended from ancestors both known and unknown and we have inherited physical, emotional, and spiritual aspects of ourselves from them. But ancestors are also those who precede us through the door of death and into the otherworld. In that sense, ancestors are before us as well as behind; they are within us and buried below us. Knowing more dead people means paying attention to the unseen things all around us that, though rarely considered, make up who we are and precede what we do. Knowing more dead people means developing an imagination for all that inhabits the world and contributes to our being, to our being human, and to our being alive.

In the tribal world, ancestors are involved with the living and must be honored, placated, learned about, and listened to. As forebearers they can either guide when life becomes difficult or interfere when origins are ignored. Usually considered to include all who have lived before, the ancestors form a community that surrounds the living society of souls. At the deepest level of meaning the ancestors become the ancient and ongoing pool of human spirit naturally communing with animal and plant spirits. Seen that way, the ancestors become valuable inner relations who mirror the weird Companions and helping spirits in stories the world over.

Old ideas of this world often remind that life continually emerges from death; death gives birth to life. The modern world tends to have problems with death. Being over-committed to what can be measured and proven, the point of death becomes a final end as life passes beyond the grasp of what can be measured. The problem with seeing death literally is that it creates a dead end for life. The original notion of a gravestone was to mark where the dead person entered the land of the ancestors. It served to connect the living to them as well as keeping the dead in their place. When modern ideas began to reject the instinctive and intuitive connections to the realm of the dead, life also became diminished and people developed the problem of the ancestors.

Before the tremendous migrations of people in modern times, a person would commonly be walking near or even on the ground that held their ancestors. People walked on the heads of the dead, figuratively and sometimes literally. Today, people often don't know who their actual ancestors were or even the original place from which they came. In fact, under the banner of progress, many prefer not to be connected to ancestors who remind them of inferior ways or terrible deeds.

Yet, at crucial intersections and turning points in life the idea of having ancient knowledge and wise ancestors can provide a steadying and encouraging sense of not walking the path alone. There may be confounded skeletons rattling in the family closet and in the national records, but ancestry has levels that cannot be held by history's seemingly solid grasp. Besides specific forerunners on one's family tree, there are those ancestors who represent the best qualities of a tribe or a culture. These are specific individuals who have lived in a meaningful way and who, after their death, are claimed as ancestors even by unrelated people. Beyond both literal predecessors and heroic forefathers, a third level of ancestry includes the original and mythic ancestors. These are the radical roots of humanity, the deepest roots from which the human family tree continues to grow.

The importance of the levels of ancestry becomes apparent when we seek deeper roots of knowledge in order to cure personal or collective problems. From the first level of ancestors—the actual family members who have lived before us—we know that we have inherited diseases and other troubles. From the second level, we remain plagued by the misguided and ill-intended actions of past cultural leaders. If we are trying to change some cycle of damage passed down through our family or trying to escape forefathers who represent historical calamities and atrocities, we may turn away from the idea of ancestry altogether.

Strangely, though, we can find healing ancestors on the family trees of others. The second level of ancestors—those who are chosen for their admirable and desired qualities—can help to heal problems inherited from direct predecessors. Revered individuals who lived nobly yet are unrelated to us by blood can become like tribal or clan ancestors. We can honor them and they can connect us to inner sources of imagination, endurance, and healing.

The third level of ancestors involves a more mythic inheritance, a layer of human imagination and resilience that transcends the history of tribal wars and human vengeance. While tribalism tends to continue the bloody history and folly of humanity, many tribal groups carry the tradition of universal ancestors who speak through living people with the voice of healing and renewal. Tribalism doesn't go far enough to find the level of universal humanity that lies deeper than the levels of partisan mania. The way to approach ideas of ancestry is similar to the attitude of the huge man in the story when he says, "If you think this is large, you should see me when I become three hundred times larger." The third level of ancestors involves the great pool of prototypes, archetypes, deities, and spiritual figures who appear in many guises but who form the common heritage of humanity. There is a hidden unity to the individual psyche and a mythic unity that humanity shares and secretly seeks to touch each time the dark times return.

The Old Queen in our story appears in all cultures and in many guises: She is the Hag of Beara who made the world and fierce Kali who can easily destroy it; she is Persephone, queen of the underworld, and the virginal Kore ever being born anew; she is the Baba Yaga who collects skulls and Isis who gathers all the dismembered members. She is the tomb of death and the womb of life; the "kiss of death" and the well of inspiration from which life renews again and again.

The seemingly impossible tasks that she requires create the circumstances that cause people to imagine in a greater way and to remember how wild and diverse and extreme life truly is. The Strange Companions are part of her gift to life, part of the ancestral human heritage, and also aspects of human imagination waiting to come to life again through us.

When the obstacles in the world become greater and more complex and seem to be coming from all directions at once, there are two great tendencies in the psyche. One is to simplify and quickly adopt some form of fundamentalism. The other is to accept the multiplicity and the great tension that come from embracing the world as it presents itself. The weird companions represent a person's sudden, increased capacity for life once the incurable nature of the world has been accepted. Accepting the Companions also means being willing to travel along paths that are creative and uncertain at the same time.

Ancient peoples used imaginative rituals to create bridges from the common world to the land of ancestral imagination and the ground of human origins. Rituals help to break the lock of linear time and open the gates of perception to things eternal. In ritual time and sacred space seemingly impossible things can be experienced for a time. Every genuine appearance of the beautiful shatters the march of time and leaves the soul in a timeless state. Most often a person needs to separate from the exacting limits of the daily world to find some peace, to see some beauty, to be touched by inspiration from beyond the inevitable conflicts of life.

The chorus of men who have been responding to these ancient tales and who offered their lives as material for exploring the plight of the soul in the modern world were part of an ongoing experiment with ritual as well. Whenever a group of people comes together to deal with meaningful issues the soul thinks a ritual has begun. More often than not a ritual is trying to be discovered or rediscovered. Art and ritual are ancient and instinctive ways to shape and display the essential expressions of the human soul.

Bringing groups of serious men together stirs the old radicals of the soul and awakens old longings for meaningful adventure and the gaze of beauty. Gathering groups of men for serious purposes also stirs old demons and dangers as men are known to be dangerous, especially in groups. All histories depict the damage done where groups of men become simply ruled by raw passions and treacherously blinded by narrow or self-serving purposes. When passions collide or purposes conflict, men can become a danger to everyone including themselves. If the fires of youth must be suffered in order to open the heart and soul to hidden meaning and purpose, how do men handle the conflicts and confusions that persist after youth and continue to arise wherever power accumulates? The loss of connective rituals leaves the door wide open for extreme personal greed and unrestricted collective delusions.

While a man remaining solitary can become numb to his inner life and unfeeling toward other people, men in groups can become fanatically self-absorbed and brutal to nonmembers. If men isolate from each other, numbness and depression grows; yet forming groups of men can trigger increased violence and habits of domination. The instinctive glue that allows men to form factions and bands and brotherhoods remains ambiguous. The same instinct to band together can generate mindless clubs, violent gangs, musical bands, or community healers. The glue simply makes for bands and bonding. Genuine vision and a willingness to deal with the inevitable conflicts that arise wherever people gather are also required. There is a collective Litima that permeates groups of men. At one extreme brutality can occur; and at the other extreme genuine service to beauty and the common good can be renewed.

How can a group of men avoid adding to the broken visions and rampant oppressions that already dominate the world? The old stories allude to ritual patterns that form the group around the longing for beauty and the return of the imagination needed to sustain it. As the prince in the story gazes into the eyes of living beauty, the Strange Companions hold and protect the ritual embrace. Seeking beauty and truth requires awakening to the vision, as the prince finally did, and joining forces with all the strange and radical aspects of the soul. Even then there is the danger of falling asleep to the purpose again. Something is needed to keep the soul awake and to keep beauty present in the eye of the beholder.

Often the lost sense of unity and community can be found hiding where conflicts have been pushed into the shadows. Frequently groups disband, fall asleep, or become dull because the heat needed to keep the bond of unity becomes lost when the necessary issues of conflict have been avoided. Each attempt to form around a meaningful vision creates inevitable and often incurable conflicts between people. True community requires a vision big enough to allow all the Strange Companions to be present and a trust and courage strong enough to face the conflicts that inevitably arise.

The entry points to community are doors of emotion that can open suddenly, can close quickly, and can even slam shut. Each door to unity has a lock with little masterworks of protection and denial intended to separate what is genuine from what is self-serving and false. Making community means unlocking the doors that divide people through a combination of artful vision, current emotions, and a dedication to remaining present with whatever might show up. The center of community is a mystery. Thus the sense of community constantly becomes lost; each time it does, the locks on the doors to community change. Each time a group seeks to become a community again, a new key must be found.

When it comes to a community of men, the willingness to reveal and handle conflicts becomes essential. Every man carries an inner knowledge that men have argued, struggled, competed against, fought with, and killed each other since the beginning of time. The inner history of violence combines personal stories, family plots, ethnic styles, and a complex array of mostly hidden emotions. The inner stories and emotional patterns quickly awaken upon entering any group of men where something meaningful might be possible. Many men avoid such encounters because of painful experience of the violence and abuse of other men. Strangely, though, there is no other way to heal the damage; what has been wounded by the masculine must be healed by it as well.

Men sense the inner conflicts and fear in each other, especially when entering a large group of mostly strangers. The first bite of fear triggers the instincts of fight or flight. More often it feels like fight and flight, for both happen at once when the push and pull of inner emotions are part of the essence of impending conflict. Old wounds begin to itch just as old longings to belong to something meaningful stir. Even a minimal intention to address serious issues can provoke deep instincts and raise questions of manliness and courage.

In America, the diversity and mixture of ancestries can quickly fill a room with historical enemies as well as descendants of peoples who never met before. Each man comes from some tradition of seeking or avoiding conflict and there's no time to introduce all the personal conflict styles to each other. By the time everyone gathers, the spirits of families and ancestors are poking around the in the shadows asking, "What the hell is going on?"

As soon as the group starts to form, the shadow of the group also begins to form. If denied or ignored, the group shadow grows and eventually divides where people seek to unite. The group shadow begins as very subtle, yet can easily grow greater than the sum of the shadows of those in the group. That's part of what can be seen in fascist groups and whenever a group defines itself by mostly excluding and "scapegoating" others. The quickest way to form a group is to evoke an aspect of the shadow, a quality that is present but undesirable, hang it on people not wanted by the group, and keep projecting it out there, on them. As long as the threatening or repulsive thing can be imagined outside and hung on someone else, the group can keep a form of superficial unity by virtue of simple exclusion; especially the exclusion of what people fear in themselves.

Finding shared ideals can start a group in a good place. But big ideals also carry big shadows. The difference between what life ought to be and what life actually turns out to be can also be called the shadow. Every move toward what life ought to be or what we hope it to become requires encounters with the shadows of both the individual and the collective group. Refusing to admit the presence of the shadow doesn't get rid of it. Instead the shadow of a person or a group grows by being ignored or denied. Denying the presence of the shadow in one place usually means that others elsewhere will have to carry it. Each person tries to deny their own shadow; every group does it to one degree or another. Yet at some point the shadow grows strong enough to take over even the high ideals.

Visions of meaning and beauty arise incurably from the human soul; no one can completely deny the ancient longings that accompany the pulse of life. But feeling conflicted and being in conflicts with others are also incurable aspects of being human. Since the shadow areas of a person or a group become depositories of emotional heat and vital energy, avoiding conflicts means losing energy and cohesion. Even if people manage to avoid simple scapegoating but don't actually deal with shadow issues, the group eventually loses emotional heat and will forget its original purpose. This happens when the prince and the Strange Companions fall off to sleep while the beautiful daughter of the soul is right in the room with them.

Groups tend to divide and distance over shadow issues and simply lose energy as more and more attention is needed to keep fixing the shadow back on others when it begins to slip. Eventually the shadows and repressed emotions have more energy than the original group. Without conflict, there can be no progress. Conflict and opposition generate the heat needed to move forward. Even peace must ever be recreated at the edges of conflict.

Eventually the conflicts and shadowy areas must be addressed or the project or group won't go where it needs to be or longs to go. Each meaningful gathering becomes an opportunity to eat some of the shadow of the group rather than to feed it blindly. Even in the course of our experiments in finding and making temporary community, attending to conflicts became crucial for finding meaning and healing. Before we learned to seek out underlying troubles, conflict would break out on its own. Heat would gather over a certain issue or a statement and there would be an outburst. Often one individual would become the focus for all the unexpressed conflict in the group and would be in danger of being made a scapegoat. Eventually it became clear that expressing conflicts was an essential need in every serious gathering.

Conflict rituals are the opposite of projecting shadowy materials on other people. Beyond releasing the fears, tensions, and angers that inevitably occur when we encounter each other's shadows by surprise, a ritual approach can lead to healing deep and inherited conflicts. While there's more in the shadows of any group than conflict and anger, the sparks they provide can light the way when things get dark. If anger can be present without violence resulting, conflict can provide the heat and the trust needed to release the entire fountain of emotions and cleanse the soul.

Too much safety will stop creativity and block change. In the case of conflict rituals, safe doesn't mean untroubled or predictable; safe doesn't mean no mistakes. In this context, safety means being secure enough to take a risk and become exposed to the unknown. Real safety involves risks, just as real trust must be tested. Safety must be risked and re-established for each event.

When treated as a ritual, conflicts become a way of exploring the courage of the group to wander into the minefields of power, trust, and love. Each ritual finds uncharted territory. The map is made as we go with an implicit understanding that the area aimed at is mystery. We are wandering together in search of mystery, in search of the opportunity to see and feel the mystery of community. The destination of each ritual is unknown and, once it's over, the map of each event is thrown away. There are recognizable landmarks, but the complexion of the group and the lie of the land are different every time.

Dealing with conflicts requires leaders who take the role of ritual elders and try to regulate speed, heat, and direction by glimpsing what waits in the shadows to be revealed. Rituals like this are full of opportunities to learn quickly. Men who can't enter heated conflicts in their workplaces, in projects, or in their relationships get to observe how others handle heated emotions and try it themselves. Those who have inherited great fear can borrow some courage, sit with that fear, and not take flight. Those who go quickly from anger to rage can be tempered by others and learn where the line of rage lies and what triggers it in themselves. Leaders can learn where their shadows lie and how their manner affects others. Most people have conflicts with authority but lack meaningful opportunities to explore them.

Anger tends to begin the movement in the territories of conflict, as if the foothills are magnetized toward frustration and populated by stinging insects, rude neighbors, and people slamming doors. Once inside the territory many emotions arise. Fear is never far away from anger and, for some, just being in a room of potential conflict requires full courage. The heat of anger may suddenly open a pool of grief that waits below the frustrations and arguments of life. The situation just had to get warm enough and safe enough to make the waters of grief approachable. For its part, grief can have bitterness and screams in it and thereby carries conflict in its own stricken way. And there's a joy of conflict—as surprising as a sun break on a stormy day—that has to be appreciated when a breakthrough occurs. Meanwhile, humor often plays at the edges of conflict and can eventually tickle places that used to be sore.

The effort to engage conflict has to be genuine enough that the leaders are involved and not completely apart. It is essential that there be more than one person taking leadership, for anyone can be pulled into the heat of a conflict.

Sometimes the primary conflicts arise with the leadership and the whole weight of authority issues might have to come up. It's always amazing how carefully men watch the demeanor of those in authority and the ways the "authority figures" handle power. In the business world, the academic world, and the legal world questioning the authorities has become increasingly dangerous. People lose jobs, status, liberties and friends for doing so. People lose freedoms, rights, and even their lives for speaking against the misuse of authority. Freedom and authority have an innate conflict with each other.

Having a rule of no physical violence can create great opportunities for working on authority issues. Challenging authority can be a way of learning about how to hold it and how to relinquish it. It's also a way of testing a developing community.

How leaders handle authority, mistakes, and challenges affects everyone. If there isn't enough sense of authority and stability present, people won't take enough risks and events won't go very deep. If authority comes to be held to firmly, people react more than respond to a challenge. If those with authority in a situation are not able or willing to disagree with each other, everyone else will hold something back. If the leaders are not somehow separate, the authority issues won't get focused. If the leaders are always separate, the group will be divided over how much authority the leaders should have. There's no *right way* to do it; each situation clarifies through uncovering and expressing the inherent conflicts.

America was founded upon incurable conflicts over religious freedom and the importance of difference and diversity. The United States can only ever be barely united, for the old wounds and incurable issues stir and seethe below the busy surface. The origins of America remain in continual dispute, just as its borders must ever be unstable and in question. America is a dream in conflict with itself. Freedom became the aim of the founders, but theft and slavery were part of the means. America presents both the dream of liberty and the wound of manifest destiny; each national crisis will bring the conflict between freedom and power back to the surface. Ultimately, the dream that sleeps in the ground of America is more radical and diverse than most of the people who try to govern it. Because the ideals involved are high and the dream calls for freedom, the shadows can become deep and harshly restrictive.

Once, at an intentionally cross-cultural, interracial conference, fifty black men and fifty white men met at a remote camp for a week. One lone Asian man seemed to represent untold millions of people, as did two Latino men. One Native American had to stand for the First People of this land. The event intended to address man and racism, especially the clash of black and white people in America. The teachers were respected black men and white men. After an opening address and some poetry, we asked for an agreement of no violence. No one doubted the potential for deep conflict as we entered the room; the real questions were who would begin it, how hot would it get, and how would it ever end? The capacity of the group to stay present and to be honest had to be tested; the rule of no violence had to be tested; the teachers and leaders also had to be tested.

A black man tore into it right away. He'd already heard some things he didn't like, like it was cool to be at such a hip event and wasn't this the cutting edge. Well, fuck that! Already people were posturing and he didn't come all the way to this godforsaken place to see racist America created all over again. In this atmosphere drenched with historical conflict and glistening with fear, another man assumed the remarks were being addressed to him and if the brother had a problem with him why not speak directly. The history of racism and oppression began to speak through those present as if it had been waiting for just such an opportunity.

Off we went, quickly, heatedly, not knowing where we were heading and soon enough not caring. To be directly in the heat of this conflict that agitates just below the surface of life felt better than living endlessly in the daily shadow of it. Besides, this wasn't a new attempt at the melting pot. Those present had no desire to be fused into a new amalgam; they didn't want to disappear into some bland solution. They preferred to contribute to the fire rather than being melted in it.

The melting pot seems like a manufacturing image, as if there could be an industrial solution that melts people into acceptable molds. Fortunately, the melting pot doesn't get hot enough to melt core memories and ancestral spirits. It never will. Ultimately, humans are too radical to be reduced to any formula; the weird Companions inside everyone won't allow that to happen. There will never be a single religion or a single idea that can absorb and celebrate and satisfy everyone. If people become too similar there is a loss of genuine identity and only a pretense of unity. Genuine unity begins with true diversity and individuality.

America boils and repeatedly burns with racial and class warfare. But the heat doesn't melt either the disparity or injustice people suffer. The core of the American experiment involves the raw heat generated by meaningfully different people gazing at the possibilities of freedom of the spirit, beauty, and truth in this world. Take the diversity out of the picture and the meaning of the struggle will disappear as well. Those who gathered to test the waters of community in the face of conflict came with embodied knowledge of what burns in the soul of America. It became more important to sift the ashes of burnt hopes than to stir the fantasies of a unifying melting pot. The ashes of the Civil Rights Movement came into the room hidden in the folds of our clothes. From those collective ashes a different fire needed to be tended. How soon would it be before America fell asleep again and the dream of truth and beauty and the possibility of freedom be smothered in again?

Some things at the core of people don't melt down no matter the pressure or the oppression. The radical aspects of the psyche are like the Man of Tempers who withstands the extremes of heat and cold. You set up a melting pot, a cultural smelting industry, and he'll step right into it. But, being essentially contrary, he'll freeze. The hotter the fire, the more he'll move into the opposite state. You won't wind up with a smelted, molded individual. You'll come face to face with a fiercely frozen radical. In our culture, if you try to freeze people out, keep them out in the cold, in the haunts of poverty, or beyond the bounds of hope some radical part of the soul begins to burn. The more cold shoulders you turn on them, the more the temper of the excluded heats up. When justice turns a cold eye, the Man of Tempers begins to burn with a furious fire.

Either we would fall asleep to what brought each of us to this soul fire and rage in age-old violence and mutual blame, or we could find ways to hold the heat and suffer the conflicts until the hidden ground of real purpose is found again. The radical beauty of gathering enough Strange Companions became evident as flames of the dream of freedom awakening from the sleep of oppression flickered all about the room. Forget the melting pot and raise the heat enough to melt the veneer of sameness and reveal the radical and healing depths of meaningful difference. Once we had an agreement that this fire would not burn to violence, we had a chance to step past the usual American solution to the presence of genuine conflict.

In order to stay present we had to call upon ancestral ideas. We had to slip past ancestral battles long enough to place some beauty in the room so that we would remember the sense of meaning and healing we sought. If we were to take up the courage of our ancestors we had also to resume the dedication to the art and beauty that all traditional groups used in order to keep mystery more present than history. We made shrines and altars and opened each session with music and poetry. We learned songs and chants that held the heat yet shaped it toward hidden harmonies that also entered the room with us.

We also sang to ease old fears that haunted us as the burning story of racism and other tales of denigration of the soul poured into the room. At night, sleep couldn't find us. People met in small groups to further question and further release the pain inherited from the confused history of America: so dedicated to freedom, yet so afraid to learn what that truly means. The houses of our souls were burning with rage and fear and frustration, as if everyone's ancestors received word that the wounds to the soul were being uncovered and some sorely needed healing might be possible for a moment.

Family stories had to be told as anguish erupted from dark- and light-skinned bodies alike in the repression of the soul of things. A black man and a white man spoke quietly about their origins because they happened to have the same last name. When the revelation came that they were descended from the same plantation, slave and master met again. Although an old battle could have resumed, it was the shared tragedy that broke both their hearts as the wound of hate and violence spoke from a painful loss of dignity that affected both souls. The descendent of slave masters had a tear in the tissue of his soul that could only find ease though a depth of forgiveness carried by his darker brother. Forgiveness is a radical capacity of the human soul that can appear exactly where interminable hatred seems most justified.

The possibilities of finding some healing kept stirring all kinds of wounds. No sooner did we sense how much wished to be aired out and cured between us than a man insisted that the all the black men meet separately. His argument was that back in the daily world such meetings couldn't happen. This was an opportunity not to be missed. Yet it raised ghosts of all kinds and threatened the shaky unity of the newly found trust in the event. Just as the sense of a community hiding behind cultural divisions began to appear, it would be tested in the glare of distrust. Even a feeling of unity can create a division. No one knew what to do or what might be right or best for everyone. We might have to divide in order to learn better how to be together; then again dividing might cause us to fall asleep just when the opportunity for beauty came near.

The answer came from those who were neither black nor white. Those whose heritage was Asian, Latino, and Native American didn't want to be absorbed into black or erased by white. They feared they might lose an essential ancestral presence that they were beginning to feel. The lone Native American man stood to speak. Dignified and deliberate, he held up a little stick painted in ascending rings with five colors. Black, white, red, yellow and green showed from his hand. As representative of the native peoples, he told how they honored the colors as five energies and five ways to be in this world. He told how this knowledge came as part of wisdom of the human heart. He said that the white man knew this because he had a heart, but that it had been forgotten.

He said that we could separate as the colors do in order to paint the world, but we had to hold the stick of truth in order not to lose the understanding of how the colors and the ways work together. For a moment it became clear how ancestral knowledge arose in him and held us all together. It became clear how something ancestral in the ground now called America tries, at painful expense, to hold the diverse peoples of the world together.

For this trial, we survived the old divisions. But soon another conflict rose to the surface and tested the equanimity of the group. Two men stood at the same time and spoke of the necessity to recognize gay men. One was a black man; one was white. You could hear the fires crackle and blaze up again. It was as if a pattern had become established and the community fire had to accept whatever radical aspects of life might be present. It was also another aspect of great good fortune. We had started with the question of whether black men and white men could honestly work together. Behind that came the question of whether men of greater diversity could find ways to work together and heal. Now the question of whether all men could work together arose. Behind that waited the question of whether all people could not gather around the pole of many colors despite the conflicts and shadows we all have inherited.

Many of the men gathered there had never faced homosexual issues directly either in the lives of others or in themselves. Suddenly here it was. Does the fire of community go out? Or does each one face the fears of homophobia and the suffering and hate caused by those fears? Gay seems to be another radical of the soul that exists wherever humans exist, often forced into the shadows and frequently a cause of intense conflict. Yet it is another piece of common ancestry, another edge of diversity, and another radical element that won't melt down in the melting pot.

Once again the question of whether the group forms by excluding and scapegoating others or forms by deepening and including the otherness of each person was on the floor. A man responds by saying that he didn't know that gay men were present. It's as if he's having a kind of reverse-phobia, as if to say, "How could I have slept peacefully when there were gay men sleeping nearby?" Various fears crackle about the room. The racial fears became revived in new ways: Are there more gays among my culture? Do other groups deal with this better than we? The room began to wobble; cracks appeared, chill winds began to blow, and dark shadows flitted across the community fire. The same questions that were there at the beginning have returned in a new way: Can the group hold together? Is there yet more room at the communal fire?

The men look at the line-up of teachers. One of them says emphatically that although he is heterosexual, two of his mentors in the art world were gay men. If he accepts the gifts that they have given to the culture and to him, how can he refuse their need to be who they are sexually? He praises their courage and their generosity to him and their integrity regarding the sexual orientation of others. Still standing, the two men have to be seen in that light. Another stick has gone into the fire and there's less shadow in the room. Another teacher recites a Whitman poem, as if to say, "Are you going to keep Walt Whitman out? If you do, you'll wind up burning books to keep false fires alive."

The two men remain standing as each tells part of the story that carried him to this room. One weeps while telling how an uncle was the only one in his family who saw him with an open heart and blessed his way of walking into life. His manner makes clear that he will keep walking if there's no room at this fire. The other man speaks more defiantly, ready to fight if need be, for a place at the fire.

Two more teachers, one black and one white, speak about the role of gay people in diverse cultures around the world, but specifically in African tribes and European groups where traditions have them keeping the gates between worlds. If someone doesn't fit into the simple division of male and female genders, they stand between the two and, being in-between, they become go-betweens where the issues of gender become troubled. They represent a third place where seemingly fixed positions become less determined. At different ceremonies they may put on the clothes and manners of either group.

Since their basic way of being in this world has this quality of in-between, they also can learn to open the gates between any polarity. Often they would take on shamanistic roles and do spiritual work at the gates between earthly and spiritual realms. The gowns worn by priests and ministers are a remnant of the old understanding of the betwixt and between aspects of spirituality.

We entered the room dragging our inherited fears, our exiles, and privileges with us. The truth was that at least one of those present was homeless, having been standing nearby as a couple of participants discussed the event. Having nowhere elseto go, he asked if he could go along. At each step we had to consider whether we would be inclusive or simply another exclusive group justifying its existence by hanging the cloak of tragedy on someone else. On the road where greater imagination and the beauty of life return, the Strange Companions wait to be invited along. Each has a unique and necessary gift that can never be found if fear and timidity guard the gates of awareness.

CHAPTER 26

THE WRITING ON THE WALL

THE CORE STRUGGLE of America will continue to revolve around issues of inclusion and exclusion. That struggle will provide the heat needed to change and grow and can generate the grieving necessary to heal. Conflicts don't end until the grief engendered has been fully felt. Meaningful conflict opens the doors of grief where the wounds of the soul wait to be washed. Oppositions heat the psyche and move obstacles, but sorrow must follow and wash the soul clean again. As the poet Vachel Lindsay wrote:

> *Only boys are afraid to cry. Men thank God for their tears*
> *Alone with the memory of their dead, Alone with lost years.*

Conflict ends on the ground of grief where the losses are counted and the wounds of the soul washed. The greatest conflicts occur where the felt sense of the sacred has been lost. One reason that wars don't seem to end and treaties never last is because peace is a sacred agreement. Unless something sacred enters in, agreements revert to conflicts rather easily. Some sacrifice is required to make things whole and holy again. The modern world is awash with unresolved conflicts and unconscious sacrifices that don't return the sacred to the world.

The search for the sacred is another way to imagine the longings woven into the old stories. Unless the sacred is touched now and again, the suffering in the world only increases and conflicts can only grow. Conflicts feed on the inability of people to sacrifice in the present and the refusal of most to reflect on the atrocities of the past.

One of the few shared and sacred places in the unsettled land of America can be found where the Vietnam Memorial Wall sinks into the ground in Washington, D.C. Unlike the heroic and ascendant memorials to other wars, the this wall descends as if seeking a ground of unity below the ongoing conflicts of American culture. The blackness of the wall, the way it descends into the earth like blood soaking soil, and the fact that the names on it reflect a wild array of ethnic groups drawn from the far reaches of the world, all contribute to its sorrowful language. It speaks of wide diversity and a hidden unity at once.

How many ancestries speak from the grave below that wall? How many tears wash it day by day? Differences of color and belief, of status and inheritance, disappear into the dark uncertainty that holds the fallen commonly present. If we follow where the wall enters the ground, we enter a common grave where mutual sacrifice and ancient lament speak below the seats of power and prestige. America begins to become itself somewhere below the base of the wall, somewhere in the sacrificial ground that unites below what continues to be in conflict above the ground.

It's not insignificant that the design of the wall came to an Asian American woman, and it is very significant that years after the conflict ended, a ritual of grieving occurs at it each day. Unlike heroic statues of a single warrior or a few soldiers, the black wall names all who fell and acts as a conductor continuing to move emotions from living people to the land of the dead and realm of the ancestors. Holding sacred the confusing sacrifices of so many, the wall is more ritual center than memorial edifice. Mourners come and go, pouring tears that fall to a well deep below the fires of conflict that continue to flare in the capitol background. It seems to balance the bravado of "bombs bursting in air."

Groups that cannot find a common language anywhere else in the country find a shared sorrow at the wall as all form a line to pass before the dead, meeting silence with silence. The accumulation of grief, tears, and the sacred presences invoked moves visitors slowly, quietly along the road of death. The open weeping and silent tears fall on all the souls connected by the common black gravestone. It's as if the old idea—known to native people in the Americas, in Asia, Europe, Australia, and Africa—that the dead have to be helped along the road to the underworld returns through the grieving wall. If the living don't release their grief through tears and prayer and song, the dead become stuck on the road to the ancestors.

I first went to the wall to look for the names of friends who had died in the war, but soon found myself in the confusing waters of my own grief over that war. I entered the ritual of the place, following the dark-etched names chronologically, day-by-day, like a procession of death or a funeral in stone. The name of a friend from college stopped me like a blow newly struck. I remember the drunken night he spoke of all the pain in his family and announced his decision to volunteer, to throw himself at the war and make something of himself. Reading all the names around his, I imagined them connected to him because they all died on the same day. I stood in the spell of the permanent litany as families of the dead took rubbings of the names the way people take rubbings of art in old cathedrals. Others felt their way along the wall, as if needing to touch the dead and feel the Braille of sorrow as they went.

After following the wall as it disappeared into the earth-dark ground, I sat still as evening gathered into night. I wanted to sing as well as cry. Thinking of the way death ripped through the young lives of those not expecting to end in silent sacrifice, I wanted to sing the laments intended to ease the dead on their way, in the old way. I wanted to lay candles and leave food the way many people make "spirit plates" to nourish the subtle presence of the ancestors in the deceased.

Years later, during the heavy bombing that began the Persian Gulf War, a group consisting of veterans of the Vietnam conflict and people who were heavily affected by the new war received a permit to make a procession to the wall. The idea was to make the connection between one war and another, to mark the procession of wars with a walk of grief in this land as the bombs fell mightily in foreign lands again.

Hundreds of people gathered in the streets of the capitol at dusk. Candles passed from hand to hand as people learned an old lament for the dead from South Africa where the war of apartheid also raged at the time. As the song gathered strength, we went down through the darkening streets. Suddenly a police motorcycle contingent pulled in front of the group. They announced that the permit did not allow a public protest and that no form of protest was allowed at the wall. I explained that we didn't intend to protest; rather, we needed to express a sense of grief born of the old war and triggered by the new one. I explained that the point was more ceremony than protest and that we weren't seeking a confrontation or a conflict; they cited federal laws regarding the area of the wall.

As lights flashed from the motorcycles, the crowd continued to grow and more candles appeared in the gathering darkness. The song spread to the new arrivals as its indelible sense of sadness echoed into the night. People came to their windows and stopped along the streets drawn by the old sound, even as the tension with the police grew.

The police insisted that the crowd disband or they would break it up themselves. That seemed sure to convert the sense of grief into a conflict. We were stuck. Many of those who had gathered had relatives and friends named on the wall. It was too late and too complicated to simply turn back; there was nowhere else to go and the crowd behind continued to grow. The song rolled from behind us and the candles sought a way to go forward. Quickly we formed into pairs and began to walk slowly past the motorcycles. Although more officers appeared, they didn't stop us and the procession moved ahead.

As we approached the vicinity of the wall motorcycles were waiting for us. Stopping the procession caused the tension to mount again as people had no choice but to condense into a crowd. The song swelled as people pressed together in some confusion. The lead officer insisted that federal regulations prohibited all group activities in the vicinity of the wall. If we persisted we would be in violation of federal law and they would bring reinforcements and begin arresting people. They were adamant that the law only allowed individuals to approach the wall. We were moving deeper into the feeling of the song and the meaning of lamenting the results of the bigger conflict that gripped us all. I said we would proceed in single file as individual citizens; word was passed and people lined up to move forward.

The officer said that federal law made it illegal to sing or make any group expression on those grounds. I explained that we came to sing for the dead and the dying. He said we would not be allowed to do so. Tension grew again and conflict seemed the inevitable outcome. We couldn't simply give up the song; it united us and made increasing sense in the face of the immediate and overall conflict and confusion of the world. Stopping, even waiting any longer, would turn the procession into chaos; you could feel the edges unraveling as the lights flashed off the helmets and face guards of the police. The officer stated emphatically that singing would not be tolerated.

We shifted quickly to humming the song softly and we began to walk forward again. In a strange way the song felt stronger as it softened, as if it carried something that could be muffled but not silenced altogether.

The cops seemed to soften up as the song became the steady humming of more than a thousand throats; but they weren't finished yet. They announced that it was illegal to enter the memorial area with lighted candles. There was a hint of apology in the officer's voice when he repeated the ordinance, as if it began to feel a little foolish even to him. By now the style of the ritual was becoming clear: they would raise a rule to stop us and we would bend the rule but not directly break it. Each move forward would generate a new conflict that would then be shaped into a new ceremonial style. I asked a stout man nearby to stand where the wall began and blow out the candles as they appeared one at a time.

There was a long line of people, each with a flickering candle, and all humming the lament. As each person stepped toward the wall their candle would be snuffed out and they would disappear into the darkness along the wall. The procession moved slowly past the long lines that named the dead. As each person reached the end of the wall someone would light their candle and they would shift from humming back to singing again. One by one the lights of the living went out as each communed with the dead. One by one each person received the light again, rejoined the living, and added to the song of life. No one had to explain it or comment on it; the doing of it made complete sense and gave each person their own sense of the road that holds the living and the dead.

By this point the police realized that we had no intention of being disrespectful. They were used to the song and to the way that each objection simply created another element of the ritual. They turned off the flashing lights and withdrew as the long procession descended to the wall and disappeared into its dark confines. As the line of mourners rose from the wall of the dead and the song grew in strength on the other side, the lead officer simply asked, "Where to now?" The police had joined the procession and were seriously offering to lead it on. We indicated the top of a hill nearby and they aimed the motorcycles and lead the way as the line of lights sang the way up the hill.

There's something about walls and breaking through what separates and keeps things opposed. At the prison wall we weren't able to break through literally. That is what made the ceremony of writing on the wall possible. The literal barrier becomes the threshold for breaking through metaphorically and releasing both emotions and imagination. Seeing each letter-of-the-law restriction at the memorial wall as a new element of the ritual trying to occur also shifted the literal to the imaginal, thus releasing a beauty hidden behind the apparent conflict.

There's an old idea in which the otherworld is termed the "world behind the world." The implication is that the daily world of facts and factions rests upon an unseen world from which all facts arise. The real world with its grave laws and persistent wars is less real than what exists behind it, the unseen source of all that comes to seem solid and real. The world behind the world tries to break through wherever the veil between the worlds becomes thin. Sorrow thins the veil, as does beauty and anything that releases authentic ideas and imaginations.

If you had observed the memorial procession from above, you would have seen a crowd of people carrying little lights as darkness gathered around them. As a song began to rise from them the mass of lights becomes a line of little flames that proceed to where flashing lights seem to wait for them. At a point marked by the flashing lights, each little flame flickers and goes out. As the flames disappear, a deep humming rises from the darkness deepened by the loss of light. Then the flashing lights appear at another point and the little flames begin to come back, each flickering up from the same place as the humming gives birth to the song again. The line of flames follows the flashing lights in a gradual ascent to a higher place and the song rises as well. After the song echoes again and again against the darkened earth and moonless sky, all goes silent again until a siren sounds somewhere and the sounds of the city return.

That was a ritual in the old sense, the radical sense that inspired all of our ancestors to make ceremonies when the pain and suffering and confusion of this world became too much to bear and there were no words to convey the burden falling on the hearts of people. The point, at that point, wasn't simple protest or complicated politics; the point was to be fully present in a way that redeems the suffering and death... just a little. By the end no one wanted it to be over. The same officer who adamantly opposed us at each step asked if we were sure we were finished. People left slowly, unwilling to leave the song and enter the night again and face the great uncertainty of the modern world.

For a few hours we were able to hold the conflicts and confusions, the sorrows and sufferings that force people into separate camps and obscure the painful beauty of being alive. By the time we all stood singing at the top of the hill we knew that we were the living and those below were the living dead. It is an old name for the ancestors: the living dead, the ones who precede us into the land of the dead and somehow remain part of the living as well. For a few hours we participated in a beauty that encompassed both death and life and gave respect to both.

The Strange Companions represent inherited imagination and radical inner forces that remember the soul's incurable love of beauty and meaning. They are strange and important capacities inside people that can convert an overwhelming crisis into an initiatory step. They are the inner resources that make a person an elder. They are the roots that connect the elder in a person to ancestors. In modern times it takes greater and greater national tragedies or natural disasters to stir the sense of a genuine community of the living that can honor the dead and relieve the pain that feeds the cultural divisions.

Being modern means going the new way; but modern also means, lost. In critical moments it becomes more important to recall what is old and even ancient in the human soul. We are each the descendants of those who survived long enough to generate more life. When we lose the sense of elder and meaningful ancestry we loose both the instincts for survival and the sense for genuine reverence for life. Life is the long ritual procession everyone makes on the way to the realm of the ancestors. Those who forget that death waits for everyone lose sight of the beauty of being alive and are truly lost.

In most old stories the radical change occurs at the last minute, often after people have fallen asleep to the purpose of the whole journey. In most stories it becomes a close call in which the oppressive conditions deepen or a breakthrough occurs. The story of the Strange Companions seems to say that all the strange elements of the soul are needed to keep a meaningful vision alive. When the obstacles in the world become greater and more complex and seem to be coming from all directions at once, we witness two great tendencies in the psyche: either a people blindly simplify the issues and adapt some form of fundamentalism that seems to explain everything; or else they accept the surprising multiplicity and creative tension that comes from embracing the world. The weird Companions represent a person's sudden, increased capacities should they accept the incurable nature of this wounded world and the radical qualities hidden within it.

Joining the Strange Companions means being willing to travel an uncertain path while remembering the beauty the soul seeks to know and trusting that the capacities of other people will be equal to the dangers of the road.

THE STRANGE COMPANIONS
Part III

The beautiful daughter of the Old Queen wanted a fire. In order to settle her doubts about the prince, the daughter of the Old Queen caused three hundred bundles of wood to be brought to the palace hall. She called the prince and said that although he had accomplished the three tasks she would not consent to be his wife until he seated himself in the midst of the great fire that she was about to set burning. The prince asked if it were allowed that someone do the sitting for him. The princess said that it was allowed, for she was sure that none of the companions would let themselves be burned for him, that he would have to enter the fire himself, that he would be burned, and that she would regain her former freedom.

The companions gathered and said that each had done their part except the Man of Tempers, so he must now set to work. He was placed in the middle of the great heap of wood and it was set on fire. The fire blazed up and burned with intense heat, driving away all the onlookers. It burned that way for three full days, until all the wood was consumed and the flames died out. Then, as the smoke settled and to the great surprise of all, the Tempered One was seen standing in the pile of ashes, trembling like an aspen leaf, saying, "Oh, it was a killing frost. I never felt such a frost in my whole life; had it lasted any longer, I would have been benumbed and turned to stone."

The last test being done, no other pretext to delay was found and the beautiful daughter of the Old Queen was forced to take the unknown youth to wed. When they set off together the old woman said, "I cannot endure it, the loss, the disgrace." So she sent her warriors after them to cut down everyone and bring her daughter back. But the Listener had his ear to the ground and heard the secret discourse of the Old Queen.

"What shall we do?" he said to the Stout One.

The Stout One didn't speak but turned back and spit out some of the water he had earlier consumed and caused a sea to form suddenly and catch the warriors as they rode, drowning them. One escaped and reported back to the queen, who railed at him and sent another army.

This time when the Listener heard the sound of the soldiers' pursuit he undid the bandages of Piercing Eyes and turned him toward them. Piercing Eyes looked rather fixedly at the charging troops and they all broke into so many pieces like shattered glass.

There were no more attacks and they were able to go on their way. At a certain point the companions said, "Your wishes are now satisfied; you need us no longer. We will go our ways." After many embraces each went his way.

Near the palace of the prince's father was a village, and near that was the hut of a swineherd. When they reached the hut, the prince said to his new wife, "I wish I were the prince of that great palace, but truly I am a herder of swine, and this is our family hut, and that old man is my father. Now that we have arrived we two must set to work and help him with the swine." He passed word of what he was doing to the villagers and in the morning the princess was given an old gown and was escorted to the herd. To herself, she thought, "Well, he accepted the fire I set for him, so I guess I must accept the little hut, the common clothes, and a number of pigs." She set to work and so did he.

One day people came and asked her if she knew who her husband was. "Yes," she said, "he is the swineherd, and you can find him now on his way to market with pigs and ropes, hoping to drive a good bargain when he gets there."

They said, "If you'll come with us, we will take you to meet him." She agreed and they took her straight to the palace. There, they didn't hesitate at the entry gate, didn't stop at all until they were in the throne room. There stood her husband in kingly raiment. In her amazement she did not recognize him. But when he came close and they gazed into the each other's eyes she knew at once who he was. It was as if they were gazing at each other, bathed in moonlight, guarded by the companions again. After that they began to prepare a great wedding feast in order to celebrate the union of the son and the daughter of the two realms. It was a great feast, one that was celebrated with poetry and song, one that was remembered even to this day.

CHAPTER 27

ON THE WAY TO THE WEDDING

THE WHOLE STORY of the Strange Companions takes place on the way to the wedding of the prince of one realm and the beautiful daughter of the other. The king who rejects the vision of the prince and the Old Queen who imprisons her daughter represent the conservative, restraining forces present in nature and in human nature. Yet the longing for wholeness and union with the Other also lives deeply in each person. Whatever divides things participates in the wounds of life and whatever genuinely joins makes a healing. The oppositions within a person and the opposing realms seek even brief moments of unity and wholeness.

The prince becomes stricken by the absence of real beauty; he will die if he cannot seek the vision that represents beauty, truth, and wholeness to him. Seeking beauty gives life meaning and purpose. Finding a beauty more than skin-deep means facing the truth of things and learning where one's life intends to go. Truth and beauty go hand and hand, with one generating the presence of the other and both offering ways to find a sense of the whole. Healing comes from the word "whole," and whatever heals makes whole again.

The first test demanded by the Old Queen involves finding and returning to the world above the ring lost in the depths of the unconscious. Approaching the source of beauty and meaning intensifies the opposing forces in a person, while also revealing hints of unity. The wounds of life will be experienced and the hidden unity of things will be touched somehow. That's part of the small print written in every soul, a gift of the road of life, and the first test of being conscious while on it. Some sense of the underlying unity of life must be experienced or a person won't have the resiliency necessary for the other ordeals.

Meanwhile, the old, gold ring of sovereignty and unity keeps disappearing into the depths. It glimmers at the bottom of the dream of life. If the ring can't be recovered the seeker will simply lose his or her head. Either a person can bring the hidden treasure up to conscious awareness and sustain a connection to its inner source... or they lose their head. On the way to becoming a genuine individual and, thus, un-divided, a person loses their head over and over. Whole cultures lose their head. Religious groups, through which people hope to find the Way, also lose their way.

Like the gold ring, one's head keeps getting lost and misplaced. During moments of wholeness, head and heart, mind and body become integrated and undivided long enough to initiate the next stage or phase or step in life.

Once the missing ring is found, the desire of the prince must be tested. Does he have an appetite for the whole thing, for all of life, for the gristle and the bone, for the quantities and strange qualities of the things that must be digested along the way? Can he handle it when things become difficult to swallow? Will he simply get drunk when the wine appears and stumble when the heady stuff of life flows? Will he lose his head in that familiar way? Will he recover himself in time and remember the purpose in his soul no matter the tempting goods and interesting fare found along the way?

To be fully initiated and become oneself a person must make a bigger life, one which doesn't shrink from the extremes of the basic hungers or the sublime states. Proving he has the stomach for life qualifies the prince for a prolonged state of vision in which beauty and truth are palpable and within his grasp. Will he be able to stay awake when close to the longing of the soul or will he succumb to one of the myriad spells that life has to offer?

Failure to reach a meaningful goal discourages many, but achieving what was desired confounds the rest. The Old Queen knows how easily we fall asleep when near the soul's radiance. Spiritual practices weren't simply for getting there, but also for staying awake once in the vicinity of the vision that compels the heart and soul.

The initiate becomes the one who suffers artfully enough that the two realms become present in him at the same time. For a moment everything stops. The eternal and the time-bound coincide in the soul and a beauty is born shaped by both. The embrace of the opposites joins everyone and everything. That's the nature of love, the working of art, and the motion of ritual. The ancient longing and the immediate breath consummate the presence of life everlasting and ongoing.

An eternal moment occurs in a recessed chamber of the soul. For a moment a hidden unity touches the soul and all the strange hungers, longings, and weird capacities make sense. The moon pours a light of blessing down, hearts fill to the brim, and a cup of the Water of Life passes all around. Life becomes blessed and can bless. The flow of life reaches a point of reversal and all that was wasting away returns to life again. A millennium occurs in the soul. Yet the stunning experience of fullness in the soul cannot be held for long. The moon moves past the window, its soft rays suffusing the night but no longer bathing the moment in full, unbearable reflection. Even the Companions fall asleep when the mysteries at the center of the chambers of the heart are finally seen and felt.

The Old Queen whisks the beautiful woman away, back to the sea of life where she must be found and released again. Now begins the back and forth that tests the presence of and sense of unity in the psyche. Even after the tests seem completed there are doubts. Doubt is another incurable companion of the human soul. The Old Queen simply whispers softly in the ear of her daughter and the same man who once seemed to draw the moon looks common and awkward in the bare light of day. Is he a genuine noble soul who knows something of beauty and truth or just a common man? The answer is yes, of course. Even the Companions look common and unremarkable when not blessed with the glow of vision and purpose. When not engaged in great tasks they look awkward, weird, unseemly. The Old Queen of the world requires ordeals that test one's courage and desire, but she also knows that plain old doubt has ruined many great designs and shattered untold visions.

On the road of initiations tests occur both going and when coming back. Whatever has been found—be it the innate gifts of one's soul, the awakening of lifelong purpose, the song of love, symbols imbued with meaning—will be tested when it must enter the common round of day in the daily world. The back and forth of initiation, the alternating of fire and water, suffers to temper the initiate's temperament which will also be tested against the hard edges of the world of facts and figures.

Anyone who has read this far has followed a long road that began where the young son, just entering the world, received a crushing blow from his father. The quest and the questioning began: Is this the son of a king or a common consumer and hunter of rats? At the burning cauldron of the Half-giantess the young son saw the endless, devouring hunger of the spinning world. In other guises he entered the deep waters where even the horse that carries faithfully must be sacrificed. Later he leapt willingly into the boiling cauldron in the great hall of the Firebird story. By now the initiate has faced many fires and tasted many waters. Early on he had leap into the fires, he had to burn fully in order to awaken fully. As things progress, acting in the same way might destroy all that has been created.

The daughter of the Old Queen has taken up the question of the nobility of the seeker and once again a great fire must be built in the center of things. It's as if the old hunter wanders over from the story of the "Lizard in the Fire" and says, "Now, the situation is like this: If the son can stand in the fire fashioned by the daughter of the Old Queen, they can find a way in life together. If he can't survive this tempering, the Old Queen of Fate will reclaim her daughter and another head will roll after all."

The temper of the prince who will be drawn through the fires one more time. This time he must ask for help, for simple heroics might ruin everything. Something else is being tested and leaping straight into the fire might put him back in the Firebird story or further back with the lizard again. The prince faces a new dilemma. He can't refuse the fire or he loses the beautiful daughter of the queen; yet he can't simply jump into it either. It's as if the issues of Litima return and the initiate must forge the last part of his character before settling the doubts for the queen's daughter and for himself.

When he asks whether his companion can enter the fire for him the prince passes another test. He has learned that it is not exactly he who undergoes the ordeals. His ego or common self has come to recognize that when truly faced by the impossible conditions in this world, help comes from the otherworld. Standing in the tension before the fire of three hundred bundles of wood, the prince remembers the odd nature of one of the soul's Strange Companions. The only helper left happens to enjoy heat that no one else can stand and stand cold that no one else can endure. The only companion not yet tested is the Man of Tempers who handles the heat easily.

Some tribal initiations involve long periods of testing. Only after ten or twelve years of ongoing rites do the elders see the genuine character emerge in a particular initiate. Young men tend to enter initiation as a group. But they only complete the process when their individuality shines through. Too much fire and they will be brittle and lack flexibility in times of trouble. Too much water and they will remain green and lack clarity and firmness when confusion boils up. The elders evaluate the temperament of each initiate before inviting them into the next stage, that of the "practice elder."

Seen from the view of the elders, an inner elder is being forged in the young initiates. In the old sense of things, knowledge—especially self-knowledge—makes a person older and eventually elder. Has the one seeking knowledge come to know who and what they are in this world that tests a person's spirit? Can he withstand the heated issues of life and death without resorting to violence or lose his tempering? Can he keep his cool in the midst of threat, be it outer or inner? Has he found inner integrity and the ability to maintain it under stress or duress?

Part of the cure of the incurable lies in developing the capacity to withstand the fires and to remember the Water of Life when things become overheated. The Man of Tempers offers a model of the integration characteristic of elders serving the community and those who serve something beyond their little self. He cools his heart when others become agitated and stirs the embers if people become overly complacent or cold-hearted. Elders have *cool*, but don't loose touch with the flow of emotions that nourish life and attract the spirit to human endeavors.

After the Man of Tempers withstands all the heat the daughter of the queen can muster, she accepts the prince as he appears: a common man with uncommon qualities. The initiatory ordeals are essentially over and the time has come for a return to the community in order to be recognized by others as a new and renewed person. Of course, the Old Queen has to send an army after them just to remind them not to forget where they have been and to restate that life is not tame and every act has consequences.

When the prince and the daughter of the Old Queen reach the border between the worlds, the Companions remained behind. Those old souls have done their work and can return to their resting places. The Stout One lay down again, content to look like a great hill in the terrain of the psyche. The Listener settled back into the earth where his extraordinary power came from. The Man of Great Vision relaxed and turned his gaze upon some still water. Piercing Eyes covered his intense glare again, the Tall One stretched all the way out to sleep, and the Tempered One found a tree with just the right amount of shade and sun.

The son of the king and the daughter of the queen continue on together and all is well. But entering the common world again precipitates another test. What happens in the inner-under-otherworld must be tested against the down-to-earth, rough-and-tumble goings-on of everyday. From the point of view of the common world, the otherworld seems inflated, exaggerated, and too much to tolerate on a daily basis. It's always the last minute in the otherworld, everything appears just about to transform or explode or fall under the spells of love or some other foolishness. The radical rituals that can change a life, that can change a relationship, and that can change a society, cannot be sustained for great lengths of time. The extremes of the human soul, represented by the Companions, the tyrannical old kings, the old hag at the well, the dwarf, the lady of the fountain, the Half-giantess, and the old king who demands the Firebird cannot be suffered for extensive periods of time. They come and they go. They are seen and they disappear again like the old ring slipping back into the timeless ocean.

The otherworld is like utopia, a word whose Greek roots mean no place. It isn't anywhere exactly, but is found in different places at different times. It could suddenly appear anywhere, but often it is nowhere to be found. It moves around and is always temporary. Living out utopian ideas and ideals never works for long because people, being bound to place and time, must be somewhere. Even when touched by the golden wing of eternity, even when imbued with the beauty of love, and even when inspired by the ancient imagination people must weave the wonder of the Other back into the world of limitations. In the otherworld everything partakes of the great sensibilities or the great tragedies of life. The daily world keeps to the basics of survival and the yardstick of ground-level common sense.

The human soul opens to the eternal drama of the world, yet also must participate in the quotidian give-and-take of the marketplace of life. Upon return the prince and the daughter of the Old Queen become common enough. They enter a pig herder's hut and live with those who work with animals and move the waste of the world. The royal clothes of the daughter of the Old Queen become the worn and stained garments common to those struggling on this earth. Whatever happened in the otherworld must be worn on the inside where it can be digested and reflected upon before integrated fully.

The camp of the pig herders represents a return to daily life and a period spent seasoning the experiences and time spent with the old Companions of the soul. What could be more earthy and earthly than the rutting of pigs and the proximity of pig shit? The psyche seeks a sense of balance—not a stasis, but a radical balance that holds the highest and lowest together. The value of all that happened, like the inner effects of an initiation, must be contained within and shaped to fit the daily world. The inner life grows around experiences that either cannot be fully told or else diminish if they can be explained. A sense of secrecy attends each transformation of the soul, and some things must be held the way prayers wait within until the time comes for their saying.

Although considered lowly and unclean by some, the pig was once a robust representative of the Great Mother in her guise of fertility mother and abundant giver of life. Like any great symbol, the "sow mother" can be seen many ways, as destroyer of life or as benefactor. Here the meaning would seem to be the opposite of the Old Queen who would hoard and withhold the her beautiful daughter. But the princess enters the great give-and-take of the worldly marketplace through the pig's run.

The prince must join the pig world as well. Remember old Ulysses who faced trial after trial? Who became lost and wandered through many realms? He enters his old kingdom as a pig herder. He had to pass before the old grandmother, the matriarch of the tribe and keeper of the pigs. She accepted him and she also inspected him. While washing the dust of the road from him she sees the scar of an old wound on his thigh. Through the presence of the wound she recognizes Ulysses, now returned from adventures in the otherworld. The old, double-minded wanderer bears a mark similar to that of the youngest brother in the Water of Life. By such marks a person becomes known both in this world and in the other. What marks us makes us indelibly part of the whole thing, unique and recognizable to those both common and extraordinary who have eyes to see.

In this instance, the prince returns to where he had wasted almost to death with the incurable condition of his soul. He was a prince in this world, albeit a stricken one. In the otherworld he appeared common, whereas the daughter of the Old Queen radiated beauty that rivaled the moon. Now the situations must reverse long enough to balance the qualities of the two realms. He wore common clothes in seeking her and she must now appear quite common to dwell with him. She must tend the pigs awhile and work for the old the sow mother. In each world something must be earned.

The time spent in the hut of the pig herder can be a long time or a short time or whatever time it takes for all of the elements of one's life to find a place within the psychic economy. The princess has mostly forgotten the moment of eternity once shared, the way a person long out of love can forget the tender glory of that embrace. When invited to see her husband she expects to find him in the marketplace, bargaining and arguing for a good price like everyone else. She has come to know a common enough life and expects him to be in the usual human circumstances, "in the shit," trying to hold together something that never seems to come out quite right. At this point there are no great expectations. If the meal that evening can be a little better than usual, it's something to be thankful for. If there's a little less work the next day, it's enough to give thanks. If a little more love flows between the two, that's something worth savoring.

One day, however, things go differently. As was the case with the youngest brother after he retrieved the Water of Life, something earned in the otherworld eventually appears in this one. The radiance of the soul can be lost if shown too soon; yet it cannot be lost altogether. The value of an initiatory experience may be primarily internal, yet it must be seen in the common light of day to be confirmed and completed.

Instead of arriving at the marketplace where the value of the soul and its connection to the otherworld can be easily forgotten and mightily obscured, her appointment takes her to the palace. There she finds her common enough common-law husband; only now he sits on the throne dressed in royal garments. She doesn't recognize him without his pig-herding gear or understand why people bustle all about in preparation for a great feast.

What is going on?

On the way to the wedding the question that began this whole series of quests arises again: Is this the son of some common family or the son of a king? Is he a pig-herder, a rat hunter, an incurable wreck? Or, if he is a royal prince, does he have the sense and sympathy to stop and stoop low enough to learn the common suffering of the human soul? If he comes to rule, will he act as the older brothers and forget the vision of healing that moved his own soul? On the other hand, who is she who comes from afar and suddenly appears? Is she noble herself or just a common woman of the herds? Will she jump into the fire when the issue comes to his life or that of the lizard? When given her chance at sovereignty will she withhold the beauty of her soul as the Old Queen seemed determined to do? Is she actually a woman? Is he a real man? How many parts of him can marry how many parts of her? Can they find more moments of beauty together? Well, in the realm of stories where all things are possible, the only answer is ... yes.

She looks past the appearance of things that distract so many in these dark and darkening times. She looks carefully into his eyes and he gazes back into the windows of her soul. In that moment it's as if the light of the moon embraces them again. For a moment they find the gaze of beauty again. Deep memories move within and they feel the presence of the old Companions around them. For now the tests are over. The two realms can be joined again and abundance can return to anyone who attends the wedding and who tends to the marriage trying to happen over and over.

Each story we have entered here has sought to find the nobility of spirit and soul that inevitably becomes lost somewhere along the road of life. At first there was a question of whether the son of the village could survive the blow struck by his father and the shock of seeing the insatiable Half-giantess. Further along, the question became whether he could enter the deep waters of the soul and learn to reflect his actual place in the game of life. Could he sacrifice his high opinion of himself in order to release that which truly carries him and avoid the fate worse than death? Once in contact with the vitality of life and the horse of power the next question involved the burning feather. Could he enter life more fully? Could he handle the heat and grasp the beauty at the heart of things? And, if he could manage that, could he recognize the importance of healing and turn aside from the obvious in order to seek the healing Water of Life?

The goal seemed to shift in the territory of each story, yet it remained the same. The question changed again and again, yet it is all the same quest. A burning question arises on the internal sea of the soul or a burning feather falls right onto the road of life. Either way the question remains: Will he, will she, take up the thread that winds through the tests and obstacles in order to heal the inevitable wounds and find the beauty hidden in the soul?

Each time a person answers even a part of the question echoing from with their life, a kind of wedding occurs as the two realms meet in the awakening soul. Each occasion of unity is temporary, be it a marriage of mind and heart, of outer and inner lives, of passion and purpose, of masculine and feminine, or of nature and spirit. What comes together goes asunder until it can reunite at another level and be found in another territory of the soul. Once the honeymoon passes, the old, gold ring becomes lost again and unity must be sought in a darker, more uncertain place. The ring that can unify the opposites always falls to the very bottom. What brings the opposites of the world together can only be found in the dark depths; otherwise the endless bright ideas and solemn beliefs would do the job.

Each initiatory experience raises something that was hidden from view and attempts to wed it to the conscious life of a person. Each time that happens there is a reason for everyone to celebrate and confirm, to bless and anoint the initiates. In that third step, the return to the community for blessing, everyone can become a little blessed. The effort of initiation and seeking of the hidden gifts can only be accomplished by the individual, by the one undivided; yet the knowledge and the gifts that are found can never be just for the individual. What was lost became lost to everyone; what is found and received must also be given. Beauty polishes the soul and the shine becomes visible and encouraging to others. An initiation won't be over, it won't solidify in consciousness, and won't generate more life unless it is celebrated and shared with everyone.

Weddings used to be part of the initiatory path through which the mysteries of life were encountered and celebrated. Like the little figures of the bride and groom set atop the concentric rings of a wedding cake, the two willing to take the vows represented a high state of coming together. For a moment they stand atop the circles of life and enter a sacred state more than a civil one. For just a moment they stand at the apex of the cosmos with its concentric layers of life. They represent a "lifting of the veil" through which everything can join together. The old, gold ring is passed. They embrace each other and kick the "round of life" into gear again.

Each wedding repeats, to one degree or another, the motions and emotions of old rituals of uniting the two worlds. Bride and groom represent the opposites in the world and their union is a reunion of all things opposed. A wedding intends to wed everything in the world, at least for a moment. That's why people watch carefully, why some laugh and some cry. A wedding joins what can only come together with great effort, some luck, a little fate, and sometimes a touch of destiny. Call it the hidden unity of life being enacted; call it a *conjunctio*, which joins all things; call it an open invitation to find something in this incarnate world to cherish and marry for a long moment, for a lifetime, or until the end of time.

Whereas a funeral intends to separate the living from the dead, a wedding would join the living to what is most alive and capable of generating more life. The soul longs for that union and it fears it as well. To accomplish it some chains will have to be broken and replaced by the ring of trust. And that too will be tested, just ask anyone who has walked down the aisle that joins the two separate souls and separate families. Two people agree to represent the beauty of the world in contrasting forms and everyone present is invited to touch the underlying unity of life.

A wedding is an imagined and imaginal event. It's best done when no expense is spared. Not necessarily buying expensive things as much as expending all of the imagination possible at the time. For what becomes wedded together are the soulful imaginations and inner dreams of the bride and the groom. That's why the bride is always beautiful and the groom handsome; with any luck they enter the imaginative state of the "gaze of beauty."

At the wedding of the son of the king and the daughter of the Old Queen, honey was gathered from the bees and fish from the seas. Foods of all kinds were cooked in many kitchens. Great barley beers were freshly made and fine old wines were hauled up from the basement of the palace. Something old and something new would bring together ancient practices with immediate feelings; a wedding would preserve the age-old traditions of celebrating life by uniting its opposites and by making something new, all the old parts wedded together in some new and unusual way.

An old rule says that anyone encountering a funeral must drop their common errand and pay their respects to the dead. At the time of a wedding, a place must be set for a stranger who will represent the unknown. If the other is not invited in, it will appear in the marriage in the wrong way. The stranger at a wedding also represents the strange old Companions of the soul, who may overeat, drink too much, stare too hard at the bride, help spread all the gossip, or step on everyone's toes. A wedding has to awaken the weird in everyone and invite it to dine and dance and shatter the confines of daily life.

At the wedding of the prince who had been incurable and the princess who had been unattainable, people came from far and wide and they came in all sizes and ages and shapes. They came wearing the many-colored garments that people used to wear to great occasions to show their relationship to the earth and the trees and the stars above. They came bearing a wide array of instruments made from the shells of animals, from the wood of trees, and from the sinews of whales. They brought drums that spoke in many rhythms and had to be answered with dances. They brought stringed instruments that could draw out the old sorrows and release the great joys of humankind.

When the music played people danced with an abandon that lifted the weight of the world even from the shoulders of the poor. In the midst of the dancing people felt free for a time; time broke apart as the dancers became the dance. People began to remember that life is a dance, that dance imitates the swirling of the heavens, that it releases the imagination of the body, and that it reconnects humans to the animated, animal sense of the world.

Dancing means breaking time and making time, finding the right timing and letting go of everything out of tune with the song of life—living. There is a dance within the dance through which each person can gather themself fully and feel whole, even if just for a moment. In letting go of who they are supposed to be, the dancer becomes who they already are. A true dancer surrenders to the dance, dances away the little self with its fears and worries and practiced uncertainty. A genuine dance becomes an act of wholeness, and a shedding of weight, a shifting of rhythms that puts a person back in touch with the spinning of the world and the singing of the spheres.

Duende they call it in old Spain, the dark spirit that rises from the depths of the earth when people allow it, the old power of the earth pulsing and rising through the dancers and singers making music of them and through them. *Duende* that stamps its foot to state the anguish and grief of the world as well as to evoke the ecstatic joy of creation, for the real dancers don't dance out of simple joy, but also because they know sorrow. Dance remembers the sorrow of life before releasing it back to the world.

Dance includes the visible and the invisible; it pulls the dancer into time, through time, and out of time—into rhythm where the touch of the eternal can be found and felt again. That's the real dance, the dance within the dance: each dancer dancing with an Otherness usually hidden. It is the wholeness of the dancers making the whole thing possible again.

A real dance and a real wedding awakens something sleeping in the world. The sound of it reaches the ear of the Listener who awakens all the old and Strange Companions of the soul. The Stout One arrives at the wedding and opens all the kegs to let the age-dark wine flow, releasing its power of causing people both to remember or to forget. Characters from the old stories stir inside the bones of the living and the otherworld secretly weds this world again. The wedding hall converts to the great hall where the burning feathers of the Firebird fall again amidst the dancers and people feel the flame of life flicker within.

For a moment a fire burns at the center of the hall that seems to sit in the center of the realm, which seems to be the center of the waking world. The bride and the groom approach a fire that could consume them body and soul or else make them new and make them over again. If they leap into the flames wholeheartedly something shifts a little in the world. For a moment all the stories born of the human heart and of the otherworld with which it dances come to life again. For a moment the bride is the daughter of a queen, the groom clearly the son of a king. Everyone fortunate enough to be present at such a wedding is part of the village of life, standing around the fire that holds the lizard of change. Each person brings an aspect of the Strange Companions; each becomes necessary to hold the moment as the princess and prince enter the gaze of beauty, not simply for themselves or even for their overwrought families, but for the meeting of the two realms and the marriage of the opposite energies which pull life apart yet which alone can make a new union.

If the fire becomes hot enough even the stone men in the hall awaken from stony sleep and pass out old, gold rings of unity. For a moment the counselors forget to manipulate the circumstances and "spin" the event for political advantage. For a moment the older brothers give up their twisted aspirations and look for a way to serve something other than themselves. For a moment even the ministers of war forget why the next battle has to happen. For a moment the fire, which could forge even more devastating weapons, becomes the heat that softens the glue of the world and makes beauty possible. For a moment the Water of Life flows again and diminishes the wasting of the world.

In the flow of things, in the throes of the music and the height of the dancing, and in the poetry of the vows spoken and unspoken, the great imagination of life returns. People recall the old stories and understand why they can't be forgotten. They must be learned anew, studied again within the context of a world at odds with itself and only able to be redeemed by the brush of the wing of the great bird of spirit or the wisdom possible when people drop the reins and allow the faithful little horse below us to lead the way again.

What is wounded in this world can only be healed by the touch of the otherworld where time began, where it can be found when no one seems to have any time. What's wounded in the world can only be healed by a willingness of actual people to become completely changed and initiated to the meaning imbedded in their own souls and willing to become wedded to the soul of the world.

In the old way of seeing, everyone attends the marriage ritual: the little children as well as the ancestors. What happens at the wedding is the stage upon which new life will play. Children who are present will never forget the sight and sound of all those people dancing and leaping, singing and weeping. The memory of it will dance inside them and encourage them at their task of growing. On the other side of life the ancestors also watch to see how the strange twists of fate will treat the newly entwined couple and the family trees they represent.

Does the beautiful couple live happily ever after? Not really. Not usually. Due to a small error in translation a great misunderstanding has occurred. The original saying was not that "they lived happily ever after." Originally, it was that "They lived happily in the ever-after." They lived happily whenever they remembered that the otherworld was part of their dance together. In this world, if we find happiness as often as we find sorrow and if we remember the sorrow when happiness happens along, that would be enough grace to start things all over again.

ACKNOWLEDGEMENTS

THE SECOND BIRTH of The Water of Life would not have occurred without the encouragement and skillful support of a team of radical cultural midwives. In particular I wish to thank: Luis Rodriguez, Orland Bishop, Alice Walker, Jack Kornfield, Anthony Crispino, Chris Armstrong, Lou Dangles, Lisa Thompson, Olivia Oso, Carl Hay, Sarah Ghiorse, Jordan Good, Sandi Miller and Rick Simonsen.

Great thanks to Tracy Lakatua for jumping into the editing process and bringing a sharp eye and willing heart to the project. For stalwart editing and generous reviewing I want to thank Duncan Allard. I cannot express enough gratitude to Jacob Lakatua for the design of the book and its cover, for, reading and editing, for seeing the vision and helping to shape the work, for always working above and beyond the call.

In the course of the difficult and surprising work of Mosaic Multicultural Foundation young and old companions and teachers have crossed over to the land of the ancestors. Their spirits accompany us and continue to guide us along the way. May peace and blessings be with: Joe Ranft, Elegba "Legs" Earl, Dumisani Maraire, Etheridge Knight, Terry Dobson, William Stafford, Juan "Bosco" Luna, Griffin Blackswan, Dadisi Sanyika, Lazar McDaniels, Terrell Sherrills.

Any faults or omissions are my own, or else they are errors made when my little horse stumbled in the dark as I was trying to write this down.

Select Bibliography

Afanasev, Aleksandr. *Russian Fairy Tales*. Translated by Norbert Guterman. New York: Pantheon Books, 1945.

Beckwith, Carol. *Maasai*. New York: Harry N. Abrams, 1990.

Bly, Robert, James Hillman, and Michael Meade, eds. *The Rag and Bone Shop of the Heart*. New York: HarperCollins, 1992.

Campbell, Joseph. *The Hero with a Thousand Faces*. Princeton, NJ: Princeton University Press, 1968.

Eliade, Mircea. *Rites and Symbols of Initiation*. Putnam, CT: Spring Publications; Reprint edition, 1994. Preface for the new edition by Michael Meade.

Eliade, Mircea. *Shamanism*. Princeton, NJ: Princeton University Press, 1964.

Feldman, Susan, eds. *African Myths and Tales*. New York: Dell, 1963.

Guest, Lady Charlotte. *The Mabinogion*. London: John Jones Cardiff, Ltd., 1977.

Hall, Nor. *The Moon and the Virgin*. New York: Harper & Row, 1981.

Hamilton, Edith. *Mythology*. Boston: Little, Brown and company, 1942.

Kerényi, C. *The Gods of the Greeks*. London and New York: Thames & Hudson, 1951.

Knappert, Jan. *Bantu Myths and Other Tales*. Leiden, The Netherlands: Colon Brill, 1977.

La Fontaine, J.S. *Initiation*. New York: Penguin Books, 1985.

Neumann, Erich. *The Great Mother*. Translated by Ralph Manheim. Princeton, NJ: Princeton University Press, 1963.

Rees, Alwyn, and Brinley Rees. *Celtic Heritage*. London and New York: Thames & Hudson, 1961.

Saitoti, Tepilit, and Ole Saitoti. *Maasai*. New York: Harry N. Abrams, 1980.

Turner, Victor. *The Ritual Process*. Ithaca, NY: Cornell University Press, 1969.

Van Gennep, Arnold. *Rites of Passage*. Chicago: University of Chicago Press, 1961.

Zimmer, Heinrich. *The King and the Corpse*. Princeton, NJ: Princeton University Press, 1948.

Index

About the Author

Michael Meade, born and raised in New York City, is a renowned storyteller, author, and scholar of mythology, anthropology, and psychology. He combines hypnotic and fiery storytelling, street savvy perceptiveness, and spellbinding interpretations of ancient myths with a deep knowledge of cross-cultural rituals. His ability to tap into ancestral sources of wisdom to help people of today heal their communities inspires thousands of men and women throughout the United States, Canada, and the British Isles. His unique translations of age-old myths and symbols into culturally relevant, everyday language earned him an honorary Doctorate in Humane Letters from Pacifica Graduate Institute. Michael is also the founder of Mosaic Multicultural Foundation, author of *The Water of Life*, co-editor of *The Rag and Bone Shop of the Heart*, and editor of the cross-cultural anthology on rites of passage: *Crossroads: A Quest for Contemporary Rites of Passage*.

About Mosaic

Mosaic Multicultural Foundation is a 501(c)3 nonprofit organization, a network of artists, social activists and community builders formed to create cross-cultural alliances, mentoring relationships and social connections that encourage greater understanding between diverse peoples, elders and youth and those of various cultural and spiritual backgrounds. Mosaic recognizes the need to put essential pieces together in order to form a whole, even if it means looking in troublesome or unexpected places. Efforts at problem solving rely on locating the genius of the situation, the unique spirit of an individual, group, or community that becomes a key to understanding problems and fitting the pieces together in new ways.

GreenFire Press and **Mosaic Audio** are imprints of Mosaic Multicultural Foundation that serve to foster cultural literacy, mythic education, and multicultural community development. Proceeds from sales of books and recordings directly benefit Mosaic's work with at-risk youth, refugees, and intercultural projects.

For more information or to order additional titles contact Mosaic:
4218 1/2 SW Alaska, Suite H Seattle, WA 98126
(206)935-3665, toll free (800)233-6984
www.mosaicvoices.org ~ info@mosaicvoices.org

Mosaic Audio Recordings by Michael Meade

Alchemy of Fire: Libido and the Divine Spark, Michael Meade
Branches of Mentoring, Michael Meade
Entering Mythic Territory: Healing and the Bestowing Self, Michael Meade
The Eye of the Pupil, The Heart of the Disciple, Michael Meade
Fate and Destiny: The Two Agreements in Life, Michael Meade
The Great Dance: Finding One's Way in Troubled Times, Michael Meade
Holding the Thread of Life: A Human Response to the Unraveling of the World,
    Michael Meade
Initiation and the Soul: The Sacred and the Profane, Michael Meade
Poetics of Peace: Peace and the Salt of the Earth, Michael Meade
Poetics of Peace: Vital Voices in Troubled Times, Alice Walker, Luis Rodriguez,
    Michael Meade, Jack Kornfield, Orland Bishop

Books edited by Michael Meade

Crossroads: The Quest For Contemporary Rites of Passage,
    edited by Louise Carus Mahdi, Nancy Geyer Christopher, and Michael Meade
The Rag and Bone Shop of the Heart: A Poetry Anthology,
    edited by Robert Bly, James Hillman, and Michael Meade

Books including contributions by Michael Meade

Rites and Symbols of Initiation, Mircea Eliade
Teachers of Myth, Interviews on Educational and Psychological,
    Maren Tonder Hansen

For more information or to order additional titles contact Mosaic:
4218 1/2 SW Alaska, Suite H Seattle, WA 98126
(206)935-3665, toll free (800)233-6984
www.mosaicvoices.org ~ info@mosaicvoices.org